Earth Time

Earth Time

EXPLORING THE DEEP PAST FROM
VICTORIAN ENGLAND TO THE
GRAND CANYON

Douglas Palmer

WILEY

Published in 2005 by   John Wiley & Sons, Ltd, The Atrium, Southern Gate
Chichester, West Sussex, PO19 8SQ, England
Phone   (+44) 1243 779777

Copyright © 2005   Douglas Palmer

Email (for orders and customer service enquires): cs-books@wiley.co.uk
Visit our Home Page on www.wiley.co.uk or www.wiley.com

Other Wiley Editorial Offices

John Wiley & Sons, Inc. 111 River Street, Hoboken, NJ 07030, USA

Jossey-Bass, 989 Market Street, San Francisco, CA 94103-1741, USA

Wiley-VCH Verlag GmbH, Pappellaee 3, D-69469 Weinheim, Germany

John Wiley & Sons Australia, Ltd, 33 Park Road, Milton, Queensland, 4064, Australia

John Wiley & Sons (Asia) Pte Ltd, 2 Clementi Loop #02-01, Jin Xing Distripark, Singapore 129809

John Wiley & Sons Canada Ltd, 22 Worcester Road, Etobicoke, Ontario, Canada, M9W 1L1

Wiley also publishes its books in a variety of electronic formats. Some content that appears in print may not be available in electronic books.

Library of Congress Cataloging-in-Publication Data

(to follow)

British Library Cataloguing in Publication Data

A catalogue record for this book is available from the British Library

ISBN 0-470-02221-3 (hb)

Typeset in 10/13pt Plantin by Mathematical Composition Setters Ltd, Salisbury, Wiltshire.
Printed and bound in Great Britain by T.J. International, Padstow, Cornwall.
This book is printed on acid-free paper responsibly manufactured from sustainable forestry in which at least two trees are planted for each one used for paper production.
10 9 8 7 6 5 4 3 2 1

For Becky and David

Contents

vii

Acknowledgements

My thanks to Dr Alan Smith of the Department of Earth Sciences in the University of Cambridge for helping to lubricate my thoughts and to Professors Hugh Torrens and Martin Rudwick who, through their publications, have unwittingly encouraged my interest in Earth Time. At Wiley, Sally Smith, Grace O'Byrne, Jill Jeffries and the production team have been very helpful and worked wonders with some difficult material.

Introduction

Our present measure of around 4.5 billion years for the Earth's age is only some 50 years old, astonishingly recent considering that scientists have been trying to work it out for well over 200 years. Everyone now knows that dinosaurs lived in Jurassic times and some enthusiasts may know that this period of Earth Time persisted for around 54 million years from 199.6 to 145.5 million years ago, but what of the rest of Earth Time? How is the history of the Earth divided up and dated? Surprisingly few people seem to have much knowledge about the life and times of our blue planet – Earth.

Maybe it is not entirely comfortable to be reminded just how old the planet is and how recent we are by comparison? Perhaps as egocentric humans we do not like to feel diminished in any way? After all, the Inquisition had the Italian philosopher Vanini burned at the stake in 1616 for suggesting that humans might originate from apes, and in 1632 it had Galileo recant his support for Copernicus's claim that the Sun and not the Earth is at the centre of the Solar System. More recently there was a popular belief that the Earth is only some 6000 years old, a belief that persists today in the minds of some fundamentalists.

We are all familiar with subdivisions of historic time based on a variety of events and people such as pharoaic dynasties, political administrations such as the Kennedy years, epochs of colonisation such as Roman Britain and periods of war such as the 1914–18 First World War. By comparison, we have very little knowledge or understanding of the subdivisions of the history of the Earth, or Earth Time as I am calling it.

As we shall see, there is some overlap with history, especially through phases of technological change such as the stone age, iron age and so on. Recent discoveries have pushed the beginning of the stone age back as far as 2.5 million years ago in Africa. In geological terms this is late Pliocene in age, but who, outside the professional world of geology and archaeology, has heard of the Pliocene? Not nearly as many people as are familiar with the Jurassic period of Earth Time, I'll warrant.

So how has the depth of Earth Time been 'plumbed', carved up and named? Who, what or where were the Jurassic, Cambrian, Pliocene and so on? When were these divisions created and how is it that they can be recognised around the world? Nowadays geologists from the USA, Britain and China all use the same major divisions of Earth Time such as Jurassic. However, there has not always been the same degree of unanimity and even today there are still ongoing boundary disputes about many of the finer subdivisions of Earth Time. How is it that a division of Earth Time, based on rock strata forming a series of hills on the western flank of the European Alps, is taken to represent a period of time dominated by extinct dinosaurs?

As we shall see, the basis for the division of Earth Time is not hugely different from historic time. Major eras, for example the Mesozoic, are based on major developments in the history of life and their boundaries are often linked to catastrophic events or relatively sudden changes in the environment, both of which have had a significant impact on life and the raw data of Earth Time – the rocks of the Earth.

The raw material of Earth Time

One of the problems of living in the 'jungle' of geology for so long is that it becomes proverbially difficult to see 'jungle for the trees'. As in most endeavours, when you work very closely with a subject, aspects that initially are quite alien become taken for granted. To the uninitiated (that is, the majority of people) many geological phenomena such as folded rocks or the opening and closing of past oceans can seem really weird, surprising or plain crazy. For me, thinking and talking about geological Earth Time is now almost second nature. But when I first ask normal, intelligent non-geologists how Earth Time is measured, they look askance and then volunteer 'years perhaps' as an answer. They suspect that either I am simple or it's some sort of devious question, since the answer seems so obvious.

'Yes, but where do we get this measure of years from?' To that replies invariably include 'rocks I suppose' and 'radiocarbon dating' from those who have some familiarity with archaeology as opposed to geology. There is an intuitive acknowledgement that somehow or other, since the material of the Earth is basically rock and mineral matter, that must be the ultimate source of Earth Time. But how?

Most people with any scientific background do know something about radioactivity and have heard of radiocarbon dating, because it is the measure of prehistoric time most frequently mentioned in the media. Geologists use the same radiometric method but have to employ different chemical elements. Radiocarbon measures can only be used for carbon-based materials that have been formed over the last 40,000 years or so. Those 40,000 years or around 1000 human generations might seem a long time by our egocentric human standards, but they barely signify in the immense 4,500,000,000 year span of Earth Time.

However, rocks and minerals also play another important role in the measure of Earth Time. Like diary pages that record the months, weeks and days in a year, rocks record time intervals in the history of the Earth. The problem is that the diary for Earth Time is not easily read. Over the last 200 and more years, many generations of Earth scientists have struggled to decipher the testimony and chronicle of the rocks. Despite the seemingly impossible task of recovering the record of the rocks, there was an expectation that as the pages of the chronicle were pieced together, deciphered and put into correct order, the details of the Genesis account would be verified and amplified from the testimony of the rocks. Curiously, as we shall see, some of the geological evidence did seem, at first, to verify some aspects of the Genesis account, especially that of the Flood.

4004 BC

I have a copy of the Bible that was given to my grandfather in 1893, probably so that he could prepare himself for confirmation in the Anglican Church of England. It is a standard edition, 'Appointed to be read in Churches', of the protestant version of both the Old and New Testaments dedicated to 'The Most High and Mighty Prince James, by the Grace of God, King of Great Britain, France, and Ireland, Defender of the Faith, &c.' This edition was published by Cambridge University Press presumably around 1890, a time when it had generally become accepted by the scientific community that the Earth had to be many millions of years old, although nobody knew for sure just how many millions.

The introduction to The First Book of Moses called Genesis has the text arranged in two columns down each page with narrow margins on either side. At the top of each margin is a date 'Before Christ 4004' and by Chapter IV the date is '4003' and continues to decrease throughout the books of the Old Testament, following the accepted chronology to the end of the Book of Malachi, which is dated at Before Christ cir. 397. As the New Testament begins the chronology continues, *anno domini*, to the end of the Book of Revelation AD 96.

Whether my grandfather believed the authority of these dates I do not know, but I suspect that as a boy living in a very authoritarian social environment at the end of the Victorian era, he probably did. After all, it was generally assumed that you could not get a better authority than the Bible, even though the intellectuals of the day were well aware of the German theological 'Higher Criticism' of the exact nature of the biblical texts. This close reading and comparison had shown up many discrepancies and contradictions, which suggested that the texts had been gathered together from different sources over centuries, initially from oral traditions, before eventually being written down in a number of versions. By the end of the nineteenth century intellectuals and academics knew that the Old Testament could not be read simply as a historical document and that the calculation of the date of the Creation being in 4004 BC was no longer tenable. And yet here we have editions of the Bible still being printed with this date firmly in place.

Through marriage this same grandfather acquired an 'uncle' who was to help change the popular conception of the biblical chronology and the status of the biblical Flood as a historical event. Harold Peake was a well-known archaeologist and writer of an influential series of books on the subject. In 1930, 'Uncle' Harold published *The Flood: New Light on an Old Story*. In his preface he explained that he was concerned that understanding of the reality of archaeological data about the chronology of prehistory and the reality of such events as the Flood were taking too long to be completely accepted in churches and schools – and this was in 1930! As he wrote, 'the reforms in the teaching, though advocated for long, have not yet been fully effected'. My own 'discovery' of this relative's writing has been instrumental in the gestation of this book.

Rock records

Exactly how a rock can record the passage of time is one of the main themes of this book. It has long been recognised that much of the rock material of the Earth is preserved in layers that were originally laid down by natural processes, one upon the other. Look at any ancient sandstones or limestones used as building stone. It is not too difficult to see layered grains of sand or fossil shells that give clues as to how they were originally formed.

And it does not require any great imaginative feat to realise that this successive layering could be interpreted as some measure of time passing – if only we knew how quickly or slowly the layers were laid down. By comparison with everyday depositional events, it was apparent that earlier deposited layers were to be found at the bottom of the pile, younger ones were to be found higher up and the most recent would be on top – pedantically known by geologists as the 'law of superposition of strata'. Observation of how mud and sand become layered in riverbanks and on beaches, how snow accumulates in glaciers and ice sheets, how volcanic ash blankets landscapes or even how trash accumulates in a waste bin, all illustrate this very simple law and allow us to understand how layered deposits build up on the Earth's surface under the prevailing influence of gravity.

Johann Scheuchzer's *Herbarium of the Deluge* (1709) explained the deposition of fossils in mountain rocks by the waters of the Noachian Flood.

My aim is to tell the story of how the existence of the Earth's deep prehistoric geological past was first discovered, recovered from the rock record and then reconstructed into our present understanding of Earth history – what I am calling Earth Time.

Earth to earth, ashes to ashes, dust to dust

So what does the data of the Earth Time record consist of? Mostly, it is the flotsam and jetsam of all those earth processes that affect the surface of the Earth. These processes range from the familiar everyday work of wind and water to the more dramatic eruption of volcanoes, crumpling of rocks into mountains and the fortunately much rarer visitations by extraterrestrial impactors. The resulting flotsam and jetsam are predominantly rock and mineral debris, mostly in the form of mud and sand sediment, along with volcanic 'products' such as ash and lava.

Of great interest to us is the further additional data left by life and its past activities – in other words, fossils. Human activity has played an increasing impact on Earth's surface processes and deposits. While this human impact was initially recorded solely by the bones of our ancient relatives and their animal food, it quickly became more complex and diverse. From discarded tools and other cultural artefacts such as artworks, the human-generated 'fossil' record has grown to include the remains of settlement, technological development and modification of landscape.

So many lives of plants and animals over millions of years, so much activity, so many earth-shattering events, all reduced – 'earth to earth, ashes to ashes, dust to dust'. The 'sure and certain hope' here is that all this activity leaves some preservable debris. It does, but most of it is stored in the Earth's mineral and rock data bank along with some organic materials. Much of this data accumulates in layers piled successively through time one upon another. As we have noted, the oldest layer lies at the bottom of the pile and the youngest on top. However, just to complicate matters, there are also deeper-seated processes that can 'inject' other rock material data into the pile from below.

Most of what we think of as the diary of the Earth Time rock record is sequentially layered and any interpretation of the chronicle of the Earth has to be gleaned from this material rock and fossil record. Needless to say, it can be very difficult to read this diary and from it to reconstruct past environments, events, life and its development.

One of the keys to understanding the Earth Time chronicle is the appreciation that the layers are like the consecutive pages of a written narrative or diary, but with an important difference. First, the book has been vandalised, torn apart and scattered over the surface of the Earth. Bundles of unnumbered 'pages' lie here and there, but with many missing altogether. Secondly, many other pages are torn and damaged by being left to the destructive vagaries of the elements so as to be virtually indecipherable.

As a result, any attempt to follow the original narrative closely can be very difficult, as it has to be pieced together from the surviving pages. Another complication is that there are several different regional versions of the diary, as if they were in different languages, and in places the versions have become mixed up. Furthermore, to begin with none of the geologists who were trying to piece the diary together knew exactly how long each recorded chronological division was, but many of them thought they knew the overall duration of the chronicle, around 6000 years. The early 'brethren of the hammer', as they saw themselves, also thought they knew the outlines of Earth's story, because the Bible told them so. It was the Old Testament's Genesis narrative of creation followed by the Noachian Flood or Deluge and subsequent repopulation of the Earth by the descendants of Noah and the animals and plants he had saved from drowning in the ark.

Historians suffer from very similar problems with fragmentary, gappy data that can be difficult to read and interpret. Nevertheless, one of the great fascinations of geology and the 'testimony of the rocks' is that we have only scratched the surface of the Earth and the story of Earth Time. There is plenty of scope for new generations of enthusiasts really to make their mark on our understanding of the rock record. New finds, new techniques of investigation and even just taking a new critical look at received wisdom can produce startling results.

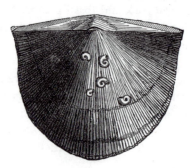

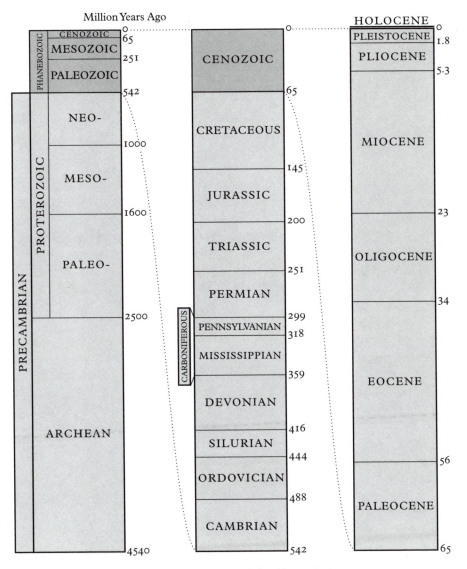

Million Years Ago

Earth Time as divided and dated by geologists.

PART I

Cutting through Earth Time – Mr Smith's Section from London to Snowdon

I

Recent Earth Time –
The Holocene

Measure for measure

The now or present of Earth Time is not exactly the same as what you and I normally mean by now or the present. After all, when you are some 4.5 billion years old what does a day or so, a week, a month or even a century or two matter? Earth Time is normally measured in years before the present (BP). And, although our Earth Time clocks are getting more and more accurate, they still cannot resolve time much better than a few hundred and sometimes thousand years or so at best. So tomorrow's 'now' is effectively much the same as last year or next year.

Whether standing on the rim of the Grand Canyon or by the River Thames in the middle of the city of London, the common concept of the present time that we live in is based on a western and Christian-dominated cultural chronology rather than the geological one. It is globally accepted (at least for general purposes of travel, commerce and international law) that we are living in the first decade of the twenty-first century and the third millennium AD (*anno domini*).

Geologically, this is year zero. The present is always zero: the past recedes from now because geologists do not use a fixed traumatic point in the past as our

3

prehistoric 'ground zero' from which all else is measured. This is fine when we are dealing with the remote past, but it creates problems when dealing with the recent past. Consequently, the AD–BC scheme is widely used for Holocene dates and older dates are referred to as Before Present (BP).

The Holocene Epoch began 11,500 years ago, the Pleistocene Epoch, famous for its ice ages, began 1806 million years ago (often abbreviated to ma or mya) and the Jurassic Period, famous for its dinosaurs, began around 205.7 million years ago.

The dating of the geological past is largely extracted from the rock record using a complex technology and it is a topic to which we will return (see p. 399 *et seq.*). However, it is important to realise that geological dates are essentially calculated estimates that often include margins of error in the order of a few per cent. So a relatively recent date of, say, 3000 BP will have an error margin of around 100 years, that is + or −50 years, and 200 ma might have an error of + or −4 million years. This kind of error margin needs to be borne in mind when any date from the remote past is talked about. Precision of geological dates, in the everyday sense, there is not. Consequently, claims that for instance an extinction event dated in one place is really the same as that in another place, just because the calculated dates seem to be the same, is not necessarily true. But with the accumulation of many dates clustering closely around the same point, the probability of synchroneity increases.

The success of western economic growth and global dominance has ensured that other cultural, religious and historical chronologies have become largely subservient to the international hegemony of a Christian-based chronology. Nevertheless, other chronologies and calendars such as the Buddhist one, which is based on the death of Buddha (544 BC), or the Islamic one, based on the flight of the prophet from Mecca (AD 622), may still be dominant in their home territories. In a similar way, a single geological chronology has developed over the last 200 years and come to dominate the division of deep time and the development of an international geological timescale. There is an importance difference in that this timescale has been achieved through international cooperation. Although for various historical reasons British and European geologists controlled most of the early development of the chronology and subdivision of Earth Time, subsequently finer divisions have been recognised in rock sequences all over the world and named accordingly. Indeed, there has been a lot of competition among geologists from different parts of the world to get some part of their geological home 'patches' officially recognised within the international timescale.

The details of how our present Christian-based Gregorian calendar, a reformed version (in 1582 by Pope Gregory XIII) of the older Roman Julian calendar, came to dominance was extensively discussed and dissected at the turn of the twentieth century by writers such as E. G. Richards (whose fascinating book is entitled *Mapping Time: The Calendar and its History*, 1998, Oxford), much better qualified than myself. The historical multiplicity of calendars is largely the result of the astronomical fact that an Earth year has the awkward length of 365.242199 solar days at the moment. This is not the easiest of measures to subdivide into neat calendar packages of days, weeks and months that are repeated on an annual basis. Nor is our year length fixed. In Devonian times, over 350 million years ago, the Earth year was some 400 days long; the planet's rotation has slowed due to tidal friction. Counts of diurnal growth rings laid down in lunar cycles and recovered from fossil corals and clams verify these measures.

Apart from calendar-based chronologies, we also divide historical time up in a number of different ways. Traditionally, many cultures have recognised time intervals based on reigns and dynasties. Acts of Parliament in England are still dated in this way, for instance those passed in 2004 will be dated as 51 Elizabeth II because the Queen came to the throne in 1953 – but then England does like to hang on to its traditions. Of particular significance is the Christian Era, a mainstay of the Gregorian calendar, which was first proposed by Dionysius Exiguus, an Abbot from Scythia, now Moldavia, in AD 532. AD 1 was taken as the supposed birth year of Christ, although it is almost certainly incorrect, the more likely date being 4 BC. Even historians have problems with accurately dating important events and have error margins to take into account.

As we have seen, the Dionysian calendar was not widely accepted until it was taken up in 1582 by Pope Gregory XIII – and the rest, as they say, is history. Several more recent reforms have been attempted, of which the most radical was that by French revolutionaries of the late eighteenth century. They tried to

introduce a whole swathe of reforms ranging from a 10-hour republican day to a
new era – the Republican Era (RE), beginning in 1792 – but it did not catch on.
Even more recently, members of the international Baha'i religion recognise a
Baha'i Era that began in 1844, the year Ali Muhommed was declared Bab.

Earth Time – trends and events

For historians, recent political, economic and cultural trends are of importance,
especially global economic trends and events such as stock market crashes. And
as we know, such crashes are sometimes the result of specific events such as
the September 11th, 2001 attack on the World Trade Center in New York.
As we shall see, such catastrophic events have parallels in geological history.
However, very few of these historical events are likely to leave any trace in the
future geological record, only those that leave widespread evidence of collateral
damage.

Even evidence (of a purely geological nature) for a large-scale conflict such as
the 1914–18 First World War will be hard to come by outside of the battlefields.
In regions like Flanders on the French–Belgian border, where there was intense
and prolonged fighting, there will be some 'debitage' remaining. Bones and even
metal degrade on the geological scale, although concrete as used in the building
of the Maginot defence line is more persistent. Military hardware or ships that
end up on the seabed also persist quite well but can be difficult to find. The event
associated with the 1939–45 Second World War that is most likely to be picked
up is the dropping of the atomic bombs on Japan. Radioactive particles (isotopes
of caesium and plutonium) from the nuclear test explosions carried out by the
American military in the Nevada desert in the 1950s were carried through the
atmosphere and around the world by the jet stream within days. Recently they
have been recovered from soil samples taken at the time in Hertfordshire,
England. Although present in extremely minute traces that do not endanger life,
they still reside in measurable quantities even 50 years after being released into
the atmosphere. Similar man-made potentially dangerous pollutants can be found
in ice cores from Greenland and Antarctica.

Archaeologists of the future may be able to recover evidence of some economic developments and trends, especially from their favoured haunt – the rubbish dump. Our huge landfill dumps will provide rich pickings in the future. Resistant and preservable items such as glass bottles will be one of the mainstays, with chronologies based on the evolution of shape, design of the stopper and chemistry of the glass. No doubt the ubiquitous and globally distributed cola bottle will provide an excellent international standard for the chronology of the twentieth century. However, the large-scale replacement of the bottle by the metal can will severely limit the usefulness of the bottle timescale into the twenty-first century.

Nevertheless, most of the archaeological record will be swept away over geological time. Very little of the archaeology of human prehistory and history will remain except for eroded stone tools and rock-derived material used for building. Much of the Earth's landsurfaces will eventually be inundated by future seas. And, as the waters transgress across any low-lying areas, they will destroy all but the most resistant structures. Wave action and marine currents will redistribute and deposit the bits as new sediment on the seafloor, where they will stand a better chance of being preserved as future marine strata, but very little of the original terrestrial structures or materials will be recognisable. Much of the record of the long-extinct, land-living dinosaurs is preserved in this way. The sheer size and toughness of their bones have allowed them to persist through destructive processes of decay, erosion, transport and redeposition offshore from the lands they originally occupied.

However, there are a number of other important processes and events that are currently recording the passage of time in newly formed rocks and sediments. These range from chemical traces and signatures to changes in the Earth's magnetic field. Some of the former can record climate change, industrial activity and largescale volcanic activity as well as the explosion of nuclear devices.

No doubt with our hominocentric view of the world we expect that the future rock record will be replete with evidence of our human triumphs and disasters. But this is not necessarily so, and it is worth considering just what the rock record typically consists of. All the average human can expect is that, if buried, our remains might be preserved in the short term. However, on the longer geological timescale our remains, like most deposits on land, will be eroded away. As more and more people are cremated, it is probably best to be 'green' about your futurity and hope that gases derived from incineration will be recycled through the atmosphere into some plant and not contribute too much to global warming.

Earth Time – the rocks

Most people do not realise that the vast majority of the rock record of sedimentary strata (otherwise known as the stratigraphic record) is made up from deposits (inorganic sediments and organic remains of dead organisms) that were originally laid down on the seabed – sands, muds and carbonates (lime-rich sediments that subsequently become limestones). So enormous has been the public 'puffing' of dinosaurs, which were solely land-living reptiles, that it is often assumed that there must be a good rock record of terrestrial deposits. Dinosaur fossils are not nearly as common as you might think. The fossil remains of our extinct human relatives are even rarer, partly because our ancestors lived on land but also because there are far fewer human-related species than there are dinosaur species, and ancient human-related populations were small and mostly confined to Africa. The existence of the fossil record of our immediate ancestors is largely thanks to the geological nature of the Great East Africa Rift Valley, in which great thicknesses of relatively recent deposits have accumulated and been preserved.

Overall, land-based sedimentary strata are uncommon in the rock record, although there were times, such as parts of the Devonian, late Carboniferous (known as the Pennsylvanian in North America), Permian and Triassic periods and regions of the continents (especially the flanks of major mountain belts), when significant thicknesses of land-based sediments accumulated.

Why are they not so common? In a word – gravity. Land is for the most part above sea level and subject to all the processes of weathering and erosion by wind, rain, ice, running water and biochemical attack that tend to reduce land surfaces. Loosened material is carried away from uplands and temporarily dumped in lowlands before eventually being removed to the sea.

Preservation of land-based sediment is certainly possible, witness the plant-derived coal deposits that fuelled the Industrial Revolution. But certain geological conditions have to be met. First, there has to be some largescale 'trap' or 'sink' in which sediments can accumulate in significant thicknesses, such as a deep lake basin or down-faulted valley. Secondly, the deposits have to be covered over by younger sediments and protected from subsequent erosion by being buried to a considerable depth (in the order of kilometres). And finally, the deposits have to be lithified (turned into rock), a process that normally results from burial, which also compacts and chemically transforms sediments into tougher and more long-lasting sedimentary rocks. When brought back to the surface through earth movements, such rocks are more resistant to weathering and erosion than unconsolidated sediments.

So the stratigraphic rock record is highly biased towards deposits that were laid down in seas that developed on and around the continents, as opposed to the much deeper oceans that lie beyond the edge of the continents. At present global sea levels are relatively low and not much of the continental surface is extensively flooded, except for regions like Hudson's Bay in North America, the Black Sea and the Caspian Sea in southwest Asia.

Of course, it is also true that some two-thirds of the Earth's surface is covered with sea, but most of this is deep ocean, with an average depth of some 3000 m (9000 ft). While sediment and organic remains do accumulate on the ocean floor, very little of these deposits are recruited into the rock record in the long term because of the movements of the Earth's crustal plates. The oldest ocean floor is no more than about 180 million years old, which might seem old enough but is not when compared with the 4.5-billion-year age of the Earth.

We will return to this topic, but in general as much ocean floor is destroyed in subduction zones (marked by deep ocean trenches) as is created in ocean-spreading ridges, otherwise the Earth would expand, which it is observably not doing. Consequently, ocean floor sediments and their organic remains tend to be destroyed by being dragged down into the Earth's interior rather than being added to the stratigraphic rock record on the continents. Nevertheless, as we shall see, there are interesting and important exceptions.

Matching Earth Time deposits around the world

At present a vast range of deposits are being laid down in many different environments over the Earth's surface. So there are river muds, now being deposited in the Thames estuary in southern England, that are the same age as glacial debris generated in polar and alpine regions and muds accumulating on the deep ocean floor. The latter are full of the remains of minute planktonic organisms and the odd whale bone, not to mention the occasional shipwreck. They, in turn, are the same age as sediment derived from the Grand Canyon and carried by the Colorado River into the Gulf of California. However, there is no direct means of measuring the exact age and contemporaneity of these deposits by any kind of geological date stamp.

Nevertheless, there is a chance that they can be closely correlated by a variety of indirect measures and especially from their organic content. 'Closely' is the critical word here. I mean close in the geological sense, which means that you have to read the small print before laying any serious bets on the correlation. This problem of correlation of sedimentary deposits and rock strata has consumed the professional lives of countless geologists since the days when

James Hutton, 1726–97, Scottish Enlightenment natural philosopher who studied medicine in Leiden, Holland, pioneered agricultural improvement and geological studies of volcanic and stratified rocks. His *Theory of the Earth*, 1788, was highly influential but mostly through Playfair's 1802 version.

John Playfair, 1748–1819, Scottish professor of mathematics and geology at Edinburgh who was a close friend of Hutton's and wrote *Illustrations of the Huttonian Theory of the Earth*, 1802, a more 'user-friendly' version of Hutton's ideas, especially those about stratification and the 'depth' of time.

———————— • ————————

James Hutton and friends, such as John Playfair, first stared into the abyss of geological time at the end of the eighteenth century.

So how will future geologists know that a layer of Thames river mud was laid down at the same time as a layer of Colorado river mud nearly 9000 km away and bordering different oceans (the Atlantic and Pacific respectively)? What would you actually find and see if you were to take a handful of sediment from both locations and compare them? For most people a mud is a mud is a mud, with not much to choose between them, nor anything much to distinguish one particle of mud from another even if you could see an individual particle, which you cannot without a high-powered microscope. Mind you, muds do vary enormously. If they did not many criminal prosecutions that depend on tracing and matching the origin of mud on the victim, suspect and so on would fail.

The composition of mud can vary because there are many different kinds of clay minerals that comprise mud and their chemistry is wonderfully complex. If it were not so we would not have the range of pottery and ceramics and many other clay-based products that we do. Even so, neither the layperson nor many geologists can distinguish one mud from another, although with the right kind of analytical equipment and know-how a great deal can be distinguished. It is possible to tell what kind of parent rocks the mud was originally derived from, what kind of climate weathered the parent rock and what kind of transport mechanism carried the mud to its final resting place.

Muds themselves cannot be directly dated, but they often contain pieces of wood or other carbonaceous organic material that can be radiocarbon dated, provided the dating is done within some 40,000 years of the life of the organism from which the carbon was derived. But even carbon dates are calculated estimates, with margins of error that amount to tens or hundreds of years, so no very precise date can be obtained by this method. Nevertheless, they are often good enough for most archaeological or geological purposes. The muds will contain a variety of microfossils, some of which belong to small organisms, especially single-celled plants (such as diatoms) and animals (such as foraminiferans) that live within the environment of deposition, plus others that have been transported by river waters, especially pollen from land-living plants.

Because our two sites – the Thames and the Grand Canyon – have a difference of more than 20 degrees in latitude and thus belong to very different climate zones and indeed continents, there will be no plant or animal species in common between them. So there is no way that the sediments can be directly matched on the basis of their contained fossils. However, indirect correlation is possible.

All species occupy finite spaces in space and time. Species' geographical range can vary from a single lake to virtually global, such as the barn owl and modern humans. Such a global distribution for a single species is unusual. Originally (around 200,000 years ago) humans were confined to Africa, so our distribution has expanded enormously since then. We have also changed over this time (evolved) and will continue to do so. The life of a species ranges from hundreds of thousands of years to several million years. Those with the widest geographical distribution but the shortest duration in time are the most useful for correlation, always providing they have preservable and identifiable fossil remains.

Thames mud is full of pollen derived from vegetation typical of the south of England, but today that includes many species that are not native and have been cultivated. Such sudden appearances can still be very useful for correlation because within a few years their pollen will be found over a wide region. Our future geologist may be able to pinpoint species in the fossil assemblage that only became common around the turn of the twentieth to twenty-first centuries, but it will still not provide a precision greater than + or − several years and will not help direct correlation with our Colorado muds in the north of the Gulf of California. The latter will also contain a great diversity of pollen typical of the vegetation found throughout the river's huge drainage basin.

A great deal is known about these plant species and their chronological ranges in North America. Consequently, there is a good chance that it will be possible to match the pollen with a particular pollen assemblage that has a restricted range in time (a so-called pollen biozone). But again, such zones are difficult to pin down to intervals much shorter than a few thousand years. Then again, matching of pollen biozones between North America and Europe is not simple because the two continents have different native species.

Estuaries and deltas are stressful environments for life because they are subject to marked changes, often on a daily basis. The presence of tides introduces changes in water salinity, temperature, clarity, level, flow direction and speed. Only tough creatures and plants can survive under such conditions. Indeed, these environments are well known for their special biotas, which include various oyster and mussel species and strange small crustaceans called ostracodes, shrimp-like creatures just a millimetre or so in size whose bodies are enclosed within tiny clam-like bivalved shells. They can be very abundant and their shells are commonly fossilised. Ostracode biozones are well developed and correlated around the world. Although they evolve quite rapidly by Earth Time standards, the relative degree of resolution that they provide is no finer than hundreds of thousands of years.

Matching strata

With the right equipment and techniques it may be possible for our future geologist to eventually get a reasonable if not exact date match between these two mud samples. But what about the poor field geologist, someone like the pioneer English surveyor and mapmaker William Smith, tramping back and forth across the British Isles by horseback, carriage and on foot trying to match strata on a regional scale? In the early days of geological mapping, the main problem was just trying to obtain any kind of match between strata that are only visible in scattered outcrops across England's 'green and pleasant land', in rock quarries, canal cuttings and boreholes excavated for wells and coal.

Fortunately, there are often reasonably distinct differences between whole sequences of strata of different age. At times particular kinds of sediments were deposited because they were laid down in distinct environments such as deserts

William Smith, 1769–1839, an English land surveyor and civil engineer, compiled and published the first *Delineation of the Strata of England and Wales* in 1815. He recognised that successive strata contained distinct fossil assemblages that could be used to match and map the rocks over wide areas. Awarded the first Wollaston medal by the Geological Society of London (1831) and an honorary doctorate by Trinity College, Dublin.

or lakes or under particular climates such as those of tropical rainforests (coal) or glacial conditions (till deposits). More often, environment and climate combined to produce a characteristic sediment that subsequently became a distinct rock type (or lithology, as it is technically called).

For instance, warm tropical waters with high evaporation rates promote the development of lime-rich (calcium carbonate) sediments and the growth of reefs with all their diverse organisms. When solidified into limestone rock, such strata are easily distinguishable from other kinds of sedimentary rocks such as sandstones that were originally laid down offshore, in river deltas or in deserts. Everywhere on Earth has, over time, experienced environmental change. Consequently, the nature of sediments deposited in each location changes and this can be readily seen in the layered nature of the resulting strata. In most places on the Earth's surface, a hole drilled straight down into the Earth will pass through successive layers of rock strata that reveal a history of dramatic change at that location.

Although distinct environments of deposition produce characteristic sedimentary rocks, such environments and their sediments have recurred throughout much of Earth Time. For instance, any one sandstone or limestone can appear, superficially at least, very much like another sandstone or limestone. Various types of detailed analysis will be able to tell just how similar or dissimilar they are in composition, but proof of similar or relative age can be more difficult. William Smith and his French contemporaries Georges Cuvier and Alexandre Brongniart found a solution to the problem. Independently, they realised that successive strata were generally characterised by particular kinds of fossils.

Smith made collections of the characteristic strata and fossils for much of England and Wales and arranged them in the order in which they were found to lie one upon another. For instance, around Oxford, Smith found a distinctive series of limestones, the youngest of which was called the Cornbrash by quarrymen. Below lay the Forest Marble, Freestone and Blue Marl, all with particular characters and fossils, before a major change occurred with the appearance of the Lias clays and limestones and then Red Marl and so on. Smith found that he could often identify and trace some strata across the landscape purely by the appearance of the rock.

But there were also many instances where limestones, sandstones and shales from different levels in the overall sequence could be easily confused. In these instances he had to rely on the fossils to help determine their relative age. It

Baron Georges Cuvier, 1769–1832, professor of animal anatomy at the National Museum of Natural History in Paris and author of many pioneering studies on extinct animals such as the mammoth. He also compiled a geological map of the Paris region with Alexandre Brongniart.

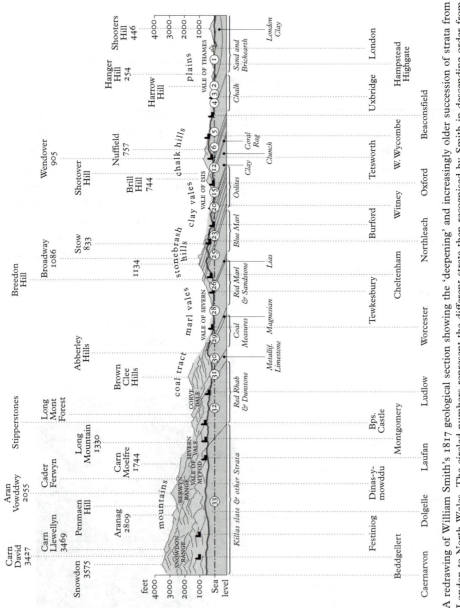

A redrawing of William Smith's 1817 geological section showing the 'deepening' and increasingly older succession of strata from London to North Wales. The circled numbers represent the different strata then recognised by Smith in descending order from youngest to oldest.

Alexandre Brongniart, 1770–1847, a French army engineer (1794–1800), director of the Sèvres porcelain factory (1800–47) and professor of mineralogy (from 1822), coauthored with Cuvier a ground-breaking geological *Essay on the Mineral Geography of the Paris Region*, 1808, and map, 1811.

was a method that worked remarkably well, although Smith did not know or perhaps even care why it worked so well. We now know that thanks to evolution organisms change through time. And, once we have worked out how exactly they change and what organisms are typical of the successive intervals of time, we can use them as crude relative 'chronometers' for Earth Time. To illustrate how the scheme works and how it developed we are going to trace William Smith's line of section from London to Snowdon.

Investigating the geological 'now'

This leg of our journey in the company of William Smith begins in London, beside the River Thames. This is where Smith's 1815 groundbreaking vertical section of British strata begins. For the first time, the whole outline succession of stratified deposits that underlie the country's landscapes were laid bare in their correct sequence, from the youngest in the Thames Valley to the oldest in the Snowdonian mountains of North Wales. The material basis of a vast chunk of Earth Time was revealed for the first time, a story that we now know takes us through more than 540 million years.

Smith must have had very ambivalent feelings about the metropolis. He had been attracted, like so many others from the rural provinces, by hopes of fame and fortune. Geologically, London was where it was all happening at the beginning of the nineteenth century. A select group of enthusiasts for the newly emerging science of the 'study of the Earth' (*logos*, a Greek word meaning discourse + *ge*, Greek for earth) founded the Geological Society of London on November 13th, 1807, initially as 'a little talking geological dinner club'. By the 1820s it was on the way to being the centre and arbiter of all things geological. Its influence spread well beyond the capital and Britain. Having a headstart over most other geological societies, it achieved an international status through its publications.

But with Britain's highly 'stratified' social system, Smith was not a member of the Geological Society and never would be. He had tried to set himself up in the capital and had high hopes for the publication of his geological map, but an 'unlucky speculation' ruined everything and he ended up spending 10 weeks in the King's Bench debtors' prison in Southwark. Any hopes of being elected a Fellow of the élite Geological Society were dashed and he had to sell up and on his release move to the north of England when his debts were paid off. It took another decade before he was re-established and his contribution to geology was formally recognised by a new generation of geologists. The Society awarded him the first Wollaston Medal in 1831, but he was still not a Fellow of the Society.

The centre of a modern capital city might not seem to have much to do with Earth Time, but it provides important examples of how present processes, especially those mediated by humans, will become part of the future geological record. In order to get some sense of what living geology is about and how it can become part of the rock record, I want to explore two distinct aspects of Holocene London. One is through a brief history of the built environment. The other is through the River Thames and its recent deposits, known geologically since William Smith's days and before as Alluvium.

What's in a name?

Alluvium is not exactly a buzzword today, but it is an ancient term simply derived from the latin *alluvius*, meaning 'washed against' or 'an inundation'. Its use in English and that of the closely related though now antiquated 'alluvion' dates back at least to the early sixteenth century. Scientifically, the name was first transformed into part of Earth Time chronology by continental scholars such as the eighteenth-century German heavyweight Abraham Gottlob Werner, who became internationally famous for his ideas about the materials and formation of the Earth. Numerous acolytes flocked to Freiburg, sat at Werner's feet, took in every word he uttered and then dispersed the Wernerian 'gospel' abroad. Many Wernerians became important and influential geologists in the early decades of the nineteenth century, including such eminent alumni as Alexander von Humboldt and Robert Jameson.

Of special importance and interest to us was Werner's attempt to order and classify all strata known at that time and provide an explanation for their occurrence at the surface of the Earth. Although his geological studies were largely confined to his home territory of Saxony, Werner was not afraid of drawing general lessons from this limited experience. Like other scholars before him, he assumed that the Earth had once been fluid and had gone through an initial and incomplete sorting into concentric layers of fire, air, water and earth according to density. For Werner, that original global and primitive ocean was a turbid and hot chemical mixture of minerals and water. The first formed rocks were deposited by chemical precipitation. Thus most rocks were aqueous in origin and were laid down one upon the other in a more or less orderly fashion. First formed and most primitive were crystalline rocks such as granite, gneiss, slate, basalt and so on. They were to be seen preserved in the highest mountains and underlay all other rocks.

———————————— • ————————————

Abraham Gottlob Werner, 1749–1817, a German professor of mineralogy at Freiburg and a charismatic teacher who attracted students from all over the world. He published little, but his *Short Classification and Description of the Various Rocks*, 1786, was highly influential.

Werner's 1786 Division of the Earth's rock formations

Aufgeschwemmte-Gebirge (Alluvium)
Flötz-Schichten (Stratified rocks)
Transition Series
Primitive Rocks

Above lay the Transition rocks, which were less crystalline chemical precipitates such as greenstone and some stony layers deposited by running water such as greywacke. These layers were to be found dipping or inclined against the flanks of mountains. Their presence suggested that the waters of the primitive ocean had begun to subside and that some of the primitive rocks were already being eroded. Recycling of their debris deposited new layers of strata, some of which included fossil remains, indicating that this was when life first began.

However, for Werner the majority of fossiliferous stratified strata belonged to the *Flötz-Schichten*, which were subsequently laid down above the Transition rocks. The *Flötz* layers were described as mainly stony and mechanical, rather than chemical, deposits of stormy running water such as sandstone, limestone

Baron Friedrich Wilhelm Heinrich Alexander von Humboldt, 1769–1859, a pioneer German polymath and geographer. Humboldt travelled to South America with his lifelong companion Aimé Bonpland. His journal influenced Charles Darwin and Humboldt authored the multivolume *Kosmos*, 1845 *et Seq.*

Robert Jameson, 1774–1854, a Scots naturalist who became professor of geology at Edinburgh. He wrote an influential Wernerian textbook, *Elements of Geognosy*, 1808, and in 1811 founded the Werner Natural History Society and journal.

———————————•———————————

(much of which is now known to be a biochemical deposit) and coal (now known to be an organic deposit), but still included some chemical precipitates such as greenstone, salt and gypsum layers. He argued that there must have been two inundations separated by a period when the global ocean was at a significantly lower level. And, since the *Flötz* were to be seen in low-lying horizontal layers, they presented evidence that overall the ocean had retreated from its original global extent.

Finally, according to Werner, there followed a prolonged retreat of the sea with the emergence of land masses on which there was a fourth series of deposits, *Aufgeschwemmte-Gebirge* or Alluvial layers. These were sands, gravels and rolled masses laid down by running water flooding over the land, carrying any loose material and dumping much of it in the sea. Volcanoes erupted spewing out lava and ash that accumulated in patches over the land along with clay and peat deposits. How and why the sea invaded the land and where it subsequently withdrew to were unanswered questions.

Werner was disinclined to speculate about the Earth's interior – 'we want to leave the dark abyss of the earth, where we can only wander about along the giddy paths of conjecture and return to that upper region of the solid earth, where the light of experience of searching minds illuminates the path'. He believed that processes going on today were the same as those in the past. And from his Saxon homeground the Earth seemed a fairly stable place undisturbed by catastrophic earth-shattering events. For Werner it seemed that geological processes were gradual, with transitions from one phase of deposition into the next.

Many students of the emerging science of geology were persuaded by Wernerian ideas and used them effectively in carrying out the first geological surveys in many parts of the world. For instance, William Maclure produced

William Maclure, 1763–1840, Scots geologist and student of Werner's who compiled and published the first geological map of America in 1809 using Werner's classification.

the first geological map of the United States in 1809. In Edinburgh University, Robert Jameson's teaching of Wernerian theory and ideas was highly influential and he probably directly recruited as many if not more to the 'cause' than Werner himself.

Famously, Jameson's performance as a teacher of geology severely 'turned off' from the subject a young English student called Charles Darwin (and his brother). Darwin subsequently remarked that Jameson's lectures were 'incredibly dull' and that as a result he determined never 'to read a book on geology or in any way study the science'. Curiously, other students do not seem to have complained about the professor's performance and luckily Darwin was to return to the geological 'fold' and accepted with more enthusiasm further instruction from a Cambridge professor Adam Sedgwick, whom we shall meet again.

In 1853 Charles Lyell defined Alluvium as 'earth, sand, gravel, stones, and other transported matter which has been washed away and thrown down by

Charles Robert Darwin, 1809–82, Cambridge-educated naturalist of independent means whose global voyage on HMS *Beagle* provided him with formative data and specimens for his theory of evolution, published in book form as *On the Origin of Species etc.*, 1859.

Adam Sedgwick, 1785–1873, student and fellow at Cambridge, appointed 7th Woodwardian professor in 1818; president of the Geological Society of London (1829), canon of Norwich from 1834, collaborated with Murchison in defining the Cambrian, Silurian and Devonian Systems of strata, but later bitterly disputed the position of the Cambro-Silurian boundary.

rivers, floods, or other causes upon land not permanently submerged beneath the waters of lakes or seas. Etym., alluo, to wash upon, or alluvio, an inundation.' By comparison Diluvium was, according to Lyell, 'those accumulations of gravel and loose materials, which, by some geologists, are said to have been produced by the action of a deluvian wave or deluge sweeping over the face of the earth.

Sir Charles Lyell, 1797–1875, Scots-born, Oxford-educated barrister who took up geology and became professor at King's College London (1831–3) and wrote the highly influential *Principles of Geology* (1831–3), president of the Geological Society of London (1835, 1849), created baronet 1864.

Etym., diluvium, deluge.' We will delve into the Diluvium in more detail below (see p. 31 *et seq.*).

Recording a built environment

A significant modern form of geological 'deposition' that does stand some chance of being preserved in the future is the result of our human habit, at least since around 8000 BP in Mesopotamia, of constructing very large structures out of reasonably durable materials. We call them towns and cities. The fact that archaeological remains of early permanent human settlements in regions such as Mesopotamia, made out of brick and stone, have lasted for such a time suggests that our much more massive modern structures are potentially of some geological significance. The Great Barrier Reef off the northeastern coast of Australia is normally quoted as the largest rock structure created by living organisms. But major cities such as London and New York are very big, with areas of around 2000 sq km (600 sq miles). Like the Barrier Reef, they can be seen from space and have similar preservational potential.

All modern cities can be seen as object lessons in the continuing economic need for rock materials and the importance of understanding geological processes that have generated these natural resources. These days, most of us, and city dwellers in particular, are far removed from any direct dependence on the natural world. Unlike our early ancestors, we do not need to know what stone makes a good hand axe, spear point, spark or even a mill stone or roofing material. However, there are plenty of people in the so-called third world who still are very close to such raw materials and have a good knowledge of rocks and minerals that are useful or valuable. Today rural markets in China have stalls selling lumps of minerals such as sulphur, rock salt, cinnabar (a mercury sulphide) and haematite (iron oxide), which have been used in medicine for millennia.

Just look around a city and reflect for a moment on its material basis. Virtually the entire external fabric and infrastructure is made of concrete, steel, glass, stone and perhaps brick – all derived from rock. And yet, very little of this huge mass is derived locally, most has been imported for construction over the decades and centuries, sometimes from considerable distance. Old cities like London grew in a fairly organic way and were founded on small settlements that were originally built using local materials. In London these were essentially organic – wood and rushes plus mud, as there is no local rock that can be used as a building stone.

London rocks

Our British geological 'hero' William Smith might not recognise many of London's buildings today, but there are still plenty of landmarks that would be familiar to him. He could spot the dome of St Paul's (founded in 604, finally rebuilt by Sir Christopher Wren over a period of 35 years from 1675), the White Tower of London (built in 1097) and the remnants of London's Roman Wall (built around 200 AD). And Smith could still find his way from the Tower to St Paul's because so many of the street names are the same as when he lived in London in the early decades of the nineteenth century.

London, like many great cities of the world such as New York, Paris, Moscow or Beijing, can be seen and thought of as a very particular kind of geological phenomenon – environments built of enduring rock materials that stand a good chance of being 'recruited' in some form into the future geological record. Just as archaeologists today grab any opportunity to probe the deep foundations of modern cities, as they try to unravel the early development and history of settlement, future archaeologists will be trying to recover information about what happened in the first decades of the twenty-first century.

Already, so much of the London environment that was familiar to William Smith has gone, mostly destroyed by the Luftwaffe but also greatly helped by really uninspired and ugly post-war 'redevelopment'. Some idea of late Georgian London can be recovered from historical documents, but by no means all. Examination of the foundations of today's new buildings often exposes artefacts and other material evidence of older buildings and activities. Furthermore, the construction of high-rise modern buildings has required deeper and more substantial foundations than previously used. The excavation of these deep foundations penetrates far below merely historic ground levels into prehistoric Pleistocene or earlier times. In doing so, it has revealed some fascinating insights into Ice Age environments, a few hundred thousand years ago (see p. 53).

The growth and development of human settlements are just like many natural geological processes. Construction and destruction combine to leave a cumulative record of layers piled one upon another, although the layers mostly consist of debris and the footings of successive edifices that were originally much grander. Both the city archaeologist and the geologist are frequently confronted with fragmentary 'palimpsest-like' records from which they struggle to reconstruct that past.

I know that many people have difficulty seeing what archaeologists or geologists find so fascinating about a muddy building site, quarry, roadcut or cliff face. Why do they spend as much time as possible grubbing about nose to the ground, backside in the air, in all weathers, scraping away with small trowels and hammers and peering at miniscule details through magnifying glasses? Well, they are like detectives or forensic scientists at the scene of a crime, often racing against time or developers to recover that elusive story of a lost past and trying to reconstruct the scene as best they can. It can be a surprisingly seductive and addictive pastime and one that is not just confined to the common caricature of bearded archaeologists dressed in shorts and sandals no matter what the weather.

Being a civil and mining engineer, William Smith had a unique knowledge of stone quarries around the country and would recognise many of the rock materials used for London's buildings. The construction of stone buildings in London has always been a problem because of the lack of any hard rock in the vicinity, as the Romans discovered. Growth and changing function required that at least some buildings, especially any fortifications, be made of tougher stuff that could not so easily be destroyed by fire. All of London's stone has been imported from elsewhere in the country and nowadays from all over the world. Being on a navigable river allowed building stone to be brought in quite easily. Certainly the Romans were past masters in the business of heavy seagoing transport, masonry and engineering construction.

When Julius Caesar's legions overran Gaul between BC 58 and 51, they found a region rich in rock suitable for building, but with no vernacular tradition of domestic stone working. However, when the Roman Emperor Claudius conquered Britain nearly 100 years later in AD 43, he found that the southern part of the country did not have much in the way of readily available rock for building. The Romans must have been taken aback by the lack of stone, but they were great improvisors and apparently good geologists because they soon 'sniffed out' what building stone was available. They found a well-established trading centre on the banks of the Thames, which they took by surprise and easily subdued. Roman London was firmly established (between 43 and 50 AD) and they built the first bridge across the river out of wood.

The Roman habit of enslaving the locals did not go down too well and in AD 60, a local heroine by the name of Boudicca and her wild army of Iceni and Trinovantes from Norfolk wreaked revenge on the Roman settlement of Colchester, routed Emperor Nero's 9th legion and then burned London to the ground. Archaeological traces of the fire can still be found in a layer of charcoal and red oxide from incinerated mud and wood. Needless to say the Romans, led by Suetonius Paulinus, were soon back in force. This time they set up shop with their standard city kit, including a public forum, basilica, temple, amphitheatre, baths, shops and markets, along with a fort. Finally in AD 200 they built a great 6 m (20 ft) high surrounding wall of stone about 5 km (3 miles) long and reinforced the river embankment to protect the 30,000 or so inhabitants.

The one local rock-derived material that the Romans did use was clay to make bricks, again a technology at which they were expert. But the stone for the fort and wall had to be shipped in by river from quarries near Maidstone, 70 miles downstream in Kent. The rock is known as Kentish Ragstone and was to become one of the most important stones for building purposes in southeast England. It is a grey limestone of early Cretaceous age (some 116 ma old) and although hard is not very good for carving or ornamental work.

Elsewhere in Britain the Romans used whatever stone was locally available and they found excellent freestone in the southwest, such as around Bath. Good-quality material they were prepared to move over considerable distances by road and water. A large ceremonial arch over 25 m high at Richborough in Kent was built of Ragstone and then clad in 400 tonnes of Carrara marble imported from Italy. And even the much smaller London ceremonial arch required the transport by road of over 100 waggon-loads of limestone from Lincolnshire 145 km (90 miles) away. Altogether London's Roman remains show that over 20 different ornamental stones, mostly marble, were imported from France, Italy, Greece, Turkey and Egypt, although the total bulk would not have been great.

The Kentish Ragstone was also exploited by the Normans some 800 years later when the next phase of significant building took place in London. The Ragstone was used to construct the impregnable walls of the White Tower, now part of the larger Tower of London. However, when it came to important ceremonial buildings such as Westminster Abbey, the Norman masons imported from France the rock material they were most familiar with, the beautiful white Caen limestone.

Smith would have recognised the Ragstone, but many of the foreign stones in use today, such as the orbicular granite from Finland and limestones from Turkey, would certainly have puzzled him. Nevertheless, the fabric of the city today, just like that of most modern human settlements, is still largely constructed from natural earth materials. Whether its modern glass, steel and concrete or the more traditional stone, brick and slate, they are essentially all derived from rocks. At any moment of the day or night, somewhere there are vast quantities of rock and mineral material being mined or quarried, then transported and processed from their raw state and finally fabricated into the buildings, roads, walls, bridges and so on that we take for granted.

These days the proportion of rock used straightforwardly as building or dimension stone, as it is called, is very small because it is so expensive. Less than 0.25 per cent of all geological materials used in construction is dimension stone (even so, around a million tonnes of dressed stone is used each year in the UK). The vast majority is crushed into rock aggregate for road construction and concrete along with sand and gravel, in total some 250 million tonnes a year in the UK. Most of us never really witness the extraction end of the business because it is unsightly, noisy, dirty and dangerous and we do not like it in our own backyards, but it still happens – out of sight, out of mind. Worldwide we are talking about over 11 billion tonnes of solid rock being quarried for construction, along with another 9 billion tonnes of sand and gravel, not to mention all the rock material excavated by the mining industry.

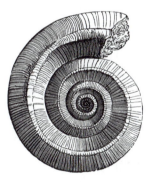

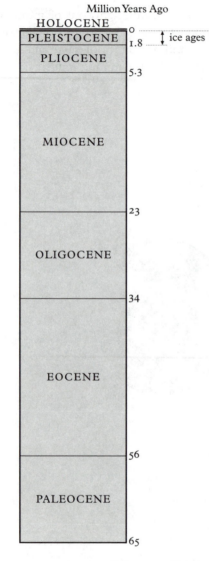

Holocene to Pleistocene.

2

The Diluvium –
The Flood and the Ice Ages

PLEISTOCENE TO EOCENE

London's Diluvial or Pleistocene park

The discovery of large animal bones buried a few feet below the ground in central London came as quite a surprise when the foundations for some of the grand buildings around Trafalgar Square were dug out in the late nineteenth century. The same rich seam was uncovered with post Second World War redevelopment of some of the surrounding 'empire' buildings such as New Zealand House, Uganda House and the Royal Bank of Scotland. Identification of the bones revealed an extraordinary bestiary of elephant, rhino, hippo, giant deer, oxen, horse, hyaena and big cats. What were animals normally associated with Africa doing in central London?

The soft riverbed silts containing the bones were fairly superficial deposits but were covered with soil or Alluvium, so they were not modern in origin. Although King Charles II had kept a menagerie of wild beasts in the Tower of London in the seventeenth century and the Emperor Claudius's Roman legions brought elephants to Britain in AD 43, these remains were evidently still older.

By the early decades of the nineteenth century, patches of near-surface, 'soft' sediments were found plastered over the landscapes of the British Isles, northern

31

Europe, Asia and North America. Sometimes similar remains of recognisable large mammals were found and the deposits were commonly referred to as the Diluvium. They were not much more ancient than the superficial Alluvium, since these diluvial sediments are still soft and have not been lithified into rock strata. Also, diluvial fossils tend to be very well preserved and can easily be mistaken for the bones and shells of living creatures. However, when closely examined by experts they generally turn out to belong to extinct species.

As we have seen, the name Diluvium is Latin and means flood or deluge. The word was in use by the mid-seventeenth century when the famous English diarist, John Evelyn, referred in his entry for August 15th, 1655 to 'the calculation of coincidence with the diluvial period'. The following year Blount's *Glossary* defined Diluvium as 'belonging to a deluge or flood, especially to the Flood as recorded in Genesis'.

———————————— • ————————————

John Evelyn, 1620–1706, an English traveller, diarist and scandal-monger, who proposed to the chemist Robert Boyle the foundation of the Royal Society (in 1660), the oldest-surviving scientific society, of which Evelyn became secretary in 1672.

———————————— • ————————————

Diluvial records of the Flood

Occasional discoveries of very large, well-preserved bones in deposits of this kind caused a stir even as far back as mediaeval times. In 1171, the English chronicler Ralph of Coggeshall in Essex recounted how the collapse of a local river bank revealed huge bones that he thought belonged to a 'man' who 'must have been fifty feet high'. However, by the seventeenth century the idea that such bones had belonged to mythical giants had faded away, as naturalists began to recognise their true affinities even if they were still greatly puzzled by how the remains of such exotic animals had 'arrived' in northern Europe. There was one explanation that at the time was the most obvious one: the animal remains and

Gigantis Sceleton
in monte Erice propè Drepanum
inventum Boccatio *teste 200 cu-*
bitorum .

In *Mundus subterraneus* (1665), the Jesuit Athanius Kircher accepted the common idea that large fossil bones were the remains of giants but protested at the tendency to exaggerate their size.

the muds and sands that contained them had all been swept north from their natural habitats by the Flood or Deluge.

It is hard for us today to fully appreciate the mindset and religious 'wiring' that connected society throughout most of Europe and the domains of Christendom. For well over 1000 years the Judeo-Christian Old Testament with its story of Creation and the subsequent Flood, as related in Genesis, was generally accepted as historical fact and, more than that, it was the word of God and therefore indisputable. Virtually all the major philosophers and naturalists, including revolutionary thinkers such as Newton, were at least Christian deists and often much more literal in their reading of the scriptures. We have to remember that as late as 1697, Thomas Aikenhead, an 18-year-old medical student in Edinburgh, was arrested for heresy. He was overheard repeating part of an 'infidel' tract and despite his recantation and plea for mercy was hanged. You did not meddle lightly with the received wisdom of the Church and Bible.

The unearthing of a huge tooth from a peat bog near Albany, New York caused a stir in 1706 and was claimed as belonging to a sinner drowned in the Flood. Governor Dudley of Massachusetts forwarded it to the polymathic Boston preacher Cotton Mather with the recommendation:

> I suppose all the surgeons in town have seen it, and I am perfectly of the opinion that it was a human tooth. I measured it, and as it stood upright it was six inches high ... and round 13 inches ... and its weight in the scale was 2 pounds and four ounces ... I am perfectly of the opinion that the tooth will agree only to a human body, for whom the flood only could prepare a funeral; and without doubt he waded as long as he could keep his head above water, but must at length be confounded with all other creature and the new sediment after the flood gave him the depth we now find.

The tooth was not very convincing evidence and was in fact the molar of a mastodon, but in Europe new victims of the Flood were being uncovered.

One of the most eminent of early eighteenth-century naturalists was the Swiss scholar Johann Jacob Scheuchzer. His 1709 book *Herbarium of the Deluge* illustrated a wide range of fossil plants that he regarded as the remains of land vegetation that had been swept away by the Flood, buried in its deposits and subsequently revealed when the waters subsided. One thing puzzled Scheuchzer

---

Cotton Mather, 1663–1728, a Harvard-trained American protestant mystic involved with the Salem witch trials. Mather also founded Yale with a grant from a London merchant, Elihu Harvard. He pioneered innoculation against smallpox in America and became a Fellow of the Royal Society in 1713.

Johann Jacob Scheuchzer (1672–1733), a Swiss naturalist and physician who amassed one of the largest collections of fossils in Europe. His *Herbarium of the Deluge* (1709) and *Physica Sacra* (1731) portrayed natural objects including fossils within the context of the Judeo-Christian Old Testament.

and that was the apparent lack of fossil remains of the human sinners who were also victims of the Flood.

In 1725 Scheuchzer seized on the reported discovery of a human-like fossil in strata quarried for lithographic stone at Oeningen on the shores of Lake Constance in his native Switzerland. Excited by the find, he wrote to Sir Hans Sloane, a rich and famous English dilettante whose extensive collections later formed the basis of the British Museum.

We have obtained some relics of the race of man drowned in the Flood ... what we have here is no vision of the mere imagination, but well-preserved bones, and in such number, of a human skull, quite clearly distinguished from the bones of other species.

The fossil named *Homo diluvii testis*, meaning 'a Man, a Witness to the Deluge and Divine Messenger', was thought to have drowned in 2306 BC according to Scheuchzer's reading of biblical chronology. Deacon Miller of Leipheim, a friend of Scheuchzer's, composed a couplet describing the victim as 'Unhappy evidence of past transgression,/Let these stones move the wicked to contrition.'

The flattened skeleton, still preserved today in the Tyler Museum in Haarlem, the Netherlands, has a curious helmet-like skull and backbone with limb bones

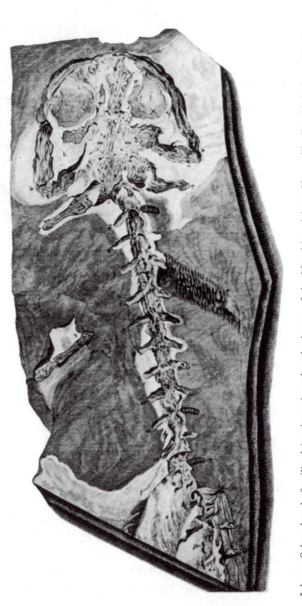

Johann Scheuchzer's fossilised 'ancient sinner' and witness of the Noachian deluge *Homo diluvii testis* is in reality the skeleton of a giant salamander.

Sir Hans Sloane, 1660–1753, physician to King George II who trained in France and became secretary (1693–1712) then president (1727–41) of the Royal Society and was created baronet in 1716. His collection was purchased for the nation and formed the basis of the British Museum.

---

sticking out from the side. But Scheuchzer's enthusiasm and desire to find a fossilised human 'witness' got the better of his critical faculties for the niceties of human anatomy. In 1809, Georges Cuvier used his predictive skills based on comparative anatomy to demonstrate publicly that the skeleton is in fact that of a large salamander (scientifically known as *Andreas scheuchzerii*).

Cuvier was unusual in being a French Lutheran and generally made a separation between his science and his religion. Just as astronomers were bursting through the perceived limits of space, so Cuvier wrote in 1813, 'would it not also be glorious for man to burst the limits of time, and, by a few observations, to ascertain the history of this world, and the series of events which preceded the birth of the human race?' He interpreted the deposition of the fossiliferous strata of the Paris region as the result of a succession of catastrophic flood events, but he refused to speculate on their extent and origin. However, he suspected that they were not global, otherwise they would have required a succession of creation events to restock the life of the planet. Instead, he thought that there must have been refuges where life survived to repopulate the lands and oceans.

But Cuvier did also believe that the catastrophic Flood, as recorded in the Old Testament, had occurred. For Cuvier this Deluge had indeed 'extinguished' the extraordinary mammal fauna that included such magnificent beasts as the mammoth and thus brought an end to the prehuman world. For Cuvier 'l'homme fossile n'existe pas', but what he did not know was that back in England a discovery had been made that presaged a revolution in the understanding of human antiquity.

At a meeting of the Society of Antiquaries in London in 1797, it was announced that a Suffolk gentleman by the name of John Frere had found flint stones carefully fashioned in the shape of pointed axes. Frere argued that these flints from Hoxne in Suffolk were so well fashioned that they must have been made by the hand of man rather than by any accident of nature. The flintstone tools were found several feet below ground level, buried in sands and gravels from which the remains of extinct animals had also come. Consequently, Frere concluded that the humans who made them must have lived alongside these ancient extinct beasts and that therefore 'the situation at which these weapons were found may tempt us to refer them to a very remote period indeed, even beyond that of the present world'. The cracks were beginning to appear in the generally accepted prehistoric chronology, especially that of humans, but it was to be nearly another 100 years before human antiquity was finally accepted by the scientific community.

———————— • ————————

John Frere, 1740–1807, a Fellow of Caius College, Cambridge, member of parliament, high sheriff of Norfolk and antiquarian who published the first description and illustration of an ancient stone tool as an object worked by human hand.

———————— • ————————

But the idea that the Diluvial Period and its fossil remains represented the biblical Flood event was still very much alive and kicking through the first few decades of the nineteenth century. This was largely thanks to energetic advocacy by some well-placed and influential geologists in England, especially William Buckland. On appointment as Reader in Geology at the University of Oxford in 1819, the Reverend Dr Buckland gave an inaugural lecture entitled 'The Connexion of Geology with Religion Explained'. For Buckland one of the prime objectives of geology was 'to confirm the evidence of natural religion; and to show that the facts developed by it are consistent with the accounts of the creation and deluge recorded in the Mosaic writings'.

The Earl of Bridgwater, Francis Egerton (1756–1829), a Fellow of All Souls in Oxford, gave £8000 for the publication of the best work on 'The Goodness of God as manifested in the Creation'. The money was divided between eight authors in what was to become known as the 'Bridgwater Treatises'. Buckland was an obvious choice to be one of the authors and took his task seriously.

The Very Rev. William Buckland, 1784–1856, reader in geology at Oxford (from 1813), author of *Reliquae Diluvianae* (1823), the Bridgwater treatise volume on geology (1836), Canon of Christchurch (from 1825), Dean of Westminster (from 1845) and twice President of the Geological Society of London (1824 and 1839).

William Buckland was one of the most influential and well-known geologists in England during the first few decades of the nineteenth century. Like Werner, he was a charismatic if sometimes eccentric teacher and lecturer who inspired many famous students of geology such as Charles Lyell. A Dickensian figure, Buckland was famous in Oxford for his menagerie of sundry pets, ranging from guinea pigs to a jackal that was occasionally to be heard crunching one of the guinea pigs under the sofa and a bear, named Tiglath Pileser, after the founder of the Assyrian empire. He also liked culinary experiments and claimed that he had tried eating most living things from mice to crocodile. Both at the University of Oxford and at the newly founded Geological Society in London, Buckland was famed for his rhetoric, often spiced with unusual demonstrations and examples. Eventually, as can so often happen, he became over fond of the sound of his own voice, something of a caricature of himself, increasingly irrational. Eventually Buckland descended into real madness.

More importantly, Buckland was also a leader of the British theological geologists, along with clergymen such as the Reverend William Conybeare. They assumed that the investigation of the Earth's history would confirm the Mosaic tradition of the Flood as a major event. Buckland and his supporters searched for geological evidence of the Flood, expecting to find both sedimentary

debris, drowned 'sinners' and remains of all the animals and plants that had
inhabited the Earth. Culturally, catastrophism was in the air, with romantic
ideas and images of revolution attracting both fear and fascination in the minds
of poets, writers and artists.

William Conybeare, 1787–1857, Dean of
Llandaff (from 1845), geologist and coauthor,
with W. Phillips, of *Outlines of the Geology of
England and Wales* (1822). He was a major
contributor to Greenough's geological map and
pioneered the investigation of extinct marine
reptiles.

The poet Byron's (1788–1824) preface to his drama *Cain*, published in 1821,
spells out his clear understanding of catastrophism as promoted by Cuvier.

The reader will perceive that the author has partly adopted in this poem
the notion of Cuvier, that the world had been destroyed several times
before the creation of man. This speculation, derived from the different
strata and the bones of enormous and unknown animals found in them, is
not contrary to the Mosaic account, but rather confirms it; as no human
bones have yet been discovered in those strata, although those of many
known animals are found near the remains of the unknown.

Likewise, whether in his home Lake District or the French Alps, Wordsworth's contemplation of the sublime mountain landscapes led him to question whether they had been 'fashioned by the turbulence of waves,/ Then, when o'er highest hills the Deluge pass'd?'

William Wordsworth, 1770–1850, the famous Cambridge-educated (1787–91) poet laureate (from 1843). He renounced his early revolutionary sympathies and became deeply concerned with landscape, especially that of the Lake District and its inhabitants, where he lived from 1799. Through his brother Christopher who was master of Trinity College, Cambridge, he met Sedgwick and asked him to write a geological introduction to his *A Complete Guide to the Lakes*, 1842.

The aspirations and excesses of the French Revolution were still very much in the popular imagination. A series of monumental canvases by the English artist John Martin (1789–1854), on historical and biblical themes such as *The Fall of Babylon* (1819), *The Destruction of Pompeii by the Eruption of Vesuvius in AD 79* (1822) and the *Deluge* (1826), attracted hordes of viewers when publicly displayed. The *Deluge* was so popular that Martin issued mezzotint copies for sale in 1828.

In 1821, Buckland heard that a huge cache of strange bones had been found in a Yorkshire cave and he hurried north to see for himself. He discovered to his amazement and delight the well-preserved bones of elephant, rhino, hippo, big cats, even birds, some 24 species altogether. Most common were hyaena bones and Buckland concluded that the cave had been an antediluvian hyaena den. In one of the earliest studies of how animals of the past lived, Buckland's examination of chew marks on many of the bones and an analysis of fossilised faeces showed that the hyaenas had scavenged the bones of the other animals, dragging them back into the safety of their den to chew at their leisure. He concluded that the den had been submerged by the waters of the Flood, drowning the hyaenas that lived there and covering their bones with sediment. From the number of stalagmites growing up from the cave floor, he further estimated that

William Conybeare drew this cartoon of William Buckland entering Kirkdale cave in Yorkshire as if it were still inhabited by ice age hyaenas and scavenged bones. Buckland saw the fossil remains as evidence that the Flood had drowned the hyaenas.

the Flood had occurred between 5000 and 6000 years ago. Not surprisingly, this age conveniently coincided with the generally accepted date of the Flood.

Buckland presented his results in his 1823 book *Reliquae diluvianae; or, Observations on the Organic Remains Contained in Caves, Fissures, and Diluvial Gravel, and on Other Geological Phenomena, Attesting the Action of an Universal Deluge*. For Buckland, the geological detail 'by affording the strongest evidence of a universal deluge, leads us to hope that it will no longer be asserted as it has been by high authorities, that geology supplies no proofs of an event in the reality of which the truth of the Mosaic records is so materially involved'. With his blinkered passion to reveal the 'true' nature of the geological record of the Diluvium, Buckland could not see any contradictory evidence. The most famous of his missed opportunities was his 'reading' of the evidence he had found in Goat's Hole Cave, Paviland in South Wales.

From 1822–3 Buckland excavated layers of cave deposits in which he found a complete human skeleton, numerous stone tools and ornaments made of mammoth ivory, all buried below the surface deposits of the cave. The human skeleton had clearly been purposefully buried in a shallow grave with the ornaments and then dusted with red ochre (a naturally occurring oxide of iron). The scattering of ochre and placing of the ornaments suggested to Buckland that the body had been buried with some ceremony. Buckland was a very acute observer, concerned with accuracy, and he produced a detailed description and plan of the find. From his examination of the skeleton, he could find no significant differences from the modern human frame. However, he mistakenly thought that it belonged to a young woman and it has been known as the 'Red Lady of Paviland' ever since, although it is in fact a young male, aged about 25 and 1.7 m (5 ft 6 in) tall.

Although Buckland knew that the mammoth was an extinct animal commonly associated with Diluvial deposits, he could not make the connection between the presence of ornaments made of mammoth ivory and a contemporaneous age for the skeleton. Instead, he had to produce an unnecessarily complicated story to explain the facts. Accordingly, the 'woman' was from a Welsh tribe who lived and died during the Roman occupation of Britain. Her relatives had buried her in the cave where they found the ancient 'fossil' mammoth tusks and made them into the ornaments that they then placed in her grave.

We now know that the skeleton is around $26,350 \pm 550$ years old and that he was one of the Cro-Magnon people who first migrated into western Europe around 40,000 years ago. There was no way that Buckland could have known the age in years. But he missed the chance to become the first person to find and describe the remains of our most immediate human relatives, who made stone tools and did indeed coexist with the animals of the Diluvium as John Frere had claimed. Buckland's sincere attempt to reconcile the Old Testament account with the emerging geological facts further delayed the recognition of the scientific facts of the matter. However, Buckland was not a dogmatic fundamentalist. Continental geologists were about to cause a major upset in the interpretation of the Diluvium.

Ice from the Alps

The phenomenon of Alpine glaciers had fascinated naturalists for hundreds of years, but it was not until the mid-eighteenth century and the pioneering work of Scheuchzer that there was any real scientific research on them. Part of the problem was the occasional presence of huge boulders of rock (called 'erratics') scattered over northern Europe and northern North America. Often they were demonstrably different in composition from the underlying rocks where they were found. What mechanism could possibly transport such massive 'alien' rocks and then dump them unceremoniously on the landscape, often many miles from the nearest mountain?

In and around the Alps there was the possibility that they had been carried by glaciers, since it was an observable fact that glacial ice could indeed support and carry very large rock masses over considerable distances given time. A Swiss pastor, Bernhard Kuhn, first suggested in 1787 that such boulders were evidence that glaciers might have in the past extended far beyond their present extent. However, Buckland and his theologically minded colleagues had a ready explanation for the 'erratics' – the Flood. Just to complicate matters, evidence was emerging from polar exploration demonstrating the power of sea ice and icebergs to transport rocks far from their original source by flotation.

Interest in the extraordinary snow- and ice-bound environments of the poles had grabbed popular imagination. Increasing publicity had attended the expeditions of British whalers such as William Scoresby (senior) in the first decade of the nineteenth century into northern polar waters and their conflicts with the French, with whom the British were at war. Appreciation of the sublime power of icy wastes was further enhanced by the growing popularity of Alpine tourism. Byron and the Shelleys were ardent fans of the mountains and glaciers. The Shelleys' 1816 visit to the Mer de Glace glacier above Chamonix they described as:

> a scene of dizzying wonder ... the vale itself is filled with a mass of undulating ice ... we walked to some distance upon its surface – the waves are elevated about 12 or 15 feet from the surface of the mass which is intersected with long gaps of unfathomable depth, the ice of whose sides is more beautifully azure than the sky. In these regions everything changes & is in motion – one would think that Mont Blanc was a living being & that the frozen blood forever circulated thro' his stony veins.

Mary Shelley used this new-found information about the icy wastes to great dramatic effect in her novel *Frankenstein*, published in 1819 when she was just 22 years old.

Perhaps Buckland's Flood could be modified by drowning landscapes with marine waters charged with icebergs that dumped their load of boulders wherever they melted? The retreating waters then exposed the stranded erratics. The idea, promoted by Charles Lyell in the 1830s, became known as the 'Drift theory', with the deposits simply referred to as 'drift'. The discovery of modern-looking seashells stranded high on Welsh and Scottish hills seemed to support this version of events. There was a lot of often heated argument in London's newly founded Geological Society on such matters. With immediate access to living glaciers and the opportunity to study both their erosional and depositional powers, Swiss geologists had a significant advantage in assessing the reality of the matter.

Jean de Charpentier (also known by the German version of his name, Johann von) first mapped the former extent of the Rhône glacier onto the central plain

Louis Agassiz's illustrations of glacial phenomena such as moraines and erratic boulders (here on the Aar glacier) eventually persuaded British geologists of the reality of the Ice Ages.

of Switzerland based on the distribution of 'erratic' boulders. Charpentier had proved that most of the rocks had not been transported by flood waters or floating icebergs and that the commonly found scratched and grooved rock surfaces in Alpine terrains were the result of glacial ice charged with rock debris. By 1824 Jens Esmark was describing evidence of formerly extensive glaciers in Norway, and in 1832 Reinhard Bernhardi argued that a polar ice cap had once spread as far south as central Germany. The study of glaciers and theorising about their former extent and influence on the landscape were becoming popular. While English geologists were still arguing the toss about the merits of the ice-raft Drift theory, the greater explanatory power of the glacial theory was common knowledge in Switzerland.

Jean de Charpentier, 1786–1855, son of German geologist Wilhelm von Charpentier, student of Werner's. Jean described (1823) the geology of the Pyrenees, became a director of saltworks and pioneered the mapping of the former extent of Alpine glaciers using the distribution of the so-called erratic boulders (often simply referred to as 'erratics').

———— • ————

Charpentier recounted that in 1834 he met a woodcutter who recognised an erratic boulder and that 'the Grimsel glacier transported them and deposited them on both sides of the valley, because that glacier extended in the past as far as the town of Bern, indeed water could not have deposited them at such an elevation above the valley bottom, without filling the lakes'. Charpentier encouraged the young Swiss naturalist Louis Agassiz to pursue and emphasise his studies of glaciers over those of fossil fish. Not that Agassiz needed much pushing: he steamrollered ahead on his own accord promoting his own ideas and often neglected to acknowledge the role of other scientists such as Charpentier and the German botanist Karl Schimper in developing them.

———— • ————

(Jean) Louis Rodolphe Agassiz, 1807–73, Swiss born, published pioneering research on fossil fish (1833–44) and developed Schimper's idea of a recent Ice Age (*Etudes sur les Glaciers*, 1840). Emigrating to America in 1846, he became professor of zoology and geology at Harvard in 1847 and was a vehement opponent of Darwin's theory of evolution.

Karl Friedrich Schimper, 1803–67, German botanist who presented many of his ideas as poems and never secured an academic post. He was one of the pioneers of modern plant morphology and from his studies of fossil plants developed a theory of alternating hot and cold climates in the past.

———————————— • ————————————

Schimper was a fellow student with Agassiz and initially his friend. In the mid-1830s they conducted their glacial studies together. Schimper developed his concept of a great Ice Age (*Eiszeit*) in a series of lectures in Munich. From his studies of fossil plant and animal remains, he suggested that there had been alternating phases of destruction and 'reanimation'. The youngest of these phases of desolation was an Ice Age during which the erratics had been scattered over the landscapes, carried there by glaciers flowing out from the mountains. Schimper even wrote an ode:

Ice of the Past! Of an Age when frost
In its stern clasp held the lands of the South,
Dressed with its mantle of desolate white
Mountains and forests, fair valleys and lakes!

By 1837 Agassiz had formulated his theory of a relatively recent *Eiszeit* (borrowing the term from Schimper) in which he claimed that a marked fall of temperature had happened before the upheaval of the Alps. He developed his ideas into a book, *Etudes sur les glaciers* (published privately in 1840). His reconstruction imagined that following the accumulation of the Earth's ancient geological formations, repeated falls in temperature produced an enormous ice sheet that extended over the greater part of Europe and across the Mediterranean as far south as the Atlas mountains, over northern Asia and northern North America. Only the highest peaks rose above the blanket of ice. Then upheaval of the Alps caused rocks to break from mountainsides and onto the ice, to be carried away by the glaciers. There were many things that Agassiz did not explain, such as why the temperature had fallen and what had uplifted the Alps. But he was an excellent self-publicist and his ideas were soon being broadcast all over Europe and in Britain, where they attracted the attention of eminent geologists such as Buckland and Charles Lyell.

Buckland had heard Agassiz lecture on his theory at Freiberg in 1838. After the meeting Buckland and his wife travelled south to Neuchâtel, along with Agassiz and a wealthy amateur naturalist by the name of Charles Lucien Bonaparte, Prince of Canino and brother of the deposed emperor. The Bucklands already knew Agassiz, since he had previously stayed with them in Oxford

Buckland's 1836 version of stratigraphic succession

Alluvium Diluvium (Glacial Deposits)	
Tertiaries	Tertiary Series
Chalk Greensand Oolite Lias Keuper Muschelkalk (New Red Sandstone) Bunter Magnesian Limestone New Red Conglomerate Great Coal Formation Carboniferous or Mountain Limestone Old Red Sandstone	Secondary Series
Transition Limestone and Shale (Wenlock Limestone) Grauwacke Series	Transition Series
Clay Slate Mica Slate Gneiss	Primary Stratified Series
Granite	

when he was researching fossil fish. Now Agassiz tried to convince the stubborn Diluvialist of the error of his ways by showing him the abundant and clear evidence for glaciation in the Alps. But Buckland was not to be swayed so easily.

However, Agassiz found a better opportunity to address his theory to a larger audience of British geologists in September 1840. He travelled all the way to Glasgow to attend the annual meeting of the British Association for the Advancement of Science. There he lectured on his glacial theory and emphasized once again that 'at a certain epoch all of the north of Europe and also the north of Asia and America were covered by a mass of ice'. Needless to say, it did not go down too well and Lyell led the attack on Agassiz. However Buckland, unusually for him, remained silent, perhaps because he had been mulling over the evidence that Agassiz had shown him in the Alps. Anyway, Buckland invited Agassiz and another rising star of the British geological firmament, Roderick Impey Murchison, to make a joint expedition to study the British field evidence of drift in Scotland and the north of England.

Sir Roderick Impey Murchison, 1792–1871, Scottish-born army officer (1807–15) in the Peninsular War, who on retirement married Charlotte, daughter of General Hugonin, and took up geology. He went on to define the Silurian and Permian Systems and the Devonian with Sedgwick. President of the Geological Society of London (1831, 1841), co-founder of the Royal Geographical Society, he was knighted in 1846 and created baronet in 1866.

This time Buckland was converted and set about bringing Lyell round, although he could not convince Murchison. By mid-October Buckland could write to Agassiz:

Lyell has adopted your theory *in toto*!!! On my showing him a beautiful cluster of moraines within two miles of his father's house [at Kinnorchy?], he instantly accepted it, as solving a host of difficulties which have all his life embarrassed him.

The following month (November), Lyell, Buckland and Agassiz all presented papers on the evidence for glaciers in Britain at the Geological Society in London. Murchison protested at the way Buckland viewed all Diluvium as glacial moraine and if so did that mean that London's 'Highgate hill will be regarded as the seat of a glacier, & Hyde Park & Belgrave Sqre will be the scene of its influences?' But the glacialists responded well with authoritative 'chapter and verse', with Buckland allowing for the additional action of drift and floating ice as well as glaciers.

One observer noted:

with a look & tone of triumph [Buckland] pronounced upon his opponents who dared to question the orthodoxy of the scratches & grooves, & polished surfaces of the glacial mts (when they should come to be d—d the pains of eternal itch without the privilege of scratching!)

(Woodward 1907, pp. 138–42)

Buckland's *volte face* did not go unnoticed by the London press. A cartoon appeared showing the Oxford professor complete with his characteristic geological field clothing topped off with academical robe standing on a deeply grooved rock surface. Two specimens lay at his feet, one labelled 'Scratched by a glacier thirty-three thousand three hundred and thirty-three years before creation' and the other 'scratched by a cart wheel on Waterloo Bridge the day before yesterday'.

The following year, a somewhat aggrieved Charpentier published his *Essai sur les Glaciers*, in which he took care to give credit where it was due, especially to mountaineers like Jean-Pierre Perraudin from Chamonix, who was a chamois hunter and back in 1815 had seen evidence of scars on hard rocks produced by

A cartoon ('scratched' by Sopwith) lampooning a 'glacially regaled' Buckland for his *volte face* on the glacial question. At his feet are rocks labelled 'scratched by a glacier 33,333 years before Creation' and 'scratched by a cart wheel on Waterloo Bridge the day before yesterday'.

glaciers and voiced the opinion that glaciers had once filled the Alpine valleys, leaving erratic boulders when they melted away. Importantly, Charpentier argued (correctly as it turned out) that the maximum advance of the ice occurred after the uplift of the Alps. Furthermore, he thought that normal river valleys had been eroded before the glaciers developed and exploited pre-existing valleys (again a correct interpretation).

Encouraged by Lyell, Agassiz took the opportunity to visit North America and Lyell waved him goodbye from Liverpool in September 1846. Docking briefly at Halifax, Nova Scotia, and eager to find evidence of glaciation in North America for himself, Agassiz

> sprang on shore, and started at a brisk pace for the heights above the landing ... I was met by the familiar signs, the polished surfaces, the furrows and scratches, the line engravings of the glacier ... and I became convinced ... that here also this great agent had been at work.

The following year a professorship was created for Agassiz at Harvard and he was to remain in America until his death in 1873. American geologists had already accepted his theory, but Agassiz was as over-enthusiastic as ever. Lyell reported that as a result of an expedition to South America in 1865 Agassiz 'has gone wild about glaciers ... the whole of the great [Amazon] valley, down to its mouth was filled by ice' and yet 'he does not pretend to have met with a single glaciated pebble or polished rock'. Agassiz had indeed let his imagination run away with him. Luckily for the development of the Ice Age theory, enough steadier hands had become convinced by the real evidence and the Flood theory was finally 'dead in the water', at least in scientific circles.

Ice Age bones and stones

Now we can begin to understand what animals normally associated with Africa were doing in central London. The ancient river sediments that contain their bones reveal an astonishing history of rapid climate change throughout the Ice Age or Pleistocene times, as it is scientifically known (see later discussion).

There were 'good' times when the climate was warm. Landscapes were lush enough for hippos to wallow in the rivers, while elephant, rhino, hyaenas, big cats and the occasional small band of our ancient human relatives, such as the *heidelbergensis*, Neanderthal and Cro-Magnon *sapiens* people, roamed through woods and valleys, over hills and dales. But there were also 'bad' times when catastrophic swings in climate brought glaciers and ice sheets down from the north. The ice sheets breached the northern flank of the Thames Valley and was not far from overwhelming the whole country. With subzero temperatures all life that could leave did so; the rest dwindled and died out over just a few generations.

The testimony of the Thames terrace gravels shows that such disastrous swings in the mood of the climate happened not just once or twice but many times. Indeed, the valley has one of the best records of climate change throughout the middle and late part of the Pleistocene Ice Ages to be found in Europe. The story has important lessons for the future.

Today a visitor to London may be forgiven for wondering how ancient names like Tower Hill and Parliament Hill came into being, since there are no significant topographic prominences to be seen. Nevertheless, these 'hills' do rise above the river and any elevation above flood level has value for those that live beside a river. The Thames is today very small by global standards, but not so very long ago it was, along with the Rhine, one of the major rivers of Europe. And it does not take much flood water to threaten life and habitation. Not until the banks of the Thames were reinforced and its channel better secured was the risk of flooding in the city diminished. Outside the city and the marshes that originally surrounded it, the flanks of the river valley rise in a series of low-stepped terraces onto the chalk downlands that form the rim of the Thames Basin.

The terrace surfaces have well-drained sandy soils with heathlands such as at Hampstead in the north and Dulwich in the south. From the mid-nineteenth century onwards these sands and gravels were increasingly exploited for building purposes and it was discovered that in places they were very extensive – all the way up river to Oxford and beyond in the west and to the old Roman fort of Colchester in the northeast. To the geologists of the day these were regarded variously as 'drift', valley gravels or glacial gravel deposits and were generally considered to be marine rather than genuine river deposits. And yet the bones of land-living animals such as elephant, deer and even rhino were occasionally found within them.

Now we realise that the sands and gravels are river deposits of a vastly larger Thames and tributaries that received huge volumes of melt water and sediment during the Pleistocene Ice Ages. The headwaters of the Thames may have even drained parts of North Wales. The original downriver outflow was further north than it is today and ran through Norfolk to the North Sea. There it joined the even bigger Rhine. Sea levels were at times much lower than today, as much as 120 m lower, and Britain was just an extension of the European continent with much of the North Sea being dry land. Animals and people were free to migrate to and fro.

This was because so much ocean water was locked up in the greatly expanded glaciers and ice sheets. At other times sea level was much higher, as much as 200 m higher than present levels, and this occurred through a combination of depressed land and more water in the oceans from the reduction of ice sheets and the release of their meltwaters into the oceans. We have good cause to worry

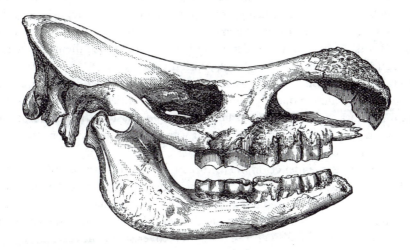

Remarkable fossils of large mammals such as this skull of an extinct rhinoceros were found within the Ice Age deposits of the Thames Valley in the 19th century.

about changing sea levels, because the record shows that they constantly change both globally and regionally from different causes and there is nothing very much we can do about it except get out of the way.

The lower course of the Thames was pushed south around 400,000 years ago by ice sheets during the Anglian cold phase, which produced one of the most extensive of the glaciations. The ice front reached what is north London today – Watford, Finchley and Hornchurch. Ice-dammed lakes ponded up as the ice melted and retreated, with their meltwaters feeding an engorged river. A hugely bigger lake filled up in the southern part of the North Sea with water from the Thames and Rhine, until it eventually spilled over and flooded out southwards through what are the Straits of Dover today.

Over nine different terrace levels have been recognised throughout the Thames Valley. Higher terraces in the upper reaches are thought to have been formed under intensely cold or even glacial conditions and low sea levels. So it is not surprising that most of the deposits do not contain many plant or animal remains. But the terraces of the lower reaches are thought to have been formed in response to rising sea levels during interglacial warmer climates when there was abundant life around. Luckily, some of these interglacial deposits and their fossils have been found in the Thames Valley. Plant pollen, preserved in the clays and silts, is used to match deposits of similar age, place them in a relative time sequence and tell us what the vegetation was like.

Overall, British land-based Pleistocene history has been subdivided into nine alternating climate phases, from a first cold Baventian glacial stage (around 1.6 million years ago) up to the last Devensian cold phase (between 110,000 and 10,000 years ago), followed by the present warm Holocene post- or interglacial (Flandrian) phase of the last 10,000 years.

However, there is evidence on the continent that the British record is far from complete, especially for early Pleistocene times. Indeed, the start of the Pleistocene record and times is recognised in Italy. It is now realised that the offshore ocean floor sediment record is even better than the land-based one and the technology has become available to recover it. Trying to recover sediment cores using ship-borne drill rigs from water depths of 3 km or more is not easy. Nevertheless, thousands of ocean sediment cores have been recovered from ocean depths around

British Quaternary Stages	Northwest European Stages	
Holocene (warm) from 10,000 BP	Holocene	
Devensian (cold) from around 110,000 BP	Weichselian	
Ipswichian (warm) from 128,000 BP	Eemian	
Wolstonian (cold) from around 380,000 BP	Saalian	PLEISTOCENE
Hoxnian (warm) from 423,000 BP	Holsteinian	
Anglian (cold) from around 478,000 BP	Elsterian	
Cromerian (warm) from around 860,000 BP	Cromerian	
Beestonian (cold) from ?1.77 ma	Bavelian from 1.2 ma Menapian Waalian Eburonian from 1.77 ma	
Pastonian (warm) from ?1.9 ma		PLIOCENE
Baventian (cold) from ?2.0 ma	Tiglian from 2.44 ma	
	Pretiglian from 2.56 ma	

the world and these reveal that there were many more climatic cycles during Pleistocene time, which is now known to have extended back to 1.8 million years ago.

In the deep oceans sediment accumulates slowly on the seabed virtually without interruption. Luckily for historians of Earth Time, the continuous oceanic 'rain' of fine-grained sediment includes the debris of ocean life, especially the tiny shells of minute single-celled protists called foraminiferans (or more conveniently forams). Most importantly, in the 1950s, it was discovered that the composition of foram shells is influenced by the chemical composition of ocean water when they were growing and that in turn reflects global ice volume and ocean water temperature. So the shells provide a proxy measure of past climates. By analysing the shell composition of forams from successive layers in sediment cores retrieved from the ocean floor, an excellent detailed record of climate change over the last 2 million years and more has been recovered. This has been supplemented by evidence of iceberg abundance and distribution in the North Atlantic. The drifting bergs carry rock debris, which is released when they melt with the debris falling onto the oceanbed. In addition, ice-core records from Greenland and Antarctica provide an independent measure of climate change in both the northern and southern hemispheres over the last 300,000 years.

Altogether, these records tell us that there have been frequent and often rapid changes in climate over the last 2 million years. At least 30 cycles of cold and warm oscillations have been measured from the ocean sediment record over the last million years. By comparison, the land-based record of glaciation is much more problematic. Much of the difficulty arises from the tendency for one glacial ice advance to disturb or eradicate evidence of the previous cycle of glacial erosion and subsequent deposition. Researchers have had great difficulty in finding good records of the succession of events. Nowhere on land is there a continuous record. Short sequences have been discovered, but they are scattered all over the place and the problem has been to match them together to form a more continuous history of events. Over 150 years after it was first realised that there has been a recent succession of ice ages, we are beginning to get somewhere. Much has been due to the discovery of the oceanic and ice-core records plus improvements in dating methods, so that there is now an increasingly reliable chronological framework within which the sediment and fossil record can be placed.

For many years now there has been a considerable problem of matching the classic land-derived record of the Ice Ages to that of the ocean floor sediments with the oxygen isotope stages (OIS). Only recently has it become clear that some parts of the early Pleistocene are preserved in East Anglia by deposits representing the Baventian (perhaps over 1.5 million years old), the Pastonian, Cromerian (around 500,000–600,000 or perhaps as much as 800,000 years ago) and Anglian stages (around 450,000 years ago).

Reconstruction of early Pleistocene river floodplains shows that an enormous amount of rock material was worn away from British landscapes since that time. Furthermore, during cold phases river flow was much more powerful and effective in both erosion and deposition. The removal of such a weight of rock material, in addition to the loss of the weight of the glaciers and ice sheets, resulted in the landscapes rising through a process known as isostatic readjustment. Just as icebergs continue to float as they melt, so do continents tend to rise as rock (or ice) is stripped off their surfaces. The added complication is that as the ice melts sea levels rise, but the two processes work at different rates and so they are rarely synchronous.

The Anglian Stage is generally matched to OIS 12 (around 478,000 years ago), which was one of the coldest phases of the mid-Pleistocene record. The following warm Hoxnian interglacial (around 423,000 years ago) represented at Swanscombe seems to equate with OIS 11 or perhaps 9. Stanton Harcourt in the upper Thames Valley is Wolstonian and OIS 7 at between 245,000 and 186,000 years ago. The latter is similar in age to the famous Pontnewydd Cave in North Wales with its Neanderthal remains, which is one of the few sites that can be dated using radiometric and thermoluminescence dating methods. The Trafalgar Square deposits are considered Ipswichian in age (OIS 5e) and around 125,000 years old.

Among the fossils found in the Thames Valley are stone tools and very rare human remains, which show that our ancestors walked across from mainland Europe when sea levels allowed them to do so. As hunters they were probably following the migrations of the animals such as horse, deer, wild oxen, bison and even mammoth, which they relied on for food, and a variety of materials for clothing, shelter and tools. When it was first accepted that our ancestors lived alongside these extinct animals of the Ice Ages, the possibility arose that their development of stone tool technology would follow a recognisable chronology. The assumption was that the evolution of the technology would be linear from crude basic forms to more advanced and sophisticated forms. All that had to be done was to work out the evolution of form and type of tool and wherever tools were found the deposit could be dated relatively within the overall scheme.

However, it was soon realised that such technological developments are culturally determined and develop at different rates within separate peoples, especially those isolated by geography, language and so on. Correlation can work, especially within contiguous regions such as northwest Europe, but it requires very detailed and meticulous studies backed up by modern dating techniques.

Naming names

The names used to label the various phases of prehistory can be really quite difficult to cope with. Even students of geology have a hard time trying to remember even the main subdivisions of Earth Time and usually have to fall back on various handy mnemonics, which can be unprintably rude. The problem is that the divisional names have grown in an 'organic' and historical way, from terms first used by quarrymen and miners as far back as mediaeval times. When the more academic geologists began to try to systematise matters they adopted the standard scientific procedure of using words derived from classical Latin and Greek. Most of these scholars knew these languages, which were the 'lingua franca' of science for centuries. Today we can no longer assume that students can automatically access the etymology of the words and they just seem incredibly arcane and meaningless. The Ice Ages form one phase of Earth Time that has a readily recognisable common name, although its scientific equivalent (Pleistocene) is much less familiar. Since even 7-year-olds today have at least heard of the Jurassic, perhaps there is some hope that in the future the Ordovician and Triassic might be just as familiar once their characteristics become better known, although I will not bet on it.

———————— • ————————

M. Jules Desnoyers, 1801–77, French stratigrapher, vertebrate palaeontologist and librarian at the National Museum of Natural History in Paris who first formally defined the Quaternary (1829) in the modern scientific sense. He also co-founded the Geological Society of France in 1830 with Ami Boue, Constant Prevost and Paul Deshayes and became its secretary in 1831.

Giovanni Arduino, 1714–95, Italian mining engineer and agriculturalist, inspector of mines in Tuscany who became professor of mineralogy in Venice. From studies in northern Italy, he first proposed a division of rock strata into Primary, Secondary etc., recognised the igneous origins of granite and basalt and that mountain building was a long process.

————— • —————

In modern scientific terminology the epoch of the Ice Ages is referred to as the Pleistocene epoch of Earth Time and its deposits as the Pleistocene Series (the old Diluvium). The name Pleistocene, meaning 'most recent', was coined by Charles Lyell in 1839 to include those deposits that lie on and and are therefore younger than the older Pliocene Series deposits. Lyell distinguished the deposits of the Pleistocene Series on the high percentage of modern molluscs they contain.

Lyell had previously (in 1833) developed an earlier series of divisions using the proportion of living as opposed to extinct molluscs found within them. He named the divisions, in descending order of age, as Pliocene (meaning 'more recent'), Miocene ('less recent') and Eocene ('early recent'). It might have seemed a good idea at the time, but it created a lot of problems. Furthermore, the latter three divisions when grouped together formed the Tertiary System of strata, as we shall see. The Pleistocene and younger Holocene series of

Arduino's 1760 divisions of the Earth's rock formations

Pianure – alluvium

Tertiary
monti terziari – fossiliferous sands, clays and gravels, volcanic rocks

Secondary
monti secondari – fossiliferous limestones and marbles

Primary
monti primari – sandstones and conglomerates (unfossiliferous)
vetrescibili – mineral-rich crystalline rocks
roccia primigenia – schists

sediments form a post-Tertiary division, and have been grouped together as the Quaternary System. The name Quaternary was used as long ago as 1829 by the French geologist Desnoyers for certain geologically young deposits in the Paris region that were originally laid down on the seabed, although in strict historical terms the name is even older and was used by an eighteenth-century Italian naturalist Giovanni Arduino. In 1759 Arduino wrote to a colleague, Professor Vallisneri, proposing a fourfold division of the succession of rock formation on Earth into Primary, Secondary, Tertiary and Quaternary.

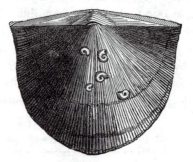

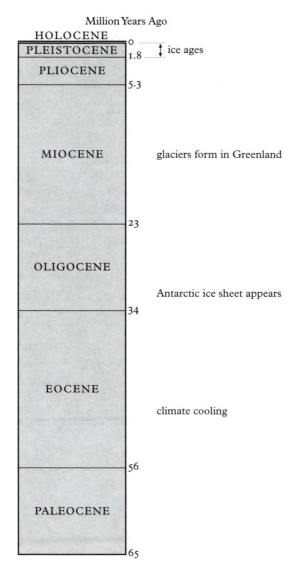

Pleistocene to Eocene.

3

Below the surface –
Into Tertiary times

PLIOCENE TO PALEOCENE

By the late eighteenth century and the beginning of the nineteenth century, wells were being dug deeper and deeper below London in an attempt to get a sufficient supply of clean drinking water. The population of the metropolis was fast outgrowing its water supply and the capacity of its primitive drainage system to deal with sewage. Human waste from leaking drains often contaminated the underground water table and wells sunk into it. Water-borne disease such as typhoid was on the increase.

William Smith knew from local enquiries about the nature of the rock encountered when these deeper wells were sunk that 'the same Clay under London [is] proved by deep Wells as in the opposite high ground of Epping Forest and the same as in Highgate and Hampstead Hills'. As a result, Smith depicted the London Clay as extending from Hounslow Heath to the west of the city, right under it eastwards nearly to the sea, with outcrops at the mouth of the Thames estuary, around Southend and the Isle of Sheppey, or 'Sheepy' as Smith called it.

This London Clay was also employed for the manufacture of cement in the latter part of the eighteenth century using a mixture of limestone and clay. Although the Romans had invented the process, it was reinvented and again manufactured about 1791. Initially the raw material was limestone nodules

'Strata' Smith's Succession of 1815	*European Divisions (Werner, 1786)*
	Aufgeschwemmte-Gebirge (Alluvium)
London Clay Clay and Brickearth	
Chalk Green Sand Purbeck Limestone Iron Sand Clunch Clay	
Cornbrash Limestone Forest Marble Oolyte or Freestone Blue Marl Blue and White Lias Limestone Red Marl Magnesian Limestone	Flötz-Schichten (stratified rocks)
Coal Measures Mountain Limestone	
Red Rhab and Dunstone Killas and Slate	Transition Series
Granite, Sienite and Gneiss	Primitive

found in the London Clay, but as demand outstripped the supply of the nodules, a mixture of river mud and chalk was used. Meanwhile, London Clay was increasingly used for the manufacture of the bricks required to build the sprawling suburbs of London as it became industrialised. Wood became expensive as forests were felled and supplies dwindled. Also, it was a notorious fire hazard as a building material, especially when combined with thatched roofs and open fires as the city's numerous major conflagrations over the centuries had shown, none more so than the Great Fire of London in 1666.

Until the 1830s, bricks were made from roadsweepings and refuse and were fired by the combustion of their inflammable content. But then demand became so high that new sources such as the London Clay had to be used and coal imported to fuel the kilns. Smith also noted that the same wells sunk through the Clay penetrated 'into the Chalk [which] shows the absurdity of the common opinion that Blackheath contains coal'. As we shall see, London's coal had to be brought a long way by cart and ship.

It had been known for some time that, in places, the London Clay was very fossiliferous. John Evelyn had first reported the existence of plant-related fossils from the London Clay back in 1668. Since then, some 300 species and 35 genera of fossil plant have been described from the Isle of Sheppey in the Thames estuary.

The proximity of these fossil-bearing deposits to London meant that many gentlemen collectors who were generally interested in natural curios came to hear about them through intricate supply chains. Networks of working-class locals, especially women and children, searched out specimens, commonly known as figs because of their brown wrinkled appearance, on the muddy and often fog-swathed foreshores. Prize specimens were fed through dealers and middlemen to the people who were prepared to pay for them. Most of the fossils are the mineralised seeds of flowering plants along with the teeth of many different kinds of sharks, bony fish and reptiles, along with bits of turtle and so on.

In 1757, James Parsons described and illustrated some of the fossil seeds, including striking specimens of the palm fruits *Nypa*. He declared that because of the evident ripeness of the fruits, the Flood must have overwhelmed the plants in autumn. By the end of the eighteenth century, Francis Crow had amassed such a collection of the fossils over a period of 20 years that in 1810 he was able to describe 100 species. From his diagnosis of their taxonomic affinities, he concluded that they once belonged to a tropical or high southern

———————— • ————————

James Parsons, 1705–70, London physician, antiquary and naturalist who published medical treatises and was foreign secretary of the Royal Society.

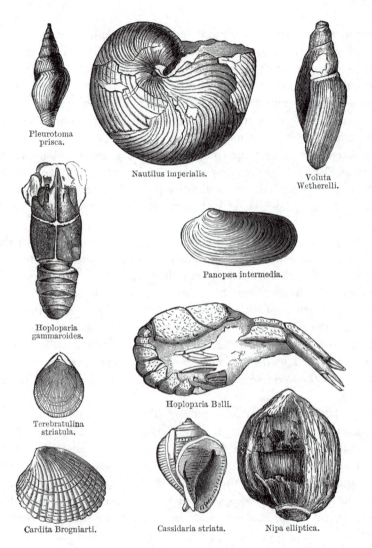

Pleurotoma
prisca.

Nautilus imperialis.

Voluta
Wetherelli.

Hoploparia
gammaroides.

Panopæa intermedia.

Terebratulina
striatula.

Hoploparia Belli.

Cardita Brogniarti.

Cassidaria striata.

Nipa elliptica.

The foreshore muddy outcrops of the London Clay in the Thames estuary provided rich fossil 'pickings' for locals who sold them to gentlemen collectors, not that the locals were paid much for their efforts.

latitude vegetation. This was one of the first connections to be made between fossil plants and ancient climates, and a remarkably accurate one at that.

The tradition of collecting at Sheppey, which was then some five hours away from London even by steam packet, continued throughout the nineteenth century. James Bowerbank, a city businessman, published in 1840 a *History of the Fossil Fruits and Seeds of the London Clay*, which was the first descriptive catalogue of the flora. Bowerbank also instructed would-be collectors how to penetrate the Dickensian world of the fossickers, such as 'a woman named Mummery, and several others who work upon the beach ... these people will direct the traveller to the cottage of a family named Crockford ... [who] will direct our fossil-hunter to many other parties who also work upon the beach ... At Hensbrook enquiry should be made for a man named Pead ... from this point ... he must enquire for Mud Row, many of the inhabitants of which work upon the beach.'

———— • ————

James Scott Bowerbank, 1797–1877, partner in a London distillery and lectured on botany (1822–4). He was co-founder of the London Clay Club (1836) and the Palaeontographical Society (1847) and elected as a Fellow of the Royal Society in 1842.

———— • ————

Charles Lyell subdivides the Tertiary

Modern analysis of the fossils of the London Clay supports Francis Crow's view that they are the remains of a lush coastal subtropical broadleaf forest that was washed into a nearby warm shallow sea teeming with fish, turtles and crocodiles. Plant fossils include representatives of the sumac, custard apple, palm, dogwood and frankincense families, along with newly evolving mammals such as dog-sized primitive horses. And we now know that the London Clay is of early Eocene age and some 50 million years old.

Consequently, there is a big time gap between the overlying Pleistocene deposits and these Eocene ones. Not that Smith was aware of it, nor was he particularly concerned with the new academic fashion for producing hierarchical classifications of strata such as those generated by Lyell.

While a student in Oxford in the first decade of the nineteenth century, Lyell had attended some of Buckland's lectures on geology. Like many others who were stimulated by both the content of the lectures and Buckland's unusually popular style of delivery, Lyell soon set off for the continent to make his own geological Grand Tour, investigating any geological phenomena he encountered along the way and collecting fossils. On graduating from Oxford, he began training as a barrister at Lincoln's Inn in London and soon became a Fellow of London's newly fashionable scientific clubs, the Geological Society and the Linnaean Society.

Membership (or fellowship as it is called) was not automatic: new recruits had to be proposed and seconded by two or more existing Fellows, which was a well-established means of retaining their social exclusivity. Being a mere surveyor of a rural artisan background, Smith was not acceptable, but Charles Lyell was a 'gentleman' of well-to-do Scottish background. With his Oxford University education, Lyell was eminently acceptable. He soon became more interested in geology than studying the law and in 1823 was elected as Secretary of the Geological Society. He managed to resist his father's continuing pressure to continue with his legal studies. Lyell was of sufficiently independent mind and means to devote the rest of his life to the new science of geology and made a very great success of it too.

The honorary office of Secretary in the organisation of the Geological Society involved a considerable amount of unpaid work. But it brought him into the close network of the most active and eminent geologists of the time and before long he was off on geological excursions to Scotland with his old professor Buckland and to the continent, where he met von Humboldt, Cuvier and Brongniart. In 1828 Lyell returned to the continent with the newly married Roderick Murchison and his wife Charlotte.

The two young men geologised wherever they went, making arduous excursions on foot into the surrounding mountains and hills, while Charlotte Murchison made accomplished sketches of the scenery and geological phenomena and collected fossils. Towards the end of 1828 Lyell went his own way and travelled the length of Italy right down to Sicily, making a careful study of the Tertiary strata as he went. He took every opportunity to quiz local experts and examine their fossil collections, discovering similarities with fossils he had seen in the Bordeaux region of southern France. On his way back to London, Lyell visited Jules Desnoyers in Paris and discussed the possibility of subdividing the Tertiary strata with him. Desnoyers told him that his colleague and fellow countryman Gerard Deshayes had been thinking along similar lines and was basing his ideas on 'the comparative proportion of living species of shells found fossil in each (subdivision)'.

Gerard Paul Deshayes, 1796–1896, French naturalist and professor of conchology at the National Museum of Natural History in Paris (from 1869).

Lyell later recalled that by January 1829 he had

fully decided on attempting to establish four subdivisions of the great tertiary epoch, the same which are fully illustrated in the present work [the 3rd volume of his *Principles of Geology*, published in 1833]. I consider the basin of Paris and London to be the type of the first division (the Eocene); the beds of the Superga, of the second (Miocene); the Subappenine strata of northern Italy, of the third (older Pliocene); and Ischia and Val di Noto of the fourth (newer Pliocene).

His purpose in publishing this retrospective claim that he had intended making his subdivision before he visited Desnoyers and Deshayes was to help establish the priority of his developing ideas and subdivision.

Lyell visited Deshayes as soon as possible and heard that he recognised three not four subdivisions. Deshayes agreed to look over Lyell's Italian shells and prepare tables showing which species were in common between the different chronological divisions and which belonged to still-living species. It was some task and took Deshayes the best part of two years, as Lyell had amassed a collection of over 40,000 specimens belonging to some 8000 species.

While Deshayes was hard at work, Lyell returned to London where he finished writing the first volume of his monumental work, which was to establish him as one of the foremost geologists of the century. This first part of Lyell's *Principles of Geology, being an Attempt to Explain the Former Changes of the Earth's Surface, by References to Causes Now in Operation* was published in 1830, in time for Charles Darwin to take a copy with him on the voyage of the *Beagle* with Captain Fitzroy.

By the time the third volume was published, Deshayes had finished his tabulation of the chronological distribution of fossils through the Tertiary strata. From this Lyell carried out a simple mathematical analysis of the proportional distribution of species in the subdivisions of strata that he recognised. He found that 90 per cent of the fossils of the newer Pliocene were still living, whereas in the older Pliocene

> the proportion of recent species varies from upwards of a third to somewhat more than half of the entire number; but it must be recollected, that this relation to the recent epoch is only *one* of its zoological characters, and that certain *peculiar species* of testacea also distinguish its deposits from all other strata.

Lyell noted that the relationship of the Pliocene and underlying Miocene is to be seen in northern Italy. The Miocene is distinguished by having a proportion of 'rather less than eighteen in one hundred' living species. Lyell had originally selected the Superga Hills near Turin as exposing typical Miocene strata, but by 1833 had changed his mind and selected the Touraine basin of France, where the relationship with the underlying and older Eocene strata can be seen. Finally, the latter have the lowest proportion of living species – around 3.5 per cent.

Importantly, he also said that further divisions might be recognised in future, which indeed they were. The Oligocene was distinguished between the Miocene and Eocene and was named by the German palaeontologist von Beyrich in 1854. And then another German, W. Philipp Schimper, carved out the Palaeocene as the oldest of the Tertiary divisions below the Eocene.

Italy's geology also provided Lyell with first-hand experiences of other geological phenomena not available to him in Britain, especially 'live' volcanoes

Charles Lyell realised that these Roman columns were bored by marine molluscs and had therefore been submerged and resurrected by earth movements associated with the nearby volcano of Vesuvius.

Heinrich Ernst von Beyrich, 1815–96, defined the Oligocene System in 1854. He was a German professor of palaeontology in Berlin, co-founder of the German Geological Society (1848) and first director of the Prussian Geological Survey.

and evidence for changing sea levels. At Pozzuoli near Naples he visited the seaside ruins of a Roman building (known as the Temple of Serapis). Its three remaining stone columns are conspicuously bored by marine molluscs (similar to 'shipworms') at some height above their base, showing that they had been submerged at some time in the past and then re-elevated from beneath the waves. As Lyell realised, the implication is that over some 2000 years since it was built the 'Temple' had been down and then up through some 10 metres without being completely toppled. And he concluded that significant geological change could occur gradually, not catastrophically as Cuvier claimed. However, the lower part of the columns is not bored, showing that at least a significant part of the elevation happened rather suddenly. The controlling factor is the nearby volcano of Vesuvius.

All was grist to Lyell's geological mill, for he was becoming an assiduous gatherer of geological information and ideas about its interpretation. With his legal training and ability to argue any case from either the 'prosecution' or 'defence' side and then come to a judgment, it was a role he was ideally suited for. Lyell was building on the work and principles of his great Scottish geological hero, James Hutton. Accordingly, it was only through the study of present processes that the geological past could be interpreted and understood, a methodological approach that was soon labelled (in 1832) as 'uniformitarian' by the Cambridge polymath William Whewell. Moreover, although there is constant gradual change manifested by many geological processes, the changes are cyclical and without progression.

Wilhelm Philipp Schimper, 1808–80, cousin of Karl and also a botanist, author of the *Traite de Paleontologie Vegetale* (1869–74), director of the Strasbourg Museum and professor in the university.

William Whewell, 1794–1866, professor of mineralogy at Cambridge (1828–38), then moral theology (1838–55), master of Trinity College and Vice-Chancellor of the University who wrote an highly influential *History of the Inductive Sciences* (1837).

In Sicily Lyell also studied Mount Etna and the history of its eruptions. Knowing its height and approximate rate of increase from eruptions of lava (assuming that its rate of growth was constant – a false assumption, by the way), he estimated that it must have taken over several hundred thousand years to grow to its present size. Now, Lyell also found fossiliferous strata beneath the oldest lavas and observed that many of the species were identical with those still living in the nearby Mediterranean, thus these apparently 'recent' strata had to be of a yet greater age than the volcano and were consequently very ancient compared with the human historical timescale. The further implication was that stratigraphically lower Tertiary strata with fewer extant species had to be even older, and so on.

Mind the Gap – the British Tertiary

It was soon realised that the British record of Tertiary deposits is limited to a certain few intervals of the Eocene, which were laid down in relatively quiet water nearshore and transitional marine–freshwater environments. Some of these (such as the outcrops of London Clay at Sheppey and Bognor Regis in Sussex) have become of international importance for their fossil record of the life of the times and the nature of the environments. Interpretation of such deposits and their fossils tells us that global climates changed significantly through the Tertiary. Initially, temperatures rose to a peak in Eocene times and then progressively cooled, with the first ice sheet appearing in Antarctica in early Oligocene times, although permanent glaciation did not appear until mid-Miocene times when glaciers may have formed in Greenland.

In more detail, the Palaeocene–Eocene transition, around 56 million years ago, was a phase of warm global climates and generally high sea levels, with polar broad-leaved deciduous forests extending high into the Arctic circle. Nevertheless, the fossil plant records show variation in vegetation throughout the interval, in response to both climate change and latitudinal position. During the latest Palaeocene times, around 55.1 million years ago, there was a very short-lived phase of warming followed by a marked cooling around 54.2 million years ago.

There has been speculation that the warm phase was a greenhouse effect caused by a catastrophic release of gas hydrates from within ocean floor sediments, perhaps initiated by contemporary volcanism. Southern Britain supported freshwater mires and relatively low-diversity, patchy forest–woodland populated with warm-loving, deciduous flowering plants. Further north in Scotland, similar flowering plants were more associated with conifers and ferns. By contrast, the floras of the earliest Eocene (lowest strata of the London Clay) indicate the early development of a frost-free paratropical rainforest-type vegetation, very similar in structure to that of the present-day paratropical rainforest.

There were significant differences between the geography of Tertiary times and that of today, including a northward plate movement of Britain over some 8 degrees of latitude. Also important in the Northern Hemisphere context was the persistence of a land connection between Europe and North America, which allowed continued interchange of plants and animals. However, by late Palaeocene times increasing igneous activity related to increasing heat flow within the Earth's crust below East Greenland led to extensive extrusive vulcanicity. The whole region was elevated to form a landmass that encompassed much of present-day Scotland and what is now the largely submerged area between Orkney and Shetland. The uplift and erosion of this landmass led to large-scale deposition of eroded sediment in the adjacent basins of the North Sea and Faroe–Shetland regions, where Tertiary sediment reached maximum thicknesses of 3 and 4 km respectively. There is no doubt that the Tertiary age deposits were formerly more extensive over Britain. It is thought that the 'clay with flints' that blankets much of the Chalk is made up of the weathered residues of these deposits.

The widespread vulcanicity eventually led to extensive rifting, both to the northwest and northeast of the British Isles. And in turn, this led to progressive opening, beginning around 55 million years ago, of the North Atlantic as new ocean crust was formed. The new ocean extended northwards from the Central Atlantic and finally severed the land connection between Europe and North America and isolated Greenland. For the first time, the British Isles came into existence as a geological entity separate from North America and became part of Eurasia instead.

As we shall see (p. 220), the original geological 'parentage' of the south-eastern part of the British Isles and Ireland is very surprising, but for around 350 million years the region had been an integral part of an extensive continental mass, known as Laurussia, stretching north through Scandinavia and northern Europe into Russia. In early Tertiary times as the Atlantic opened northwards, this continent was rent in two. North America and Greenland were left on one side, while Scotland and northwestern Ireland, which had been part of North America, were torn away as part of Eurasia, the eastern continental mass of Ireland, Britain, northern Europe and, by now, the vast mass of Asia.

In the west of Scotland and northeast of Ireland, this phase of intense volcanic activity formed widespread flood basalt sequences associated with lava shields, large volcanoes and shallow intrusive centres all spanning the interval from around 60.5–55 ma. The geological evidence for this is spread over the Western Isles of Scotland from Skye south to Mull, the small isle of Staffa with the famous Fingal's Cave, celebrated by poets, painters and composers such as Mendelssohn, and on to the equally famous Giant's Causeway of County Antrim in the north of Ireland.

The strange columnar formations of the lavas intrigued artists from the seventeenth century and puzzled naturalists. The rocks were central to a long-running debate between Wernerians, who argued that they were evidence for a primeval ocean, and Huttonians, who argued that they were evidently the result of volcanic eruptions of molten magma. The latter were right and we now know that the columns result from cooling and shrinking of thick lava flows, which then crack into polygonal jointed columns.

The igneous activity was intermittent with periods of rapid growth of the lava fields and intrusion of a variety of igneous bodies, followed by significant hiatuses during which weathering and erosion allowed the development of relatively mature vegetated landscapes, whose deposits and fossil remains are to be found within the plateau basalts. Evidence of this Palaeocene volcanism is also present in the south of England, where airborne pyroclastic material has been preserved as ash layers in the basal strata of the London Clay.

In comparison, southern Britain was less elevated and two structural basins, known as the London and Hampshire Basins, were formed from a single structural 'low' that originally covered much of today's North Sea region, the Low Countries of Belgium, northeast France and southeast England. The formation of the elevated Weald–Artois 'high', which just extended into southeast England from Europe, split the original structural basin in two. High global sea levels resulted in these structural lows also being sites of shallow water deposition, with extensive alluvial plains and marshes and brackish to freshwaters dominated by fine-grained mud deposits. Open marine conditions lay to the northeast in the North Sea region and to the southwest in the Western Channel.

By latest Palaeocene to early Eocene times, the shallow seas had extended over much of southern England, interconnecting the London and Hampshire Basins and flooding over the Low Countries. Subsequently, in late Eocene to early Oligocene times, retreat of the shallow seas led to separation of the two basins and extension of the Weald–Artois 'high' as a land bridge to Europe.

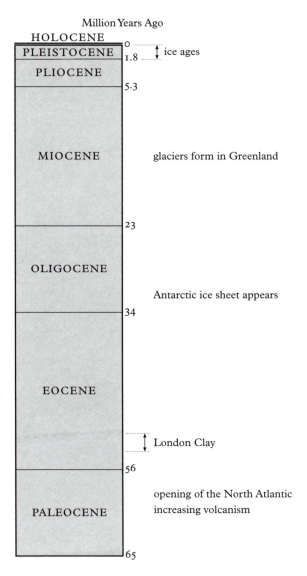

Pliocene to Paleocene.

4

Layer upon layer – Deeper and deeper into Earth Time

CRETACEOUS

Up onto the Downs

The road north out of London follows an old Roman road known as Watling Street. Climbing up the side of the Thames Valley gives a view across the whole of London. In Smith's day, much of the city would have looked like a smouldering ruin covered by a pall of smoke, as thousands of household fires wafted strands of wood smoke into the atmosphere. Several decades later at the height of the Industrial Revolution, the city would have barely been visible at all as coal-burning fires belched thick acrid fumes into the atmosphere, blackening all the buildings around with the sooty pollution. Only in recent decades has this industrial grime eventually been cleaned off the more prestigious of London's buildings, but there are still plenty that retain the disfiguring layer of soot.

In places the grey, silvery glint of the river is just discernible as it wends its weary way down through the port of London to the sea. Smith would have seen a busy port with a forest of wooden masts belonging to sailing vessels that plied their trade from all over the globe to one of the world's busiest centres of commerce. Only in the twentieth century with the growth of much bigger steam-powered vessels did the shallow waters of the Thames make the port more or less redundant. Downstream at Greenwich there was the famous Observatory, from which the Greenwich meridian of longitude was established in 1884, and the fine Regency buildings of the Royal Naval College, with direct access to the Thames estuary and eventually the sea.

The landscapes surrounding the estuary were low-lying muddy marshes made famous or rather notorious by Charles Dickens' novel *Great Expectations*. The criminal Magwitch, one of the main characters, escaped from one of the prison hulks moored offshore these bleak and damp mistbound seascapes.

Right across the Thames Valley to the south another line of low hills can be seen rising in the distance, forming the southern rim of the geological basin in which London lies. The lines of hills that rim both sides of the basin are established on the same kind of rock strata – the distinctive white and soft limestones known in England as Chalk Downs. Historically, chalk has been all too familiar to countless generations of schoolchildren as the material by which the wisdom and information of the ages has been transmitted from teacher via the blackboard to pupil, although it has been largely superceded by clay-based chalk- and whiteboards.

'Downs' is a typically topsy-turvy English name for hills. It is very ancient and is derived from the old English and Celtic word 'dun', meaning 'hill'. It was famously used by Shakespeare in *The Tempest* (iv, i, 81), 'my boskie acres and my unshrubd downe'. This accurately describes the characteristic features of downland for 1000 years or more since the original tree cover of beech and elm was cut down and land turned over to grassland pasture. As Smith noted, 'great flocks of sheep are kept upon these Downs and supplied with early spring feed from water meadows in the vallies'.

The thin soils can easily be broken through to reveal white patches of limestone that underlie the landscapes, but rarely are there any natural rock outcrops because the limestone is so easily weathered and eroded. Seldom is chalk hard enough to be of any use as a building stone, although there are places in Norfolk where it is used because some layers are harder than usual. Since most of the trees have been cut down the hard chalk is the only vaguely durable material available locally, apart from flint and bricks manufactured from clay.

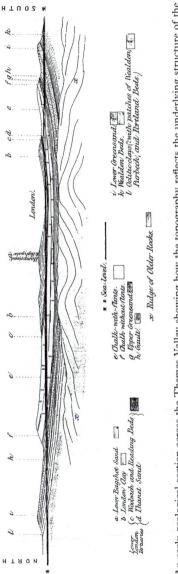

An early geological section across the Thames Valley showing how the topography reflects the underlying structure of the younger strata of the London Basin.

Shallow pits and quarries have been excavated over the centuries as the chalk has been dug out for various purposes. Smith remarks that 'much chalk ... is used on the land either in a crude state or burned to lime .... and for the recovery of its hard siliceous nodules called flint'. Lime was extensively used as a cheap form of cement and the ubiquitous 'whitewash' form of paint. But chalk has also played an important role in the history and development of fine art in Europe (see box on Painting with chalk).

Painting with chalk

Chalk has played an important role in the painting of fine art over the ages. A particularly important historical painting, known as the Thornham Parva retable, is the oldest oil painting in Britain and one of the oldest in Europe. Its three panels originally formed a backdrop to an altar and inevitably it was a religious work painted on wooden panels. The magnificent depiction of Christ flanked by his disciples has recently been restored. In order to carry out the work in a way that used original materials, the technical details of the painting's construction have been scientifically analysed. Dendrochronological study of the wood's growth rings revealed that the panels were cut from tough, slow-growing Baltic oak, which was felled in 1336. The age has been further constrained by Dr Sophie Stos-Gale of Oxford University. She analysed the lead pigments in the paint and showed that the original lead mineral used to make the pigment has a characteristic isotopic 'fingerprint'. This identifies it with lead ore from a specific lead mine in Derbyshire. Historical records show that the mine had closed by the end of the fourteenth century.

A microscopic sample of the white 'ground' or base paint layer from the Thornham Parva has been examined to check its provenance. With a scanning electron microscope it became evident that the paint was clearly made from micron-sized fossils of unicellular organisms called coccoliths, which comprise the bulk of chalk rock. By identifying the fossils, Professor Katharina von Salis of the Swiss Federal Institute of Technology in Zurich has shown that the artists obtained their chalk from a particular layer of rock, which she identified as coccolith biozone CC 17 of the Late Santonian, which was deposited some 84 million years ago, near the end of the Cretaceous Period of Earth Time. A soft limestone that is common throughout large regions of northwest Europe, it was commonly ground up for use as a ground for paintings over hundreds of years and has only been replaced by other base paints since the late nineteenth century.

Since prehistoric times peoples have searched for the best type of rock to make stone tools and weapons. Flint, along with a volcanic glass called obsidian, has been recognised as one of the best materials. The mineral is so tough that its strange, irregular-shaped cobbles or nodules persist when the surrounding chalk enclosing them has been worn away. Consequently, there are places on the land surface, such as beaches and riverbeds, where flints accumulate in great numbers.

The mineral has many of the properties of glass. It is both hard and brittle and can be broken into flakes and shards with exceedingly sharp edges. Blades and points can be fashioned from it, along with blunter axes or hammer stones. In places it is so abundant that prehistoric peoples used the sites as centres of manufacture. Smith thought it worth noting that in Norfolk Chalk landscapes, 'The plougher land between Swaffam and Castle Acre [is] strewn with Flints.' But flints that have been exposed at the surface for a long time become weathered and discoloured and are weaker than ones freshly dug out of the chalk.

Quarries and even mines, such as Grimes Graves in Norfolk, were excavated as long ago as Neolithic times to obtain the best flints and the industry persisted right through into the eighteenth century. As its use for stone tools became redundant, flint was still knapped (meaning shaped) to make small, brick-shaped blocks for building and for use in old-fashioned flint-lock percussion weapons. Again, Smith notes that 'Gunflints formerly manufactured at Salisbury', in Wiltshire, from flint nodules occur in the Chalk there. There was a particular demand for flints in the region because it was and still is a military barracks town. The striking of a hammer flint against an iron metal sheet generated sparks that ignited the gunpowder, which exploded and propelled the ball-shaped bullet down the weapon's barrel. The actual generation of flint within the chalk rock is a complicated process.

The chalk landscape consists of rolling downs dissected by narrow tree-filled 'hangars' or valleys. The valley bottoms are often filled with weathered clay and flints and, as Smith observed, 'copious springs of clear water flow from the foot of the chalk hills'. Rarely do the streams seem nearly big enough to have carved their valleys and in many places the chalk valleys are completely dry, without any sign of running water even in the wettest winters. Rainwater falling on the soft and porous chalk limestone generally soaks straight into the ground and percolates down until it reaches the local water table or an impervious layer of clay. Here the strata are soaked in water and wherever the water table reaches the ground surface springs occur. In chalk landscapes they are often found along the bottom of the valley sides, so that historically farms and even hamlets have been sited where there are naturally occurring and persistent springs that provide beautifully clean hard, lime-rich water.

The formation of the dry valleys found higher on the downs was seen as a puzzle for many centuries. Again, Smith remarked that 'the scarcity of water and other reasons for the paucity of habitations on the hills accounts for the numerous sites of population in the vallies'. Since the mid-nineteenth-century discovery that even the landscapes of the British Isles had suffered extensive glaciation in the not too distant geological past, it has also been realised that beyond the southernmost extent of the ice sheets, the ground would have been permanently frozen just as much of northern Alaska and Siberia is today.

If the chalk was frozen, it would have become impermeable during the brief periods of summer thaw. Any rainwater would not have soaked into the ground but would have run across the surface and eroded normal river valleys. When the glacial climates modulated and the permafrost melted, the chalk would have resumed its normal porosity and rainwater sank more or less straight down into the water table, leaving the distinctive upland dry valleys and grasslands that formed ideal pastures for domesticated sheep and cattle.

William Smith described the Chalk as forming 'Extensive sheep pastures on the Downs' and 'Water Meadows in the Vallies' and noted that 'fossil oyster shells and echini' (sea urchins) were to be found within it. Indeed, he went on to collect, describe and illustrate the common clams, ammonites and other seashells found in this ancient seabed deposit. What Smith was not able to observe are the fossils that make up the bulk of the chalk rock, because they are far too small for the microscopes available in Smith's day to resolve.

We now know that chalk is largely composed of the remarkable microscopic fossil skeletal remains of myriads of tiny unicellular marine algae known as coccoliths. A single sugar-cube-sized piece of chalk contains hundreds of thousands of these calcareous skeletons, which accumulated on the seabed when

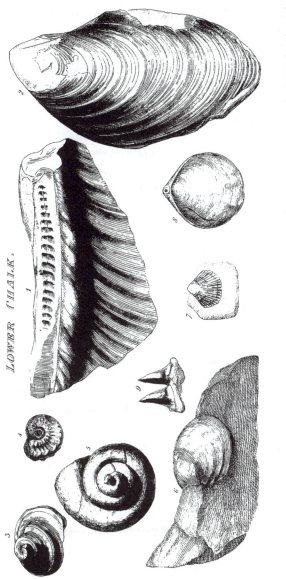

William Smith's 1816 selection of fossil shells characteristic of the Cretaceous Chalk rock strata. Apart from the shark's teeth they are all extinct species of shellfish.

the parent organism died. Today similar organisms live in subtropical waters and are known to have bursts of reproduction, known as 'algal blooms' or 'whitings', when trillions of organisms are suddenly generated and discolour the sea locally. So many are produced that they soon use up whatever nutrients are available and then die off, with their minute calcareous skeletons sinking onto the seabed, where they accumulate as a white calcareous mud, which eventually is compacted and hardened off to form chalk.

The shellfish of the chalk seas were largely creatures that are still familiar today, such as clams, snails, sea urchins, crabs, lobsters and shrimps, along with quite modern-looking bony fish and cartilagenous sharks, some of which were significantly bigger than today's Great Whites (*Carcharadon*). Two less familiar groups of fossil shellfish are the extinct belemnites and ammonites of the chalk seas. Both were abundant, squid-like, swimming cephalopods, some of which lived in vast shoals.

All that normally remains of belemnites are peculiar bullet-shaped fossils made of a limy mineral (calcite), which originally projected from the posterior end of the animal and acted as ballast for buoyancy control over the depth at which they swam, gave the back end a pointed shape and stiffened the body. It did not protect them from being consumed by the dozen by the voracious marine reptile predators of these ancient seas. The discovery of hundreds of small belemnites clustered on ancient seabed surfaces has been interpreted as ichthyosaur vomit. The idea is that the predators swallowed the belemnite animals whole and, rather than pass the indigestible mineral 'bullet' through their digestive system, were able to 'cough' them up, in a similar way to many other predators such as owls and dogs.

Of the coiled ammonites, altogether there were many different kinds that lived at different water depths and ranged in size from a centimetre or two up to metre-sized giants with heavy shells that could not move from the seabed. By the middle of the nineteenth century German scientists who studied ammonites in detail realised that they were very useful for helping make fine distinctions between successive layers of strata and their relative dating (see p. 144).

Much more spectacular were the giant creatures of the Chalk seas, some of which reached astonishing dimensions and were the Cretaceous equivalent of

Napoleonic forces capture fossil

In 1780, giant fossil jaws over a metre long were recovered from underground chalk workings in Maastricht. Armed with an impressive array of teeth, the jaws were soon the subject of discussion among scholars all over Europe and were described in 1786 as the jaws of a fossil toother whale. Napoleonic forces besieging Maastricht in 1795 were on the lookout for any interesting and valuable war booty. The jaws had been hidden by their owner Canon Godin, but the French General Pichegru offered a reward of 600 bottles of wine for the recovery of the jaws. It did not take long before they appeared and were shipped off to Paris, where French scholars were only too delighted to have such a famous fossil to themselves. In 1799 Faujas de Saint-Fond described the jaws as belong to a giant crocodile, but his younger colleague Georges Cuvier later changed the diagnosis to that of a giant extinct and predatory monitor lizard called *Mosasaurus* that lived in the Chalk seas. The fossil jaws are still in the Natural History Museum in Paris and the Dutch have to make do with a plaster cast.

Today we know that the mosasaurs included voracious predators that were among the top predators of the Cretaceous seas. Analysis of their teeth shows that they had some of the most advanced cutting edges of any teeth seen in marine reptiles. The teeth evolved along similar lines as those seen in predatory dinosaurs and modern sharks. Each tooth had numerous cutting or breaking facets that were capable of both crushing bone and slicing through flesh. The mosasaurs had no serious competitors except other mosasaurs. The discovery of mosasaur jaws with repaired fractures shows that they probably did fight among themselves and may even have been cannibalistic. Some grew to over 17 m in length and their fossil remains have been found from the Netherlands to North America and New Zealand; in other words they had a truly global distribution. They ruled the oceans of the world for some 27 million years in the latter part of Cretaceous times, but apparently died out as suddenly as they had appeared.

Barthelemy Faujas de Saint-Fond, 1742–1819, a successful lawyer but, influenced by Buffon, took up geology and became professor of geology in the National Museum of Natural History in Paris and authored the *Natural History of the Mount St. Pierre, Maastricht* in 1799.

Miners discovery of gigantic fossil jaws of an extinct marine reptile in underground workings at Maastricht became a late 18th century *cause célèbre*. Faujas St Fond dramatized the scene in his 1799 scientific description of the 'Grand Bête'.

today's mammalian whales. The discovery of one particular chalk seamonster was part of an important development in the overall understanding of the history of life. This particular fossil monster was found in the chalk limestones of Maastricht just across the North Sea near the Dutch/Belgian/German border.

The recovery of the 'Grand Bête de Maastricht' in 1780 (see box Napoleonic forces capture fossil) from underground chalk workings and subsequent discussion of its exact nature and biological affinities became a pivotal point in an ongoing argument about whether any of God's creatures could have become extinct. After all, why would a benevolent God allow any of his creations to die out?

Dutch anatomist and naturalist Pieter Camper saw that while the metre-long fossil jaws might superficially look like those of a giant crocodile, they also had features that were, to his mind, like those of a toothed whale. When French scholars got their hands on the fossil they decided it was in fact a crocodile, only to have their argument countered by Adriaan Camper (Pieter's son), who had inherited his father's collections. Adriaan made a more detailed study of the fossil's anatomy and concluded that it was neither whale nor crocodile but a new kind of reptile previously unknown to science – a giant marine lizard.

Adriaan Camper wrote to the most famous anatomist of the day, Georges Cuvier in Paris, telling him of his reasons for his new diagnosis, but Cuvier dismissed the suggestion and sided with the previous French diagnosis as a crocodile. But young Camper must have sown some doubts in Cuvier's mind. For once in his life Cuvier changed his mind and in 1808 named the beast *Mosasaurus*, meaning 'lizard from the River Meuse', and suggested that it was a monitor lizard of kind intermediate between the iguanas and varanids; not that he gave Adriaan Camper much credit for the diagnosis. But most importantly, Cuvier acknowledged that the 'beast' from the Chalk strata was also extinct. Once the great Cuvier had spoken, the notion of extinction became more acceptable.

Greensands, Gault Clays and some big reptile bones

The chalk downs of Norfolk, Cambridgeshire and Wiltshire look northwest out across extensive low-lying and wet vales and floodplains (the Bedfordshire

Levels, the Vales of Aylesbury, the White Horse and so on). The underlying strata are not immediately obvious, except in a few places along the foot of the chalk escarpment and where low-lying sandstone ridges occur.

Mostly the strata are too soft to form significant topographic prominences. But historically the clays have been widely exploited for making bricks and phosphate minerals in some of the clays have been quarried for fertiliser. In a few places iron has been smelted from the so-called greensands, especially in mediaeval times. As Smith notes, 'the ancient ironworks were chiefly on opposite sides of the "Forest Ridge" where Marl occurs with Ironstone and thin beds of Limestone'. The iron was smelted using charcoal made from the local trees in a tradition that stretched back to Iron Age times some two thousand five hundred years ago.

Smith also ruefully observed that 'at Bexhill the extremity of the Forest Ridge against the sea was the late very expensive and useless search for Coal'. As we shall see (p. 163), it was the search for coal that directly and indirectly provided Smith with much of his income and helped fuel the early development of the Industrial Revolution in England.

Most of the Wealden deposits were laid down in shallow seas, with the greensands accumulating in very shallow offshore and coastal waters. Although typically the sandstones are various shades of brown, orange and yellow, they are called 'greensand' because when freshly excavated, they can be seen to contain grains of a distinctive green clay mineral called glauconite, with a complex iron–magnesium silicate composition. And glauconite is so named because it only forms in marine environments ('glaucus' meaning sea).

Excavation of the clays and sands has occasionally revealed spectacular skeletons of extinct marine reptiles as well as a host of other important fossils over the ages. Historically, the most important and interesting were the bones that were turned up in strata of similar age that occur to the south of the Thames Valley in a region of the south of England known as the Weald.

Between London, nestling in the Thames Valley Basin and the south coast of England, there is a large geological 'window' that opens on these pre-Chalk Age strata in the Weald. The Chalk Downs that form the southern rim of the Thames Valley Basin also form a huge elongate semi-oval escarpment running westwards from the Kent coast in the east, through Surrey to Wiltshire and then swinging sharply south and around in a semicircle before returning eastwards through Hampshire and Sussex to the sea again. Along the southern 'limb' the Chalk escarpment faces north and thus encloses the Wealden region within a rim of Chalk hills.

The eastern half of this semi-oval structure is closed offshore and in the Artois region of France on the other side of the Straits of Dover. William Smith was well aware of its geometrical form, which geologists call an anticline or upfold. The strata have been arched upwards in a huge dome by pressures coming from far away in the south. Originally the Chalk would have arched right over the Weald, but its soft limestones were easily and rapidly eroded and worn away to reveal the older greensands and clays underneath. Topographically the original dome now forms a wide vale, although the central part is elevated with significant outcrops of sandstones, some of which have been extensively quarried in the past for building stone.

The reason for taking the southward diversion here is that historically these sandstones of the central Weald have been of enormous importance in the development of our understanding of the life of Cretaceous times and the whole era, as we shall see.

Giant saurians make their first appearance

In the first decade of the nineteenth century, a young apprentice physician by the name of Gideon Mantell had the luck to be introduced to Dr James Parkinson, the famous medic and radical reformer who advocated universal suffrage in order to avert bloody social revolution. In 1811, the final volume of his five-volume work *Organic Remains of a Former World* was published, in which he described the then known distribution of fossils within their original strata. Not surprisingly at this date, he still concluded that the Mosaic account 'is confirmed in every respect, except as to the age of the world, and the distance of time between the completion of different parts of creation' and that overall the creation of the Earth 'must have been the work of a vast length of time'. It was Parkinson

Gideon Algernon Mantell, 1790–1852, English physician who was the son of a shoemaker and subsequently devoted his energies to geology. He struggled to be recognised but described *Iguanodon*, one of the first dinosaurs to be discovered, and was elected a Fellow of the Royal Society in 1825 and published *Wonders of Geology* in 1836.

who encouraged the young and ambitious Mantell to pursue his interests in geology.

Following a London medical apprenticeship, Mantell qualified as a physician and returned to Lewes in Sussex where he had grown up. By 1819 he had become a well-established, successful medical practitioner and was married with a child, but he was also actively pursuing his geological interests in the region. From a network of local contacts, gifts of stones and fossils from the rock strata of the Weald flooded into the Mantell house to be piled everywhere, so that it became as much a museum as a home. News of his collection brought well-connected visitors who in turn spread news among the scientific élite about Mantell, the talented young country doctor.

In June 1820, Mantell was sent some fossils that had been unearthed in the Wealden quarries around the nearby town of Cuckfield. They included bits of

James Parkinson, 1755–1824, English physician who first described the 'shaking palsy' (in 1817) now known as 'Parkinson's Disease', also a radical reformer, naturalist and founder member of the Geological Society of London.

backbone, a fragment of a very large leg bone and some teeth. Greatly excited by the fossils, Mantell visited the quarries and had the luck to find more pieces of large bones and the metre-long fragment of a fossil tree trunk covered with diamond-shaped scars like tropical palms. His initial thoughts were that the fragmentary remains belonged to one of the seamonsters newly discovered in the older strata of Dorset and North Yorkshire (see below), but he soon changed his mind and was more inclined to think that they had something to do with crocodiles. At the same time, Mantell recognised that the fossil tree trunk indicated that land could not have been far away when the deposits were originally laid down.

In the early 1820s, another piece of fossil tooth of unusual appearance was found, whether by Mantell or his wife is unclear – the popular story has it that it was his wife. With a distinct wear surface on the crown, which gave it a blunt end, the tooth was clearly not that of a crocodile but more like that of a mammalian plant eater. The problem was that at the time Mantell knew of no mammal fossils being found in such ancient rock strata. Nor was he aware of any reptile that masticated plant food to produce such a wear surface.

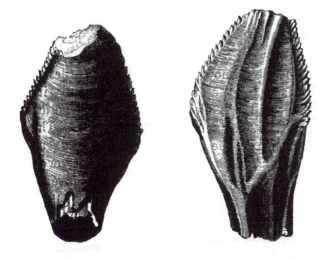

The strangely shaped fossil teeth found in Sussex in 1820 puzzled Gideon Mantell and even Georges Cuvier because they knew of no living creature with similar teeth.

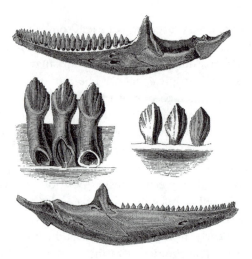

Mantell's eureka moment came when he saw the jaw and teeth of an modern iguana preserved in the Hunterian Museum in London. The marine plant eating reptile's teeth were remarkably similar to Mantell's fossil teeth from Sussex.

Among the bones he had amassed was the broken section of a thigh bone that was 60 cm (25 in) in circumference. With his anatomical knowledge Mantell understood the logic behind the comparative anatomy practised by Cuvier and the idea of scaling up from measures on individual bones to assess the overall size of an extinct animal. When he did the calculations with the figures from his fossil thigh bone, Mantell came up with an animal having the bulk of an elephant and an astonishing length of over 10 m (30 ft), far bigger than any other fossil creature known at the time.

The year 1822 saw the publication of Mantell's book *Fossils of the South Downs*, the results of his investigations into the geology of Sussex, with illustrations of strata and fossils engraved by his wife. Included was reference to 'the teeth, ribs, and vertebrae of a gigantic animal of the Lizard tribe'. Mantell hoped desperately that this book would gain him entrée into the select world of the Geological Society, but his hopes were not fulfilled. When he took the fossil teeth to a meeting of the Society, the general opinion of the 'experts' was that

Jean Baptiste Julien D'Omalius d'Halloy, 1783–1875, an aristocratic Belgian who devoted himself to geology from 1804–14 and compiled a geological map of France before becoming Governor of the province of Namur (1814), member of the Belgian Senate and President of the Belgian Academy of Sciences.

they belonged to some large fish or a more recent mammal from the Diluvium. Sales of the book were another disappointment; they did not nearly cover the cost of publication and Mantell was left with a bill for £300, which was an awful lot of money in those days.

The same year saw the Chalk strata with the older greensands and clays beneath grouped into a distinct system called the Cretaceous or rather 'Terrain Cretacé' by the Belgian geologist J. J. D'Omalius d'Halloy. The name was anglicised to Cretaceous in the same year by two English geologists, William Conybeare and William Philips. For many years different parts of the pre-Tertiary rock succession had been studied in Europe, where there are extensive outcrops extending from Sweden and Denmark through northern Germany, Poland and the low countries of the Netherlands, Belgium and into France.

D'Halloy was employed by Baron De Monbret, head of the French bureau of statistics, to gather information on the rocks in France and to make a map of their distribution. During D'Halloy's evaluation of previously known information, he concluded that of the five groups of strata recognised within the old broad division of Secondary rocks, a Terrain Cretacé could be usefully recognised. As stated in the description accompanying his map, this is 'the chalk formation, such as I have determined it ... comprising the tuffas, sands and marls, which occur beneath the true chalk, [and] constitutes the third group [of the Secondary rocks]'.

William Phillips, 1775–1828, English printer, bookseller and geologist who co-authored (with W. D. Conybeare) *Outlines of the Geology of England and Wales* (1822) and was one of the founder members of the Geological Society of London.

In 1823, with Charles Lyell's help, Mantell managed to get a paper containing his ideas on the Cretaceous Tilgate Forest strata read at a meeting of the Geological Society, but then its publication was held up for three years, perhaps because his ideas clashed with those of senior members of the Society. Lyell even took one of Mantell's fossil teeth to Paris to get Cuvier's opinion, only for the great anatomist to dismiss it as merely that of a rhinoceros. Although Cuvier later had second thoughts, the only message that got back to Mantell was Cuvier's singularly unenthusiastic initial one, much to Mantell's disappointment and dismay. After all his hard work, which not only took up his time but also meant neglect of his medical practice and his family, his hopes of rising in the scientific world seemed to be dashed.

When Mantell heard that Buckland was due to lecture at the Geological Society in London on some saurian fossils from Stonesfield in Oxfordshire, Mantell determined to be there. His intervention in the discussion alerted Buckland to the potential competition coming from the Sussex finds and Buckland tried to steal Mantell's thunder by incorporating discussion of the Sussex bones and an illustration of them in his own paper. Luckily for Mantell, the Society's publication committee rapped Buckland, their president, over the knuckles and stopped him from going too far in the interest of fair play. Even so, Buckland did mention that Mantell's Sussex giant must have been twice the size of the Oxford one and pumped the 'reptile from Cuckfield' up to between 'sixty to seventy feet', but he did not agree with Mantell that it was a plant eater.

Mantell determined to try his luck again with Cuvier, sending him tooth specimens and drawings of the other fossils. This time Cuvier acknowledged their curious form and at last asserted his true acuity by concluding that Mantell might have a new herbivorous reptile on his hands. Encouraged at last, Mantell visited the Hunterian museum in London to see if he could find anything resembling his fossil specimens. He found nothing among the fossils, but luckily a well-informed assistant curator, Samuel Stutchbury, saw that the fossil teeth possessed a passing semblance to those of living iguana. Stutchbury was familiar with iguana specimens from the West Indies because he had recently preserved one from Barbados in a bottle of spirit for the museum collection.

It was just the breakthrough that Mantell needed. The iguana's strange, leaf-shaped teeth with serrations along the edges and flat wear surfaces were an adaptation to its plant-eating habits. The only major difference was in the size: the fossils were some 20 times bigger than those of the living beast, which was only a metre long. Mantell quickly recalculated his sums and concluded that 'his' beast must have been at least 20 m (over 60 ft) long. He proposed that it be called *Iguana-saurus*, but was advised by the Reverend William Conybeare, an expert on fossils with a classical education, that *Iguanoides*, meaning 'like an iguana', or *Iguanodon*, meaning 'iguana tooth', would be better. Mantell chose the latter and so the beast has been named ever since. Cuvier's mention of Mantell and his curious new beast in a new edition of one of his books on fossils ensured that Mantell's star was at last ascending in the scientific galaxy.

In 1825 his description of *Iguanodon* was read at a meeting of the prestigious Royal Society, and later that year the 35-year-old Mantell was elected a Fellow, thus giving him an equivalent scientific status to the members of the Geological Society who had been so chary about recognising his work. But it was nearly 10 years before Mantell had any really significant new material with which to flesh out his *Iguanodon*. The basic problem was that fossils of such beasts, now known to be land-living dinosaurs, are uncommon within the predominantly shallow marine strata of the south of England. It was only because land lay not far to the north when the Wealden strata were laid down and rivers draining those landscapes occasionally washed the remains of dinosaurs and plants into the shallow coastal deposits.

Then in May 1834, Mr Bensted, a Kent quarry owner, wrote to Mantell telling him of a new find of giant bones that had been unearthed by his workers in a Wealden stone quarry near Maidstone in Kent. Mantell's luck was in again: the rock slab included some of the peculiar leaf-shaped *Iguanodon* teeth and a jumble of other bones belonging to the animal that he had not seen before. Mantell's first problem was the fact that Bensted, being a businessman, had realised the potential monetary value of the find and was determined to get as much as he could for it. Only through the intervention of some wealthy friends, who bought the specimen and presented it to him, was Mantell able to work on the new slab, which came to be known as the 'Mantell-piece'.

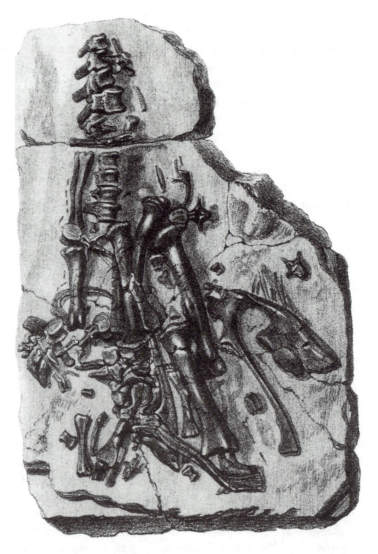

Mantell ignored his patients and spent time painstakingly preparing this rock slab to reveal the fossil bones of the giant reptile he was to name as *Iguanodon*, one of the first dinosaurs to be described.

Mantell spent long hours preparing the fossil, laboriously chipping the hard rock matrix away from around the petrified bones while trying not to damage them. He made quite a good job of it, considering the fractured nature of many of the bones. For the first time, he had part of an actual single skeleton with backbones, ribs, part of the pelvis, foot bones and a single conical spike or horn-shaped bone about 15 cm long.

Again, Mantell tried scaling up measures from the bones and found that the beast was getting bigger and bigger. Its shoulder blade measured some 30 in, which was 20 times bigger than that of the iguana, giving *Iguanodon* an estimated length of 100 ft (30 m). The Geological Society at last recognised Mantell's endeavours and awarded him its prestigious Wollaston Gold Medal in 1835; the only other recipient had been William Smith.

By this time Mantell and his family were established in fashionable Brighton and he had been doing well with his medical practice, but as he spent more and more time on his geological studies the practice began to suffer. Word was that Dr Mantell was more interested in his fossils than his patients and, whether true or not, the damage was done to such an extent that he had to sell, first his stocks

Sir Richard Owen, 1804–92, renowned English anatomist who studied in Edinburgh, became conservator in the Hunterian Museum (1827–56), its first professor of comparative anatomy, then superintendent of natural history in the British Museum (1856–83) and tutor to the Royal family (1860–4). He was knighted in 1884.

and shares, then his practice. Most of his grand, fossil-laden museum of a house was let and the family had to go into lodgings.

Eventually, in 1838, Mantell's collections had to be sold and after protracted negotiations were bought by the British Museum for £4087. Mantell moved to Clapham in south London, hoping to set up a new practice. His long-suffering wife left him, as did the older children. His son Walter, a newly qualified doctor, emigrated to New Zealand. Tragically, a younger daughter, Hannah, died and Mantell fell into deep despair. And there was a new rival in the study of the giant denizens of the geological past, a young man called Richard Owen. Neither Buckland nor Mantell, the pioneers of the terrestrial saurians, were to take the big prize: Owen beat them both to it. But Mantell was the first scientist to establish that giant extinct saurians had once lived in the landscapes of Cretaceous times.

Million Years Ago

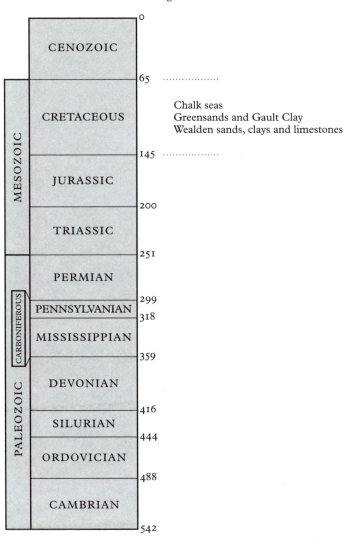

Chalk seas
Greensands and Gault Clay
Wealden sands, clays and limestones

Cretaceous.

5

Oolites and Lias – The Jurassic before the Park

JURASSIC

The Jurassic is the one period of geological time that is widely known, thanks to Michael Crichton's novel *Jurassic Park* and Steven Spielberg's series of blockbuster films. But who knows where the name Jurassic comes from or who first named the period and its system of strata? Although the name Jurassic is derived from the continent of Europe, British strata and their fossils played a major role in the history and development of the system, and the very idea that somehow Jurassic times was a period dominated by the dinosaurs. As we have already seen, the dinosaurs were just as much part of the Cretaceous as the Jurassic, in fact they originated in Triassic times. But such is the power of a blockbuster film with worldwide distribution that for most people dinosaurs are inherently Jurassic.

Initially this bit of Earth Time was not widely known as the Jurassic, but rather by the names of smaller and more regional divisions of strata. In William Smith's geological book of English strata they were known as the Oolites and Lias, names whose origin is lost in the vernacular tradition of centuries. Quarrymen characterised the limestones as Oolites because they seemed to be made from tiny egg-shaped grains (*oon* being Greek for egg, plus *lithos*, stone) and the Lias or Layers was so called simply because it typically consisted of regular alternating layers of thin limestones and shales.

The intimate association of the Jurassic with the name 'dinosaur', which could well be the world's best-known scientific term, dates back to the first identification of the dinosaurs as a distinct group of fossils in the mid-nineteenth century. It was Richard Owen who in 1842 'invented' both the name and the idea of an entirely new group of extinct reptiles that were quite different from surviving land-living reptiles such as crocodiles, snakes and lizards. But, as we have seen (p. 99), Owen was building on the pioneering groundwork of Gideon Mantell and William Buckland. A ruthless and extremely ambitious man, Owen managed to step in at a crucial moment and steal the headlines. Just think how wealthy he would have become if he had been able to copyright the name dinosaur.

The scientific importance of Jurassic strata and their fossils extends well beyond dinosaurs and their reptilian relatives, who not only dominated the landscapes of the period but also the seas and skies. It was because Jurassic strata are so well exposed in parts of Europe and are so fossiliferous that they promoted pioneering scientific work on how even small changes in fossils could be used to make fine subdivisions of strata, which could then be matched over considerable distances – the concept of biozonation (see below).

William Smith's green and pleasant land

Some of the most beautiful and picturesque landscapes of Britain, the Cotswold hills, are founded on Jurassic strata and especially the Oolitic limestones. The range of hills and valleys extends northeast from the magnificent eighteenth-century grandeur of the spa town of Bath, nestling in the valley of the River Avon where it cuts through the Cotswold Hills. The Cotswolds extend right across the country to the Lincoln and Yorkshire Wolds, where they run into the North Sea at Flamborough Head. From Bath the outcrop continues south, swinging through Dorset and out into the English Channel at Portland Bill and Durlston Head.

The gentle, rolling hills and vales have an intimate, very human scale and are largely founded on differences in hardness of the underlying rocks. These vary from hard limestones, which form the upland wolds, to softer shales and marls, which form the valleys. Many of the older houses and farms are built of the local limestone; even the roofs are 'slated' with a kind of limestone. The limestones are so abundant and easy to work that they are also used to make the stone walls that enclose fields and separate one property from another. The overall effect is to make these 'manmade' structures appear as very much a natural part of the landscape. In places, there are ironstones that were extensively exploited in the past, but the main use has been the quarrying of the limestones for building stone and more recently for cement.

William Smith was thoroughly at home in this, his geological 'backyard'. He knew all the subtle variations of the succession of strata, with ancient local names given them by quarrymen over the centuries. Smith could recognise all the distinctive local types of limestone such as the Portland Stone, Coral Rag, Cornbrash, Forest Marble and Fullers Earth Rock on how they appeared and what they were used for as well as their characteristic fossils. For instance, as Smith noted, the Forest Marble was 'wrought into slabs and chimney pieces' and Portland Stone 'provided fine stone of which Salisbury Cathedral is built' and many other of the country's most prestigious buildings.

Similar strata are exposed across considerable stretches of the landscape of Europe, from southern Sweden down to the Mediterranean coast. Limestones, sandstones and shales of coastal cliffs and inland hills have been quarried for millennia since stone fortifications and other 'public works' were built by the Romans and Normans, along with the churches, cathedrals and castles of mediaeval Europe. There were other, more specialised uses for certain kinds of strata such as very fine-grained and platy limestones, which could be used for lithographic printing. As we shall see, it was the quarrying of some Bavarian lithographic limestones that was to reveal some of the most interesting and important fossils ever found.

The late eighteenth century saw a renewed and growing demand for rock as a raw material, not just for fine buildings but for more general construction related to northwestern Europe's growing wealth. Inevitably, all this quarrying

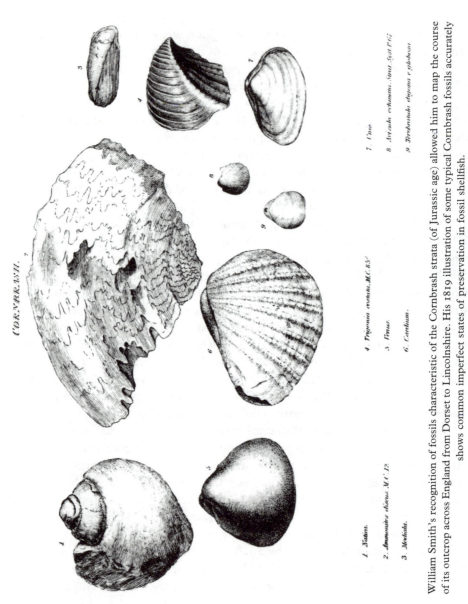

William Smith's recognition of fossils characteristic of the Cornbrash strata (of Jurassic age) allowed him to map the course of its outcrop across England from Dorset to Lincolnshire. His 1819 illustration of some typical Cornbrash fossils accurately shows common imperfect states of preservation in fossil shellfish.

and mining activity greatly enhanced the chances of finding significant new kinds of fossils and, most importantly, there was a growing intellectual interest in these fossil finds.

Since the European Secondary (now known as Mesozoic and Tertiary) strata that were being quarried are largely marine sediments, most of the fossil remains were of creatures that lived in ancient seas. If the Mesozoic strata had been made of terrestrial deposits full of dinosaurs, such as is the case in much of the midwest of North America, the history of discovery would have been very different.

First recognition of the Jurassic as a distinct system dates back to observations made by Alexander von Humboldt. At the end of the eighteenth century, as he travelled around the flanks of the Alps, through southeastern France, western Switzerland and northern Italy, Humboldt noticed that the limestones of the Jura mountains, which are full of certain kinds of fossil corals and shellfish, seemed to form a distinct and separate rock unit in their own right, which he called the *Jura-Kalkstein*. However, it was not until 1839 that there was a more widespread use of the name Jurassic on the continent, with the publication of a general description of 'Jura' strata in Germany by another German, geologist Leopold von Buch.

Baron Christian Leopold von Buch, 1774–1853, German geologist and student of Werner's. He became inspector of mines in the Prussian civil service (from 1796), compiled the first geological map of Germany (1832) and, in 1839, was first to describe the Jurassic System.

In Britain, from the seventeenth century, a whole range of curious and unfamiliar fossils were being turned up by intensive quarrying along the several hundred miles of outcrop of Oolitic limestones and Liassic shales. Some of these finds were donated to the Ashmolean Museum in Oxford, which soon built up an internationally famous collection of petrified remains, including large bones of some unknown animals.

These included the 10 kg knuckle end of a thigh bone that had been found in the seventeenth century in a local quarry and was described in 1677 by the first keeper of the museum, Dr Robert Plot, in his *Natural History of Oxfordshire*. Plot's initial diagnosis was that the bone was from an elephant imported into Britain during the Roman invasion. However, when he had the opportunity to compare the specimen directly with that of an elephant thigh bone, he had to admit that it was different and was forced to conclude that the fossil had 'exactly the figure of the lower most part of the Thigh-bone of a Man' who must have been a victim of the Flood. However, as we shall see it was actually much more interesting and was in fact one of the earliest discoveries of a dinosaur bone.

———— • ————

Robert Plot, 1640–96, landowner and antiquarian, who became the first keeper of the Ashmolean Museum and professor of chemistry in Oxford (from 1683) and wrote a *Natural History of Oxfordshire* in 1699.

———— • ————

At the end of the seventeenth century, the Oxford scholar and Keeper of the Ashmolean Museum, Edward Lhwyd, illustrated some fossil vertebrae in his 1699 book *Lithophylacii Britannici Ichnographia*. The fossils probably came from strata exposed along the banks of the river Severn, which we now know were deposited from the end of Triassic times into the beginning of Jurassic times. Lhwyd thought that they were fish backbones and so he called them *Ichthyospondyli*. We now know that they belonged to large, extinct marine reptiles such as ichthyosaurs and plesiosaurs.

Over 100 years later, the Reverend William Buckland also became Director of the Ashmolean Museum, which by the end of the eighteenth century had

Edward Lhwyd, 1660–1709, antiquarian and Celtic scholar who became keeper of the Ashmolean Museum in Oxford and wrote *Lithophylacii Britannici Ichnographia sive Lapidorum aliorumq.* (1699) and *Archaeologia Britannica* (1707).

---

acquired yet more puzzling bones, including teeth, which were found locally in the so-called Stonesfield slate. This Jurassic limestone was actively quarried in Oxfordshire because it could be split into thin slabs that were extensively used as roofing slates in the region. The limestone is often quite fossiliferous and when the quarrymen came across curious shells and bones they put them aside to be sold to collectors; some of these ended up the museum.

The fame of the Oxford collection drew the eminent French anatomist Cuvier to the museum in 1818. From his examination of these problematic bones, he concluded that some of them were more likely to be reptilian than mammalian. One of the fossils was a 30 cm (12 in) jawbone still armed with impressively long (15 cm, 6 in) backward-curved teeth and some unerupted smaller ones still within the jawbone. Cuvier recognised this as a typically reptilian mode of continuous tooth replacement, but could not be sure what kind of reptile the jaw

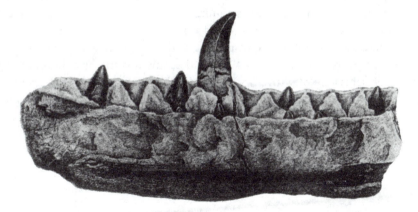

The fossilised lower jaw of Buckland's giant reptile from Stonesfield, Oxfordshire still retains some of the serrated and blade-shaped teeth of a predatory carnivore.

came from. The most obvious comparison was with a crocodile, but the fossil teeth were flattened and quite blade-like with serrated edges, while crocodile teeth are more conical and not serrated, although sometimes ridged. From the size of the thigh bone, Cuvier calculated that the original owner must have been more than 12 m (40 ft) long, with a bulk equivalent to that of an elephant over 2 m (7 ft) high.

Although Buckland was alerted to this revolutionary diagnosis by Cuvier in 1818, he did not rush to publish it, perhaps because it hardly fitted into the biblical scheme of things that he wanted to promote. Not for another six years, until 1824, did Buckland get around to doing so, and then it was mainly because there were reports of some new giant bones being found in Sussex that were, he heard, being studied by Mantell. So on February 24th, 1824, Buckland took the opportunity to describe 'his' giant reptile at a meeting of the Geological Society in London, of which he just happened to be President at the time. He described the fragmentary Oxfordshire remains and explained how, from the teeth alone, the remains could be assigned to the lizard 'Order Sauria', within the 'Class Reptilia'.

Since the bones had been found associated with the fossils of sea creatures, including crocodile and turtle remains, Buckland concluded that this extinct lizard 'was probably an amphibious animal', but could probably emerge to creep about on the land. The image he created was that of a very big but still 'lowly, creeping serpent-like animal' and he gave it the name *Megalosaurus*, meaning 'great lizard'. In retrospect, we now know that this was the first dinosaur in the world to be 'christened' with a formal scientific name and it was found in the Jurassic age strata of southern England within deposits that are predominantly marine. But it was not the only historically important fossil of a terrestrial animal to be found in these shallow marine deposits.

Jurassic mammals

The tiny lower jawbones from three different kinds of mole-sized mammals were also found in the Stonesfield Oolites of Oxfordshire. Although biologically important, the discovery of these mammal fossils and any publicity associated with them was largely eclipsed by greater interest in the much more exotic extinct reptiles. The small size of the mammal fossils contributed to their lack of allure. Subsequent discoveries of early mammals have verified the fact that the first mammals were all small, shrew to hedgehog-sized creatures. Like the poet Robert Burns's 'wee, sleekit, cow'rin, tim'rous beastie', these tiny Jurassic mammals would probably also have suffered the 'panic in thy breastie', and would need to be able to 'start awa sae hasty', considering the company they kept. Their world was populated by an enormous diversity of reptiles, not only dinosaurs of all sizes.

Cuvier also cast his expert eye over these fossils during his Oxford visit of 1818 and thought that they belonged to marsupial mammals, but noted that they differed from living marsupials and all known mammals in having 10 molar cheek teeth. One of the specimens was illustrated and described as a fossil marsupial with the name *Thylacotherium* by the French palaeontologist Constant Prévost in 1825. Richard Owen pointed out that the jawbone must belong to an extinct genus because of the number of molars. He also claimed that it might have an affinity with the newly discovered numbat, a squirrel-shaped, termite-eating marsupial technically known as *Myrmecobius*, which was first found in a hollow tree, surrounded by anthills, near the Swan River in southeast Australia. The mid-nineteenth century was a great period of biological discovery, with new animals and plants being found all over the world and brought back to fill the new natural history museums of the great metropolitan centres of the western world.

When another, better-preserved fossil jaw was found at Stonesfield, Richard Owen was able to show that *Thylacotherium* was not a marsupial but rather a placental insectivore. He renamed it *Amphitherium* in 1846, although it does

----

Constant Prévost, 1787–1856, French student of medicine who, encouraged by Brongniart Sr., turned palaeontologist and professor of geology at the Sorbonne, collaborated with Lyell and was co-founder of the Geological Society of France in 1830.

preserve some features similar to the marsupials. The other Stonesfield specimen, *Phascolotherium*, seemed to him to be a genuine marsupial.

Charles Lyell, in 1853, was so impressed by the occurrence of 'these most ancient memorials of the mammiferous type ... in so low a member of the oolitic series. (They) ... should serve as a warning to us against hasty generalisations, founded solely on negative evidence.' He eventually gets to the point:

> it seems fatal to the theory of progressive development, or to the notion that the order of precedence in the creation of animals, considered chronologically, has precisely coincided with the order in which they would be ranked according to perfection or complexity of structure.

Remember that this was before the Darwin/Wallace theory of evolution and Lyell was, at this stage, arguing against any idea of progressive development. He thought that the fossil record of most groups of animals and plants would eventually be found to extend back to some common starting point (act of creation) in the earliest Transition strata, which were later named as Cambrian by Adam Sedgwick.

However, what had been clearly established in the early decades of the nineteenth century was that although life on land during Jurassic times was dominated by the dinosaurs, the mammals were also present. This important discovery tended to be overlooked until relatively recent times, partly because the mammals were very small and their fossils extremely rare, and partly because the dinosaurs and their reptilian relatives were much larger and, perhaps more importantly, much more spectacular. As we shall see, this view of prehistoric life was reinforced by the creation in London in 1851 of the world's first theme park with life-size models of dinosaurs.

Jurassic birds

In southern Germany, quarrying of limestone strata of similar age to England's Oolites revealed one of the most important fossil finds ever made, the oldest bird, *Archaeopteryx*, now known to be some 147 million years old. Originally

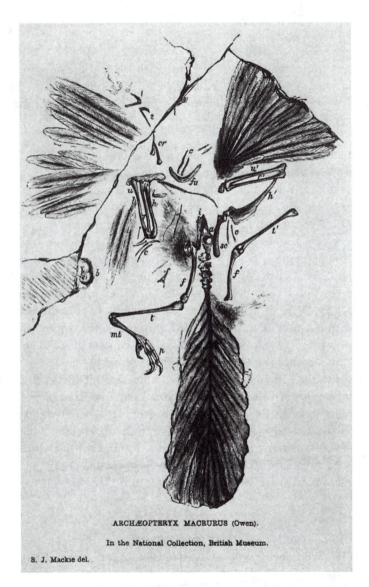

ARCHÆOPTERYX MACRURUS (Owen).

In the National Collection, British Museum.

S. J. Mackie del.

Richard Owen's drawing of *Archaeopteryx* shows the mixture of bird-related features such as a 'wishbone' (fu -furcula) and feathers along with a typically reptilian long bony tail. However, it was Huxley who recognized that it provided an excellent example of Darwinian evolution.

deposited in shallow marine lagoons dotted with islands, the fine-grained muds were lithified into limestones that could easily be split into thin flags, which were greatly valued for high-quality lithographic printing stones. Splitting the rock also often revealed remarkably well-preserved fossils that the quarrymen put on one side for sale to collectors.

In 1860 a small, 5-cm-long fossil feather was found in the Solnhofen quarry, preserved as a black impression on one of the rock surfaces. With its asymmetric shape and details of individual barbs preserved as if printed, the feather clearly had a very modern look and was evidently designed for flying. It was realised that where there was a feather there should be a bird not too far away and the following year *Archaeopteryx* was found. News of the discovery soon spread throughout the palaeontological world and Richard Owen used his considerable influence to get the British Museum to buy it in 1862, along with a magnificent collection of 1703 other Solnhofen fossils for £700, a considerable sum in those days. The owner, Dr C. F. Häberlein used the money to provide each of his six daughters with a dowry. Owen published a masterly description of the fossil, showing that while it was clearly a bird, it also preserved some features that were otherwise only seen in the embryos of living birds.

However, it was the English biologist and evolutionist Thomas Henry Huxley who first realised that *Archaeopteryx* possesses a remarkable mixture of reptilian and bird characteristics. In this, the fossil provided something that Darwin thought the fossil record would never be able to do: it represented an ancestral 'link' between two major groups of backboned animals, the reptiles and the birds. As such, it was an excellent example of Darwinian evolution and Huxley made the most of it in his proselytisation for the Darwin/Wallace theory of evolution.

Thomas Henry Huxley, 1825–95, trained in medicine, was assistant surgeon on HMS *Rattlesnake* (1846–50) and professor of biology at various institutions in London. He became a vehement supporter of Darwin and his theory of evolution and wrote many books and articles; president of the Geological Society of London (1868) and the Royal Society (1883–5).

Huxley knew that in the late 1850s, the skeleton of a small bipedal dinosaur, *Compsognathus*, had also been found at Solnhofen and that it closely resembled *Archaeopteryx*. For Huxley, there was no inherent problem, even in linking separate classes of animals despite their seemingly different anatomy and physiology. It reinforced his view, as did Owen's embryological evidence. Huxley was a particularly persuasive speaker, in a way that the shy and private Darwin was not. There is little doubt that a great deal of the growing acceptance of Darwin's revolutionary ideas was due to Huxley's powerful advocacy through his public lectures and published essays.

Archaeopteryx was a medium-sized bird like a magpie, about 300–500 mm long, from the tip of its snout to the end of its long, bony, feathered tail, and stood some 250 mm high. The skull was lightly constructed with large eyes and optic lobes in the brain, showing that it depended on sight as a key sense for survival. The narrow, pointed, beak-like jaws were armed with widely spaced, sharp teeth. The neck was curved and led into a short back and long, straight tail with 22 vertebrae. The forelimbs had three greatly elongate fingers, each ending in a long, curved claw. The pelvis was generally like that of a small theropod reptile, but there has been some controversy over the exact form of its construction.

The question is whether the pubis was aligned vertically, as in some dinosaurs, or backwards, as in living birds. Compression of specimens during fossilisation often creates such problems. The hind limbs were particularly reptile like, with the inner toe being very short and lying at the rear of the foot. However, this condition is also typical of many living birds. As Huxley pointed out, the foot of a chicken embryo is hard to differentiate from that of a reptile.

The living habits of *Archaeopteryx* and its flying ability have also been a matter of considerable argument. It has often been portrayed as a forest inhabitant and capable of climbing trees using the hooked claws on its wing fingers and feet. Its feathers were ideal wing material, since they were light, waterproof and did not tear easily. This combination provides quite an attractive model for a prototype bird, with the animal taking to the trees to escape predators and to find food, as so many birds do today. Being able to glide from one tree canopy to another would have several advantages, as squirrels, monkeys and some frogs and lizards

Within four years of the discovery of *Archaeopteryx* it was included in a 1865 reconstruction of life in Upper Oolite (Jurassic) times by Louis Figuier.

find today: it saves energy and the risks of returning to the ground all the time. Gliding could then have evolved more easily into powered flapping flight, which would have extended the animal's range.

One snag with this model for *Archaeopteryx* is that the environment in which the bird lived did not include any substantial trees. The only available land seems to have been some low-lying islands within the lagoon where the Solnhofen lime-rich muds accumulated. With the prevailing hot and fairly arid climate, these islands would not have been able to support tree-sized vegetation, but rather a sparse, low scrub of bushes separated by open ground. Hardly the sort of environment for an arboreal glider to prosper in. The plant fossils from the same deposit support this reconstruction, since they lack any wood and only preserve the remains of some small, shrubby conifers *Brachyphyllum* and *Palaeocyparis* and bennettitalean plants, which only grew to about 3 m high.

Nevertheless, there is no doubt that *Archaeopteryx* was capable of climbing and flying. The primary wing feathers were asymmetric and that means one thing only – flight, even if it was fairly clumsy and inefficient. Modern flightless birds do not have asymmetric feathers. Recently, scientists in London's Natural History Museum have been able to isolate part of the skull of their *Archaeopteryx* specimen and make a brain scan using high-resolution X-ray computed tomography. The brain is smaller than your little finger, but even so they found that its brain was remarkably similar to that of modern birds, with enhancement of those areas associated with movement and vision. Similar analysis of the brain in unrelated flying reptiles shows the same kind of organisation, indicating that such brain enhancement is probably intimately linked with active flying.

Jurassic monsters of the abyss

A number of other historical finds of isolated fossil bones and even parts of skeletons were made during quarrying operations throughout much of the English outcrop and in Germany during the eighteenth century and occasionally they were pictured in books. We only know anything about them from these published records because few of the actual specimens have survived or can now be identified in existing museum collections. One extensive collection, made by the famous Scottish anatomist John Hunter, formed the Hunterian Museum of the Royal College of Surgeons in London and was catalogued by Richard Owen in 1854. From Owen's catalogue, we know that it contained 29 specimens of marine reptile fossils.

John Hunter, 1728–93, Scottish surgeon to King George III and collector, brother of another collector William Hunter. His collection of 10,563 specimens was bought by the British government in 1795 for £15,000 and formed the Hunterian Museum of the Royal College of Surgeons in London. Unfortunately, most of the collection was bombed into oblivion in 1941, during the Second World War.

By the beginning of the nineteenth century, while such finds were regarded as the remains of marine creatures, 'the irresistible proofs of an Universal Deluge, and of a new world risen from the ancient ocean', it was not clear exactly what kind of animal they belonged to: they could be crocodile, lizard or even whale. Nevertheless, the problem was soon to be resolved.

Constant erosion of coastal cliffs made of Lias strata in Yorkshire and Dorset by the sea, especially by winter storms, broke fossils from their rock tombs and tumbled them onto the beaches. The most prized fossils were the rare skeletons of 'seadragons' preserved in the thin limestone layers. The intervening black shales are more easily weathered, so that the limestones stand out from the cliff face as ledges until they break away under their own weight and tumble down onto the beach. Unless quickly recovered, they are soon pounded to unrecognisable pieces by the waves.

Local people, who traditionally scoured the beaches for anything useful or saleable, were well aware of the strange shells and bits of bone that turned up after the storms, but it was not until the latter part of the eighteenth century, when fossils acquired some value, that they bothered to recover the heavy and awkward petrifications from the beaches. Some of the most spectacular of these early discoveries came from Lyme Regis at the southern end of the outcrop, where many of them were found by a remarkable Dorset woman, Mary Anning and her family.

The Anning family

Between 1811 and 1830, the Anning family of Lyme Regis, Dorset found and recovered several strange, vaguely dolphin-like skeletons from the Liassic limestones and shales that form the local seacliffs of this part of southern England. Richard Anning (1766–1810), the father of the family, was a carpenter and cabinet maker by trade, but was often out of work. His wife Mary, called Molly by the family, tried to supplement their precarious income by collecting and selling fossils to the growing numbers of genteel tourists. In the late eighteenth century, changing agricultural practices and enclosures of land meant that many of the peasants of rural England were impoverished.

People such as Jane Austen and her social circle increasingly frequented picturesque fishing villages such as Lyme, to admire the seascapes, the quaint cottages and their inhabitants, whose local accents were barely understandable. At the time it was becoming fashionable to collect natural curiosities to adorn glass cabinets in the reception rooms of spacious middle-class homes. The specimens could always be brought out as aids to polite conversation. Typical of their time were the three Philpot sisters, who first visited Lyme in 1806 and became avid samplers and collectors of natural objects. Somehow, the Philpot ladies met the 7-year-old Mary Anning junior and befriended her. Over the following years they bought numerous specimens from Mary and her family. Eventually, the Philpot sisters' magnificent collection of fossils was donated to Oxford University Museum.

But there were also other collectors who took a more serious financial or academic interest in unusual specimens. One of these collectors, James Johnston, wrote in 1810 to a friend that 'there is a person at Lyme who collects for sale by the name of Anning, a cabinet maker and I believe as men are, may be depended upon, I would advise you calling upon him.' By comparison, he also remarked that nearby at Charmouth there was 'a confounded rogue of the name of Lock to call upon ... give him a Grog or a Pint, this will buy him to your interest and all the crocodiles he may meet with will almost assuredly be offered to you first, you must then agree with him for he is poor and will sell within one hour after the article is found.'

The Annings probably had as many as 10 children, but such was infant mortality in those days for poor families that only two of them survived to maturity, a boy called Joseph (1796–1849), who became an upholsterer, and a girl, Mary. Disaster again struck the Anning family late in 1810 when Richard died from the combined effects of consumption (tuberculosis), an all too common disease in those days, and a serious fall. He left his family in serious debt to the tune of £120, with the result that they were dependent on parish relief until 1816. Nevertheless, in 1811 Joseph found the spectacular skull of a fossil 'seadragon' and the following year his sister Mary, just 12 years old, found the rest of the skeleton. According to a report in a local newspaper, it was dug out of the rock by workmen employed by the family in November 1812.

— • —

Mary Anning junior, 1799–1847, most famous member of the Dorset family who collected and sold fossils to supplement their income. A number of the important fossils found by Mary and her family in the Jurassic strata forming the seacliffs around Lyme Regis in Dorset are to be seen in major national collections, such as those of the Natural History Museum in London.

— • —

The specimen was sold for £23 to the lord of the local manor, Henry Henley, who was a keen fossil collector. He sold it on to William Bullock, a showman, who exhibited the petrified curiosity in his private London Museum of Natural History. Natural history was fashionable and people were prepared to pay to go and see the newly discovered wonders of the natural world. The fossil was illustrated and described in 1814 by Sir Everard Home, whose poet sister Mary was married to John Hunter. Some of Mary Hunter's verses were

An 1825 lithograph of a young woman, perhaps Mary Anning junior, out 'fossicking' with a hammer amongst the rocks by the Cobb in Lyme Regis, Dorset.

set to music by Haydn when he visited London and was befriended by the Hunters.

Home noticed some crocodile-like features in the jaw, but concluded that its affinities lay with the fish. When Bullock's collection was sold to the British Museum in 1819, the specimen was priced at £47 5d, a great deal of money in those days. The specimen now has pride of place in the Natural History Museum in London.

More and better finds of 'saurians' were made; one particularly fine ichthyosaur was sold in 1819 for £100 and the fame of the Annings spread among scholars and collectors. Mary probably had little or no schooling and yet, of necessity, she had learned to read and write and was well able to communicate news of finds to those who might be interested. Lyme was still very much off the beaten track and a long way from London by horseback or carriage. Most of her clients were well-educated gentlemen and her surviving letters are testimony to her abilities, which went far beyond finding specimens: she corresponded and conversed over matters of scientific detail.

The most spectacular and interesting specimens went to 'Oxbridge' academics such as Adam Sedgwick and William Buckland, who used them to develop their ideas about life in the geological past. It is a matter of record that many scientists, such as De la Beche, Buckland, Louis Agassiz and even the King of Saxony, visited Mary's small shop to see her latest specimens and talk of fossils. Many of them remarked on her knowledge of anatomy, especially of the marine reptiles, and she was not afraid to dispute the finer details of interpretation, even with the likes of Professor Buckland.

One of her best finds was a complete 3-m-long plesiosaur found in 1823. Henry De la Beche and the Reverend William Conybeare had previously realised that certain bones, which had been thought of as belonging to an ichthyosaur,

Sir Henry Thomas De la Beche, 1796–1855, began his career in the army (1810–15), became a geologist in the Trigonometrical Survey (from 1832), was the first director of the British Geological Survey (from 1835), president of the Geological Society of London (1847) and was knighted in 1848.

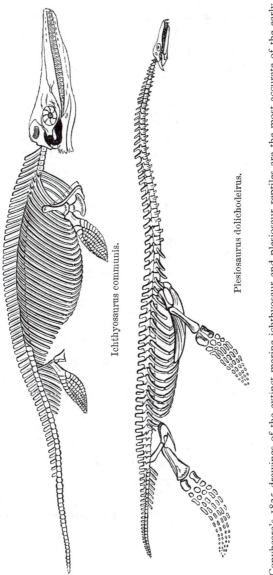

Ichthyosaurus communis.

Plesiosaurus dolichodeirus.

Conybeare's 1825 drawings of the extinct marine ichthyosaur and plesiosaur reptiles are the most accurate of the early reconstructions ever made and were based on fossils found by the Annings in Lyme Regis, Dorset.

were in fact those of a quite different reptile. They called this putative creature *Plesiosaurus* (Greek for 'near lizard'), but its recognition was disputed by other scholars and so De la Beche and Conybeare were greatly pleased when Mary proved them right by finding this complete specimen.

The following year, 1824, Conybeare described their new fossil and concluded correctly that it was a marine reptile that swam slowly, using its flippers, a bit like a turtle. He considered that its long, flexible neck compensated for its small head and weak jaws by being able to bend quickly and snap up passing prey. He also took the stance of so many churchmen of the time, who were enthused by natural science. In these pre-Darwinian days, Conybeare regarded the extreme deviation of the plesiosaur body from the reptilian norm as a perfect and purposeful example of design by the Creator. It exemplified the 'exquisite orderliness and diversity of divine creation'. This stance had the benefit of allowing Conybeare and his fellow clergymen to pursue their interests with a clear conscience, in the knowledge that they were investigating and illustrating the works of God for the greater edification of mankind.

Mary Anning's social status and sex prevented her from entering this developing world of nineteenth-century science that was rapidly becoming professionalised and was dominated by university-educated, middle-class men. Mary never married and there is much speculation of a tragic romance with a gentleman (subject of Sheila Cole's 1993 novel *The Dragon in the Cliff* and not unrelated to the plot of John Fowles's *The French Lieutenant's Woman*) but no real evidence.

She found at least three complete ichthyosaurs (1818, 1821 and 1830); two plesiosaurs (1823 and 1830); a cephalopod *Belemnosepia*, with its fossilised ink sac preserved; the first British pterodactyl *Dimorphodon* (1828); the cartilagenous fossil fish *Squaloraja* (1828); and quantities of other invertebrate shells. Mary Anning was possibly the first person to recognise the phosphatised fossil fish and reptile faeces that are not uncommon in the Lias shales. How much of her observation found its way, unacknowledged, into the scientific books and papers that Buckland and others wrote is a matter of argument, but she certainly felt that her knowledge had been used.

Until recently, very few of her fossil finds, specimens of which are in museum collections, have been recognised. It is only now, when museum curators are more interested in the history and provenance of their specimens, that her discoveries are being properly acknowledged. Of the five most important institutions to purchase her specimens, only Oxford University Museum has a direct record of a specimen originating from her, and that is a single coprolite. Over the last few years, searches of Mary's correspondence have revealed that Cambridge University's Sedgwick Museum has several of her prize ichthyosaur specimens.

Her latter years were ones of sad decline. There was less interest in fossils and the monsters of the abyss had lost their fascination for the while and Mary made no further spectacular finds, so her income fell. She suffered from breast cancer and had to give up the hard life of 'fossicking' out on the beach. Fortunately, her gentlemen had not entirely forgotten how much they owed to her industry and expertise. She became a worthy cause and at the meeting of the British Association for the Advancement of Science in 1835, £200 was raised by private subscription. Buckland persuaded the Prime Minister Lord Melbourne to add £300 in 1838 and together these sums bought Mary an annuity of £25. She died in 1847 at the age of 48.

The most famous lines that may refer to her are those of the tongue-twister:

She sells sea-shells on the sea-shore,
The shells she sells are sea-shells, I'm sure
For if she sells sea-shells on the sea-shore,
Then I'm sure she sells sea-shore shells.

Within just a few decades of the early nineteenth century, the Oolites and Lias strata were transformed from being merely the source of useful stone and mineral materials into the Jurassic System of strata that represents the Jurassic Period of Earth Time, now known to extend for some 54.1 million years from 199.6–145.5 million years ago. Fossils from these strata revealed an extraordinary ancient world occupied by a mixture of some familiar-looking animals such as small mammals and birds, but also by creatures more curious and bizarre than previously dreamt of.

The mythical dragons of mediaeval times were eclipsed by extinct but very real monsters that had lived on land and in the seas. But a full understanding of their remarkable diversity and true appearance had to await the discovery of much better-preserved specimens than were available to Richard Owen. It was only when dinosaur fossils were recovered from strata representing land environments of Jurassic times, especially those that are so well exposed in the arid badlands of the midwest of the North American continent, that the true image of the 'terrible saurians' emerged. Meanwhile, Richard Owen made a brave attempt at reconstructing the dinosaurs and their lost world with the help of a little-known but entrepreneurial artist by the name of Benjamin Waterhouse Hawkins.

Benjamin Waterhouse Hawkins, 1807–89, London sculptor and illustrator, who created, with Richard Owen, the first life-size reconstructions of dinosaurs and other extinct animals and plants for the park surrounding the relocated Crystal Palace when it reopened at Sydenham in south London in 1854.

The world's first theme park

The opportunity that presented itself to Owen was the relocation of Thomas Paxton's world-famous Crystal Palace from the 1851 Great Exhibition site at Kensington in central London to the rapidly growing suburb of Sydenham in the south of the city. With his royal connections and the ear of Prince Albert, Owen grasped his chance to put his concept of the dinosaurs into practice by recreating them as lifesize models. The whole scheme was very ambitious: there was a 'greenfield' site that could be landscaped with real rock strata. A lake was to be created and filled with fossil crocodiles and an island built on which the dinosaurs were to be 'safely' marooned and surrounded by appropriate vegetation.

Within a decade of inventing the dinosaurs, Owen, who well knew the value of publicity, made what must be one of the biggest coups in terms of scientific publicity in the whole of the nineteenth century. He redefined the concept and appearance of his invention and transformed Mantell's 'lowly, creeping', serpent-like creature into something much more ponderous and imperious, as befitted the new Victorian era. Mantell's *Iguanodon* was remodelled as a curious chimaera with a stance rather like a mammalian rhinoceros. Owen realised that the structure of the dinosaur pelvis showed that they were not like lizards with legs sticking out to one side, but that the legs were brought close in under the body to support the huge bulk with its massive tail and head. The creature was given a typical reptilian scaly skin and a rather baleful stare, curiously like Queen Victoria in her old age. Owen calculated that his *Iguanodon* might be as much as six times the size of an elephant.

Apart from *Iguanodon*, there were two other dinosaurs, *Hyleosaurus* and Buckland's *Megalosaurus*, and even more ancient amphibian labyrinthodont and younger Tertiary and Quaternary mammals, altogether representing a broad sweep of ancient life. But the ancient menagerie was never fully completed: there was a planned life-size restoration of an American mastodon, but funds were cut off by the Crystal Palace company.

The models were created by the artist Benjamin Waterhouse Hawkins, under Owen's supervision, and the construction process was closely trailed and illustrated in the popular journals of the day. Famously, on New Year's day 1853, a celebratory seven-course dinner for the great and the good of the day was held within the cast of the *Iguanodon*, surrounded by a panoply of heroes' names – Buckland, Cuvier, Owen and Mantell. The idea may have come from another earlier famous fossil dinner in 1801, held in his Philadelphia museum by American artist and museum owner, Charles Willson Peale. Dinner for 12 was held inside the partly reconstructed skeleton of a mastodon, which Peale had excavated. Patriotic toasts were made with rousing choruses of *Yankee Doodle*.

The Crystal Palace invitation card, drawn by Hawkins, had its text written on the outstretched wing of a flying reptile. Again, the occasion was pictured in the *London Illustrated News*, giving further publicity to the project. Attended by

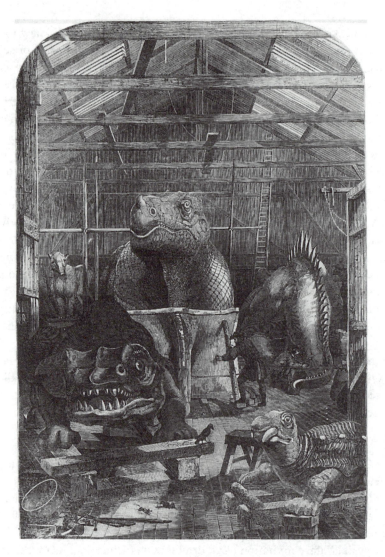

In 1853 the *Illustrated London News* showed the lifesize model dinosaurs and other extinct animals under construction in Waterhouse Hawkins studio at the relocated Crystal Palace in Sydenham, south London.

the likes of Charles Lyell and of course Owen, there was an elaborately joky 'fossiliferous' menu and special song composed for the occasion:

A thousand ages underground,
His skeleton had lain,
But now his body's big and round
And there's life in him again!

His bones like Adam's wrapped in clay
his ribs of iron stout,
where is the brute alive today
That dares turn him out.

Beneath his hide he's got inside
The souls of living men,
Who dares our Saurian now deride
With life in him again?

with the chorus:

The jolly old beast
Is not deceased
There's life in him again!

The chorus presumably referred to the dinosaur, but it may also have been a dig at Owen. He managed to sound the only sour note of the evening by publicly attacking Hawkins for getting the *Iguanodon* wrong, which was a bit rich considering he was supposed to have been supervising the construction. Owen was probably covering his own back, as recently fossil footprints had been found, which suggested that *Iguanodon* walked upright on its two hind legs. Owen seems to have been a thoroughly unpleasant man and few of his contemporaries had a good word for him, but nevertheless his anatomical talent does have to be acknowledged.

The grand reopening of the Crystal Palace at Sydenham on June 10th, 1854 by Queen Victoria drew a crowd of 40,000. The first theme park in the world was open to an incredulous public and it went on to draw an average two million visitors a year until the end of the century. More engraved illustrations were reproduced in the popular press, including *Punch*, the famous satirical magazine of the day. Here, a Victorian top-hatted father is portrayed, intent on improving his young son's mind by visiting the antediluvian reptiles. The child is screaming with horror but, unperturbed, the father walks on and the punch-line reads: 'Master Tom strongly objects to having his mind improved'. The giant models have recently been renovated and are still to be seen at Sydenham, so young minds can continue to be improved by viewing them, although Paxton's wonderful Crystal Palace was unfortunately burned down in 1936.

News of the huge success of the venture soon spread and Hawkins was invited to New York for a repeat performance in Central Park. He set up his studio and began producing an even more ambitious scheme with many more fossil reconstructions. Unfortunately, it fell foul of local politics and came to nothing, although some of the completed models are reputed to have been broken up and buried in the park; despite some modern searches nothing has been turned up.

The plants the dinosaurs ate

In the late 1820s, John Phillips, William Smith's nephew, was gathering information for his pioneering book on the geology of the Yorkshire coast. The coastal strata are often well exposed and in places highly fossiliferous, something that generations of locals had realised. Like their counterparts at the other end of the country in Dorset, a network of local collectors and dealers was established as soon as money was to be made from the sale of fossils to the gentry and those interested in the study of rocks and fossils. Students of geology ranged from amateurs, who were often members of the local literary and philosophical societies that became fashionable in the latter decades of the eighteenth century and persisted into the early nineteenth century, to the occasional but growing bands of professionals, mostly but not always university men, and those who struggled to make a precarious living from surveying and map making, such as William Smith and his nephew.

By 1825, fossil plants had been found in rocks of the Oolitic Period (later referred to as the Jurassic Period) at a number of localities on the Yorkshire coast north of Scarborough and Saltwick, south of Whitby. Specimens collected by locals were bought by societies such as that in York for their museums. Indeed, Adolphe Brongniart, on his way to Scotland, was shown the collection of plants in York by John Phillips. And in 1826 Roderick Murchison arrived to view them and the coastal sections from which they originated, in preparation for a trip to Sutherland in Scotland. There, on the northern shore of the Moray Firth in the village of Brora, was a coal mine.

John Phillips, 1800–74, was orphaned and adopted by his uncle William Smith, whom he assisted in the compilation of his county maps. Phillips became keeper of the York Museum and subsequently professor of geology in London, Dublin and Oxford. He was president of the Geological Society of London (1862) and coined the name Mesozoic in 1840.

Coal at Brora had been exploited from surface exposures since 1529 and the first pit was dug in 1598. New mines had been opened in 1810 and Murchison wanted to see if the Brora coal strata were the same age as those of the Yorkshire oolites. Coal was mined sporadically from a number of small pits in Yorkshire strata of Jurassic age since 1648. Birdforth Colliery was the largest mine with a shaft 46 metres deep sunk in 1760, but even at the height of its productivity it

only employed some 30 men and it closed in 1798. Murchison was always keen
to try and apply geological knowledge to economic ends and subsequently made
considerable efforts to deter land owners, ignorant of the geological constraints,
from wasting money searching for coal in rocks that would never yield any.

The 1827 discovery of fossil plants at Gristhorpe on the Yorkshire coast was
to put the district firmly on the fossil collector's map. There was some dispute
over who first discovered the fossil locality. Two local collectors who were
cousins, William Bean and John Williamson, both claimed priority. Since then,
over 300 different plant species, many new to science, have been found in the
Jurassic strata of the region and 100 of these come from the strata exposed on
the coast at Gristhorpe, which is now internationally recognised as the best
locality in the world for fossil plants of this age. Brongniart named four new
species after Williamson and Bean's contribution was subsequently acknowledged
by the naming of a cycad genus after him.

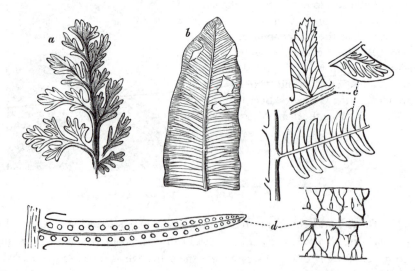

Some of the best preserved fossil plants were ferns found in the first decades of the 19th century
within Lower Oolite (Jurassic) age strata exposed on the Yorkshire coast of northeast England and
were studied by the French naturalist Adolphe Brongniart.

John Williamson, 1784–1873, gardener employed by his cousin William Bean, also a naturalist and collector, who became curator of the Scarborough Museum from its inception in 1827.

The modern interpretation of the deposit is that the plants were part of a diverse vegetation of bryophytes, clubmosses, ferns, caytonias, cycads, ginkgophytes, conifers and so on that grew around a lagoon. Bits of the plants were blown or fell into the lagoon where, over the years, they were buried and preserved in fine mud. Several fossil plants, such as the cycad *Beania* tree, have been reassembled from Gristhorpe fossils.

William Crawford Williamson, 1816–95, son of John W., surgeon and professor of botany and geology at Queen's College, Manchester (from 1851), he made a particular study of Coal Measure plants and was one of the founders of the science of palaeobotany.

The fossils were first brought to the attention of the wider geological community by John Phillips's 1829 book *Illustrations of the Geology of Yorkshire*. John Williamson's son, William Williamson, provided many of the specimens, descriptions and drawings of the plants for Phillips's book. William Williamson later became professor of botany and geology at Queen's College in Manchester (later becoming the University of Manchester) and effectively founded the academic study of fossil plants in Britain. A decade or so later, it was realised that the remarkable fossil floras that had been preserved in these Jurassic strata were the basic food supply of the dinosaur food chain, consumed by the innumerable herbivorous dinosaurs of all dimensions, from ostrich-sized bipedal forms to the biggest land-living animals of all time, the giant sauropods.

Million Years Ago

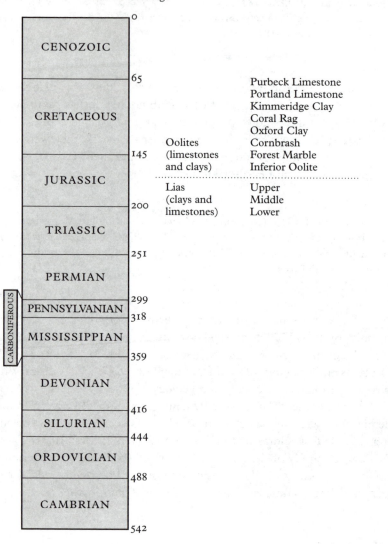

		Purbeck Limestone
		Portland Limestone
		Kimmeridge Clay
		Coral Rag
		Oxford Clay
Oolites		Cornbrash
(limestones		Forest Marble
and clays)		Inferior Oolite
Lias		Upper
(clays and		Middle
limestones)		Lower

Jurassic.

6

Red beds in the Midlands and Russia

TRIASSIC TO PERMIAN

From the heights of the Cotswolds the great lowland of central England spreads out northwestwards – known as the Midlands for many centuries. The wide vales of the rivers Avon and Severn, which lie on either side of the great industrial conurbation of Birmingham, converge at Tewkesbury before flowing into the Bristol Channel. Stratford-upon-Avon is perhaps the most internationally famous of the River Avon's historic communities because of its association with Shakespeare, but from the point of view of industrial history there are also Rugby and nearby Coventry.

Geologically, the Avon flows over both Lias strata of Jurassic age and older rocks, which Smith knew as Red Marl and Sandstone but the strata soon became known as the New Red Sandstone. These rather unimaginative names did at least attempt to differentiate it from the more ancient Red Rhab and Dunstone or Old Red Sandstone, as it is more commonly known. However, as we shall see, there was at times a lot of confusion over their separate identities. The overall outcrop of the New Red Sandstone parallels that of the Jurassic strata from the south coast northeast to Durham and the North Sea. But from the Midlands northwards there is also a considerable northwestern extension to Lancashire and the Irish Sea known as the Cheshire Basin.

The uppermost and relatively younger strata of the New Red Sandstone are mostly mudstones, which can be difficult to differentiate from the Lias. The older and lower New Red Sandstone strata are predominantly sandstones, as their name suggests. In places the dark red-brown and occasionally almost blood-red sandstones outcrop at the surface to form low hills. Historically, the sandstones were widely used for building and many of the low hills are surmounted by ancient prestigious buildings such as churches, castles and the grand houses of wealthy landowners.

However, in Cheshire the deposits are interbedded with layers of rock salt and gypsum, which have been extensively exploited commercially. As a mineral formed by the evaporation of seawater, rocksalt is equally easily dissolved by rainwater, so that in fairly wet climates like those of Britain today, layers of rocksalt do not outcrop at the surface but may persist below ground. To begin with the rocksalt was mined by the ancient method of pillar and stall, whereby caverns were excavated deep below ground with the roof supported by pillars of rock left in place. Britain's last surviving rocksalt mine was still producing nearly 2 million tonnes of rocksalt a year by this method in the late 1980s. But nowadays most salt is extracted from the Cheshire deposits as brine. Hot water, pumped into the salt-bearing layers, dissolves the salt and the resulting brine recirculates to the surface where it is evaporated to recover the salt. The downside of the extraction process is widespread subsidence as the land sinks and closes the underground spaces. Large holes can suddenly appear that are big enough for houses to collapse into.

The occurrence of evaporite minerals such as salt and gypsum in the New Red Sandstone tells us that the deposits bearing them must have been laid down in tropical climates. The climate needs to have been hot and dry enough to repeatedly evaporate large, shallow bodies of seawater to form salt pans over a significant period of time so that substantial thicknesses developed (one of the Cheshire salt horizons is over 290 m thick). The relative age of the deposits in England proved very difficult to determine because of the lack of marine fossils. The resolution was first found on the continent and especially in Germany, where there are extensive strata of New Red Sandstone and associated strata.

Over the last 200 years a significant variety of fossils have at last been recovered from the Triassic deposits of Britain and record the kinds of life inhabiting the tropical landscapes of the time. Fossil bones are very rare, but many footprints and trackways have been found showing that vertebrate animals were much more common than their skeletal remains suggest. The plant record is particularly poor apart from some pollen and spores but there was a typical Mesozoic vegetation of clubmosses (lycopsids). seedferns (pteropsids), primitive conifers and cycadopsids and it was substantial enough in places to feed plant-eating reptiles such as the rhynchosaurs (1–2 m long) and occasional large, primitive sauropod dinosaurs such as *Thecodontosaurus* (up to 7 m long). There were even some of the earliest reptiles (*Kuehneosaurus*) capable of gliding 'flight', which presumably lived in the tree-sized plants from where they could launch themselves. Numerous rivers and lakes were important habitats for aquatic life ranging from clams to arthropods, fish and a variety of predatory amphibians that were somewhat crocodile like in body form. *Haramiya*, a tiny, shrew-sized and primitive mammal, lived a precarious life among the vegetation and may even have been nocturnal to avoid the numerous predatory reptiles and amphibians.

The Triassic

As this name suggests, the Trias of Germany had long been known (since the mid-eighteenth century) to consist of a sequence of three distinctive series of rocks. From oldest to youngest, they are the Bunter Sandstone, the Muschelkalk Limestone and the Keuper Marls and Clays. Of these, only the Muschelkalk was a marine deposit, the older and younger strata were predominantly non-marine successions, which created great problems in determining their relative age and position in the overall succession. Their various fossils were well described and illustrated in the 1820s. But there was still considerable confusion and mismatching of strata, especially between the Muschelkalk and Zechstein limestones.

By 1834, German geologist Friedrich August von Alberti felt confident enough to group them together as an identifiable system. Alberti proclaimed that whoever

tabulates all the fossils of the three hitherto separate formations; whoever examines, further, the transition of the different forms one into the other, and, indeed, considers the entire structure of the mountains and the markedly different character of the fossils of the Zechstein from those of the Lias, will realise that the Bunter sandstone, Muschelkalk and Keuper are the result of a single period, their fossils, to use Elie de Beaumont's words, being the thermometer of a geological period; that their separation into three formations is not appropriate, and that it is more in accord with the concept of a formation to unify them into a single formation, which I shall provisionally name *Trias*.

———————— • ————————

Friedrich August von Alberti, 1795–1878, German mining geologist, inspector and finally manager of the Friedrichsall Saltworks, who described in detail the Bunter, Muschelkalk and Keuper strata and first suggested their union as the Triassic System in 1834.

———————— • ————————

Again, there was a problem of correlation, in that most of the European Triassic strata were continental rather than marine deposits. What did marine Triassic deposits look like and what were their fossils like? Fortunately, they did not have to look too far away, just as far as the Alps. But the tectonic complications of extreme folding and faulting of the strata presented new problems that took a considerable time to unravel. Sedgwick and Murchison had together made a foray into Alpine geology in 1830. Thanks to Sedgwick's skills in unravelling the geometry of complicated fold structures, they had published some remarkably accurate cross-sections of the folded strata.

But it was not until the 1840s that the presence of marine Triassic strata and fossils was first recognised in the South Tyrol. On the discovery of fossil-rich marls (lime-rich muds) at St Cassian, the German geologist Leopold von Buch

———————— • ————————

Jean Baptiste Élie de Beaumount, 1798–1874, French geologist and professor at the College de France who compiled a geological map of France (1841) with Dufrénoy. He also demonstrated that different mountain belts have different ages.

Count Georg Graf zu Münster, 1776–1844, Bavarian aristocrat and fossil collector who held office as Bavarian court chamberlain and whose large collection of fossils formed the basis of the state museum in Munich.

———————•———————

collected many of the fossils and sent them to Count Georg Graf zu Münster for identification.

In 1841, Münster published a description of 422 species from the St Cassian strata, including molluscs, brachiopods, echinoderms, corals and sponges, all creatures that lived in warm shallow seas. Of these species, Münster recognised some that he thought typical of Carboniferous strata, some from the Zechstein, others from the Muschelkalk and finally some Jurassic ones as well. In detail, most of these marine animals were not very widespread in their distribution, but were relatively long lived as genera and species so were not very useful for diagnosing the relative age of the strata. However, it was soon realised that the Cassian strata lay above the Alpine equivalents of the Muschelkalk and that the Hallstatt marble of the northern Alps was of similar age, since it contained similar fossils. In addition, it became clear that these fossil-rich strata were distinct from the younger Liassic limestones.

Unravelling the detailed succession of strata in the different regions of the Alps took many years because of the mountainous terrain and its structural

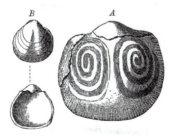

Identification of the fossils, such as this small lampshell (brachiopod) with its coiled internal spiralia, from the St Cassian strata in the Tyrolean Alps of Europe helped match terrestrial and marine rocks of Triassic age from northern and southern Europe.

complexities. Matching the strata across the Alps and beyond was even more difficult. We can now understand why and have to admire the efforts of those European geologists who struggled over several decades to make sense of it all. The strata of the Alps represent the deposits of an ancient ocean, called Tethys, which were hugely compressed, folded and faulted, with some of the deeply buried rocks being highly metamorphosed. The extensive foreshortening, driven by the northward movement of Africa, destroyed most of the evidence that would normally have linked the offshore marine and onshore continental deposits.

By the mid-1850s, the young German palaeontologist Albert Oppel had realised that an extinct group of coiled cephalopods (distantly related to the living cuttlefish and squid), called ammonoids, were particularly useful for matching strata. Often abundant in limestones, shales and marls, experts can distinguish the separate species of these sea-dwelling creatures by detailed examination of the fossil shells. These 'shellfish' were free-swimming molluscs with a buoyant shell that lived at different depths in the water column. They evolved rapidly and many were widely distributed in the seas and oceans of the world. Individual species tend to be confined to relatively small thicknesses of strata, and yet at any one level the same species are found over large regions, so they are ideal for matching strata that were originally laid down on the seabed at the same time. They could still be matched even when the contemporary sediments that enclosed the fossils were different. Since one particular fossil ammonoid species occurred in a limestone in one place and in a shale somewhere else, it meant that the limestone and shale had been originally deposited at more or less the same time and therefore could be linked with one another in terms of the overall succession of strata.

———————————— • ————————————

Albert Oppel, 1831–65, German professor of palaeontology (from 1860) and director of the palaeontological collections (from 1861) in Munich and travelled through Europe to compare Jurassic strata. He showed that successive changes in ammonite fossils could be used to distinguish stratigraphic succession in detail.

Oppel pioneered this use of cephalopods for correlation in both Triassic and Jurassic strata. Subsequently, it was found that other kinds of fossils could be used in a similar way for correlation of different parts of the geological column. For instance, graptolites proved equally useful for matching lower Palaeozoic strata. Oppel's work strengthened the whole approach to the subdivision of Earth Time through the use of characteristic fossils. In London some Fellows of the Geological Society complained that the whole business of the Society and the pursuit of geology in general was being taken over by 'fossil men'.

Oppel also found the first fossil 'keys' to the problem of matching Alpine deposits of upper Triassic age with their age equivalents elsewhere. Not one of the 1000 or so species known from the St Cassian and Hallstatt beds by this time could be found in regions beyond the Alps. But Oppel found the same fossils in the highest and youngest Triassic strata of both the Alps and Swabia. They occurred in strata that seemed to pass from the top of the Trias into the Lias above and they were subsequently called the Rhaetic Group of strata. However, experts on different groups of fossils could not decide whether they would be better placed at the top of the Trias or at the base of the Lias in the Jurassic System. After more than a century of wrangling, the Rhaetic is now placed at the top of the upper Triassic.

Oppel's approach was taken up by palaeontologist E. Mojsisovics von Mojsvar (generally known as Mojsisovics), who detailed the strata and fossils of the Rhaetian and Jurassic deposits between localities in Swabia, Salzburg and the Carpathian regions. Then he extended his cephalopod studies to the upper Triassic fossils of the Alpine region. On the basis of these studies, he recognised a threefold division into Carnic, Noric and Rhaetic, which is still used. By the 1870s, Mojsisovics linked the fossil cephalopods of the Alpine Muschelkalk (middle Triassic) with similar fossils in the Himalayas, Spitzbergen and Eastern

———— • ————

Johann August Georg Edmund Mojsisovics von Mojsvar, 1839–1907, Austro-Hungarian turned from study of law to geology with Edouard Suess, joined the Austrian Geological Survey. He made a particular study of the Mesozoic strata and fossil cephalopods of the Austrian Alps.

Siberia, and they were subsequently found in both Transylvania and California. Most importantly, these correlations showed that the Alpine region had not been an isolated one as had been thought and that Alberti's Triassic System had an international significance.

We now know that from around 200 million years ago, at the end of Triassic times when the North Atlantic began to open, a succession of plate fragments rifted away from the northern margin of the African plate. During early Jurassic times they moved north, closing Tethys, and collided with the southern margin of Eurasia. The resulting compressive movement crumpled and thickened the mass of Tethyan sediments. Some were pushed down, heated and metamorphosed, while the top of the fold pile was elevated to form the high mountain belt of the Alps and Carpathians. Similar movements pushed the Spanish Peninsula towards France and crumpled up the Pyrenean alpine chain.

During middle and late Tertiary times, Africa continued to move north and has done so ever since. Movements along major fault dislocations in Iran, Turkey and the Aegean region are a continuing expression of this movement. Much of the complex and large-scale overfolding seen in the Alps results from mid-Tertiary movements (around 15 million years ago). Similar processes continue today in the Mediterranean region, generating the numerous earthquakes and the remaining vulcanism of southern Italy. But the Alps are only part of a much larger fold belt that extends eastwards and connects with the Himalayan belt, where the intense folding was and still is the result of India driving northwards into the southern flank of Asia.

Below the Trias

Back in England William Smith was confronted with a problem. He found that along the eastern flanks of the central north–south Pennine Ridge and below his Red Marls (the New Red Sandstone), there is a distinctive succession and outcrop of what was called Magnesian Limestone and it, in turn, lay above the 'Coaliferous' strata. However, on the west side of the Pennines from the Solway Firth to the coast of Devonshire, the succession of red and brown sandstones along with pebble conglomerates extends right down to the coal-bearing strata without any intervening limestone. Again, the answer to the problem was not to be found in Britain but in the far east of the European mainland, where it faces the vast hinterland of Asia. The boundary is marked by one of the world's great geological features, the Ural Mountain chain, which extends practically all the way from the Arctic Ocean to the Caspian Sea. And it was a British geologist who carved out this new system of strata and period of geological time – Roderick Impey Murchison.

Imperial ambitions and the Permian System

Roderick Murchison was 47 years old when, in 1839, he decided to make a bold career move. With the Silurian and Devonian systems reasonably well recognised and established in the British geological world (see p. 193), he wanted to see if they could also be recognised on a more international front. Perhaps they would prove to have a global significance, which really would be a 'feather in his cap'. He knew that the one relatively nearby region that had not been geologically surveyed in any detail was Czarist Russia. And he also knew, from what geological work had been done, that there seemed to be vast tracts of probable Silurian and Devonian strata there, especially in Baltic Russia.

Apart from questions of finance and energy, which were no problem to Murchison, the main problems were bureaucratic and logistical. Even European Russia was huge, excessively bureaucratic and suspicious of foreigners. It was also very backward in terms of communications. But this is where Murchison's years of soldiering came in very useful. He knew better than anyone else in the world of British geology that meticulous advance planning and organisation were the key to any successful campaign on such a grand scale. And he must have realised that he was better placed than anyone else to undertake such an ambitious survey, but that if he did not do it soon, one of his continental rivals might beat him to it.

Murchison also knew that he would need as much help as he could get from his well-placed connections in the scientific, diplomatic and political world.

He needed a team that he could work with and trust, preferably competent gentlemen scientists like himself but also people who would not try to steal the limelight. Murchison had already collaborated with the French palaeontologist Philippe Edouard Poulletier de Verneuil, so he knew he could trust his scientific judgement and got on well with him. Then, through the auspices of the well-known Berlin geologist Leopold von Buch, Murchison was introduced to the young Russian gentleman scientist Count Alexander Andreevich von Keyserling, and he knew that he had found just the right collaborators and travelling companions.

Philippe Edouard Poulletier de Verneuil, 1805–73, French lawyer turned palaeontologist who collaborated with Murchison, especially on the palaeontology of the Permian of the Urals and in 1846 visited North America to compare Transition Series strata. He was awarded the Wollaston Medal of the Geological Society of London in 1853.

Murchison realised that accurate and speedy fossil identification was of the essence for the successful establishment of stratigraphic order, relative dating and correlation of sedimentary strata. The deal was that de Verneuil and von Keyserling would be co-authors (with Murchison first in the pecking order) on any joint publication arising from their work. It subsequently turned out that in the major two-volume work called *The Geology of Russia*, the second volume, devoted to the palaeontology, was in French and authored by de Verneuil.

The total membership of the expedition was of course much larger. Rural Russia could be a dangerous place and unprotected travellers were not only

---

Count Alexander Andreevich von Keyserling, 1815–91, Russian aristocrat, studied law in Berlin where he met Humboldt and became interested in geology. He was employed in the Russian Department of Mining (1842) and collaborated with Murchison on the geology of the Urals. Marriage in 1844 secured his financial independence.

frequently robbed but also sometimes murdered. For the ex-soldier and his military companions this was perhaps all part of the challenge. Nevertheless, they travelled with all manner of Cossack guards, drivers, servants and assistants, including the highly accomplished Nikolai Ivanovich Kokscharoff, a young army officer and mineralogist. In addition, Murchison also took enough creature comforts in the form of his favourite cigars and madeira wine to last the whole trip, along with a folding iron bed.

———————— • ————————

Major-General Nikolai Ivanovich Kokscharoff, 1819–93, Russian officer selected to accompany Murchison and his expedition to the Urals. He was also a mineralogist and became director of the Institute of Mines in St Petersburg and author of a multivolume work on the minerals of Russia.

———————— • ————————

A brilliant and indefatigable networker, Murchison used his social skills and contacts very effectively. The help of people like Count Brunow, the Russian ambassador in London, was invaluable. As a result of Brunow's highly placed connections at the court in St Petersburg, Murchison was offered not only diplomatic and logistical but also financial support. And they were invited to join a non-geological fact-finding expedition to Russia's northern territories from St Petersburg led by Baron Meyendorff.

However, there was a condition – that Murchison should return to Russia and extend his survey beyond the northern territories to the rest of the Empire. So the complete work would take two trips. He could not have asked for a better remit and Murchison's passport was endorsed by Czar Nicholas I himself. Nicholas tried to hold the reins of his vast Empire by being a workaholic bureaucrat and was personally briefed by Murchison at the beginning of the trip and received reports on its completion. Murchison seized on the chance to make a good impression on the imperial personage and it worked very well.

Murchison's preparation was meticulous. He searched out copies of all relevant previous publications and maps and he used his linguistic fluency to contact all the most eminent and useful European geologists for advice and information, and he got it. Despite the continuing and ever-changing European alliances and occasional wars, scientists were rarely prevented from travelling or communicating, even between otherwise warring nations. Murchison consulted Alexander von Humboldt, the well-known German traveller and naturalist, who had tutored von Keyserling, while Alexander Brongniart and Jean Baptiste Élie de Beaumont were two of the French scientists he knew well. But his network extended to North America, where he corresponded with Yale scientist Benjamin Silliman, George Featherstonhaugh, one of the first professional geologists in America, and William Logan, director of the Geological Survey of Canada.

Benjamin Silliman, 1779–1864, Yale-trained lawyer, admitted to the bar in 1802 but never practised, becoming instead professor of chemistry and natural history at Yale in 1804. He founded the *American Journal of Science* in 1819 and was a founder member of the National Academy of Sciences in 1863.

The 1840 expedition essentially tagged along with Meyendorff for some time through Baltic Russia, but it soon became clear that for Murchison's purpose it was not an ideal arrangement and that his team would be better off as masters of their own destinies. Soon, Murchison negotiated an amicable parting of the ways. This first season's field work did in general seem to support the identity of both the Silurian and Devonian as distinct and recognisable systems of strata and fossils, but there were still some boundary problems. The lower boundary

George William Featherstonhaugh, 1780–1866, Oxford-educated traveller who visited America in 1802, organized the first Board of Agriculture for New York State, obtained the first charter (1826) for a passenger railway and became the first federal government geologist in America in 1834 and surveyed the disputed boundary between Canada and Maine. Appointed British consul in Le Havre, France and effected the escape of Louis Philippe and his Queen from the revolutionaries.

Sir William Logan, 1798–1875, Canadian geologist who mapped part of the South Wales coalfield then returned to Canada to initiate and become the first director of the Geological Survey of Canada (1843–70), wrote a *Geology of Canada* (1836) and was knighted in 1856.

of the Silurian was crudely resolved by Murchison pushing it down as far as it would go, encompassing any fossiliferous strata on the way. Sedgwick's Cambrian was swept aside and obliterated by Murchison's geological empire building.

Murchison had a very personal proprietorial view of 'his' system, typically referring to the landscapes of 'my Silurian Region' or to fossils as 'my published Silurian types'. He developed the argument that 'the great mass of the rocks which Sedgwick had called Cambrian, but without defining their fossiliferous contents, were nothing but replications, in a more altered and slaty condition, of my Silurian types'. Murchison was wrong, Sedgwick's Cambrian strata do contain separate and distinct fossils, but Sedgwick was partly to blame because of his long delay in describing them.

Other palaeontologists, such as Salter, tried to fight Sedgwick's cause, but they had an uphill struggle because Murchison had 'outflanked' them by redefining 'his Silurian'. He claimed that the Silurian included the oldest fossils known, thus lowering its base to incorporate all more ancient fossiliferous strata. Murchison used the first Russian expedition to gather supporting data for this view but it was, of course, something of a 'self-fulfilling prophecy'. He summarized his views in *The Geology of Russia* as:

we have indicated the existence over large tracts in Scandinavia, the Baltic provinces and northern Russia, of those Lower Silurian strata, which by extensive examination of various countries, have been found to contain the earliest vestiges of animal life. This point has, indeed, been rendered singularly clear in Sweden, where Lower Silurian rocks, perfectly identified with those of their typical regions in the British Isles, rest at once on crystalline or azoic rocks of antecedent date, in which the remains of all organized beings, if such there ever were, have been entirely obliterated.

Representing as elsewhere the lowest recognizable stage charged with organic matter, the Lower Silurian rocks of Sweden and Russia teach us, that among the earliest animals known to us were crustacean, with eyes suited to the recesses of the seas in which they lived, and that these, with certain Mollusca, Zoophytes and Crinoidea, which have long since passed away, were associated with marine fucoids, the latter being, as far as we know, the only vegetables of which there is trace in this protozoic group.

In August 1840, Murchison finished his first round trip with a few days around St Petersburg and encountered reddish cornstones with 'an absolute identity of structure with our Herefordshire cornstones' and full of fish scales, teeth and a kind of brachiopod (spiriferid). He concluded:

QED – The mixture of Devonian shells of Devonshire with fishes of the Highlands of Scotland demonstrates that Sedgwick and myself were right to identify the Scottish Old Red with the Devonshire rocks, under the name of Devonian ... the Devonian, based on Silurian, and overlain by Carboniferous limestone, is now completely established.

Most importantly, Murchison managed to persuade some very influential geologists of the validity of this view of an enlarged Silurian System. Foremost among these was Sir Henry De la Beche (1796–1855), who in his capacity as the first Director of the British Geological Survey was particularly useful because he ensured that the Survey adopted Murchison's extended version of the Silurian System in all survey maps and publications. De la Beche's death in 1855 vacated an all-important post in the development of British geology and Murchison stepped into it and remained Director until his death in 1871. Unsurprisingly, the Survey persisted in the habit of ignoring the Cambrian and using an enlarged Silurian until the end of the century, even though most of the geological community had by then accepted Sedgwick's Cambrian as a valid system.

Murchison's position allowed his influence to extend into the far reaches of the Empire as well, especially through the auspices of directors of the various colonial geological surveys. His good friend the Canadian geologist Sir William

Logan, Director of the Geological Survey of Canada, was particularly influential in North America.

Towards the end of the 1840 expedition, Murchison and his party reached Archangel and began their long trek east and then southwards, following the course of the River Dvina. In places along the valley, they found cliffs with interstratified limestones, layers of white alabaster (the calcium sulphate mineral gypsum), along with red and green marls. At first they were puzzled and did not know whether they were part of the Carboniferous or Triassic. The few fossil clams they found were not diagnostic, but then they found fossils of a particular kind of lamp shell (productid brachiopods) in the limestones, which look very like those known from the Carboniferous and so opted for that designation. However, the occurrence of the gypsum plus the red and green marls, which was rather more typical of the younger Triassic strata, created something of a problem and they did not feel enormously confident about their diagnosis.

They subsequently found that the red deposits formed a vast basin and so were much more than just a local development. Their redness also suggested the possibility that they were older than the Carboniferous and perhaps some equivalent of the Old Red Sandstone, but they did not contain any fossils typical of these strata such as the characteristic jawless fish. The party decided to hedge their bets until the next year.

Murchison was supremely confident, writing:

> I leave Russia with the desire of exploring the Eastern regions of the Empire, and of putting them into direct connection with those of the west. This is merely a work of detail. The great points are fixed, and if I could see the Ural, I should get them all in order.

As we shall see, the following year he did just that.

During that second expedition, Murchison and de Verneuil did indeed change their opinion, but not before they had indulged in a little socialising. Murchison attended a grand court ball held to mark the marriage of the Czar's eldest son and was presented to Czar Nicholas himself, who engaged him in conversation about the prospects for coalmining and other matters geological in Russia. Murchison was particularly concerned about the waste of money and

Palæoniscus comptus.

Fossil from the Permian.

effort that was generally expended at this stage in the Industrial Revolution throughout Europe in fruitless searches for coal in unsuitable rocks.

Murchison was mightily impressed by the Czar and noted:

> when the Emperor is in full costume, it is impossible to behold a finer sample of human nature. The tight breeches are unusually well fitted, and especially on the upper part of the thigh, so as to delineate even the virile member with great precision. Your eye glances from these to his beautiful family, and the animated but épuisé Empress, and the history is told.

She had 15 pregnancies. Apparently, the Czar was also impressed, Murchison recording that Nicholas remarked that 'you must have good stout legs' whereupon he passed 'his hand ... to the side of my thigh, which he pinched'. Their mutual admiration continued through several subsequent meetings, but then, the marriage celebrations over, Murchison's expedition got down to the real work, although not before Murchison had 'agreed' to attend the Moscow continuation of the celebrations.

The first record of Murchison's change of heart and mind regarding the nature of the strata his party encountered above the Carboniferous is recorded in a letter he wrote to the German naturalist and director of the Natural History Museum in Moscow, Johann Fischer von Waldheim, in October 1841. In the letter Murchison says:

> The Carboniferous System is surmounted, to the east of the Volga, by a vast series of beds of marls, schists, limestones, sandstones and conglomerates, to which I propose to give the name of 'Permian System'.

Johann Götthelf Friedrich Fischer von Waldheim, 1771–1853, German vertebrate palaeontologist and naturalist who coined the word 'palaeontology' in 1834 and became director of the Natural History Museum in Moscow.

————— • —————

The name was derived from the city of Perm, the regional capital of the Urals.

Murchison translated and published the letter because he wanted to make sure of his priority in naming the new system. In addition, he gave some important information about the fossil content of these strata:

> of the fossils of this system, some undescribed species of producti might seem to connect the Permian with the Carboniferous aera; and other shells, together with fishes and Saurians, link it on more closely to the period of the Zechstein, whilst its peculiar plants appear to constitute a flora of a type intermediate between the epochs of the New Red sandstone or 'Trias' and the Coal Measures. Hence it is that I have ventured to consider this series as worthy of being regarded as a 'System'.

The presence of Saurians in such old strata was particularly interesting. Fossils of this kind were first discovered in the 1770s by Russian mining engineers working the belt of copper-rich sandstones that stretched for hundreds of kilometres along the western flank of the Ural Mountains. But it was not until 1838 that a Russian professor in St Petersburg, S. S. Kutorga, first described some of the fossil bones. He thought they were mammals, one of which he called *Brithopus*, as a relative of the sloths, and the other *Syodon*, a relative of the elephants.

This was an extraordinary claim, since the bones were much more ancient than any other then known mammal fossils. Kutorga had indeed spotted features of the bones that were mammal like. We now know that these creatures belong to an early group of extinct reptiles called the synapsids (technically they are dinocephalian therapsids), which were very important in the early evolution of the mammals, but it was many years before this was fully realised.

Independent of Kutorga's work, a German geologist and manager of copper mines in Ufa and Orenburg, Major Wangenheim von Qualen, had amassed one of the best collections of 'saurian' bones from these strata. With his German background, von Qualen was familar with the German Zechstein succession, especially the copper-rich (*Kupferschiefer*) strata that lies in the lower part of the Zechstein. Von Qualen published a number of reports about the bones in Russian journals and suggested that the Russian saurian-bearing strata could be matched with the German *Kupferschiefer*. His fossils were studied by Kutorga and two other German fossil experts living in Russia, J. G. F. Fischer von Waldheim, who named (in 1841) a new reptile with mammal-like features as *Rhopalodon* (now regarded as a dinocephalian), and E. I. von Eichwald, who in 1848 named another new reptile as *Deuterosaurus* and an amphibian as *Zygosaurus*.

In August 1841, Murchison called on von Qualen near Troitsk and the Kazakhstan boarder to quiz him about his local knowledge. Von Qualen obliged and gave Murchison the general order of these Russian *Kupferschiefer*-like strata that Murchison realised lay above the Rothliegende. He subsequently assigned both successions to his new Permian System, but not before getting some palaeontological checks made on the fossil saurians and plants that also occurred in the copper-rich strata. Murchison suspected that the saurian fossils could be very useful in helping to establish his new system.

Murchison passed the saurians on to Richard Owen in London. Owen was the up-and-coming star of the anatomical study of fossil vertebrates in Britain and was seen as the English Cuvier. As we have seen (p. 106), Owen secured his place in the international scientific hall of fame when, in 1842, he coined the new name 'Dinosauria', now known by practically every educated 7-year-old on Earth. Owen was aware of the published descriptions of the Russian fossils and identified Murchison's fossils as belonging to von Waldheim's new animal *Rhopalodon*, but thought that it was some kind of crocodile. As far as Murchison was concerned, the reptile was most like those previously found in the Triassic strata of England and Germany and radically different from any found in younger Jurassic strata or older Carboniferous strata, and it was one of the oldest saurians known from Europe.

As seen in their typical Russian formations, the Permian strata were a mixture of freshwater (especially the red beds) and marine deposits (especially the limestones), with an interplay between the two environments resulting in interfingering of intermediate deposits. This meant that matching deposits of similar type and age was going to be difficult, because the specific kinds of animals and plants that live under such conditions tend to be restricted to the region. At least there was a better chance of matching the marine deposits and Murchison went on to note that, in England, the well-developed strata, known as the Magnesian Limestone, occupied a similar position in relation to the Carboniferous. The Magnesian Limestone could thus be considered as being part of 'his' new Permian System, which was therefore developed over a very extensive area, although it remained to be seen whether it could be recognised worldwide.

International recognition was not as guaranteed as Murchison hoped it would be. German miners and mining geologists had recognised a distinctive metalliferous *Zechstein* group of strata for many centuries. Werner's *Flötz* formations included the ore-rich *Zechstein* (which means 'mine stone') and their structure and succession of strata had already been explored in considerable detail by the eighteenth-century German mineralogists Johann Gottlob Lehmann and Georg Christian Füchsel. Their tabulation and illustrations presented the succession of strata from what they called the 'Red Underlyer' or basal series of conglomerates, shales and sandstones through to the uppermost limestones, dolomites and marls of the *Zechstein*, in other words what Murchison was calling the Permian. Lehmann's vertical section through the rocks, published in 1756, showed a very clear understanding of stratification and its continuation below ground. And Füchsel's 1761 map of Thuringia presented a remarkable

———————— • ————————

Johann Gottlob Lehmann, 1719–67, teacher of mineralogy and mining in Berlin who wrote extensively on chemical, mineralogical and geological topics. He became professor of chemistry and director of the Imperial Museum in St Petersburg in 1761, but died in 1767 from injuries received from an exploding retort of arsenic.

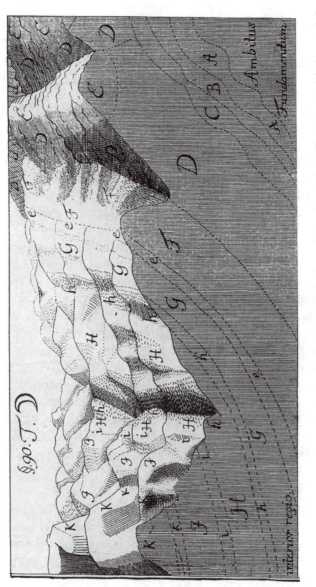

German mineralogist Georg Christian Füchsel's pioneering illustrations of 1761 showed how 3D structure might be revealed by extension of the surface arrangement of strata underground.

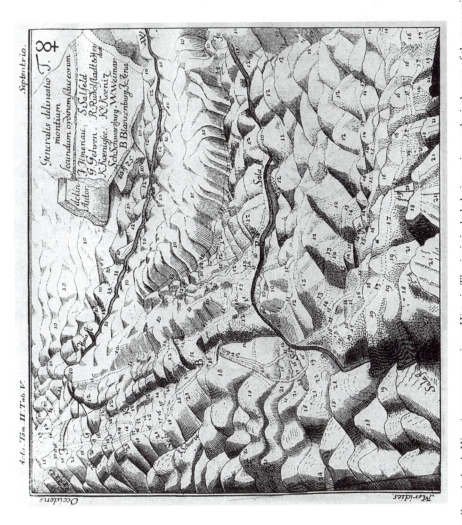

Füchsel's 1761 book *Historia terrae et maris, ex Historia Thuringia* included pioneering geological maps of the succession of strata (numbered) across the landscapes of Thuringia.

Georg Christian Füchsel, 1722–73, a German physician in Rudolstadt who wrote important works describing and illustrating the geology of Thuringia, which demonstrate a considerable sophistication in understanding of the structural geometry of strata as they affect topography and are arranged below ground.

———————————— • ————————————

oblique 'bird's eye' view of the strata in relation to both the surface topography and the underground 3D structure and succession – some 50 years before Smith or his French competitors, Cuvier and Brongniart, presented their 'pioneering' work.

The upper limit of the new system was defined by overlying 'red deposits which occupy a great basin in the governments of Vologda and Nijni Novogorod', which Murchison was 'disposed to think they may at some future day be identified with a portion of the "Trias" of German geologists'. He was right.

Million Years Ago

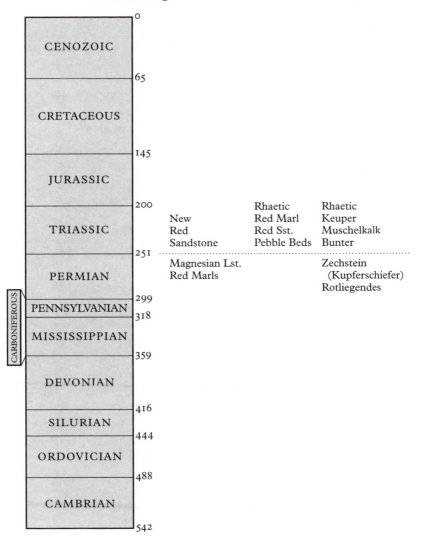

	Million Years Ago			
CENOZOIC	0			
	65			
CRETACEOUS				
	145			
JURASSIC				
	200	New Red Sandstone	Rhaetic Red Marl Red Sst. Pebble Beds	Rhaetic Keuper Muschelkalk Bunter
TRIASSIC	251			
PERMIAN		Magnesian Lst. Red Marls		Zechstein (Kupferschiefer) Rotliegendes
PENNSYLVANIAN	299 318			
MISSISSIPPIAN				
	359			
DEVONIAN				
	416			
SILURIAN	444			
ORDOVICIAN				
	488			
CAMBRIAN				
	542			

CARBONIFEROUS

Triassic to Permian.

7

Fuelling the Industrial Revolution

PENNSYLVANIAN TO MISSISSIPPIAN

Great Coal Formation

Coal, or 'black gold' as it became known, was literally the fuel of the Industrial Revolution. For much of the nineteenth century Britain led the world in the exploitation of its coal and iron ore deposits, along with those of tin, copper and lead, and it was largely self-sufficient in minerals until the end of the century. Within less than 200 years from the early decades of the nineteenth century, the industrialised western world burned up a significant proportion of the planet's reserves of solid organic fuel. Made essentially of plant remains that originally accumulated within ancient tropical rainforests, the coal measures took the best part of 18 million years of Earth Time (from 318.1 to 299 million years ago) to be laid down. Many but by no means all of the global coal deposits were laid down during what we now know as Carboniferous times. But in the early decades of the nineteenth century this fact was not generally appreciated, except by geologists such as William Smith. Huge amounts of private money were squandered and fortunes lost on fruitless searches for coal in strata of the wrong age.

In William Smith's day, the name Carboniferous was yet to be adopted by English geologists, although it was first formally used on the continent of Europe as early as 1808 by D'Omalius d'Halloy. For Smith there were the Coal Measures or Great Coal Formation, as it was also known, and below lay the Mountain

Limestone strata, which he was particularly familiar with from his work in the West Country around Bristol and the Forest of Dean.

The initial realisation of where coal was to be found depended largely on coal-bearing strata outcropping at the surface. The natural occurrence of such outcrops is relatively restricted, since many coal-bearing strata can easily be eroded and do not generally form prominent topographical features, except in a few places where the seams are thin and interlayered with much harder strata such as sandstones and limestones. In those situations exploitation of the coal is difficult, time consuming and costly. There are, however, some places where the coal measures are well exposed in coastal cliffs such as around Blyth on the North Sea coast of Northumberland, around Workington and the Solway Firth on the northwest coast, and to a lesser extent around Carmarthen Bay in South Wales.

The coals of Northern England and South Wales were first mined and used by the Romans. However, it was not until the ninth century that coals were again exploited on a regular basis in Northumberland. Monastic records show that by the twelfth century coal was regularly used as a fuel, and by the thirteenth century exported from Newcastle by ship to London and other major centres of population. The noxious and polluting properties of coal burning were first recognised as early as the thirteenth century, when for a time King Edward I imposed the death penalty for anyone found burning coal as a fuel.

As early as 1800, England was producing some 10 million tons of coal a year, and by 1847 production had tripled. In comparison France, despite extensive coal fields in the north of the country, was only producing five million tons by 1847. Coalmining continued to develop and expand in England, Wales and Scotland and rose fairly steadily until 1910. Then production peaked, with a total of nearly 300 million tons a year, and Britain was still the world's leading producer. There was a related rise in pig-iron production from 68,000 tons in 1788 to 1,347,000 tons in 1839. By contrast, China was producing well over a billion tons of coal in the mid-1990s.

From the point of view of the history of the Industrial Revolution, the most important coals were exposed in the steep valley side of the River Severn at a place called, appropriately enough, Coalbrookdale, near Ironbridge in the Welsh

Borderland county of Shropshire. Here, the combination of coal and sedimentary ironstone bands within the Coal Measures, along with limestone, water power and a navigable river with access to Bristol and the sea, produced one of the earliest centres of the Industrial Revolution. The first metal bridge in the world was made in 1779 at Ironbridge to span the Severn gorge. However, the Shropshire coal deposits turned out to be very restricted in their extent and it was not long before other, bigger coal fields began to be exploited. But this required new types of communication to transport the bulky and heavy coal to where it was most needed and new technology to follow the coal seams from the surface deeper and deeper underground.

Canals and strata

From the geological point of view, expertise was required in the construction of canals to carry materials such as coal and other ores, stone for building and grain to help feed the growing populations of certain cities that were becoming increasingly industrialised. And it was in this pursuit that William Smith made his mark and developed his ideas about the distribution of the strata of southern Britain.

Smith's knowledge was built up through years of practical experience as a freelance civil engineer and surveyor, working on any project that would provide some income. From sinking wells for water and trial shafts for coal to cutting canals and land evaluation, he travelled the length and breadth of the country from one job to another. The 1790s and first decades of the 1800s were a period of growing industrialisation and an intensifying search for coal, with as we have seen large sums of money being wasted sinking shafts through strata that would never lead to coal deposits. Transport of bulky raw materials like coal and building stone was much more efficient and cheaper by water. Unfortunately, few of the country's rivers were navigable and so a network of canals was developed, but building canals is a very costly business. Being able to predict the underlying geology before construction started could save huge amounts of money. The trouble was that there were very few useful geological maps available in the 1790s. Nevertheless, there was information that had been gathered and occasionally documented so that even Smith had something to build on.

For instance, information about the coal seams and other related strata in the Somerset coal field south of Bristol had been published by John Strachey as long ago as 1714 and he also described those of Northumberland in 1725. A diagrammatic vertical section cutting through some 82 m (250 ft) of the former showed eight inclined seams of coal beneath horizontal layers of 'red earth or malm or loom', 'yellowish spungey earth', 'marle' with 'lyas or limestone' on top. The coal seams all had individual and characteristic names given them by the miners. For example, the 'stinking vein' was probably so called because it had a high sulphur content and smelled of rotten eggs (hydrogen sulphide gas), and 'three coal vein' had three thin, closely spaced coal seams. Strachey also noted the depths of the seams and the occurrence of fossils – 'cockle shells and fern branches' in some layers.

———————— • ————————

John Strachey, 1671–1743, Oxford-educated antiquarian who studied law in London (1687–8) but took an interest in coalmines and minerals and published some of the earliest cross-sections of underground strata and a map of Somerset in 1737, which located its coal and mineral deposits.

———————— • ————————

Today we can recognise the succession extending down from Jurassic oolitic limestones through the Lias strata early Jurassic age, the Rhaetic marly passage beds between Jurassic and underlying Triassic, and then the soft red strata of Triassic age. The angular discordance between these younger horizontal layers and the older and inclined coal deposits has great temporal significance.

The feature is known as an unconformity (see p. 295) and tells us that there was a major time gap between the deposition of the two sets of strata. It had to be long enough for the older coal-bearing deposits to be contorted by a major phase of major earth movements, uplifted and deeply eroded. The weathering and erosion were extensive enough to remove all the rocks forming the upper parts of the folds as if they were planed off, exposing the tilted edges of the

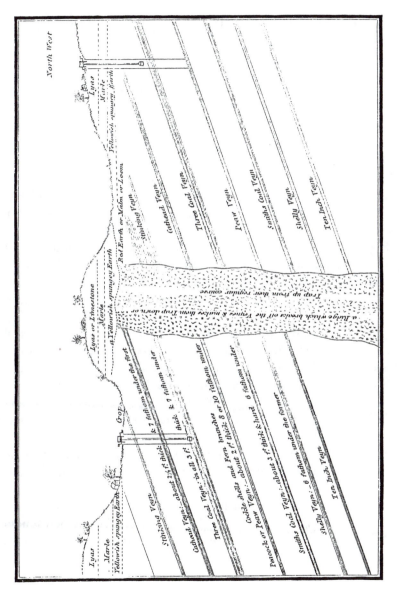

John Strachey's 1719 section through faulted 'coaliferous' strata (subsequently identified here as Carboniferous in age) in the Somerset coal field south of Bath shows how individual layers were identified primarily by their physical features.

strata as a landscape surface on which Triassic-age terrestrial deposits were laid down.

The Terrain Bituminifere becomes Carboniferous

Because of the historical use of coal in northwest Europe and its identification with a particular sequence of strata, the deposits and their associated strata were first formally named as the Terrain Bituminifere by the Belgian geologist Jean Baptiste Julien d'Omalius d'Halloy (1783–1875) in 1808. D'Halloy came from a rich aristocratic background and his interests in geology were stimulated by contact with the likes of Cuvier, Brongniart, Lamarck and Faujas de Saint Fond in Paris. He had a special interest in the coalmining region of Belgium and northern France and became Governor of the Province of Namur in 1814. Applying the stratigraphic principles of succession of strata identified by their characteristic fossils described by Cuvier and Brongniart, he produced an outline geological map of France, Belgium and parts of Germany and Switzerland in 1822.

D'Halloy's Terrain Bituminifere included the coal seams and related shales and sandstones as the upper part and the thick succession of limestones beneath them. This continental sequence of strata was similar to that mapped out by Smith in England. Here the overall name Great Coal Measures included an upper sequence of coal deposits and related strata and a lower sequence of sandstones, which are in places hard, gritty rocks. Their resistance to weathering and erosion has resulted in their surface outcrop as small, craggy hills and ridges beloved by climbers. The rock has been quarried for centuries as a building stone and more especially as mill stones, so much so that the strata were called the Millstone Grits.

Below the Millstone Grits lie thick limestones similar to those found on the continent. In England these were called the Metalliferous or Mountain Limestones, because they typically form the hilly landscapes of much of the north of England and in places were rich in mineral deposits. A central line of limestone hills of this age separates the west and east of the north of England. It runs from Derbyshire and the famous ancient mining area of the Peak District north to Northumberland and into the southeast of Scotland around Berwick-upon-Tweed. And in Ireland much of the centre of the country is underlain by limestones of similar age.

Such limestones form very particular landscapes because of their geological structure and chemical composition. Rainwater soaks down through natural cracks in the rocks (called joints) so that there is little or no surface drainage on upland limestone landscapes. The calcium carbonate minerals of the limestone can be dissolved by slightly acidic rainwater to form bare fretted and fissured surfaces (called grykes in the north of England), with underground drainage systems of interconnected caves and passages. Such topographical surfaces are known as karst landscapes, a name derived from the Slovenian word 'kras', because they are particularly well developed in the limestones along the eastern border of the Adriatic.

Smith's stratigraphy and naming of strata were very much based on old vernacular and regional practice, largely derived from quarrymen's terminology. One of the first more formal and academic attempts to regularise the nomenclature was produced by Conybeare and Phillips in their 1822 book *Outlines of the Geology of England and Wales*.

As they wrote, 'the class of rocks thus constituted will contain not only the great coal-deposit itself, but those of limestone and sandstone also on which it reposes ... the epithet Carboniferous is of obvious application to this series'. At this time they included in the Carboniferous System a thick succession of sandstones known as the Old Red Sandstone, which occurs below the Mountain Limestone. Conybeare and Phillips thought that this Carboniferous System was distinct from both Werner's *Flötz-Schichten* and Transition Series, although, if anything, they considered it to be more allied to the latter than the former. The anglicised name Carboniferous has since become an internationally recognised system of strata and period of Earth time, but, as we shall see, without the Old Red Sandstone. The strata represent the Carboniferous Period of geological time, which we now know lasted from 354 to 290 million years ago.

However, as we shall also see (p. 323), North American geologists recognise two separate systems, an upper Pennsylvanian for the Coal Measures and the lower Mississippian for the Mountain Limestones. The fossil content of the strata had long been a subject of debate, especially with regard to the true nature and formation of fossils.

The nature of fossils

The discovery of fossils that looked like plant remains dates back to the seventeenth century and earlier. Collectors such as John Woodward, an English physician, amassed a diversity of crystals, minerals and organic remains, which were all then regarded as fossils since they had been dug from the ground (the word 'fossil' is derived from the Latin *fossa*, meaning a digging or ditch). Woodward left his collection or 'cabinet' as it was then known to the University of Cambridge, along with an endowment for a 'chair' or professorship. Both still survive in the university, with Woodward's cabinet forming the basis of one of the oldest continuing university museum fossil collections in the world.

———————— • ————————

John Woodward, 1665–1728, physician, professor at Gresham College, London (from 1692) and author of an 'Essay toward a Natural History of the Earth' (1695); he bequeathed his collection of books, minerals and fossils to the University of Cambridge and endowed a chair in mineralogy.

———————— • ————————

Among Woodward's fossils are some plant fossils that were originally classified as 'snakestones' because they were long, cylindrical and sinuous petrifications with a regularly patterned surface, which superficially at least does indeed look a bit like a snake skin. In Woodward's time, the whole question of the true nature of fossils was still a matter of intense debate. Fossils tended to be grouped according to their resemblances in external form rather than any insight into their true organic or inorganic nature. It is only in retrospect that we can recognise that Woodward's 'snakestones' were in fact the remains of the 'rootlike' structures of some characteristic Coal Measure plants called clubmosses (technically known as lycopsids).

Oxford also had its historically important collection of 'fossils' amassed by Edward Lhwyd, who, apart from being a well-known scholar, was an indefatigable explorer of the highways and byways of rural Britain. He was curious about almost everything to do with the past, whether it was historical buildings, ruins or fossil petrifications, as well as the living organisms of the natural world. Lhwyd was not convinced by either the organic or inorganic theories for the origin of fossils and proposed a 'middle way'. In a book published in 1699, he illustrated a selection of fossil ferns and insects from Coal Measure strata, but was particularly intrigued by the appearance and origin of the ferns. The puzzle was that they looked so plant like but were not preserved with any plant-like material; they seemed to be just the impressions of fronds on the rock surface. Furthermore, they were not quite the same as any living plant then known. Lhwyd concluded that the fossils must have grown within rock strata from 'seed' (pollen) that had percolated into the rocks from living plants that they most resembled.

The Swiss naturalist Johann Scheuchzer still had the same problem with fossil plants when he published his *Herbarium of the Deluge* in 1709, as he illustrated some inorganic mineral dendrites alongside what can be seen today as genuine fossil plants. And as Scheuchzer's title suggests, he interpreted the preservation of plant-like fossils in rock strata far inland as the result of the Noachian Deluge.

By the end of the eighteenth century, these problems with the true nature of fossils had been resolved and William Smith was well aware of the genuine botanical character of the plant-like fossils of the Coal Measures. He also knew that, like fossil shells elsewhere, they could be used to distinguish the relative age of the strata in which they were found. But there was a major problem with establishing any deeper botanical understanding of the plants from which they originated. The problem arises from the way plant remains are recruited to the fossil record. Very rarely does a complete plant, from the extremities of its roots to its leaf tips and reproductive structures, get preserved in its entirety in the rock record. That would require the plant to be uprooted and instantly buried in sediment, not impossible but nearly so. Normally life and death processes

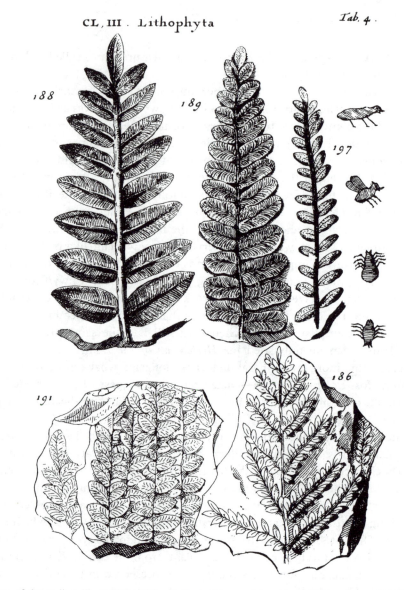

CL. III. Lithophyta

Tab. 4.

Some of the earliest illustrations of fossil plants from coal bearing strata are those reproduced in Edward Lhwyd's 1699 *Lithophylacii Britannici Ichnographia* etc.

separate out the various parts of plants (stems, leaves, pollen and so on) and bury them at different times in different places.

Rarely, in fossil forest or swamp-like situations such as the Coal Measure deposits, tree-sized trunks with their roots may be preserved still standing upright, but the rest of the canopy cannot be preserved intact. Branches, leaf fronds and reproductive structures might be found in the surrounding sediment, but there is no guarantee which root and trunk they originally belonged to. Leaf fronds may be blown from plants and carried some distance by wind and water along with other light plant components, especially pollen. Flowers are particularly delicate structures and very difficult to fossilise, although seeds, nuts and fruit can be much tougher. They generally become separated from the parent plant and buried in fine sediment such as lake or river muds, along with pollen and other buoyant plant debris. But the sedimentation processes tend to mix up bits and pieces from many different plants in all this flotsam and jetsam. As early investigators found, it can be very difficult to reassemble the parent plant from the fossil fragments. Just to confuse matters, each different fossilised plant element was given its own name. So a leaf frond might be placed in one species, its stem in another and so on.

Discovering plant prehistory

One of the most important of the early nineteenth-century studies of fossil plants was made by the French naturalist Adolphe Brongniart. In his 1828 pioneering book on fossil plants, *Histoire des Végétaux Fossile*, Brongniart *fils* concluded that there had been four distinct phases in the prehistory of plants, within each of which there had been gradual change. These gradual phases

---

Adolphe-Théodore Brongniart, 1801–76, son of Cuvier's collaborator Alexandre, palaeobotanist and professor of botany at the National Museum of Natural History in Paris and author of *Histoire des Végétaux Fossile* (1828).

were, however, separated by abrupt breaks. The first phase was dominated by
the primitive land plants of the Coal Measures; the second contained the first
conifers; cycads appeared in the third (Mesozoic) phase and along with the
conifers dominated the flora; finally, the flowering plants took over (Cainozoic).
Altogether, to Brongniart, this represented a progressive history of increasing
complexity and diversity similar to that which seemed to be emerging from the
fossil record of animal life.

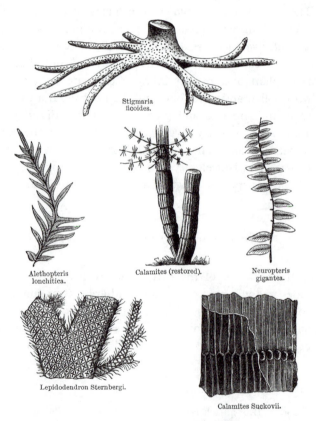

These fossils of Coal Measure plants illustrate the difficulty of relating various parts of individual
plants separated by the fossilization process.

In the 1830s Adolphe Brongniart reconstructed Carboniferous plants using modern examples such as this tropical tree-fern and drew appropriate conclusions about the climates of the time, i.e. that northern Europe was significantly hotter. However, he was not in a position to realize the very different geography of the day and the effects of plate tectonic movements.

Brongniart also discerned another important feature of the plant fossil record. The fossil plants of the first phase, the luxuriant fossil tree ferns, clubmosses and horsetails, although extinct, showed characters similar to plants that grow only in hot, humid tropical rainforests today. So he concluded that the global climate of the Earth must have been significantly warmer than that of today, since tropical warmth extended as far north as regions of northwestern Europe such as Scotland from where such fossil plants had been found. We now know that there are other explanations for this phenomenon (see below), but at the time it was an important breakthrough that resurrected Buffon's theory of a cooling Earth (see p. 401).

Even more ahead of its time was Brongniart's proposal that the abundance of plants during Coal Measure times was a measure of high levels of carbon dioxide in the atmosphere. Moreover, the effect of abundant plant life was to lock up carbon from the atmosphere in coal deposits and consequently CO_2 levels and global temperatures rose sufficiently to allow air-breathing reptiles to thrive. We now know that he was basically correct. Atmospheric CO_2 levels were very high, perhaps some 20 times higher than present in Devonian times (around 600 ppm). However, as terrestrial vegetation flourished through the Carboniferous Period, it 'drew down' CO_2 from the atmosphere and locked it up in the plants. The accumulated debris from the plants was so extensive and voluminous that it built up thick enough layers in places, which in turn were buried and compressed over time to form coal deposits. Indeed, there was so much vegetation globally that atmospheric CO_2 was reduced close to that of today at around 354 ppm, drastically cooling global climates from a high point in Devonian times. This ice-house climate state precipitated an ice age from the end of Carboniferous times into the Permian Period. In the equatorial regions climates became drier and the rainforest cover was drastically reduced, although coal deposits were still forming in China in early Permian times.

Today's global distribution of Carboniferous coal-bearing rocks can be explained by plate tectonics. When the coal-rich parts of the continents are reassembled, as they were in Carboniferous times, they all fall within an equatorial belt from Arkansas and Kansas in central North America, through the Maritime Provinces of Canada, northwestern Europe (British Isles, northern Germany, Netherlands, Belgium, northern France and Poland) and extend across to the Ukraine and China.

The Mountain Limestone

The Belgian geologist d'Omalius d'Halloy responded to Conybeare and Phillips's attempted 'capture' and anglicization of his 'Terrain Bituminifere' by claiming that there were in fact two separate and distinct 'terrains'. The younger 'Terrain Houiller' was comprised of the coal-bearing strata and below it lay the older 'Terrain Anthraxifere', which he claimed should include the British Mountain Limestone and the underlying Old Red Sandstone. He thought that they could be distinguished one from another by their fossils.

D'Halloy's distinction of the two successive groups of strata or 'terrains' as he called them was accepted in part by most European geologists, with a recognition of a separation between upper and lower Carboniferous but with the Old Red Sandstone excluded from the latter. However, as we shall see, it was North American geologists who were more insistent about the importance of the division and who recognised it at the system level.

The great diversity of ancient seabed life preserved within the Lower Carboniferous Mountain Limestones suggested that the deposits had been formed in warm, shallow tropical seas, which again seemed to indicate that there had been dramatic changes in global climates in the remote geological past. Furthermore, there must also have been drastic changes in sea level, since the plant-rich Coal Measures and unfossiliferous Millstone Grit strata had originally been laid down in continental environments of deposition, while the older coral- and shell-rich Mountain Limestones had formed in shallow seas. But in the nineteenth century nobody had any idea why this had happened.

Fossils of the Mountain Limestone

The distinctiveness of the abundant shell fossils of the Carboniferous (Mountain) Limestones was first studied in detail by William Smith's nephew John Phillips, who described the fossil shells of the Carboniferous Limestones of Yorkshire in 1836. There are numerous kinds of reef-related organisms such as corals, moss-animals (bryozoans), sponges, calcareous algae, sea-lilies (crinoids), clams, snails, lamp-shells (brachiopods) and occasional cephalopods and trilobites.

The palaeontology of the Mountain Limestones was greatly developed in succeeding years by research in Belgium by Laurent G. de Koninck and in Ireland by Frederick M'Coy. Since then astonishing levels of detailed understanding of both the sediments and their fossils have been achieved. The sediments are much more varied than the name Mountain Limestone suggests. In places over 1.5 km of strata are preserved, ranging from very shallow-water carbonates to deep-water shales and turbiditic deposits. The underlying geological structure of the basins within which the sediments accumulated is complex, with numerous faults and fault blocks actively moving during deposition. Despite over 100 years of continuing research deposits of this age still throw up remarkable finds that give new insights into the life of the time.

Laurent G. de Koninck, 1809–87, Belgian professor of industrial chemistry in Liege who was also a palaeontologist and stratigrapher, noted for his studies of fossil corals and crinoids, especially those of Devonian and Carboniferous age.

In 1981, a specimen of a little 'eel-shaped' fossil turned up among a collection of fossils in the Edinburgh office of the Geological Survey of Great Britain. It was spotted by palaeontologists Euan Clarkson (of Edinburgh University) and Derek Briggs (then at Bristol University, now Yale), an expert on fossilisation processes, while they were scanning an unusual collection of fossil shrimps that came from the Granton 'Shrimp Bed', near Edinburgh, which is of Mountain Limestone (Lower Carboniferous) age. Normally shrimps are exceedingly rare as fossils because their carapaces (shells) have little mineral content and do not fossilise. But within this rare deposit, there is some preservation of soft tissues.

Sir Frederick M'Coy, 1823–99, Irish geologist who studied medicine in Dublin and Cambridge and was employed by Sir Richard Griffith on the compilation of his 'Geological Map of Ireland'. He became professor of geology at Queen's College, Belfast (1850–4) and then Melbourne, Australia (1854–99), knighted in 1891.

The palaeontologists realised that the eel-shaped fossil was not a shrimp but instead looked as if it might be something that many people had been trying to find for over 120 years – a conodont animal.

Fossil conodonts were discovered in 1856 by Christian Heinrich Pander, a German biologist who worked mostly in Russia, pioneering embryological studies and evolutionary ideas. He was the first to describe and illustrate conodonts and regarded them as minute, millimetre-sized fish teeth. As the name given to them by Pander implies, conodonts are minute, conical, tooth-like structures found, often quite commonly, throughout a wide range of time (Cambrian to end Triassic) and different seabed deposits. But it took nearly another 130 years before anyone had much of an idea what the conodont animal actually looked like and Pander's diagnosis was finally acknowledged for its general insight. Meanwhile, conodonts were shuffled around from one phylum to another within the Kingdom Animalia. As recently as 1981, conodont expert Klaus Muller could still claim that 'the origin of conodonts is considered by many palaeontologists to be one of the most fundamental unanswered questions in systematic palaeontology'.

Christian Heinrich Pander, 1794–1865, medically trained German biologist who worked mostly in Russia, especially on embryology, and made important studies of fossils, including pioneering work on conodonts.

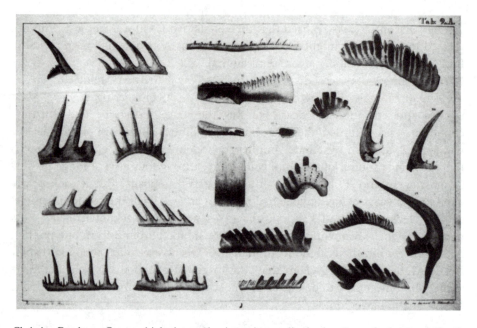

Christian Pander, a German biologist, made pioneering studies in the 1850s of microscopic fossils
which he considered to be a kind of fish teeth which he called conodonts.

Not until the 1930s did anyone in the palaeontological world bother much
with conodonts, but from then onwards new techniques, such as acid dissolution
of limestones, became commonplace in the search for useful microfossils within
economically important strata. Residues from work on Palaeozoic and early
Mesozoic limestones frequently included conodonts among other microfossils.
Being made of calcium phosphate mineral, conodonts could survive gentle acid
solution of the rock material. The problem with their identity arose because
mostly they are found isolated from one another and without any other preserved
clues as to the shape or size of the animal to which they belong.

Because conodonts are so abundant in some deposits and evolved relatively
quickly, they became very useful indicators of stratigraphic age for marine strata
of late Cambrian to end Triassic age. Consequently, a great deal of effort was

put into identifying their innumerable taxa and trying to classify them. But the nomenclature was originally based on the identification of individual conodont 'elements', as they are called. Their general tooth-like form varies from single simple cones, through serrated bars, to flatter platform-shaped elements. So there was a proliferation of names without a sense of which elements belonged together, as happened with the different parts of fossil plants.

Ever since 1879, occasional clusters of particular conodont elements have been found together on shale surfaces. We now know, in retrospect, that those clusters found in the late nineteenth century, by the English palaeontologist G. J. Hinde, were actually assembled by animals that had eaten conodont animals and that the conodont elements had passed through the gut of the predator quite unharmed. Not until 1934 were natural conodont assemblages first found in the rock record and then it was not until the late 1950s that the penny dropped and it was realised that these were true natural assemblages and gave important clues about how conodonts were arranged in the parent animal.

Different elements occurred in overlapping and elongate pairs, with the points of the teeth facing one another to form a kind of narrow basket with the most sharply pointed cones at one end and the platform elements at the other. But there was still a great deal of disagreement among experts as to what the apparatus represented, how it worked and where it was placed in the original animal. By the late 1950s and 1960s conodont experts were recognising that different element types form recurring associations, thus reinforcing the idea of natural assemblages, which was then incorporated into the taxonomy.

Realising the importance of what they had found, Briggs and Clarkson called in British conodont expert Richard Aldridge. Meanwhile, a student of Clarkson's, Neil Clark, who had just finished his final exams and was awaiting his results, asked Clarkson where he might usefully go fossil hunting. Clarkson jokingly suggested that he could always go and find some conodont animals among the fossil shrimps on the Granton foreshore. Much to Clarkson's surprise, his protégé returned with several specimens.

Close examination revealed that *Clydagnathus windsorensis*, as it was called, had at one end a cluster of conodont elements arranged as a bilaterally symmetrical apparatus. At last, a conodont animal had been found. Between 21 and 55 mm long, it looked as if fossilisation processes had preserved traces of a notochord running the length of its narrow body, with serially arranged, V-shaped muscle blocks on either side, paired eye capsules and a tail fin with numerous small finrays. With the discovery of this remarkable find, palaeontologists had to seriously consider the possibility that conodonts were chordates and what that status implied for the early phylogeny of the vertebrates.

Million Years Ago

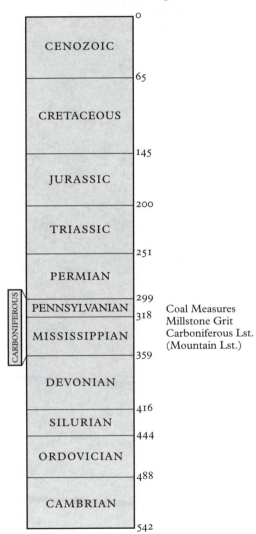

Pennsylvanian to Mississippian.

8

A boundary dispute in the Welsh Hills

DEVONIAN TO CAMBRIAN

The distant hills of Wales can just be seen from the lowlying plains of the English Midlands. The Borderlands between the two countries have been greatly disputed over the centuries, although today they are occupied by picturesque market towns such as Oswestry, Shrewsbury and Ludlow. But the presence of castles is a reminder of past conflicts. This history makes the Welsh Borderlands an appropriate setting for one of the most rancorous, personally embittered and long-running battles in the history of geology – a border dispute over the boundary between the Cambrian and Silurian strata and the divisions of Earth Time that they represent.

Historically, it was a combination of rugged and inhospitable upland terrain in central and west Wales and the warlike nature of the Welsh clans that deterred even the Roman legions from venturing too far to the west. Nevertheless, the Romans did occupy areas of significant economic interest to them, such as Anglesey with its substantial copper deposits and the gold deposits near Lampeter in South Wales. Hill tops are often capped by the barely discernible remains of ring forts constructed by Celtic Welsh clans in Roman times. Major Roman garrisons were established at strategic points along the border, interconnected by typically straight Roman roads.

Several hundred years later, Offa, King of Mercia, even went to the extent of having a dyke (a ditch and wall) dug along the 150 and more miles of the border just to make an indelible mark as to what was Welsh and what was English territory. The passage of the dyke across the landscape of the Borderlands often coincides with the Roman roads. Beneath these relatively recent human-generated demarcations lies a much more ancient and fundamental change in the geological structure and strata between the two countries.

As we have seen, the Midland plains are founded on relatively soft and easily eroded sedimentary rocks belonging to the Triassic System. In places older Carboniferous deposits outcrop along the border from the Forest of Dean through Shropshire to Denbighshire in the north. To the west lie even older rocks, which in Smith's day were largely *terra incognita*. Those he was most familiar with were what he called the Red Rhab and Dunstone, also known as the Old Red Sandstone, below which lie a great thickness of older strata that he called the Killas Slate (an ancient Cornish miner's name for clay-slate). Unlike many of the gentleman geologists of the day, Smith had not benefited from the European geological education promulgated by the likes of Abraham Gottlob Werner. Instead, Smith was using the terminology of English quarry workers. To those of the Wernerian school, the Killas Slate strata belonged to the Transition Series.

The wide triangular swathe of the Red Rhab and Dunstone forms rounded hills and high moorlands south from Bridgnorth to the Severn Estuary and west to the Black Mountains and on to Pembrokeshire and the Irish Sea, and to the west lie the Killas Slate and other strata. This was the real unknown geological territory of southern Britain and presented a considerable challenge to a rising generation of young and ambitious men. Increasingly they were calling themselves geologists rather than natural philosophers. They were part of a growing band of practitioners of a new and exciting science in the 1820s and 1830s and they were intent on building their reputations and geological careers on 'Smithian' foundations.

While much of Smith's mapping of Jurassic and younger strata was reasonably accurate, the boundary lines of older strata needed extensive revision and subdivision with the introduction of new terminology. But there were relatively few 'virgin' tracts of rocks left that had not been mapped and western Wales was one of them. The others were southwest England and the huge region of the Highlands of Scotland with their immensely complex rocks and structures, which were still completely intractable for such a young science as geology.

The 'terra incognita' of the Transition Series

Although, strictly speaking, the Old Red Sandstone is next in the succession of older and older strata that we have been following, the revolutionary work that was carried out on the Old Red Sandstone was historically preceded by the mapping of Smith's Killas Slate and so on. Furthermore, the work that revolutionised the idea and understanding of the Old Red Sandstone was done by the same geologists who first conquered the Killas, and so I am going to follow the historical narrative and deal with the Killas, otherwise known as the Transition strata, first.

The theoretical understanding of the division of Earth Time at the turn of the eighteenth and nineteenth centuries was still greatly influenced by the German intellectual tradition. Rock strata appearing at the Earth's surface had been generally classified successively from younger to older as Tertiary, Secondary and Primitive strata. But this scheme was modified by Werner, who published a more advanced classification of rocks in 1787.

Above the Primitive rocks, Werner recognised what he called Transition rocks and these were primarily seen as chemical precipitates of a global ocean, although they included some stratified deposits, which were thought to have been produced by the erosion of Primitive rocks. As we have seen, Werner called his version of Secondary strata *Flötz-Schichten* or stratified rocks, and they were made up of fossiliferous sandstones, limestones, slates, coal and so on. Above these lay his *Aufgeschwemmte-Gebirge* or Alluvial strata (equivalent to the Tertiary deposits), formed by running water carrying eroded material from the land into the sea to form sands, peats and clays. In addition, there were volcanic products, such as ash and cinder beds, all of which could be fossiliferous. To Werner, his four subdivisions reflected the history of the formation of the Earth's crust.

As we have also seen, British geologists were deeply involved in the race to distinguish and name geological systems with recognisable 'packages' of strata, representing discrete periods of Earth Time. The Transition strata were generally not differentiated or mapped in any detail, but thought to be comprised of an upper sequence of limestone and shale below which lay Grauwackes or Graywackes (another Wernerian term for a kind of dark-coloured sandstone typically associated with the Transition strata). Even the 1820 compilation map by Greenough showed the older Transition, Grauwacke and Primary rocks of Wales, the Lake District, southwest of England and most of Scotland as 'terra incognita'. Indeed, Smith's nephew, John Phillips, wrote:

> before the Summer of 1831 the whole field of the ancient rocks and fossils ... was unexplored but then arose two men ... Adam Sedgwick and Roderick Murchison and simultaneously [they] set to work to cultivate what had been left a desert.

As usual, the truth is somewhat more complex.

----- • -----

George Bellas Greenough, 1778–1855, member of parliament (1807–12), chemist and geologist, co-founder of the Geological Society of London and first President (1807–13, also 1818 and 1833). He compiled a geological map of England and Wales in 1820 that used some of Smith's work and undercut sales of Smith's own map.

----- • -----

The story generally told in books about the history of geological investigation in Britain is that the first systematic investigation of the strata of the Transition rocks of Wales was undertaken by Roderick Impey Murchison and Adam Sedgwick in the 1820s and 1830s. Murchison was of a Scottish family of landowners and minor aristocrats, but their land was relatively poor and provided little in the way of rents. Murchison knew from an early age that he had to make his own way in life and at the age of 15 went to the Military College at Great Marlow and joined a foot regiment in the British army as a subaltern. He may have got more than he bargained for, as he was immediately involved in the Peninsular War, taking part in Sir John Moore's famous retreat to Corunna over the Pyrenees in winter 1808–9. Thanks to some family influence he was then able to move to a more fashionable mounted regiment of Guards, but in 1815, on making a 'good' marriage at the age of 23 to Charlotte Hugonin, the daughter of a General, was able to resign his commission and 'do' the Grand Tour of Mediterranean Europe with his new wife.

The story has it that, although he was inclined to the usual gentlemanly pursuits of hunting and shooting, Charlotte encouraged him to do something more useful instead. Some versions of the story relate that thanks to a chance meeting at a dinner party, the eminent chemist Sir Humphrey Davey encouraged Murchison to take up geology. Maybe his well-connected wife prevailed on Sir Humphrey to do so. Anyway, Murchison attended geology lectures in London, which sufficiently enthused him to take up the hammer instead of the gun. He soon began independent researches into the geology of parts of Sussex, the northeast of Scotland and the Isle of Arran. He also made useful contacts with the rising stars of British geology and in 1828 geologised with Lyell in France and northern Italy. As a man of independent means he could afford to spend as much time as he wanted in the field, and with his social connections was able to make use of the hospitality of local gentry and aristocracy.

By contrast, Adam Sedgwick, son of the vicar and schoolteacher of the small village of Dent in Westmorland, had done well enough scholastically to gain a sizarship to Cambridge University. This meant that he had partly to pay his way by waiting on his fellow students; it was a well-trodden route for clever but poor students to gain degrees. Sedgwick did exceptionally well, was elected a fellow of Trinity College in 1810, was ordained at Norwich in 1817, and appointed to the Woodwardian chair of mineralogy in the university and a fellowship of the Geological Society in 1818, despite only having a limited knowledge of geology. He soon made up for this deficiency and was the first Woodwardian professor in many years to take his duties seriously. From 1822–4, Sedgwick made the first systematic geological survey of the Lake District (and in 1842 was asked by Wordsworth to write a geological introduction to his *A Complete Guide to the Lakes*), made the acquaintance of Murchison, and together they geologised in Scotland, Devonshire and Wales in the 1830s and began some detailed geological studies in the Austrian and Bavarian Alps. Sedgwick's time available for field work was constrained to the university vacations and even then he had ecclesiastical duties in Norwich to attend to.

In Wales, the two friends decided to see if they could make geological sense of the unknown terrain of the Transition strata. Sedgwick, with his mathematical skills and greater experience of unravelling structurally complex rocks with folds and faults, started his mapping from the oldest, Primary rocks of North Wales, with the intention of mapping his way south and east. Murchison was to work his way down from a known base line in younger rocks. He did his homework, assiduously picking the brains of any geological acquaintances who knew anything about the Grauwacke strata, such as Buckland and Conybeare. As a result of the advice he received, he started his investigation from the southern end of the Wye valley and worked his way northwards. He drew sketch sections down through the stratigraphic succession from the Old Red Sandstone strata into progressively older but richly fossiliferous strata, noting their characteristics and fossil content as he went. His young wife Charlotte went with him and, being a well-trained and accomplished sketcher of picturesque landscapes like so many genteel ladies of the time, she drew views of geologically interesting and significant features, which Murchison later used in his publications.

In retrospect, Murchison claimed that his mapping in Wales proceeded by 'Smithian' stratigraphic principles. Right from the start he certainly took care, whenever he could, to characterise his rock units by listing their fossil contents. But his palaeontological skills were limited and to begin with he was often basing his mapping on the physical appearance of the strata. For instance, he could differentiate between successions of shales or limestones, but since there is a considerable repetition of these strata types within the overall succession and their fossil content can to the inexpert eye seem similar, he sometimes got confused. In 1839 Murchison recognised an Upper Silurian made up from higher Ludlow strata and lower Wenlock Limestone, below which was his Lower Silurian comprised of the Caradoc Sandstone and Llandeilo Flags, and then below this lay Sedgwick's Cambrian strata.

Roderick Murchison's wife Charlotte was, like so many of her contemporaries, accomplished at sketching landscapes and provided illustrations such as this view of the Carneddau Hills from the Wye Valley for her husband's 1839 book on *The Silurian System*.

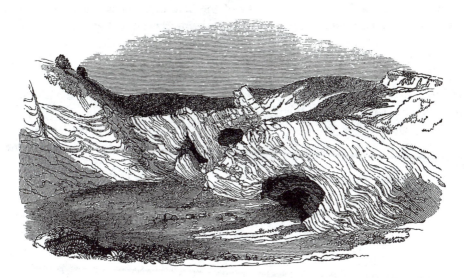

Murchison could afford to publish the lavishly illustrated *The Silurian System* by raising private subscriptions in advance. Here, a woodcut depicts the Silurian Wenlock Limestones near Ironbridge from which the carbonate rock has been quarried for use in the local iron industry.

William Henry Fitton, 1780–1861, Irish-born physician who practised in Northampton. He also studied with Jameson in Edinburgh and devoted himself to geology, determining the succession of strata between the Oolite and Chalk (1824–36), for several years was secretary and then president of the Geological Society of London (1827).

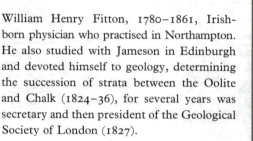

Although he did acknowledge some of the help he received, Murchison was sparing in his admission of just how much groundwork had already been laid down by a number of investigators in the region. He claimed in his introduction to *The Silurian System*, the book he wrote in 1839 synthesising his work in Wales, that 'having discovered that the region formerly inhabited by the Silures ... contained a vast and regular succession of undescribed deposits of a remote age [I had] named them.' He went on to say that 'no one was aware of the existence below the Old Red Sandstone of a regular series of deposits containing peculiar organic remains', which was seriously economical with the truth.

William Fitton, Arthur Aitkin and Rev. T. T. Lewis were just some of the people who had made serious investigations of parts of the local geology. There were many others, stretching back decades, such as the German mineralogist Rudolf Erich Rapse, better known as the author of the fantastical *Singular*

Arthur Aitkin, 1773–1854, chemist and mineralogist, founder member of the Geological Society of London in 1807 and author of manuals on mineralogy and chemistry.

Rev. Thomas Taylor Lewis, 1801–58, Cambridge-educated Shropshire vicar, antiquary and geologist who showed Murchison the stratigraphic succession below the Old Red Sandstone.

———————— • ————————

Travels, Campaigns and Adventures of Baron Munchausen, who discovered lead ores near Shrewsbury in the 1780s.

Historians of geology, such as Hugh Torrens, have recently pointed out that there is a discrepancy between our knowledge of the history of practical geology in Britain and the development of its more academic theories. And yet, the Industrial Revolution began well within the latter part of the eighteenth century. Indeed, mining and quarrying for economically valuable materials ranging from tin, copper and gold to coal was well established in certain localities in Roman times. Since the Industrial Revolution was so dependent on geological materials, how is it possible that it should have succeeded so spectacularly in Britain when it was apparently in advance of the theorising and published maps and information about the distribution of geological rock materials of economic value? There must have been a considerable body of knowledge held by practitioners who were operating outside of the gentlemanly cliques of the metropolis and the few universities that 'indulged' in science.

The Reverend Lewis was particularly important for Murchison and he recalled how he 'had the honour of conducting Mr Murchison ... along the path of an old road ... presenting a continuous section from the lower Ludlow rock to the Old Red Sandstone ... in his first visit to Herefordshire [in] July 1831.' The succession of Ludlow strata and those immediately below had been worked out by Arthur Aikin before 1812 during an attempt to survey the region geologically, an attempt that failed through lack of money, something that did

———————— • ————————

Rudolf Erich Raspe, 1737–94, German mineralogist and keeper of the landgrave of Hesse's antique gems, which he stole. Fled to England, he worked (masqueraded) as an expert on mines and minerals and wrote the *Singular Travels, Campaigns and Adventures of Baron Munchausen* (1785).

not concern Murchison. Murchison saw Aikin's notes and drawings; indeed he was still repeating Aikin's confusion of the Wenlock and Aymestry Limestones as late as 1833.

The geological situation that confronted Sedgwick was much more complex. Not only are the strata of North Wales difficult to subdivide because so many of them look similar in the field and generally lack fossil content, but they are often highly deformed by folds and displaced by faults. Sedgwick struggled to make sense of the order of the strata and, in the absence of fossils, was largely dependent on trying to match similar-looking kinds of strata between separate outcrops, a notoriously difficult and unreliable procedure. Even when he did find fossils, he was not so assiduous as Murchison in identifying them and did not at first have a supporting network of specialist 'helpers' in the way that Murchison did. Sedgwick was the only geologist in Cambridge at the time, whereas Murchison was in London where he could call on a number of experts.

Sedgwick had essentially been trained in the Cambridge mould as a mathematician and cleric; he had little or no biological background. But then very few British geologists did: geology was seen as a physical science and few of the geologists who studied fossils had much biological training, unlike many of the continental palaeontologists. Palaeontology in Britain was largely seen as a 'handmaiden' to stratigraphical geology. The only real biologically minded palaeontologists were scientists like Richard Owen, who mostly studied vertebrates and did not much concern themselves with stratigraphy or field geology.

Nevertheless, by 1835 both Murchison and Sedgwick were convinced that they had each recognised distinct new systems of strata that should replace the old Transition Series. Sedgwick named his the Cambrian, after the Roman name for Wales (*Cambria*), and distinguished it as a series of strata lying above the Primary rocks of Anglesey and below Murchison's Silurian System, which was named after a Romano-Celtic hill tribe, the Silures.

At first, Sedgwick and Murchison were happy that they had found a mutual boundary between the two systems that was geologically secure, but it did not stay that way for long. In their haste they did not pay enough attention to firmly securing the upper boundary of the Cambrian with the base of the Silurian, and there was some confusion about it right from the start, a fact that they both tended to gloss over. But it was Sedgwick's initial failure to list the characteristic fossil fauna of the various subdivisions of his Cambrian that allowed the subsequent conflict over the definition of the boundary to escalate. Both systems were predominantly comprised of marine deposits and so their fossils recorded the kind of life that inhabited the seas of the time. The few fossils that Sedgwick found to begin with in the Cambrian were in later years supplemented by more detailed investigation of the strata.

Murchison, like Sedgwick, was no palaeontologist, so he recruited specialists such as J. de C. Sowerby, who had general expertise in identifying invertebrate fossils, J. L. R. Agassiz, a Swiss glaciologist and expert on fossil fish, and W. Lonsdale, another ex-military man and pioneer in the identification of fossil corals. With their help, Murchison was able to provide good-quality illustrations, descriptions and lists of his abundant Silurian faunas in his famous three-part work of 1839, *The Silurian System*.

James de Carle Sowerby, 1787–1871, English professional naturalist, artist and collector of fossils, worked with his father James (1757–1822) and brother George (1788–1854) on numerous published compilations of illustrated natural history.

As early as 1836, propagation of the term Silurian was helped by its use in a number of popular geological books, such as Buckland's 'Bridgwater Treatise' on *Geology and Mineralogy* (1836) and the first American edition of Lyell's *Principles of Geology* (1836). By 1838, Silurian fossils were identified as far away as the Falkland Islands by Charles Darwin when he visited the islands during the voyage of the *Beagle*. Darwin had learned what expertise he had in field geology from Adam Sedgwick just before he embarked on his *Beagle* voyage.

Over the following decades, Murchison elaborated on 'his' Silurian System and in 1854 published the first edition of *Siluria: A History of the Oldest Fossiliferous Rocks and their Foundations*, which, as its title indicates, was not only a synthesis of his many academic publications but laid claim to the origin

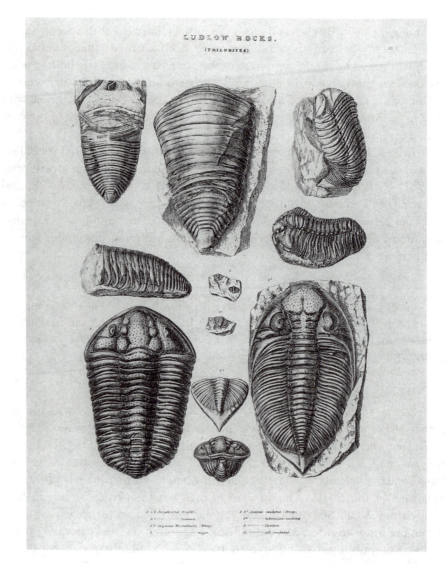

One of Murchison's plates from *The Silurian System* illustrating trilobite fossils characteristic of Ludlow strata.

Strophomena euglypha.

Pentamerus oblongus.

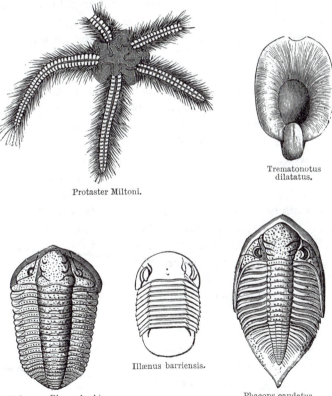

Protaster Miltoni.

Trematonotus
dilatatus.

Calymene Blumenbachi.

Illænus barriensis.

Phacops caudatus.

Repeated depiction of typical Silurian fossils in different publications helped promote the Murchison's
Silurian as a recognisable system of strata and period of Earth Time beyond the British Isles.

of life within the Silurian. He was able to do this because by this time he had already reduced Sedgwick's Cambrian to a minor subdivision in the lower part of a greatly enlarged Silurian System. The book went into a number of editions over the years and its wide distribution helped promote acceptance of the Silurian System both nationally and internationally.

It was the adoption of the Murchisonian version by the Geological Survey of Great Britain and Ireland that finally painted so much of the Lower Palaeozoic outcrop of the British Isles the characteristic Silurian blue, a situation that lasted until the latter part of the century. It was perhaps no accident that the Survey should promote Murchison's version, since he became its Director in 1855.

We now know that Sedgwick had taken on a task that could not really have been satisfactorily concluded given the state of knowledge of the time. If he had been in a position to base his Cambrian System on the strata of Baltic Russia, with its simple succession and fossiliferous rocks, the Cambro-Silurian 'problem' would not have arisen. Nevertheless, Sedgwick did start the long process of research into the geological structure and succession of the Cambrian rocks in North Wales. They are highly deformed, so much so that many of the fine-grained muddy seabed deposits have been compressed, cleaved and slightly metamorphosed into slates. Such processes destroy fossils and make the recovery of any that survive extremely difficult. Indeed, slates from the famous quarries of the Llanberis region are among the best in the world and were used to roof buildings all over Britain in the nineteenth century.

We also now know that the Cambrian strata of North Wales record a deepening succession of seabed deposits, from pebbly conglomerates and sands at the base followed by muds (now compressed into the Llanberis slates, some 1000 m thick), followed by a particular kind of sand layers called turbidites, which were laid down by sediment-laden submarine (turbidity or density) currents that flow over the seabed in a similar way to avalanches of snow. Above these relatively deep-water deposits are shallower-water sands and muds of the Lingula Flags.

Fossils are very uncommon in this region, especially in the lower part of the succession, and the first useful fossil remains are trilobites (such as *Pseudatops*

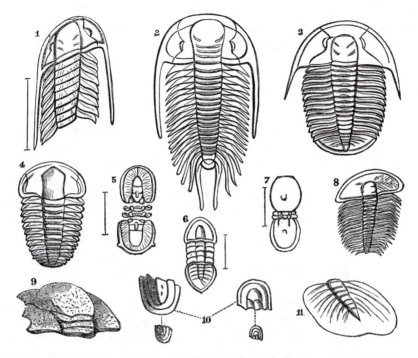

Sedgwick's tardiness in illustrating characteristic Cambrian fossils (e.g. these trilobites) was eventually overcome with the help of palaeontologists such as John Salter but it still took a long time before the Cambrian was restored to its rightful position as a valid system and period of Earth Time.

viola) preserved in some sandy layers within the Llanberis Slates. The sands are not so compressed as the muds and allow the preservation of these extinct marine arthropods, which were very diverse and evolved rapidly. Consequently, individual species are characteristic of relatively brief time intervals, which makes them very useful for matching contemporaneous strata between now separated outcrops.

The Lingula Flags preserve a greater variety of remains, ranging from the lingulid lamp-shells (brachiopods) after which the group of strata are named to several different kinds of burrows and trails made by worms and trilobites, all of which seemed to have lived in a shallow sea.

The whole succession is some 3000 m thick and must originally have been much thicker before the sediments were compressed. The fact that such a thickness of sediment, beginning and ending with shallow-water deposits, accumulated in this region shows that there must have been active subsidence of the seabed over a prolonged period. However, Adam Sedgwick would never have been able to believe the most extraordinary aspect of the Cambrian story of Wales. We now know that this Welsh Cambrian seabed originally lay many thousands of miles away from its present location (see p. 220), near the South Pole and attached to the northern margin of North Africa. But then it is only in the last few decades that the evidence for this extraordinary history has emerged.

Conquering the Devonian

Before relationships between Murchison and Sedgwick seriously deteriorated over the question of the identity and extent of the Cambrian, the two men added another prize to their collection of geological systems – the Devonian. For many years extensive ancient successions of sandstones, which are often distinctly red-brown in colour and make good building stone, had been called Red Rhab and Dunstone, or more commonly Old Red Sandstone by the early decades of the nineteenth century. There were extensive outcrops in Scotland, Wales and the Midlands, and there had been considerable confusion over their separation from a much younger series of similar strata known as the New Red Sandstone. Similar kinds of sediments occur in both series and both successions were relatively unfossiliferous, especially the latter. However, the river and lake deposits of the Old Red Sandstone were known to preserve the occasional remains of some very distinctive and strange-looking extinct fish-like animals, which were the subject of detailed study by the Swiss naturalist Louis Agassiz in the 1830s.

In the Welsh Borderland region the Old Red Sandstone could be seen to underlie and therefore predate the limestones and Coal Measures of the Carboniferous System. Murchison had used the base of the Old Red Sandstones

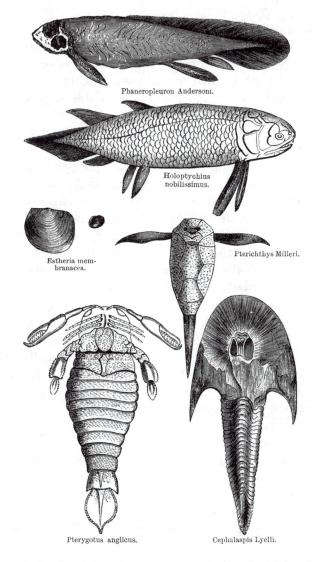

Phaneropleuron Andersoni.

Holoptychius
nobilissimus.

Estheria mem-
branacea.

Pterichthys Milleri.

Pterygotus anglicus.

Cephalaspis Lyelli.

Right from the early decades of the 19th century strange-looking fossil fish and arthropods (e.g.
Pterygotus) were found in the freshwater deposits of the Old Red Sandstone.

as a geological upper 'plimsol line' or datum from which he worked his way down into the older Transition rocks, which he was to rename as Silurian. So the Old Red Sandstone was fairly clearly defined as being older than the Carboniferous and younger than the Silurian. But there was a considerable problem and complication in the recognition of this sequence in southwest England.

Following their initially compatible and apparently successful campaign in the Transition rocks of Wales, Sedgwick and Murchison made a series of forays between 1836 and 1839 into the structurally complex geology of Devon, with its highly folded and faulted strata. Their interest in the region had been partly stimulated by some fossil plants from the region, which had been sent to them by Henry De la Beche. Like Murchison, De la Beche studied at the Military College at Great Marlow, where he received training in topographical surveying and mathematics, an expertise that helped secure his appointment as the first Director of the British Geological Survey in 1835, initially a one-man band. Prior to this he had, in 1832, started a personal investigation of the geology of Devon.

De la Beche inherited a sugar plantation in Jamaica, living there and studying the geology of the island for some years before returning to England in 1824 and settling down in Devon. That is when he started his geological investigations of the southwest, but with the abolition of slavery and a dwindling income from his plantation he no longer had independent means and so sought and obtained a government grant of £300 to produce geological maps of the region. De la Beche was an accomplished draughtsman, indeed he was also a skilful caricaturist who often made thumbnail sketches of his colleagues, especially during meetings of the Geological Society in London, which did not always enamour him to those who were the butt of his humour. They were sometimes worked up into lampoons and cartoons that were occasionally published.

De la Beche thought that the plants he had found came from 'old greywacke' strata and this aroused Murchison and Sedgwick's curiosity, because they had not found anything like them in the Transition strata that they had investigated in Wales. Murchison thought that if anything the plants most resembled those from the Coal Measures, and in 1836 he and Sedgwick confirmed his suspicions when they visited the locality from which they came in north Devon. But they were still intrigued by the highly contorted strata below the plant-bearing beds. They knew by this time that the Old Red Sandstone had not been identified in the region and this was a considerable puzzle.

Continuing their investigations in Devon, Sedgwick and Murchison could only think that the contorted rocks resembled those of Sedgwick's Cambrian 'territory' in North Wales. One difference was that in among the greywackes of Devon there are occasional fossiliferous limestones and, although many of the fossils have been distorted by the same earth movements that deformed the rocks, they were still possibly identifiable and many had been collected by local amateurs. To Murchison's eye they seemed to have a general resemblance to those of his Silurian strata, but were different in many details and he knew that he could not resolve the problem. However, Murchison was good at delegating such work and he knew a man who could help him – William Lonsdale.

William Lonsdale, 1794–1871, army officer (1812–15) who served in the Peninsular War and at Waterloo, then turned palaeontologist, became curator and librarian to the Geological Society of London (1829–42), studying fossil corals, especially those from Devonian and Carboniferous strata.

Lonsdale was another retired army man who had devoted many years to the collection and detailed study of fossils, especially the corals of the Mountain (Carboniferous) Limestone. He had also already helped Murchison with his Silurian corals and Murchison respected his judgement. However, Lonsdale reported in 1837 to Murchison that the corals from the limestones of Devon did indeed show some resemblance to those of the Silurian and also to those of the Carboniferous. To Lonsdale they seemed to be intermediate. Murchison's confidence in Lonsdale's judgement was shaken: he had certainly not considered the possibility that such contorted strata could be relatively young.

Murchison and Sedgwick continued to struggle with the structure and stratigraphy and collected more fossils, which were passed on to Lonsdale who found no new evidence to change his opinion. Eventually, Murchison and

Sedgwick had no option but to agree. After all, no matter how contorted the rocks were, their whole methodology rested on 'Smithian' principles of the identification of the relative age of strata by their characteristic fossils. There was a major implication to Lonsdale's palaeontological work: the Grauwackes of Devon with their limestones containing the marine fossils had to be of similar age to the Old Red Sandstone. It was one of the first occasions on which geologists realised that such drastically different kinds of strata were originally contemporaneous in their deposition.

Early in 1839, Sedgwick and Murchison together announced another new system of strata for which they proposed the name Devonian. Included were the slates, sandstones and limestones that had previously been referred to as Grauwackes within the Transition series of Devon and could now be seen to lie beneath the plant-bearing Carboniferous strata. Their characteristic fossils suggested that they must be younger than the Silurian and therefore equivalent to the Old Red Sandstone. But to fully justify the naming of a whole new system, the men realised that they needed to establish its applicability beyond the British Isles. Later that year they went to Germany, travelling through the Rhineland, Westphalia and the Eifel region, from where similar rocks and fossils had been reported. They needed to know if the fossils really were similar and if the strata that contained them were also bounded above by Carboniferous rocks and below by Silurian ones.

They collected plenty of fossils, which were shipped back to London to be examined by Lonsdale, George Sowerby, who had a wide-ranging experience of fossils of all ages as well as a specialist knowledge of molluscs, and Smith's nephew John Phillips, who was making a particular study of Devonian fossils. Their overall conclusions were that since the fossils were indeed similar to those of the British Devonian and the German strata were clearly overlain by Carboniferous-age rocks, they were also of Devonian age and that the System did indeed have a validity beyond Britain. The timely publication in 1841 of Phillips's book *Figures and Descriptions of the Palaeozoic fossils of Cornwall, Devon, and West Somerset; Observed in the Course of the Ordnance Geological Survey of that District* made an enormous contribution to the rapid acceptance of the Devonian as another subdivision of the old Transition Series. Phillips also took the opportunity to further argue the case for the usage of the terms Palaeozoic, Mesozoic and Kainozoic.

The name Palaeozoic, meaning ancient life, was first introduced by Sedgwick in 1838 as a grouping of two series of stratified rocks beneath the Old Red Sandstone. The younger of the two included both the Silurian and Cambrian, while the older group lay below and included highly contorted but still stratified strata. In 1840, Phillips had added the Devonian to Sedgwick's definition of the Palaeozoic and included his own new names for further groupings of younger strata – the Mesozoic Era (meaning middle life) and Kainozoic Era (meaning recent life). Then in 1841 he redefined the Palaeozoic to include the Carboniferous and Magnesian Limestone (which Murchison was soon to include in his new Permian System).

At the time the understanding of life during Palaeozoic times was that it included the origin of life itself, virtually all the sea-dwelling creatures from primitive forms such as sponges and corals to shellfish, including a lot of now extinct or uncommon groups such as the trilobites, graptolites and lampshells (brachiopods). Then there were primitive fish that arose in late Silurian and Devonian (Old Red Sandstone) times, while the first occupation of the land by plants and animals such as amphibians and reptiles was thought to have been a feature of the Carboniferous.

The Mesozoic Phillips defined as encompassing the Cretaceous, Oolites (Jurassic) and New Red Formation (Triassic). It was characterised by a significant change in life, with the extinction of some of the Palaeozoic groups of marine organisms such as the trilobites and graptolites, as well as the primitive fish groups and land plants. They were replaced by new kinds of fish both in the seas and freshwaters, new land plants, and importantly new large saurians (this was just before Owen called some of them dinosaurs), which occupied the land, took to the air (pterodactyls) and returned to the seas (the ichthyosaurs and plesiosaurs). Some of the earliest mammals had also been found, but little attention was paid to them.

The Cainozoic (as Phillips now spelled it) spanned the Tertiary and Recent, with the former including Lyell's Eocene, Miocene and Pliocene. The other Cainozoic divisions of the Palaeocene and Oligocene were yet to be established,

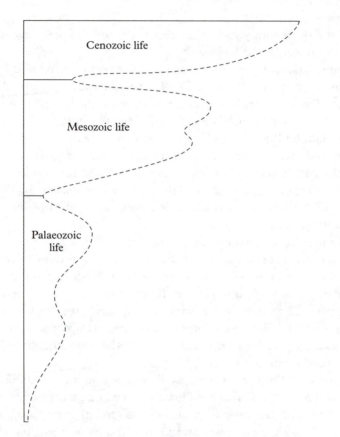

John Phillip's 1860 diagram showing the changes in fossil diversity since Cambrian times which he used to justify his recognition of three great eras in the history of life. The duration of each era was based on measures of the total thickness of strata within each era.

but the substance of the eras has stayed basically the same ever since. They were based on what were already perceived to be major changes in the overall composition of ancient life, as reflected in the fossil record. Life in the era was characterised by mammals and birds that largely replaced the Mesozoic saurians on the land, in the seas and in the air. In addition, the flowering plants became

Friedrich Heinrich Emanuel Kayser, 1845–1927, German invertebrate palaeontologist who made a particular study of Devonian strata and their fossils from the Rhineland, Devon and Boulonnais and wrote a widely used textbook *Allgemeine Geologie*, 1893.

———————— • ————————

a major feature of vegetation on land. The possibility of human-related fossil remains being found within rock strata was still not a serious consideration. Although fossil bones and stone tools had already been found, they were either ignored or construed as historical remains. And, as we have seen, the near-surface and relatively young Diluvium was beginning to be accepted as the product of deposition by ice rather than a Noachian-type flood. Phillips was to return again to his overview of the division of Earth Time and the eras of life.

The formal publication of Murchison and Sedgwick's German work in 1842 claimed that there are Devonian and Silurian strata in the Rhineland and Devonian in the Fichtel region, but no Silurian, and that Carboniferous strata overlay the Devonian in both regions. Overall they were correct, but in retrospect it was realised that they missed the Silurian rocks of Fichtel. By the 1850s the German Devonian strata had been further investigated by the likes of Ferdinand Roemer and the von Sandberg brothers, Guido and Fridolin, and shown to be rich in fossils, which were to provide a significant basis for further detailed subdivision of the system. And by the 1870s, Emmanuel Kayser's investigations of the oldest Devonian strata and their fossils in the Harz Mountains were showing links with the youngest *étages* (F, G and H) of Barrande's Silurian succession in Bohemia and raising questions about their true age that took the best part of 100 years to resolve (see below).

———————— • ————————

Joachim Barrande, 1799–1883, French engineer and paleontological student of Cuvier's who settled in Prague and spent his fortune publishing a monumental monograph series describing and illustrating the 'Silurian' fossils of the Bohemia.

The 'Hercynian question' and the Siluro-Devonian boundary

The long debate became known as the 'Hercynian question'. The Harz fossils had been accurately described by German palaeontologists such as von Beyrich and seen to characterise a Hercynian stage of development. Kayser was sufficiently convinced of the Devonian age of this fauna that he also suggested that Barrande's Bohemian *étages* F, G and H be removed from the upper part of the Silurian and placed in the lower Devonian. The strata are for the most part limestones and the fossils marine shellfish with trilobites, but interbedded with the limestone strata are dark grey-black shales containing graptolite fossils.

As we shall see, graptolites became very useful indicators of the relative age of lower Palaeozoic strata, especially for the Silurian and for the subsequent separation of the Ordovician System between Silurian and Cambrian strata. It was two British palaeontologists who made a major contribution to the study of the distribution of graptolite species through successive strata. In Britain the highest and therefore youngest graptolites are found in Murchison's Ludlow strata, but even here they disappear before the top of the series of Ludlow strata and its boundary with the base of the Old Red Sandstones. Consequently, the assumption was that this was when the graptolites became extinct – near the end of Silurian times.

Barrande's Bohemian strata contain a number of shale horizons that are also rich in graptolite fossils and the assumption was that their disappearance from the Bohemian strata must be coincident with their disappearance in the British succession; that is, before the end of the Silurian. When the graptolites were studied in more detail in the 1950s, it became clear that there were differences between the last surviving species in Britain and those found in Bohemia and the Harz Mountains. The curious thing was that, if anything, the latter seemed initially to be more like some older British Silurian species rather than the last survivors. However, the other shell fossils found in the accompanying limestones did appear to be more like the latest British Silurian ones.

Eventually, European graptolite specialists found some really well-preserved 'late' Silurian graptolites, and it became clear that they were indeed different from the British ones. The whole study of graptolites as organisms had become more sophisticated and it was realised that as with many marine organisms, it is possible to get endemic or provincial species whose distribution was restricted to particular seas and perhaps levels within the water column. British geologists also had to admit that the environments of deposition in the latest Silurian strata were strongly affected by an overall shallowing of the seas, especially in the Welsh Borderlands, and possible restrictions in their connections to the open oceans of the time. Consequently, it was likely that graptolites could have died out earlier in the progressively shallowing British region than in Bohemia and the Harz, where more open and deeper-water marine conditions lasted for longer. The question then arose as to exactly where the Silurian/Devonian boundary should be drawn.

There was an ongoing international debate about the nature of such major boundaries, with a recognition that it was necessary to have some international agreement about them so that everyone was at least talking about the same thing when trying to correlate between strata and fossils in different parts of the world. Even trying to match strata within a small geographical area such as the British Isles could be notoriously difficult: witness the problems over matching the Old Red Sandstone and marine Devonian strata of the southwest of England. Part of the problem was that many of the major boundaries between successive systems of strata were first discerned where there were major changes from one system to another between the types of deposits and their fossils.

For instance, the division between the Silurian, with its marine fossils found in limestones, sandstones and shales, and the Old Red Sandstone, with its reddish deposits and peculiar fish, had seemed pretty clear cut. Equally, there was an obvious division between the Old Red Sandstone and the Carboniferous above it with marine fossils in limestones and shales. It was realised that often such changes are more a reflection of gaps in the sedimentary record and phases of erosion rather than rapid prehistoric changes. Indeed, it is now realised, thanks to very detailed correlation by fossils, that Old Red Sandstone environments and sediments began and ended at different times in different places. Such boundaries often cut across time planes technically known as diachronous (meaning 'across time').

Equally, breaks in deposition might provide good, sharp boundaries, but they are no use as a record of the passage of Earth Time because often there is no way of telling how much 'time' is missing. The ideal boundary is one across which there has been continuous deposition of sediment with a fossil content that can be used for correlation as widely as possible. Most sequences of this kind are marine continental shelf deposits. The problem is that generally such depositional sequences show little or no significant change in sediment type and, if there is a change, it is probably recording a break in deposition.

Important boundaries not only have to be in continuous sequences of strata but the strata also have to be fossiliferous. Ideally, the fossils also have to be those of abundant and widely spread organisms that evolved rapidly, are well preserved and easily recognisable. In lower Palaeozoic strata evolving lineages of trilobites and graptolites have commonly been used in the past, but various groups of microfossils are increasingly used because they are often more abundant. The requirements are not all easily fulfilled. Consequently, to mark an important boundary in a continuous sequence of strata, it is necessary to have a good understanding of the successions of fossil assemblages and lineages of related fossils that evolve through the interval. An agreed choice has to be made about some point in the fossil record of a well-exposed sequence of strata that can be most usefully recognised as widely as possible with commonly preserved fossil species. In addition, the chosen sequence of strata should be reasonably accessible to geologists, which is a tall order.

The continuing rise and subsequent fall of the Silurian

Murchison's international network of contacts allowed him to 'recruit' a number of influential geologists, such as Verneuil, von Buch, von Keyserling and Barrande, into accepting the existence of the Silurian System within the Transition rocks of their own countries. As we have seen, Keyserling and Verneuil collaborated with Murchison in his expeditions across eastern Europe to the Urals, which culminated in the 1845 publication of *The Geology of Russia in Europe and the Ural Mountains*.

In this book, Murchison not only established the Permian System but proved the extension of the Devonian System beyond Britain, and identified and mapped what he regarded as Silurian strata lying directly above 'Azoic' or Precambrian metamorphic rocks, thus excluding any recognition of the Cambrian. The critical acclaim of this work beyond the confines of the geological world resulted in a knighthood for Murchison and seemed to put an official seal of approval on his expanded Silurian 'empire', to the exclusion of Sedgwick's Cambrian. But as Conybeare pointed out at the time, such a downward extension of the Silurian defeated the original purpose of Murchison and Sedgwick's venture, in that Murchison had effectively replaced the name Transition with Silurian, although the subdivision within it had been improved on considerably.

Among the most important and influential of Murchison's supporters abroad, from the palaeontological point of view, was Joachim Barrande, a French engineer by training, who lived in Prague and devoted his energies to describing and illustrating the abundant fossils of the Transition rocks of Bohemia. Barrande had been tutor to the French royal family and had followed them into exile in 1820, first to England, then Scotland and then to Bohemia. In 1831 he became personal tutor to Prince Henry of Chambord, but Barrande decided to stay in Prague when the royal *caravanserai* moved on.

From 1846 until 1883, Barrande published over 29 volumes entitled *Systeme Silurien du centre de la Boheme*, which describe and illustrate the wonderfully rich fossil biotas. He spared no expense, paying collectors to bring him fossils from the well-exposed limestones, shales and sandstone strata of the Prague Basin and beautiful surrounding countryside of Bohemia, which was riddled with small quarries. Altogether, Barrande described several thousand species, many of them new, and paid for innumerable high-quality engravings from which the high-quality plates (1160 in all) of his books were printed. He spent his whole private fortune on the enterprise and it remains one of the great nineteenth-century contributions to our understanding of the fossil remains of early Palaeozoic times. His fossils are still preserved in the National Museum of Prague, despite the invasion of the city by Hitler's forces in 1939 and the Soviets in 1968.

The preservational quality of these fossils was unsurpassed at the time and Barrande's monographs had a considerable international impact, helping further the establishment of the Silurian System in Europe and beyond. Barrande vehemently defended his espousal of the enlarged version of Murchison's Silurian System right up to his death in 1883. Ironically, it was because Barrande was so good at illustrating his fossils and his publications were so widely distributed in both French- and German-language editions that they were widely used for the identification and comparison of fossils from strata of similar age throughout Europe and beyond. This eventually threw up a number of discrepancies, not only concerning the question of the Cambrian but also the boundary between the Silurian and the overlying Devonian (see below).

In the pre-Darwinian world of the 1830s, the investigation of fossil remains was still to a considerable extent at the 'natural history' stage of discovery. Murchison and his palaeontological collaborators were part of a general international effort to describe all aspects of the natural world, including the history of life on Earth. Of increasing concern was the question of whether life had progressed from primitive to more advanced forms, or whether all forms of life had been present right from the original 'creation' – the gradualist view versus the uniformitarian argument of Lyell.

The investigation of the British Silurian played a significant role in undermining Lyell's concept, which had initially been supported by most British geologists, including Murchison and Sedgwick. Inevitably, it was tied into the question of how and when life had originated. And the resolution to this lay in the fossil evidence contained within what were at the time thought to be the oldest sedimentary strata within the Transition Series.

As we have seen, from the 1840s the development of the conflict between Sedgwick and Murchison over the definition of the boundary between the Cambrian and Silurian resulted in Murchison extending the base of the Silurian downwards. This allowed him to claim that the very origin of life, as represented by the oldest organic remains, was to be found within an enlarged Silurian. But if this were true, it had a very far-reaching implication for Sedgwick's Cambrian, because it excluded the possibility that Sedgwick would be able to define the Cambrian on the basis of its contained fossils.

By Murchison's definition, any fossils that were found were Silurian and therefore the rocks that contained them were also Silurian. Murchison seemed to be supported by evidence from Bohemia, where Barrande established a sequence of *étages* (stages A to G) within the Silurian. The first two were unfossiliferous but from C upwards each was characterised by its own profuse fossil fauna. *Etage* C contained what Barrande called the 'First' or 'Primordial Fauna', below which were the even older unfossiliferous rocks. Barrande visited Britain in 1851 and had found a distinctive trilobite from his 'Primordial Fauna' among the fossil collections of the British Geological Survey. And the Survey palaeontologist J. W. Salter went on to find several *Etage* C trilobite genera in North Wales in 1854.

John William Salter, 1820–69, taxonomist, engraver, curator and palaeontologist apprenticed to J. de C. Sowerby (from 1835), assisted Sedgwick (1842–6) and Forbes (from 1846) before working for the Geological Survey of Great Britain (1854–63).

Sedgwick had renewed his investigations of the Cambrian strata of North Wales in 1842, aided by Salter, and eventually, a decade later, mounted a vigorous defence of the Cambrian System, this time bolstered by fossil evidence for its independent existence and validity. He maintained that Murchison's inclusion of the Llandeilo strata in the Silurian was erronous and that their fossils showed them to be contemporaneous with the Bala Beds of the Upper Cambrian. Furthermore, the 10,000 ft of Lower Cambrian strata below this could be subdivided into two major divisions, which Sedgwick called the Festiniog and Bangor Groups, and these in turn contained identifiable sequences of distinct sedimentary rocks such as the Arenig flags and shales, the Tremadoc slates, Lingula Flags, Harlech Grits and Llanberis Slates, some of which contained fossils.

Between 1851 and 1855 Sedgwick also published successive parts of an extensive review of all British Palaeozoic strata and their fossils. Needless to say, he took the opportunity to again defend the Cambrian and tried to turn the tables on Murchison by restricting the Silurian to the Ludlow and Wenlock strata and claimed that all strata from the Caradoc downwards were Cambrian in age. But it was all too late, at least during the lifetime of the one-time friends, who became increasingly estranged. Murchison's publicity campaign had won the hearts and minds of most of the geological community. Murchison even managed to claim that vast areas of the Scottish Highlands were Silurian in age.

In the far northwest of Scotland there is a band of limestone called the Durness Limestone or 'pipe-rock', in which vertical fossil worm burrows are to be found. And there are places where schistose metamorphic rocks seem to lie above the limestone and then above these lie Old Red Sandstone strata, with their characteristic fossil fish. Although there are no fossils in the schists, Murchison argued that they had been metamorphosed in place and therefore were Silurian in age. The Geological Survey accepted the argument and so for much of the 1860s and 1870s the Highlands of Scotland were coloured Silurian 'blue' on official survey maps. Murchison's Silurian empire had reached its apogee, but nevertheless was going to be severely cut down to size.

Sedgwick took every opportunity to try to reverse the situation, to such an extent that the Council of the Geological Society in London took the extraordinary step of passing a resolution banning any further communication on the division and classification of early Palaeozoic strata by Sedgwick. It was only years later, when Murchison's wife Charlotte died, that Sedgwick tried to mend the rift and wrote a heartfelt letter to Murchison commiserating with him over his loss.

Murchison's claim that the origin of life itself was recorded within 'his' Silurian System was widely accepted. It was portrayed in one of the very first attempts to chronicle the history of life pictorially, published in an English broadsheet entitled 'The Antediluvian World'. By 1858, this view was even more widely distributed by its depiction in the second edition of a popular book on the *Primitive World in Its Different Periods of Formation* by the Austrian botanist Franz Xaver Unger. However, by the 1860s it had become clear to many geologists that there was a distinct Cambrian fauna to be found below the Silurian and that therefore life had originated much earlier than Murchison claimed.

One of the first illustrated histories of Earth Time and its fossil inhabitants (entitled 'The Antediluvian World' and omitting the Cambrian) was engraved by John Emslie in 1849.

Franz Xaver Unger, 1800–70, Austrian professor of botany at Graz, who published a *Flora of the Former World* (1841–7), a succession of reconstructed scenes beautifully illustrated by a well-known landscape painter, Josef Kuwasseg (1799–1859), followed by a similarly illustrated atlas, *The Primitive World in its Different Periods of Formation* (1851).

———————— • ————————

During the late 1840s and 1850s, fossils from Barrande's Primordial fauna had been found in Scandinavia and North America and their distinctiveness from the Silurian fauna gradually became more apparent. Furthermore, there was emerging evidence of primitive life, such as the trace fossil *Oldhamia* from Ireland, having existed in the older rocks. Murchison eventually conceded in the second edition of *Siluria* (1859) that such ill-defined fossils might be Cambrian in age, but still adhered to a Silurian age for well-defined and stratigraphically useful shelly invertebrates, such as trilobites and brachiopods.

The Ordovician compromise

The problems of definition of the Cambro-Silurian boundary took a long time to resolve. Although Charles Lapworth was able to demonstrate and justify the separation and reallocation of much of Murchison's enlarged Lower Silurian as a major division in its own right in 1879, it was several decades before this new tripartite division of the Lower Palaeozoic was generally accepted. Lapworth had named his new division the Ordovician System, after another of the Welsh tribes of Roman Britain, the Ordovices. He effected his compromise by taking the lower part of the Silurian and upper part of the Cambrian to form a new grouping.

———————— • ————————

Charles Lapworth, 1842–1920, Scottish schoolmaster (1864–75) turned professor of geology in Mason College, later Birmingham University (1881–1914), who defined the Ordovician System of strata. President of the Geological Society of London (1902).

Lapworth claimed that the successions of predominantly seabed strata that had been called, from oldest to youngest, Arenig, Llandeilo and Bala could be distinguished as a system in their own right, with a distinct fossil fauna and distinct rock types because they also contain a distinctive suite of volcanic rocks. A lot of lavas and ashes are interbedded with the marine deposits, which are mostly sandstones and slaty shales but also contain the occasional limestones. Furthermore, he claimed that the new system could be distinguished in both North and South Wales, the Lake District and the Southern Uplands of Scotland, but it had been the latter that had provided him with the means to make the distinction.

The volcanic processes that generated many of the distinctive volcanic rocks that are interlayered with the Ordovician marine sediments of Wales also produced other deposits of great historical and economic importance. Parys Mountain in Anglesey was for a time in the late eighteenth century (1768–88) the world's greatest producer of copper, with some 3000–5000 tonnes of metal being smelted each year. The mine was worked from Roman times or perhaps earlier, but was probably more or less defunct during the Mediaeval period. The sulphide ores occur within Ordovician volcanic rocks, which still contain significant reserves of zinc, copper, lead, silver and gold. Similar sulphide ores are also found in Ordovician volcanic rocks and strata in Snowdonia. Famously, gold associated with Ordovician-age intrusive volcanic-related rocks has been recovered from the Harlech region in North Wales, but the host strata here are Cambrian in age. Maximum production was at the beginning of the twentieth century, when some 1.5 tonnes of gold metal were recovered from 150,000 tonnes of ore over the decade 1900–9.

When Lapworth had been a schoolmaster in the Southern Uplands, he had spent a great deal of time and effort trying to unravel the complex structure and subdivision of the strata of this borderland region between Scotland and England, which the Geological Survey regarded as entirely Silurian. The rolling hills have many scattered outcrops of rock and are dissected with hundreds of streams (or burns as they are called here), which cut down through the thin soils to provide narrow streambed exposures of the rocks. Many of the rocks are very similar kinds of deposits with repeated alternations of sandstones and shales, but they do contain quite a lot of fossils, especially those belonging to a strange group of extinct marine colonial organisms called graptolites. Lapworth eventually realised that their fossils provided a 'key' that would help unlock the puzzling sequence of Southern Uplands strata that have been folded like a concertina and then faulted.

Graptolite fossils tend to be preserved as black carbonaceous lines on the rock surface, just a few millimetres wide but elongate, from 5–1000 mm long, looking like lines drawn with a pencil. Indeed, the name is derived from the Greek *graphos* and *lithos*, meaning 'writing on the rock', and was first given to the group by Linnaeus. However, we now know that the specimen he originally described and figured as *Graptolithus* is in fact not a fossil in the modern sense but an inorganic dendritic mineral growth. Nevertheless, it does also resemble some graptolites and moss-animals (bryozoans), so because of historical precedent and usage the name graptolite has been retained.

In more detail, graptolites also resemble bits of 'fret-saw' blades with serrations along one side, often forming curvilinear and branched geometric shapes. The serrations are flattened cups or thecae and originally housed the tiny animal zooids that make up the colony and grew by asexual budding from a parent

Carolus Linneaus, 1707–78, Swedish physician and professor of medicine and botany in Lund (from 1741), trained in Sweden and Holland, whose systematic attempt to catalogue all known life is taken as the beginning of scientific taxonomy and classification using a Latin binomial system, i.e. species and genus. His first edition of *Systema Naturae* in 1735 contained plants and by 1758 the tenth edition included some 11,900 plants and animals.

Gertrude Lillian Elles, 1872–1960, palaeontologist in Cambridge who (with Lapworth and E. M. R. Wood) made a particular study of fossil graptolites and their use in stratigraphy.

———————————— • ————————————

individual. The tubular skeleton housing the colony is a tough organic protein exuded by the zooids. Although they look like some curious kind of plant, they were in fact invertebrate animals and are related to an obscure living group of hemichordate marine creatures called pterobranchs.

Lapworth realised that subtle differences could be distinguished between assemblages of graptolites found at different levels within the thick sequence of strata. He taught himself to recognise the various graptolite species and tried to work out their evolutionary relationships. From this he was able to subdivide and correlate Lower Palaeozoic strata with a refinement and confidence that had previously been unobtainable. Detailed biozonation of this kind had been developed first by the German palaeontologist Oppel (1856–1858) within younger strata of the Jurassic using ammonites.

Lapworth's breakthrough in the development of biozonation not only helped him discern the Ordovician as a separate system, but also marked the beginning of the modern phase of subdivision of Lower Palaeozoic strata in general. Lapworth became Professor of Geology in Mason College, Birmingham (later the University of Birmingham) and encouraged the further investigation of graptolites. By the end of the nineteenth century two of his students, Gertrude Elles and Ethel Wood, were working their way through the Ordovician and Silurian strata of Wales by pony and trap and on foot, in their long dresses, hammer and chisel in hand, recovering tens of thousands of these fossils and carefully mapping which strata they occurred in.

———————————— • ————————————

Ethel Mary Reader Wood, 1871–1945 (Dame Ethel Shakespear), Cambridge-trained palaeontologist who collaborated with Elles and assisted Lapworth with his study of graptolites (1896–1906), created Dame for her public services.

The Misses Elles and Wood, later Doctors Elles and Wood, identified many new species and developed a whole new biozonal scheme based on the vertical (evolutionary and stratigraphical) distribution of graptolite species within the succession of strata. Some graptolite species are relatively short lived, but because of the way they lived as plankton in the ancient oceans they are also widely distributed. Consequently, the discovery in the Southern Uplands of Scotland and in Wales of certain key or characteristic species for a particular Silurian zone shows that the strata of the two separate localities were originally laid down at the same 'time', geologically speaking. Although the Southern Uplands of Scotland and Wales are today 300 km (220 miles) or so apart, they were much further apart in Ordovician times (see below).

Gertrude Elles went on to Cambridge University and during the course of a long career there continued to work on graptolites, producing what was for many years the standard work of description, illustration and biozonation of lower Palaeozoic graptolites, which was used as a reference throughout the world. Graptolite biozonation has continued to be an extremely valuable means of identifying and relatively dating lower Palaeozoic marine strata. New refinements have produced a modern biozonation in which each biozone represents a million or so years. The Silurian now has some 40 graptolite biozones and is known to have lasted for 27 million years, thus on average each biozone has a time equivalent of less than 1 million years, which is an astonishing level of refinement.

Despite repeated efforts of successive International Geological Congresses from 1878 onwards to standardise global stratigraphic nomenclature and its usage, it was not until the late 1950s and 1960s that the movement finally succeeded in relation to the Lower Palaeozoic systems. Murchison's power base had been the Geological Survey and it continued to display the enlarged Silurian on all its maps well past its 'sell-by' date. Only after the retirement of Murchison's protégé Sir Archibald Geikie in 1900 was a new survey regime able to change its colours and display both the Ordovician and Cambrian on its maps and other publications, but it was a very slow process. Even in 1897, Geikie's new synoptical map of the geology of England and Wales still portrayed the Cambrian

Sir Archibald Geikie 1835–1924, Scottish professor of geology at Edinburgh (1871–81), director of the Geological Survey of Great Britain (from 1882), president of the Geological Society of London (1890) and the Royal Society (1908–13), knighted 1891.

———————— • ————————

confined to the Tremadoc Group, Lingula Flags and Harlech Group in North Wales, while the Lower Silurian extended down from the Caradoc or Bala Group through the Llandeilo Group to include the Arenig Group with no recognition of the Ordovician.

Throughout the twentieth century, the establishment and international acceptance of the Ordovician and reinstatement of the Cambrian also led to a reappraisal and posthumous increase in Sedgwick's status as an important if still somewhat tragic figure in the history of geology.

The Woodwardian 'fossil' collection and other fossils subsequently amassed by Sedgwick and his successors were rehoused in a purpose-built university museum in Cambridge called the Sedgwick Museum, which was opened in 1904 by King Edward VII. The international status of the museum helped further Sedgwick's status, while Murchison's eminence and importance waned considerably. Throughout the twentieth century historians of science and the 'folklore' tradition of the increasingly egalitarian and professionalised 'middle-class' enterprise of geology turned against Murchison. He was and still is largely portrayed as a snobbish and pompous empire builder who unfairly did Sedgwick 'down' and was overly concerned with status and collecting titles, honorary degrees and medals.

While much of this may be true, Murchison's achievements were very considerable and he was evidently capable of inspiring cooperative efforts, both with Sedgwick and others such as von Keyserling and Verneuil. I doubt that any other British geologists could have organised and carried out his 'Permian' campaign in Russia. His personality and driving force might have been overbearing at times, but it is also possible that to begin with he inspired Sedgwick to achievements such as their work in Devon and in the Alps that Sedgwick might not have achieved on his own.

A remarkable story

The old sequence of Transition strata that Murchison and Sedgwick subdivided, with a little help from Lapworth, into Cambrian, Ordovician, Silurian and Devonian is now known to record an extraordinary episode in the geological story of the British Isles. The story is so unlikely that if it were not for the acceptance today of the mechanisms and processes of plate tectonics, no serious scientist would countenance it. The short version tells how southern Britain in Cambrian times was originally part of North Africa and the supercontinent of Gondwana. From the northern edge of Africa, a fragment called Avalonia (which includes southern Britain and southern Ireland) broke away in late Cambrian times and moved north. In doing so it 'closed' (subducted) the ocean in front of it (called Iapetus) and opened another (the Rheic Ocean) behind it, before colliding with North America (known geologically as Laurentia), which also lay in the southern hemisphere.

The subduction of the Iapetus ocean floor rocks generated intensive volcanicity on Iapetus, which is recorded in the Ordovician lavas and ashes of the Lake District and North Wales. These volcanoes rose above sea level, forming landscapes on which terrestrial sediments were at times laid down. Some shallow-water lake sediments in the Lake District preserve one of the earliest indications of life moving onto land. Some sandstones interlayered with ashes have been found to preserve the tracks of a freshwater, millipede-like arthropod, although the remains of the fossil itself have not been found. The transition from a supportive watery environment into the light gas we know as air was a very difficult one that required several preadaptions, such as protection from dessication and the ability to obtain oxygen from air, which is a dry gas.

By Silurian times, Avalonia was in close proximity to the northeastern margin of North America and the tropics. Overall, the marine seabed deposits on Avalonia during this period became progressively shallower and warmer. Extensive reefs were formed and the resulting reef limestones preserve a wonderful diversity of fossils, from corals, algae, sponges and moss animals (bryozoans) plus shellfish, including extinct groups such as the trilobites, graptolites and occasional remains of primitive fish. In late Silurian times the eastern part of

Avalonia emerged as a landmass and the offshore sedimentary environments became shallower and shallower. Near-shore sediments in the Welsh Borderlands record another important development in the history of life. Remains of the first land plants were washed out to sea and became incorporated in shallow offshore sediments now preserved as muddy siltstones of Silurian age in Herefordshire.

Tiny (1–2 cm) plant fragments have been found that belong to the first plants that could grow upright on land, using sunlight to photosynthsise and build their tissues. Called vascular plants, their simple stems can grow against gravity and are held upright by strengthened cells. There are no leaves, but the stems are forked and terminated by capsules that hold the reproductive spores. Reproduction was still very primitive and it was necessary for the plants to grow in watery environments so that the gametes could be exchanged via the water. So the Silurian period saw the beginnings of the greening of the land.

By the end of Silurian times, Avalonia, and coincidentally another plate fragment called Baltica (Scandinavia and northwestern Russia), collided with the northeastern margin of North America. For the first time, southern Britain was brought into contact with northern Britain, which had been part of the northeastern margin of North America. Scotland and northwestern Ireland are essentially part of the North American continent and only by the accident of geological history have become 'welded' tectonically onto southern Britain. However, the formation of what we now recognise as the British Isles had to await another 340 million years.

The margins of the continents marking the collision zone were thickened to such an extent that in early Devonian times a mountain belt was formed, extending from northern Scandinavia and eastern Greenland southwestwards through northern Britain and Ireland as well as Newfoundland, New England, and down into the Appalachians. Thus an enlarged continent of Laurussia (Laurentia plus Russia) was formed. Slowly moving northwards, it was still equatorially positioned and consequently developed vast interior semiarid desert regions. With no plants yet evolved that could exist without boggy conditions, there was no extensive plant cover nor soils to protect the landscapes from rapid weathering and erosion. But there must have been plenty of rain, as much of the

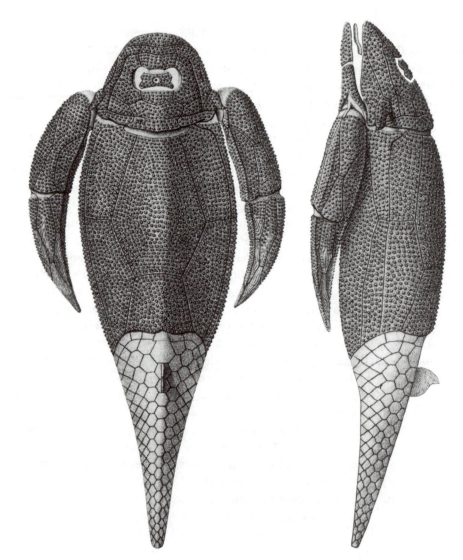

Christian Pander's biological expertise and access to well preserved fossils allowed him to produce beautiful and accurate illustrations of the strange bony jawless fish of the Old Red Sandstone in 1857.

Old Red Sandstone was deposited in large lakes and rivers draining from the northwest towards the southeast and the Rheic Ocean.

These freshwaters were occupied by rapidly evolving and very diverse groups of fish, along with the arthropods, molluscs and algae on which they fed. The most abundant fish were strange, jawless creatures largely covered (except for the tail region) in thick, leathery plates of spongey bone. In some Old Red Sandstone strata their fossils are common enough and they evolved rapidly enough to be of use as biozonal indicators, in much the same way as graptolites. Seabed deposits of Devonian age are preserved in southwest England and, as we have seen, it was their contemporaneity with the continental Old Red Sandstone that caused so much confusion and difficulty over their relative age.

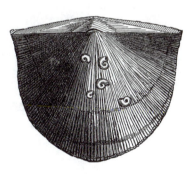

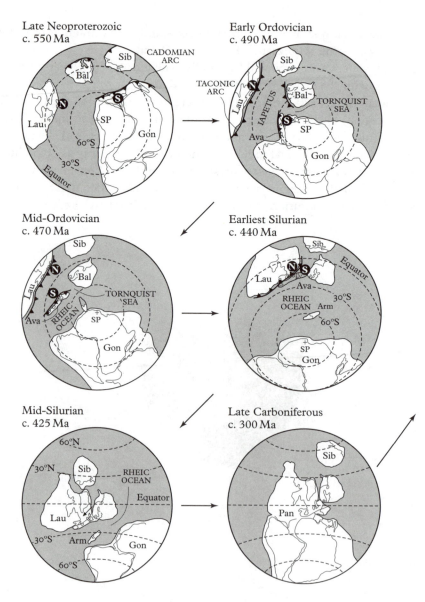

Late Neoproterozoic
c. 550 Ma

Early Ordovician
c. 490 Ma

Mid-Ordovician
c. 470 Ma

Earliest Silurian
c. 440 Ma

Mid-Silurian
c. 425 Ma

Late Carboniferous
c. 300 Ma

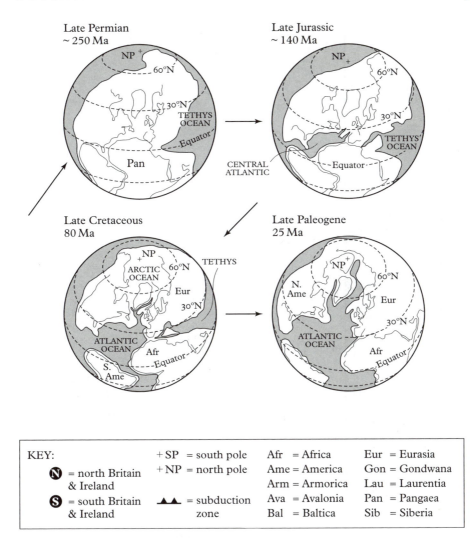

KEY:

= north Britain & Ireland	+SP = south pole	Afr = Africa · Eur = Eurasia
	+NP = north pole	Ame = America · Gon = Gondwana
= south Britain & Ireland	▲▲ = subduction zone	Arm = Armorica · Lau = Laurentia
		Ava = Avalonia · Pan = Pangaea
		Bal = Baltica · Sib = Siberia

Reconstructions of successive opening and closing of oceans and movements of continents through plate tectonic processes over Earth Time.

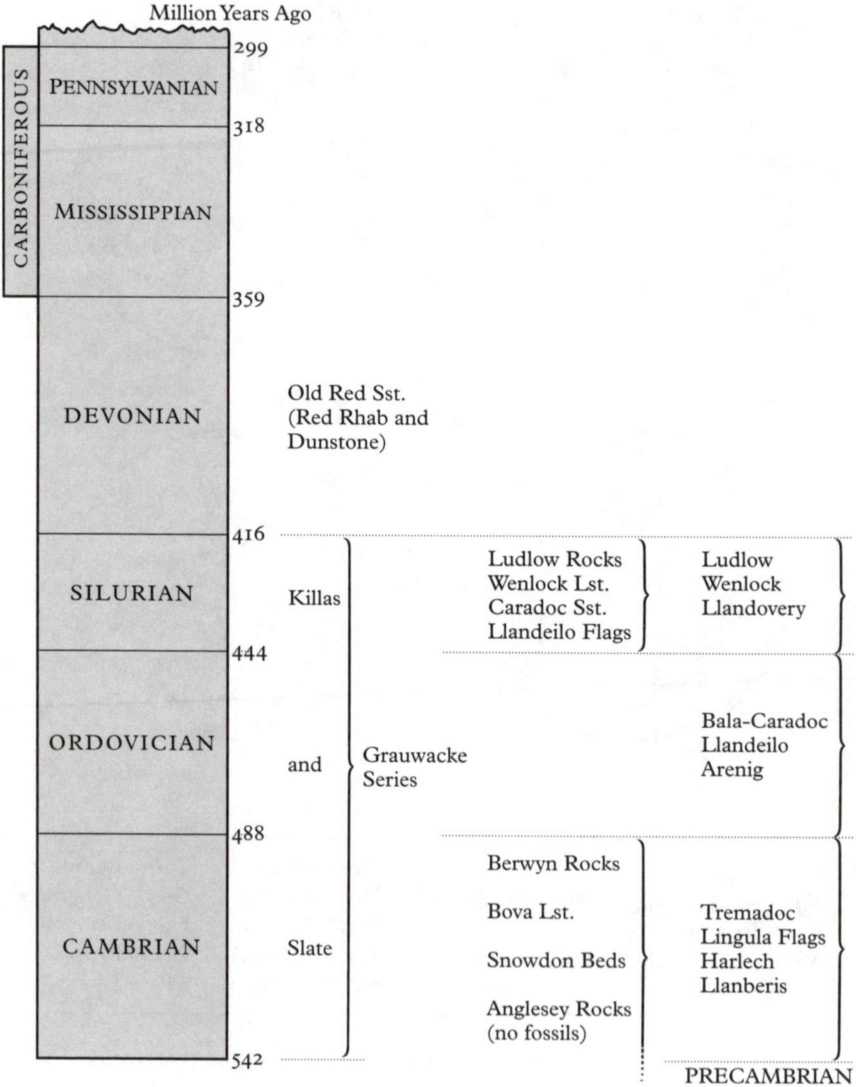

Devonian to Cambrian.

9

The end of the line –
The Precambrian

William Smith made no attempt to deal with the oldest rocks of North Wales at the northwest end of his section. Indeed, until the latter part of the eighteenth century such mountainous terrains of the British Isles were still almost completely unknown territory and generally regarded as not only useless and inhospitable, but also uncivilised, undesirable and generally to be avoided. However, attitudes were beginning to change as artists and poets, often from urban middle-class backgrounds, began to discover untramelled nature away from the fields, pastures and parks cultivated by their fellow humans and look to the savage and rugged beauty of rocky mountains, narrow passes and deep ravines, with their sense of the unknown, danger, forboding and deep antiquity.

Mountains presented an exciting challenge to the jaded senses of urbane and refined society, as portrayed by Jane Austen. Although the mountain and rocks of North Wales did not have the grandeur of the Alps, which so many of the well-to-do admired as they crossed into Italy on the Grand Tour, they did attract some very capable artists such as Richard Wilson, Cornelius Varley, John Sell Cotman and David Cox, whose paintings of their wildness attracted crowds of admirers when they were first displayed in the fashionable salons of London. Some of these North Wales localities were among the first tourist attractions of nineteenth-century Britain, but the intricacies of their geology were far beyond the understanding or interest of even the literate middle classes.

Even among the geologically minded naturalists of the day, understanding of the nature and formation of mountains was still exceedingly primitive at the end of the eighteenth century. Werner's standard succession of the oldest rocks was claimed to reflect the order in which they appeared as they crystallised out of the primeval ocean. The theory persisted in Britain into the first decades of the nineteenth century, largely due to the influential teaching of Robert Jameson in Edinburgh and Richard Kirwan in Ireland, who was a vehement opponent of Hutton.

———————— • ————————

Richard Kirwan, 1733–1812, Irish chemist and natural philosopher who was firstly a Jesuit novitiate (1754), then called to the Irish bar (1766), studied science in London, returned to Dublin as a professor of mineralogy (1787), published *Elements of Mineralogy* (1784), President of the Royal Irish Academy (1799).

———————— • ————————

By the 1820s the sequence had been elaborated to 15 or so separate rock types, ranging from the youngest 'Newer serpentine' and 'Sienite' down to 'Primitive limestone', 'Primitive trap', Older porphyry', Clay-slate', 'Topaz-rock', Mica-slate' and 'Gneiss' to the oldest and most primitive 'Granite'. All of these were seen to have some sort of stratification or foliation that was thought to be primary, except for granite. The latter with its large crystals and randomly formed, non-laminar masses had to be the oldest. Buckland was still using 'Clay-slate', Mica-slate', 'Gneiss' and 'Granite' for his illustrated succession of Primary Stratified Rocks in his Bridgwater Treatise volume on *Geology and Mineralogy* published in 1836. Early nineteenth-century attempts to unravel the geology of the oldest rocks of North Wales, such as those by Sedgwick and by Henslow, Darwin's Cambridge mentor and Professor of Botany, were doomed to failure.

Rev. John Stevens Henslow, 1796–1861, Cambridge botanist, first appointed professor of mineralogy (1822–7) then botany (1827–61), vicar of Hitcham, Suffolk (from 1839). Recommended Darwin as a naturalist to accompany Fitzroy on HMS *Beagle*.

With the development of the Cambrian/Silurian controversy and Murchison's claim that the origin of life was to be found in his 'protozoic' Silurian strata, questions arose about the nature and naming of pre-Silurian rocks. Murchison tended to refer to them as 'Azoic' or 'crystalline', but by the 1850s William Logan had found some curious organic-looking structures in limestones interbedded with ancient gneiss in Canada (see p. 266). Logan discovered that much of that country (the so-called Canadian Shield) is comprised of an extensive complex of crystalline metamorphic rocks – gneiss and schist, which form a basement to the oldest fossiliferous rocks. When William Dawson proclaimed Logan's organic-looking structures to be the genuine remains of primitive life, the options were either that life had originated in times represented by pre-Silurian/Cambrian rocks, or that the rocks were themselves also Silurian in age. Logan tried to resolve the question by differentiating older Laurentian gneisses from a younger Huronian series of metamorphosed sedimentary rocks that contained the fossils.

Sir John William Dawson, 1820–99, Canadian-born geologist educated in Edinburgh. On return to Canada as schools superintendent in Nova Scotia (1850), geologically surveyed the region, became professor of geology at McGill (1855–93), first president of the Royal Society of Canada, knighted in 1884.

Similar initial attempts were made to subdivide older rocks in Europe, but there was a growing awareness from studies of the European Alps that not all metamorphic rocks were so ancient. Therefore it was possible that the process of metamorphism could happen at any time in the geological past. If that were true then, in the absence of fossils, any attempt to give a relative age to such rocks was problematic. If they were overlaid by 'datable' fossiliferous strata, the best that could be said was that they predated those strata. By 1862 the name Precambrian was formally defined by Joseph Beete Jukes for all those rocks older than the Cambrian and has been in general use ever since. At the time, nobody had the remotest idea how much of Earth Time was represented by the Precambrian.

Joseph Beete Jukes, 1811–69, Cambridge-educated geologist and pupil of Sedgwick's, worked on the geological survey of Newfoundland (1839–40), naturalist on the voyage of HMS *Fly* (1842–6), director of the Irish Geological Survey (1850–9) and worked on the Royal Commission on coalfields, 1866.

In 1877 British Precambrian rocks were subdivided into four by Henry Hicks, namely the Lewisian in Scotland and the Dimetian, Arvonian and Pebidian in Wales. Similar attempts were made elsewhere in Europe and in North America (see p. 249) and the gradual process of trying to make some geological sense of the vast stretch of Precambrian time had begun.

As the understanding of metamorphism and structural geology improved, it became possible to attempt detailed analyses of complex Precambrian rocks. In Britain there were geologists such as Edward Greenly who devoted many years of their professional lives to mapping the Precambrian geology of particular regions. Greenly tried to decipher what had happened geologically on Anglesey and in 1919 published a two-volume memoir in which he drew comparisons with structures and metamorphic rocks found in Anglesey and the Lewisian rocks of the Highlands of Scotland. Even today, the structure and relative ages

---

Henry Hicks, 1837–99, Welsh physician and geologist who worked with Salter on the palaeontology of Cambrian rocks in Wales (1860s), the Precambrian of Anglesey, Devonian and Quaternary.

Edward Greenly, 1861–1951, British geologist who devoted many years to a geological survey of the Precambrian rocks of Anglesey, published *Methods of Geological Surveying* (1930) with Howel Williams.

———————•———————

of the rocks are far from clear, and recently comparisons have been made with rocks found in the southeast of Ireland and with rocks of Precambrian age in Newfoundland.

As we have seen, the lowest and oldest strata of Sedgwick's Cambrian strata in North Wales consist of gritty sandstones and conglomerates, which are interpreted as shallow-water deposits formed as the Cambrian seas flooded over (transgressed, as geologists call it) an eroded and subdued landscape developed on more ancient rocks. The Cambrian strata are themselves strongly fractured and cleaved and somewhat metamorphosed, so that if there were any fossils in them originally, they would have been destroyed. Consequently, their age is not really known and it is by correlation with similar deposits elsewhere that they have been assigned to the early Cambrian.

On the island of Anglesey and in the Llyn Peninsula of North Wales there are some 7000 m of older, unfossiliferous sedimentary strata with interbedded volcanic rocks, all of which seem to have been metamorphosed and deformed to a greater degree than the younger Cambrian rocks elsewhere in Wales. They include an extraordinary rock unit called the Gwna Melange, which contains blocks of older rocks ranging in size from a few millimetres to a kilometre or so in diameter. Edward Greenly thought that it had been formed by tectonic processes, but such deposits (called olistrostomes) are now known to be generated by deposition within actively subsiding and deforming ocean trenches associated with subduction.

The relative age and subdivision of these rocks are still matters of controversy and the nature of the boundary between them and undoubted Cambrian strata is still unclear. Some of the strata could also be of early Cambrian age, a possibility that has been strongly supported by the discovery of marine microfossils in some of the fine-grained sedimentary strata. Below the bedded series of rocks on Anglesey lies a considerable thickness of more highly metamorphosed and

Presently recognised major divisions of Earth Time with their 'authorship'

Holocene (Gervais, 1867)	
Pleistocene (Lyell, 1839)	Quaternary (Desnoyers, 1839)
Pliocene (Lyell, 1833)	
Miocene (Lyell, 1833)	
Oligocene (Beyrich, 1854)	Cainozoic (Phillips, 1840)
Eocene (Lyell, 1833)	
Palaeocene (Schimper, 1874)	
Cretaceous (D'Halloy, 1822)	
Jurassic (von Buch, 1839)	Mesozoic (Phillips, 1840)
Triassic (von Alberti, 1841)	
Permian (Murchison, 1841)	
Pennsylvanian (Williams, 1891)	
Mississippian (Williams, 1891)	
Carboniferous (D'Halloy, 1808; Conybeare & Phillips, 1822)	Palaeozoic (Sedgwick, 1838;
Devonian (Murchison & Sedgwick, 1839)	Phillips, 1841)
Silurian (Murchison, 1835)	
Ordovician (Lapworth, 1879)	
Cambrian (Murchison & Sedgwick, 1835)	
Precambrian (Jukes, 1862)	

presumably more ancient gneisses that Greenly compared with the Lewisian gneisses of Scotland, but their status is also far from clear. The Precambrian story will be continued on the other side of the Atlantic in the depths of the Grand Canyon.

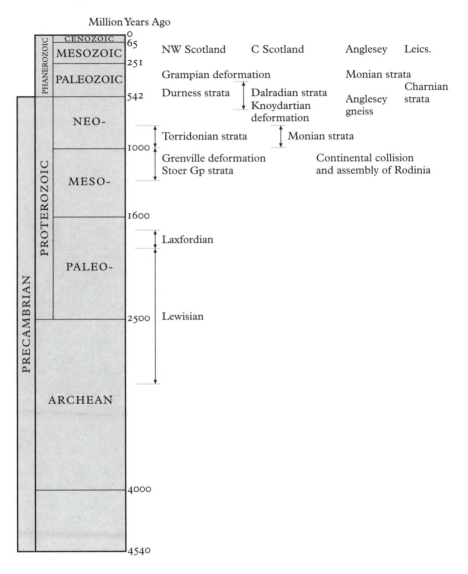

Paleozoic to Archean.

PART II

Major Powell's Boat Trip through the Grand Canyon

10

A glimpse into the abyss of Earth Time

ARCHEAN TO NEO-PROTEROZOIC

The second half or 'leg' of our journey through Earth Time takes us across the Atlantic and the North American continent to one of the world's most spectacular natural phenomena – the Grand Canyon. Here in a single river gorge we have a vertical section through some 1.7 billion years of Earth Time. We follow in the footsteps of pioneer geologists such as John Wesley Powell as they explored and mapped the Canyon's strata. The rocks revealed a peculiarly North American slant on the Earth Time story.

Some episodes, such as the vast expanse of the Precambrian, are revealed in much greater detail, while others, such as the Jurassic and Cretaceous, are missing altogether. Indeed, if Earth Time had been originally carved up according to the Canyon's rock record, its subdivisions would have been significantly different from those recognised in the European testimony of the rocks. But together the two lines of section complement one another. From such varying regional accounts of Earth Time geologists have had to find ways of recognising and matching contemporary deposits around the world. As a result, they have had to adjust the internationally accepted subdivision of Earth Time accordingly.

An engraved vista (from a photograph) of the Grand Canyon of the Colorado viewed from the same vantage point as Thomas Moran used for his huge (3.5 × 2 m) *Chasm of the Colorado* painting of 1873.

Our journey through the Canyon's strata follows Powell and begins in the oldest rocks at the bottom of the chasm and climbs up through younger and younger strata – a reverse chronology to our exploration of Smith's section.

Looking into the abyss of Earth Time

Clearly visible from space, the Grand Canyon's magnificent breadth, depth and overall extent are awe inspiring. Rapidly changing weather conditions frequently create a moving theatrical drama that no cinematic panorama can replicate. Storms can be raging in one part of the canyon while elsewhere basks in bright sunlight.

There are people who return many times and are rarely disappointed as the light and colours of the rocks regularly change from dawn to dusk, season to season. The Canyon's famous diurnal drama draws acolytes from all over the world to take part in the quasi-religious ritual of gathering at dawn to witness the curtain of darkness fall away into the depths of the gorge. The rising sunlight from the east flashes across the landscape, illuminating the younger, upper layers of strata first. Then gradually as the light brightens and intensifies, the sunlight penetrates the deeper and geologically older recesses of the gorge until there is virtually no shadow left anywhere. In the late afternoon the procedure is reversed as darkness seems to rise from the Canyon's abyss. As the sun sets in the west, the uppermost strata go through an amazing sequence of colour changes as the sunlight reddens and darkens.

The awesome beauty and drama of the Canyon have been celebrated by countless artists, beginning with the English-born painter Thomas Moran, who

———— • ————

Thomas Moran, 1837–1926, English-born painter whose weaver parents emigrated to America, became an engraver with his brothers. Joined Hayden's 1871 Yellowstone expedition. His painting of the Grand Canyon of Yellowstone was the first American landscape bought by the government (for $10,000) and helped President Grant secure the protection of the region.

Major John Wesley Powell, 1834–1902, self-taught naturalist and one-armed veteran of the American Civil War (1860–5), professor of geology at the Wesleyan University in Bloomington (1865), who led the first scientific expedition to travel the length of the Grand Canyon (1869, and again in 1871) and became the second director of the US Geological Survey (1881).

joined John Wesley Powell's second expedition to the Canyon. Moran's magnificent and enormous, 2 m by 3.5 m canvas was unveiled in 1872 in Boston and attracted huge crowds who had never before seen anything like the grandeur of the Canyon's landscape.

Powell commented on the merits of the landscape artists of the day:

Church paints a mountain like a kingdom of glory. Bierstadt paints a mountain cliff where an eagle is lost from sight ere he reaches the summit. Thomas Moran marries these great characteristics, and in his infinite masses cliffs of immeasurable height are seen.

Today, it is hard for us to imagine the impact that Moran's picture had. The scene that is so familiar today from photographs and that we take for granted was then almost unbelievable, beyond imagination and wildest dreams. Moran did not have to exaggerate what he saw and was careful to paint what was actually there in front of him – a gaping chasm broken open to reveal layer upon layer of rock descending into the abyss, all depicted in such realistic detail that it had to be true. Powell himself remarked that the canyons of this region of North America were like 'a Book of Revelations in the rock-leaved Bible of geology'.

Albert Bierstadt, 1830–1902, German-born painter who emigrated with his family to America, revisited Germany (1853–8) to train as an artist before returning to America and joining Colonel Lander's 1858 Rocky Mountain railway survey as artist. His resulting spectacular landscapes sold well in New York.

——————— • ———————

And yet, the evident vastness of such natural features and the depth of the Canyon were influential in convincing many people that it must have taken an equally vast immensity of time for such a thickness of strata to have been laid down. And then how much more time was needed to be uplifted and so dramatically dissected by the Colorado River for all to gape into the abyss of time? How could all this have been achieved in a mere 6000 years?

Although it is now one of the most visited natural wonders of the world, the Grand Canyon was ignored for three centuries by the Europeans who first explored the western interior of North America. Native Americans knew about the Canyon several thousand years ago and indeed some of them even lived within it. We now know that humans have occupied the Canyon for at least 4000 years, with over 2600 documented prehistoric ruins, including evidence of what are called Palaeo Judiou and Archaic cultures by archaeologists. The most recent native peoples to inhabit the region were the Anasazi on both the South and North Rims and the Inner Canyon, while the Cohonina were restricted to the South Rim. The Canyon appears to have been abandoned by native Americans, sometime after 1200 AD, perhaps in response to climate change, and then reoccupied some 100 years later when the Hualipai and Havasupai Indians moved into the region. These people remained undisturbed by outside forces until the Anglo-Americans arrived in the 1860s. The archaeological evidence tells a story of how these human societies adapted to severe climate change and physiographic variation. The Canyon's topographical and climate range produces environmental changes that extend over five vegetation zones and five of the seven life zones defined for the whole of North America by Dr C. Hart Merriam in the late nineteenth century.

As far as we know, the first Europeans to see the Grand Canyon with their own eyes were a small party of 13 Spaniards. In their greedy search for the fabled Eldorado – cities of gold – they were prepared to risk life and limb and go almost anywhere. In 1540, Hopi Indian guides led Captain Don García López de Cárdenas to the South Rim of the eastern part of the Canyon, but they could not find a way down the gorge to the Colorado River. Although the Spaniards were impressed by the sight of the Canyon and reported what they had seen, it was another two centuries before more Europeans were to visit it.

Inevitably perhaps in the aftermath of the Spanish invasion it was two indefatigable missionary priests, Father Silvestre Véez de Escalante and Father Francisco Domíngues, out to save 'savage' souls, who in 1776 discovered a ford across the Colorado. Even then, it was the best part of another hundred years before there was any further interest in this remarkable natural phenomenon. First on the scene in the 1830s was James 'Ohio' Pattie, who even published a description of this remarkable phenomenon, but there still was no rush to admire the view. The main stumbling block was the problem of access, but eastern entrepreneurs were soon trying to fix that by extending the railroads across the continent. The problem was what route to take.

The earliest scientific search for a suitable route was undertaken in the 1850s by the French geologist Jules Marcou. He was part of the pioneering topographical and geological search for suitable routes to which the Canyon provided something of an obstacle, to put it mildly. Marcou achieved considerable notoriety for his over-reaching geological theories and geological mapping, which either ignored or did not credit the work of his American contemporaries. A few years later the War Department sponsored the 1857–8 Ives expedition with geologist John Strong Newberry to search through the southwest looking for a railroad route to the west coast. With hindsight, Ives's conclusion about

Jules Marcou, 1824–98, Paris-educated Swiss geologist who worked on the geology of the Jura. With Thurmann visited America (1847–50), where he met Agassiz. Published one of the first geological maps of America (1853), professor of geology in Zurich (1855–9), returned to America (1861) to work with Agassiz in the Harvard Museum of Comparative Zoology and published a geological map of the world (1861).

John Strong Newberry, 1822–1902, American physician and geologist, practised medicine (1851–5), appointed surgeon and geologist to the Williamson (1855–6), Ives (1857–8) and Macomb (1858) expeditions, army medical sanitary inspector during the Civil War. Professor of geology at Columbia School of Mines (from 1866), Ohio state geologist (from 1869), palaeontologist to the USGS (from 1884), Murchison medal of the Geological Society of London (1888).

the Canyon shows the dangers of prophecy and just how wrong it is possible to be. He wrote:

> Ours has been the first, and will doubtless be the last, party of whites to visit this profitless locality. It seems intended by nature that the Colorado River, along the greater portion of its lonely and majestic way, shall be forever unvisited and undisturbed!

A decade later John Wesley Powell led a party of 10 on one of the great pioneering journeys of the continent. They voyaged for 1000 miles down the Colorado River through the Canyon from Green River, Wyoming to the mouth of the Virgin River, at what is today the north end of Lake Mead. Their frail wooden boats were at times battered, overturned and smashed against the rocks by violent currents, rapids and whirlpools. The team was reduced to nine and then six by the perils of the journey, but Powell's monumental 1876 report changed everything. With its numerous illustrations, it became possible at last to get some idea of the nature of the phenomenon, its grand scale and the unique strangeness of the Canyon's landscapes.

The inner gorge of the Colorado with the steeply inclined Precambrian metamorphic rocks forming dangerous rapids in the foreground.

Tourists started visiting the Canyon in the late 1880s and by 1901 it was possible to travel right to the South Rim by train. But how many of the millions of visitors who stare in awe of this great chasm have any real inkling about what they are actually seeing? It takes a great deal of imagination and background knowledge to turn the rocky layers into the real story of the Earth. Lifetimes of toil by countless geologists have been expended investigating these rock layers and trying to understand what they tell us about the history of the Earth and its past inhabitants.

The fact that so many visitors come from all over the world just to view the Canyon and that so many of them come back repeatedly suggests that the vista is more than merely a nice view. Perhaps the draw is the unusual combination of the huge panoramic vista of the plateau landscape around the Canyon rim, and then a sense of being inexorably drawn down into the depths and imagined dangers of the chasm. It feels as if the Earth is literally opening up in front of you and many feel a strange pull towards the Canyon's edge. No doubt it is all very symbolic and has the power to take the viewers out of themselves.

Some facts and figures

Since the latter part of the nineteenth century, the topography of the Canyon has been further mapped and measured by teams of surveyors laboriously traversing the very difficult terrain by mule and on foot, carrying heavy and cumbersome theodolites and plane tables. More recently, aerial photographs gave extra detail on some of the most inaccessible terrain and now satellite imagery can perform in a second or two what it took Powell and his team 95 days to complete.

The gorge of the Grand Canyon lies entirely in northwestern Arizona and extends for nearly 448 km (278 miles) from Lake Powell in the east, created by the completion of the Glen Canyon Dam in 1963, to Lake Mead in the west, created by the completion of the Hoover Dam (originally called the Boulder Dam) in 1936. The gorge was excavated by the powerful erosive force of the Colorado River as it cut down through the rock strata of the Colorado Plateau.

The essential ingredient in the formation of the Canyon was the process of vertical uplift of the Colorado Plateau over a period of nearly six million years to form a vast uplifted tableland over a large portion of the states of Arizona, Colorado, New Mexico and Utah. The uplift rejuvenated and re-empowered the ancient river to dramatic effect. The altitude of the Canyon and its flanking cliffs ranges from 2793 m down to 518 m above sea level. The maximum depth of the Canyon at any one location is about 1829 m (6000 ft) from rim to floor, but is more typically around 1.5 km deep, and its width varies between 0.5 and 30 km.

The water that flows through the Canyon is derived from four rivers, the Green, Colorado, San Juan and Little Colorado, and together they drain a huge area of many hundreds of square kilometres. Continuing erosion by both the permanent and seasonal rivers produces many impressive waterfalls and rapids (over 100 are named) along the Canyon. Although the Canyon is neither the deepest nor longest gorge in the world, it nevertheless has achieved icon status in global terms.

Protection of the Grand Canyon has quite a long history, dating back to 1893 when it was declared a forest reserve, but protection was very limited as mining, lumbering and hunting were permitted. The Canyon's remaining wildlife was protected in 1906 when it upgraded to a game reserve. Redesignation as a national monument followed in 1908 and eventually led on February 26th, 1919 to an Act of Congress that declared the Grand Canyon as a National Park. Finally in the US context, in 1975 the National Park was enlarged to nearly half a million hectares (4930 sq km or 1900 sq miles) with the incorporation of some adjacent national recreation areas, while 34,000 ha were removed into the Havasupai Indian Reservation. From the international perspective the Canyon was inscribed on the World Heritage List in 1979.

From the scientific investigation of the Canyon's strata we now know that it took the Colorado River a 'mere' 3–5 million years to cut its way down through what geologists call layer-cake strata of the Canyon's rocks. Layer upon layer of horizontal strata are laid out one upon the other. The youngest and most recent layers at the top of the pile form the plateau landscape surface. But these 'recent' surface rocks are now known to be some 270 million years old. Peering into the

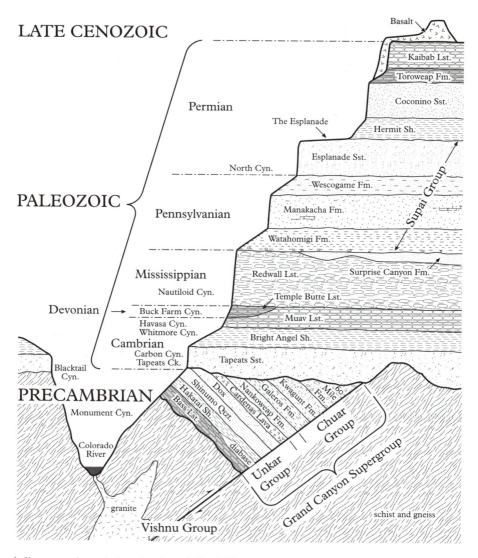

A diagrammatic vertical section through Earth Time as represented by the succession of strata in the Grand Canyon (redrawn from Beus, S. S. and Morales, M., 2003).

depths of the Canyon, the eye scans down through another 275 million years to ancient sedimentary rocks that were originally deposited on the seabed at the beginning of Cambrian times, some 545 million years ago. And beyond that it descends yet further into Precambrian time before the bottom of the chasm is reached. Even then the viewer becomes aware that the whole rock story must continue beneath our feet into the Earth. If we could descend further, how far back could we go?

Powell's perspective

For Major Powell, the view from the depths of the chasm was that of 'a stairway from gloom to heaven ... the earth and the heavens are blended into one vast structure'. We now know that, however you view it, a single sweep of the eye over the Canyon's rock strata can scan over some 1700 million years of Earth history.

Curiously, considering he was a geologist, Powell did not dwell on the Canyon's perspective on the deep past, but was more impressed by the emotional effect of its sheer physical presence, from which 'a concept of sublimity can be obtained never again to be equaled on the hither side of Paradise'. Heady words, but like Moses's 10 commandments, the testimony preserved in the Canyon's 'tablets of stone' is the story of the deep prehistoric past. The mindset, language and metaphors of the Judeo-Christian Bible permeated not merely descriptions of the Grand Canyon but, as we have seen, the whole development of our understanding of geological time.

By exploring the Canyon's rock record we can recover and sample a particular view of Earth history and its division. But the Canyon's story is just a palimpsest – a collection of fragments of the whole story. In fact, there are more gaps than records of Earth Time. No single location reveals the 'collected works', none of the rock sequences exposed on the Earth's surface tells the full story. A lot of the narrative has been lost irretrievably, so we shall have to make do with our samples. The version of Earth history preserved in the Grand Canyon is a particularly North American one.

The Precambrian rocks

'Down by the river the walls are composed of black gneiss, slates, and schists, all greatly implicated and traversed by dikes of granite. Let this formation be called the black gneiss. It is usually about 800 feet in thickness.'

Powell came to dread these rocks at the bottom of the Canyon because they were tough and dangerously sharp. Rocky points and edges threatened to impale or slice open any boat or person that was thrown against them by the powerful currents of the Colorado River. And because many of these rocks are so resistant to erosion, they tend to form the rapids and falls that constantly endangered the lives of these pioneers. Now we know that these most ancient of Canyon rocks are Precambrian in age and are immensely thick. By 1938, Powell's original estimated thickness of 800 feet (240 m) had been radically revised and had grown to between 8 and 16 km, although this is probably a considerable overestimate. Nevertheless, the pile is immensely thick and the rocks are very complex in their structure and composition. This is not surprising, since they represent over a billion years of Earth Time and a lot can happen over such a long interval.

The Precambrian rocks of the Canyon tell us about the early formation and growth of the North American continent. But we have to remember that none of the continental masses at this time looked anything like they do today and our modern names for them are not really appropriate. Geologists know this 'proto-North America' as Laurentia and it was mostly comprised of the Canadian Shield, Greenland, Scotland and the ancient 'heartland' of America.

On to this initial assembly of a few very ancient crustal 'nuclei' or 'islands', a series of progressively younger belts of rocks (or tectonic terrains, as geologists prefer to call them) have been welded by the large-scale geological processes of plate tectonics. The very oldest rocks of Laurentia are not seen in the Canyon but in Labrador and southern Greenland. Other nuclei are in the Lake Superior region and an extended belt from Wyoming north to the Great Slave Province of Arctic Canada and on into northern Greenland. In addition, the amalgamation of Laurentia was part of a more widespread global process, the assembly of the supercontinent of Rodinia around 1.1 billion years ago, to which we will return.

The awe inspiring sight of the towering spires and sheer walls of the Colorado gorge reminded
John Wesley Powell of cathedral architecture.

One possible reconstruction of the arrangement of continental plates making up the super-continent of Rodinia between 1.2 billion and 780 million years ago. The Grenville orogenic belts are shaded grey.

For many years, the most ancient rocks on Earth were thought to be the Acasta gneisses from the Great Slave Province of the Canadian Shield, dated at between 4.0 and 3.6 billion years old. These gneisses (an old German mining term) are metamorphic rocks that have been greatly altered by heat and pressure deep within the Earth's crust. They are derived from even older rocks that were part of the early formation of crustal rocks. The largest, best-exposed and most-studied area of early rocks are those of southwest Greenland. They include rocks, dated at around 3.8–3.7 billion years old, that were originally volcanic and sedimentary and deposited within water at the Earth's surface.

Even older, with ages of up to 4.4 billion years, are individual mineral grains of zircon found in Western Australia. The 'parent' rocks, in which they were originally formed, were worn away by prolonged surface erosion, leaving the exceedingly tough zircon crystals that have survived to tell the tale by being redeposited in much younger host sedimentary rocks. The more ancient end of this range of mineral dates is getting close to the estimated age of the Earth. From what we know at present of the formation of the Earth, it is unlikely that we will find any minerals much older than this. All these rocks greater than 2.5 billion years old are placed in the Archean Era of Earth Time.

By comparison, the oldest rocks of the Canyon, at a mere 1.84–1.71 billion years old, are relative 'youngsters' and are placed in the Proterozoic Era of Earth Time. Some 2 billion years long, this era is further subdivided into three intervals, the Paleo-, Meso- and Neoproterozoic, and the oldest Canyon rocks fall into the late Paleoproterozoic. Geologists interpret these as originally part of a series of volcanic island arc terranes, similar to the volcanic islands of the Indonesian archipelago today.

Plate tectonic processes welded these separate terranes on to the ancient, Archean-age, Wyoming island of continental rocks around 1.74–1.65 billion years ago. These processes initially pushed the rocks deep down (some 20–25 km) into the Earth where they were subjected to intense pressure and heated to temperatures of around 700 degrees C. Subsequent erosion stripped off some 10 km of overlying rocks before the main phase of intense deformation, between 1.7 and 1.68 billion years ago, which occurred at depths of 10–15 km. The result of all these cumulative tectonic stresses was to produce a marked vertical layering of these oldest Precambrian rocks in the Canyon. Then, over the following hundreds of millions of years, all the remaining rocks above them were eroded away and they were eventually exposed at the surface.

To the non-geologist such a history may well seem unbelievable, but there is very good evidence that vertical movements of these magnitudes have taken place all over the world through various intervals of Earth Time. The critical factors are, of course, active elevation of the crustal rocks, surface erosion and, essentially, time. The interesting problem is what internal mechanism caused the elevation. It is still not entirely clear, but rising plumes of heat from deep within the Earth's interior are the most likely cause. Heated rocks expand and the only direction that such expansion can take is upwards. As we shall see, the cutting of the Canyon itself provides a wonderful example of the remarkable rate at which erosion can occur.

It is by accident of geological history that the Grand Canyon cuts across 200 km of spectacular Precambrian rocks that underlie the Colorado plateau. The excavation of the gorge has opened this privileged window into the deepest past. Since Powell first realised the general geological nature of these rocks, a succession of geologists have refined their subdivision and argued over their nature and meaning.

The oldest Canyon rocks are gneisses, which were originally intrusive igneous rocks. Dated at 1.84 billion years old, they are the oldest-known rocks in the southwest of the USA. Their contact with younger rocks (1.75–1.73 billion years old) indicates a considerable time gap of 90–100 million years, called an unconformity, between the two. These younger rocks, collectively known as the Granite Gorge Metamorphic Suite, are made up of a wide variety of metamorphosed volcanic and sedimentary rocks, which can be generally categorised as schists. From relict structures within the oldest schists, experts in metamorphic geology have been able to discern the original presence of volcanic rocks such as ash fall deposits, pillow basalts and volcanic breccias in the oldest part of the group.

The schists above were originally sedimentary sandstones and mudstones deposited on sloping submarine flanks of volcanic islands. Individual sediment grains have been found within these deposits, which date back to 3.3 billion years ago and were probably derived from the weathering and erosion of Archean rocks to the north in the Wyoming region. The tightly constrained dates of between 1.75 and 1.73 billion years suggest that the whole succession was deposited within 10–20 million years as part of a volcanic island arc system, similar to the strings of volcanic islands that form the Indonesian archipelago, the Antilles and Aleutians today.

The metamorphic rocks were 'invaded' by numerous intrusive igneous rocks such as granite, and these date the intrusive events as occurring between 1.84 and 1.35 million years ago. This igneous invasion and formation of the Laurentian continental crust were widespread from California to Wisconsin and clearly are an expression of some profound thermal event that is not yet understood very well. They may well have been connected to the process of assembly of the supercontinent of Rodinia.

The nature of the igneous rocks produced at this time does, however, show that the Precambrian rocks were still at depths of around 10 km when they were intruded by these igneous rocks. But by 1.25 billion years ago, following this great gap of 100 million years, the vertically aligned schists, gneisses and granites of the Granite Gorge Metamorphic Suite had been sufficiently eroded to reappear at the Earth's surface, ready to receive the next episode in their depositional history.

Above the Great Gap

'Then over the black gneiss are found 800 feet of quartzites, usually in very thin beds of many colours, but exceedingly hard, and ringing under the hammer like phonlite. These beds are dipping and unconformable with the rocks above; while they make but 800 feet of the wall or less, they have a geological thickness of 12,000 feet … these quartzites vary greatly from place to place along the wall, and in many places they entirely disappear. Let us call this formation the variegated quartzite.'

Again, it was Powell who was first to note the geology of these rocks and, just over a decade later, Charles Doolittle Walcott divided them into lower Unkar

Charles Doolittle Walcott, 1850–1927, American palaeontologist and third director of the United States Geological Survey (from 1894), secretary of the Smithsonian Institution (from 1907), discovered the Burgess Shale in 1909.

———————— • ————————

(2073 m/6800 ft) and upper Chuar (1587 m/5200 ft) groups within the Grand Canyon Series (today called a Supergroup). It was Walcott who also provided the first geological map and sections, in which he agreed with Powell's measure of 12,000 feet (3660 m) for the total thickness of the 'Series'. Powell belonged to the generation of geologists who had been persuaded by Murchison's bluff and bluster to accept an enlarged Silurian extending down from the base of the Devonian to the Precambrian. Consequently, he thought the rocks to be Silurian in age, but Walcott, who belonged to a new generation that embraced new evidence and ideas, correctly reassigned them to the Precambrian by rather long-distance comparison with rocks in the Lake Superior region. Walcott was right and their age has now been confirmed on a more secure basis by radiometric dating. They are overlain by the mid-Cambrian-age Tapeats Sandstone (some 510 million years old) and thus altogether the Grand Canyon Supergroup spans over 700 million years of Earth Time. The only rocks within the Supergroup that are suitable for radiometric dating are the lavas found at the top of the Unkar Group and their age has been calculated at around 1100 million years old.

One of the most important aspects of this early geological history is the fundamental question of how and why sedimentary rocks accumulate on continents. Globally, most deposition occurs in the oceans of the world, especially around their edges where they lap onto the continental margins.

The Grenville event

The climax of Proterozoic Earth Time in Laurentia was a major event called the Grenville 'orogeny'. As an 'event' it was slow in human terms, in that the whole process took place over more than 300 million years. But its geological results were of intercontinental significance and are readily identifiable as an 'event' or well-defined episode in Earth Time.

'Orogeny' is a technical term, coined by the eminent American geologist G. K. Gilbert, for large-scale collisions of crustal rocks and the structural results of these immense collisional forces. Crustal rocks are folded, faulted and pushed about. Some are forced down into the semi-plastic interior of the Earth and others elevated to form mountain (orogenic) belts. Overall, there is considerable thickening of crustal rocks, which in the Grenville orogeny amounted to some 50 km thick. The thickened welts extend laterally over thousands of kilometres to form great linear belts of deformation, which we recognise as a particular kind of mountain range.

———————— • ————————

Grove Karl Gilbert, 1843–1918, American geologist, graduate of Rochester (1862), appointed senior geologist when the United States Geological Survey was created in 1879, who produced important descriptions of the Henry Mt. laccolith, Lake Bonneville, Niagara and Alaskan glaciation. He introduced new concepts of erosion, river and glacier development and coined the word 'orogeny' for mountain building.

———————— • ————————

The Grenville orogeny was the climactic event in a series of collisions involving the convergence of volcanic island arcs over some 300 million years. The culmination of the event was the arrival and slow but inexorable impact of a continent-sized landmass with the southern and southeastern margin of

Laurentia between 1.15 and 1.12 billion years ago. The impact occurred all along a front that extended from what today is west Texas through the Appalachian region to the maritime provinces of Canada and associated areas of Scotland, Ireland and perhaps Scandinavia.

The pace and magnitude of such events are hard for us to imagine, although similar events are going on today. The Grenville orogeny was characterised by the generation of huge thrust sheets. The collisional forces crumpled and deformed the rocks and then fractured them into huge, sheet-like slivers that were slammed together like a shuffled deck of cards. The slices slid over one another along major low-angle thrust faults for tens of kilometres. Consequently, highly deformed rock slices were driven over younger, undeformed rocks to form structures that puzzled geologists for many years.

Analysis of Grenville-age thrust sheets shows that they were pushed northwards by the encroachment from the south of a continent-sized mass impacting on the southern margin of Laurentia. Similar structures are seen in the northwest of Scotland and when Murchison saw them he could not conceive of fault movements of such magnitude. He argued that the great slice of metamorphic rocks must have been formed in place. And, since sandstone strata with traces of life (worm burrows) occur below the metamorphic rocks, he concluded that all the metamorphic rocks of the highlands of Scotland were Silurian in age.

Current opinion and assessment of a variety of evidence strongly suggest that it was the Amazon craton of older Proterozoic and Archean continental crust rocks that did the 'damage' to the southern margin of Laurentia. The collision was part of the final assembly of the supercontinent of Rodinia, which stretched from the South Pole northwards across the equator.

Rodinia and its reconstruction

Over the 420 million years or so between 1.2 billion and 780 million years ago, a global jigsaw puzzle of continent-sized pieces moved across the surface of the Earth to form a supercontinental agglomeration known as Rodinia. It is only over the last decade or so that enough information has piled up from different sources to convince geologists that such an important event in Earth Time did actually happen. There are still plenty of problems and arguments over the configurations of the continents and many gaps in the story, but the assembly of Rodinia is the earliest such event that is more or less generally accepted by the geological community.

Over the last 50 years, reconstruction of the past distribution of the Earth's tectonic plates has become increasingly sophisticated and more secure in its configurations. Most is known about recent events such as the opening of the North Atlantic from around 55 million years ago. And, as we work back in time, the basic story is pretty clear back as far as the assembly of the Pangean supercontinent in late Palaeozoic times and the even earlier formation of Gondwanaland in early Palaeozoic times. But even then, the data is becoming less secure and the constraints on plate configurations grows increasingly problematic and unreliable.

Fundamental to our understanding here is the study of the Earth's magnetic field in the past and the way in which some measures of that past magnetism are recorded in certain rocks.

Without the palaeomagnetic record it would not have been possible to attempt any reconstruction of Rodinia, but the data are still scarce and open to various radically different interpretations. The main contender for the Rodinian reconstruction at the moment has Laurentia straddling latitude 30 degrees south and rotated clockwise from its present position, so that the east coast is facing the South Pole across the Grenville orogenic belt to the continental mass of Amazonia that extends south across the Antarctic Circle. The north coast of Laurentia (today's west coast) faces north and the continental mass of East

Palaeomagnetism

Recovery and interpretation of what is known as the palaeomagnetic record are indispensable for the reconstruction of Earth Time. The Earth's magnetic field might seem pretty weak to us humans, but it is remarkably powerful and persistent. It has probably been in existence since the initial layering of the Earth's interior into a thin outer cool and brittle rocky crust, below which is the thick and hot rocky mantle and even hotter innermost metallic core with its solid centre and liquid outer layer.

The Earth's magnetic field is strong enough not only to orient compass needles but also any magnetically susceptible iron-rich particles that are moved around in a fluid medium such as a hot lava, air or water. Once deposited and solidified in a rock, the particles' record of the magnetic field is locked in for posterity as a kind of 'fossil compass'. Surprisingly perhaps, they can survive being folded and faulted, shuffled about the Earth's surface and buried several kilometres deep, all provided that the parent rock is not heated too much.

Palaeomagnetism records the orientation of the contemporary magnetic north and the declination of the field. This latter is very important because it varies from being near to vertical at the poles to horizontal at the equator. Subsequent recovery of this data informs us of the rock's latitude at the time of formation. However, it unfortunately does not inform us about the longitude. That has to be recovered from other criteria and introduces an often highly debatable and contentious element into past reconstructions.

When palaeomagnetism was first discovered and measured, scientists were puzzled to find that in some instances polarity was swapped over, with north becoming south, and that the magnetic pole seemed to 'wander' well away from its present location. For some time it was known that there is a constant slight but discernible shift in the magnetic field and that allowances have to be made on a year-to-year basis for accuracy of navigation and so on. But even so, some of these palaeopoles were way off course.

When the location of the palaeopoles was calculated through a succession of rocks and over a significant period of geological time, they followed well-defined but meandering paths. These often diverged well away from the known variation. Furthermore, measurement of polar wandering for successions of strata in different parts of the world showed that each region has its own path. When paths converge or coincide, it shows that those regions were in close proximity. For instance, polar wandering curves from northern Scottish rocks coincide closely with those of northern Laurentia (today's eastern Greenland) over a long period. This extends from around a billion years ago until 55 million years ago when the North Atlantic first began to open, as rifting and volcanism generated new ocean floor rocks between eastern Greenland and Ireland along with Britain. Consequently, Scotland was split away from its ancient Laurentian allegiance and joined the rest of Britain and Ireland to form the northwestern continental margin of Europe.

Antarctica, which extends north across the Equator to where India lay, 'docked' alongside Antarctica's northern coast. By comparison with modern geography, everything is 'topsy-turvy'. An alternative arrangement has Australia abutting against today's west coast of Laurentia and the Grenville orogenic belt extending into East Antarctica. Much more research will be needed before the picture becomes in any way clearer.

Comparison of polar wander curves for Laurentia, East Antarctica, India and Australia suggests that following some 300 million years of existence as part of the supercontinent of Rodinia, Laurentia broke away from East Antarctica and so on by 755 million years ago. It began to 'drift' away following a path that seems to have taken it right over the South Pole and eventually up into higher latitudes by Cambrian times. Anatarctica, India and Australia remained in low southern-hemisphere latitudes for the rest of Proterozoic times until the beginning of the Palaeozoic. Again, there are still big questions over the timing of the break-up of Rodinia. Some experts claim that, following the initial break-up, there was a brief re-assembly of another supercontinent that has been called Pannotia, but the waters of this issue are still very muddy. Either way, the overall result was a major reconfiguration of continents and oceans.

'Rift to drift'

Inevitably, such major changes affect the processes of sedimentation on and around the continents, and the sequence of mid to late Proterozoic strata in the Grand Canyon and nearby territories provides supporting evidence for the break-up of Rodinia, leading to what is known as a 'rift to drift' succession. They are intimately connected with the stretching of the crust – an essential ingredient of the supercontinent's break-up process.

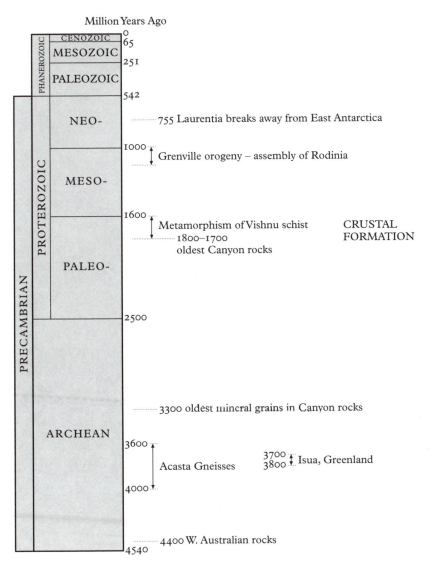

Million Years Ago

	CENOZOIC	0	
		65	
PHANEROZOIC	MESOZOIC		
		251	
	PALEOZOIC		
		542	

NEO- ········ 755 Laurentia breaks away from East Antarctica

1000 ↕ Grenville orogeny – assembly of Rodinia

MESO-

1600 ↕ Metamorphism of Vishnu schist   CRUSTAL
········ 1800–1700   FORMATION
            oldest Canyon rocks

PALEO-

2500

········ 3300 oldest mineral grains in Canyon rocks

ARCHEAN

3600

Acasta Gneisses   3700 ↕ Isua, Greenland
                             3800

4000

········ 4400 W. Australian rocks
4540

PRECAMBRIAN — PROTEROZOIC

Archean to Neo-proterozoic.

11

Signs of life appear

ARCHEAN TO NEO-PROTEROZOIC

The Canyon's Unkar Group of strata, forming the lower part of the Grand Canyon Supergroup and ranging in age from 1.2–1.05 billion years, record the situation when the Rodinian supercontinent was assembled. But the story is far from complete. There is probably a significant time gap between the top of the Unkar strata and the base of the overlying Chuar strata, which may represent as much as 250 million years (between 1050 and 800 million years ago).

Analysis of the Chuar strata shows that a major change in tectonic style was underway and that Rodinia was in the process of being broken apart as the crust was stretched and broken into fault blocks. But even the superb Canyon record is incomplete here and does not fully represent late Proterozoic time. The top of the Chuar, with the last and youngest preserved strata being somewhat more than 700 million years old, leaves another gap of around 150 million years before the beginning of Cambrian time. Fortunately, this gap is filled by strata preserved not too far away in southern California.

Unkar strata

At present the Unkar Group strata are subdivided into five different formations, which include limestones, shales, quartzites and lavas. Altogether some 1770 m

(5800 ft) of sediments were laid down in very shallow seas that spread from an ocean in the west onto a continent in the east. Ripple marks and mudcracks formed in these shallow waters are still to be seen in strata, and the occurrence of red sedimentary layers shows that at times the seas retreated, exposing the surface to weathering and erosion. The eroded continental landscape of the older metamorphic rocks over which the seas flooded was low lying with very little topography. The scene would have been a bleak and desolate one of an almost featureless plain of bare rock and rock debris, with perhaps some shallow braided rivers flowing into the sea. There would have been no discernible life on the land, despite the fact that, by this time (over one billion years ago), life had been around on Earth for over two and a half billion years. What life there was lived in the shallow offshore waters.

Right at the bottom of the Grand Canyon's pile of Unkar strata there are cliffs formed by limestones between 50 and 100 m (165–330 ft) thick. Within these strata it is possible to find surfaces covered with ripple marks, mudcracks and knobbly laminated structures called stromatolites, which were made by micro-organisms. When first confronted with such familiar sights as ripple marks, it takes some moments of reflection and a leap in imagination to realise what you are actually looking at – a seabed surface formed around one billion years ago. They can be humbling moments, especially for the geologist who may well be the first human to ever have seen that particular window on the deep past. But it is the younger Chuar strata that preserve a better record of ancient life. The discovery of this fossil record is particularly significant, in that it was one of the first realisations that life might extend back into Precambrian times.

The Chuar window on life in the deep past

As early as 1883, Walcott, employee number 20 of the recently formed United States Geological Survey, was dispatched to the Grand Canyon by John Wesley Powell who, as the first Director of the Survey, was his boss. Powell had a more intimate experience of the rocks at the bottom of the Canyon than anyone, an experience that was probably too close for comfort. Anyway, Powell suspected that it was here, if anywhere, that would provide evidence for life in rocks that predated the Cambrian Period.

Drawing of a magnified section through Precambrian age *Eozoon canadense* which Dawson (1875) claimed to show organic structures such as protozoan pseudopodia and therefore represented the oldest known fossil at the time.

For some 25 years there had been a rumbling storm over the true nature of a fossil called *Eozoon canadense* (meaning 'dawn animal from Canada'). Claimed as the oldest and most primitive organism known, *Eozoon* was found in 1858 within ancient limestones exposed along the banks of the Ottawa River, west of Montreal in Canada. John William Dawson named it and portrayed it in 1865 as the remains of a giant unicellular organism.

Dawson's reputation was so high that *Eozoon* was quickly accepted as a genuine fossil. Hailed by luminaries such as Thomas Henry Huxley, *Eozoon* was invoked as supporting evidence for Darwin's claim that there must have been a prolonged and almost unrecorded succession of primitive life forms in Precambrian rocks. As Huxley wrote in 1870, 'it is appalling to speculate upon the extent to which that origin must have preceded the epoch of the first recorded appearance of vertebrate life'. Dawson was not pleased to have Huxley's support. A Calvinist, Dawson did not subscribe to Darwin's theory of evolution and considered rather that *Eozoon* demonstrated that

> there is no link whatever in the geological fact to connect *Eozoon* with the Mollusks, Radiates, or crustaceans of the succeeding [Cambrian strata] ... these stand before us as distinct creations.

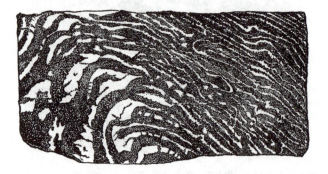

An unreconstructed section through *Eozoon canadense* does show organic-like structures but they were subsequently shown to be inorganic mineral growths.

Moreover, a gap 'yawns in our imperfect geological record. Of actual facts, therefore, we have none; and those evolutionists who have regarded the dawn-animal as an evidence in their favour, have been obliged to have recouse to supposition and assumption.'

However, there were some dissenting voices who doubted that *Eozoon* was a unicelled organism and yet others who doubted that it was genuinely organic. Even within a year of publication, Irish-based palaeontologist William King was on the attack. Just from Dawson's illustration, King observed that it was no more than an inorganic structure resulting from metamorphism of carbonate minerals in the limestone. Nevertheless, Dawson refused to acknowledge any doubts and defended his fossil into his old age. In 1894, just a few years before his death, *Eozoon*-like structures were found in a limestone block ejected during an eruption of Mount Vesuvius. As King had predicted, extreme heat within the volcano had indeed caused chemical changes of the carbonate minerals to produce *Eozoon*.

William King, 1809–86, British palaeontologist and expert on Permian fossils, was Lyell's assistant then became professor of geology at Queen's College, Galway in Ireland (from 1849), named the extinct human-related species *Homo neanderthalensis* in 1863.

By the 1880s increasing numbers of experts had come to doubt the organic nature of Dawson's *Eozoon*. And since no new convincing fossils had turned up in Precambrian strata anywhere else in the world, they had virtually given up looking for them. Powell, presumably, still held out some hope and probably knew that if anyone could find them it would be Walcott despite his lack of any formal university training in palaeontology. However, Walcott had been very well brought up in fossiliferous matters by the redoubtable and famously irascible chief geologist of New York State, James Hall. Walcott had been Hall's assistant and had closely examined some very primitive-looking organic structures that Hall had found in Cambrian (Sedgwick's Cambrian had been largely reinstated by this time) limestones of Saratoga in the east of Hall's home state.

James Hall, 1811–98, palaeontologist and chief geologist of the New York State
Survey (1836–98), first director of New York State Museum (from 1871).

———————— • ————————

These strange, cauliflower-like mounded structures were distinctly layered
and Hall was to formally name them *Cryptozoon* (meaning 'hidden life') in 1883,
but he was not able to find any definitive structures such as identifiable cell
spaces that would clinch their fundamental organic nature. Nevertheless, Hall
strongly suspected that laminated and aptly named *Cryptozoon* mounds were
small, reef-like structures made by algal communities. Having examined the
evidence himself, Walcott was also convinced of their true organic nature.

Not long after Walcott arrived in the Canyon, he was able to report that he
had found structures similar to but significantly older than Hall's Cambrian
ones. It was Walcott who first recognised that the ancient sediments, which
Powell had designated as 'Algonkian' in age (an old North American name for
the Precambrian), could be divided into what he called the Unkar and Chuar
'terranes'. Where exactly Walcott first found laminated mound structures (now
known as stromatolites) in the Chuar strata is not clear, but it was probably high
up the succession in the Awatubi Member strata where they are particularly
well developed and readily visible – if you know what you are looking for, and
Walcott did. Here, the mounds form columns 5–7 cm (2–3 in) wide and they
grew into closely packed, pipe-like forms 2.5–3 m (8–10 ft) high.

Walcott's geological survey next took him north to Montana, where again he
found *Cryptozoon*-like structures in Precambrian strata. Over the years he tried
various analytical techniques to see if he could find microscopic evidence for
cell-like structures within these laminated limestones. He tried slicing the rocks
and cutting sections thin enough to be viewed under a microscope, which was
a standard technique pioneered in the mid-nineteenth century. Eventually, he
found and described single cell-like structures and connected chains that he
thought were bacteria. He also tried dissolving the limestones and found organic
residues, which again contained cell-like structures. Although these finds should
have been slowly convincing scientists that there was life in the Precambrian,
there was a general reluctance to accept the evidence. Worse still was the deep

Sir Albert Charles Seward, 1863–1941, professor of botany at Cambridge and author of an influential textbook, *Plant Life through the Ages* (1931), knighted 1936.

———————— • ————————

scepticism of the biological community, epitomised by an eminent Cambridge (England) botanist, Albert C. Seward.

One of the most respected plant scientists of the early twentieth century, Seward took an interest in fossil plants and their stratigraphic record. In his *Plant Life through the Ages*, a well-known textbook on fossil plants published in the 1930s, Seward was dismissive of the evidence for Precambrian life:

> The general belief among American geologists and several European authors in the organic origin of *Cryptozoon* is, I venture to think, not justified by the facts ... [such forms] are precisely the same in their series of concentric shells as many concretions which are universally assigned to purely inorganic agencies ... [furthermore] it is clearly impossible to maintain that all such concentrically constructed bodies are even in part attributable to algal activity.

Seward did go on to admit:

> primitive algae may have flourished in Pre-Cambrian seas and inland lakes; but to regard these hypothetical plants as creators of reefs of *Cryptozoon* and allied structures is to make a demand upon imagination inconsistent with Wordsworth's definition of that quality as 'reason in its most exalted mood'.

Seward specifically attacked Walcott's Montana finds, commenting:

> In a very few examples the residue left after treating the rock with acid revealed the presence of a small number of cell-like structures, the organic nature of which cannot be said to have been established ... It is claimed that sections of a Pre-Cambrian limestone from Montana show minute bodies similar in form and size to [modern bacterial] cells and cell-chains ...

these and similar contributions ... are by no means convincing ... we can hardly expect to find in Pre-Cambrian rocks any actual proof of the existence of bacteria.

But in science, as in many other aspects of life, never say never. Seward turned out to be spectacularly wrong.

Over subsequent decades similar mound structures were found in Precambrian strata all over the world, but still not until the 1950s was there any great development in our understanding of them or biologically convincing evidence for the existence of life in Precambrian. The critical fossils were not found in the Canyon but in Canadian Precambrian strata of the Lake Superior region. In 1953 Stanley Tyler, a well-known American economic geologist, was investigating some curious iron-rich Precambrian strata known as the Gunflint Formation.

Stanley Tyler, 1906–63, American economic geologist at the University of Wisconsin and discoverer of the Precambrian Gunflint Chert and its microfossils.

These banded iron-rich formation (BIF) strata form economically important iron ores, but remarkably little was known about how they formed or the extent of the deposits. We now know that similar, globally distributed deposits are telling us something very important about the chemistry of ancient oceans and atmospheres. They record low but slowly rising oxygen levels in the primitive atmosphere and ocean water. A change in the iron mineral composition of the BIF, around 2.2 billion years with the formation of red iron oxides, signals a threshold in rising oxygen levels, perhaps to around 15 per cent of its present level. Importantly, this meant that life forms dependent on oxygen could at last begin to thrive. Very few of the organisms we are familiar with today would have lasted very long in the oceans or atmosphere of the Earth prior to 2.2 billion years ago.

Tyler traced the strata from the ironworks of the Mesabi Range in Minnesota along the western shore of Lake Superior for some 500 km. Taking a day off to go fishing, he took his boat around Flint Island near the village of Schreiber, Ontario. Noticing some gently sloping strata by the water's edge, he could not resist taking a look and found that it was a black layer of chert instead of the more usual red iron-rich cherts and other sediments. Breaking some off with his hammer, Tyler was impressed by the shiny, almost coaly appearance of the chert.

It was this deposit that had given the island its name, for chert is the same as flint and has been used for hundreds of thousands of years by our ancient ancestors for stone tools and weapons and in historical times as a source of gunflints for flint-lock weapons. Although the rock is sedimentary in origin, it has a hard, brittle, glassy toughness and sharpness when flaked. Made of silica, the deposits form in a similar way to carbonate nodules within wet sea and lake-bed sediments. The silica may be derived from a number of sources, but is chemically unstable in most sedimentary environments and so precipitates in irregular-shaped nodules and layers, quickly hardening into virtually incompressible and indestructible rock material. Any organic material within them can be preserved in remarkable detail without compression.

Tyler saw that the unusual Flint Island cherts were full of the enigmatic *Cryptozoon* laminated mounds, some up to a metre in diameter. Although he was mostly interested in the red beds, he collected samples of the black chert that were duly sliced into thin sections back in his laboratory at the University of Wisconsin. Whether Tyler caught any fish on that memorable day is not recorded but, although he did not know it at the time, he had landed one of the most important catches in the history of palaeontology.

Examination of the slides soon showed why the cherts were black. They were full of cloudy clumps and wisps of microscopic particles of brown to black material that looked remarkably organic in nature. Being an economic geologist, Tyler was well used to all the strange, organic-looking structures that some inorganic minerals can mimic. He knew that these were not any of the usual iron sulphide or oxide minerals such as pyrite or magnetite. They looked like organic cells and filaments. He also realised that the rock had not been metamorphosed in the way that other parts of the Precambrian red-bed strata are. There was absolutely no doubt about their Precambrian age; indeed, they were generally regarded as mid-Precambrian and we now know that they are an astonishing 1.9 billion years old and thus older than any of the rocks in the Grand Canyon.

However, with no biological training, Tyler did not feel confident enough simply to pronounce them as definite Precambrian fossils. After all, could they be some younger contaminants of the rock? Eventually, in 1953 Tyler plucked up courage to show pictures of his chert slides to Robert Shrock, an eminent palaeontologist, who enthusiastically directed Tyler to one person who really knew about plants and fossils, a young palaeobotanist called Elso Barghoorn.

Robert Rakes Shrock, 1905–93, American palaeontologist, graduate of Indiana University who taught geology at Wisconsin (1928–37) and MIT (1937–75), where he helped develop oceanographic science and co-authored the influential textbooks *Sequence in Layered Rocks* and *Principles of Invertebrate Paleontology* (with W. H. Twenhofel).

Barghoorn, as a specialist in fungae, had spent part of his Second World War service investigating fungal contamination of military equipment. Consequently, he knew a thing or two about fungae and was sufficiently impressed by Tyler's photos to realise that they had to publish some results quickly in case somebody else was working on similar material and beat them to it. Priority in publication counts in the scientific race; as in athletics, there is not much credit in being second.

Within a few months Tyler and Barghoorn had a short paper describing and illustrating five distinct Gunflint microfossils, including what they thought were two algae, two fungae and a flagellated unicell. It was published in *Science*

Elso Barghoorn, 1915–84, American palaeobotanist of Finnish extraction who studied at Miami University, Ohio and Harvard (1941). Following military service in the Second World War, he taught at Amherst College and then became professor at Harvard.

(April 30th, 1954), one of the premier international scientific journals, found in any decent university library in the world. The Precambrian 'can of worms' was definitely open and it was clear beyond any doubt that layered *Cryptozoon* mounds had an organic basis, but exactly what organism had generated them?

Stromatolites

By the 1960s, word was percolating through the international palaeontological community that living laminated mound structures had been found in very shallow and tropical hypersaline coastal waters in Shark Bay, Western Australia. Called stromatolites (meaning 'mattress of rock'), they had been known about for some time by the biological community, but the news took some time to cross the subject boundary to the palaeontological world. Now they are known from other shallow tropical waters with high evaporation rates such as the Bahama banks and Gulf of Mexico, and they have been subject to intense investigation.

Essentially, the laminated mounds are built by communities of micro-organisms (mostly cyanobacteria and occasionally algae), which grow across sediment surfaces where there is little current to disturb them. Their tiny filaments interweave, binding the sediment surface and spreading out as thin mats. The mucilagenous surface of the mats traps more sediment particles, forming a sheet-like veneer of sediment. The veneer prevents sunlight from reaching the micro-organisms, which need its 'photo' energy for photosynthesis, and so the organisms respond by growing through the surface sediment to reach the light and establish new microbial mats, which in turn trap more sediment and so on *ad infinitum*. The result is a micro-laminated sheet-like structure.

Since few shallow-water environments are entirely devoid of currents, such thin microbial mats readily wrinkle and tear. Renewal of the surface depends on the initial pattern of disrupted mats, with the result that variously shaped domes and columns develop over time. The extent of upward growth depends on subsidence or rising water levels, otherwise the mats become exposed at the surface and die off. The sediment is typically carbonate mud, which can harden (lithify) quickly; or at least in geological terms it is rapid. Once lithified into limestone, stromatolites can be remarkably resistant to erosion and therefore have a good record of preservation in the rock record.

The problem has been that, although their construction is essentially mediated by microbes, what is preserved is generally just the laminated sediment. The microbes decay without trace, which is why it took so long for the critical organic traces to be recovered and that involves the intervention of an unusual mode of preservation. At Gunflint, on Lake Superior, it was the rapid lithification of chert that did the trick.

Stromatolites are now known to be widespread throughout Precambrian times, with some perhaps as old as 3.5 billion years. The remarkable thing is that they are so conservative. Those that are billions of years old look very much like 750-million-year-old stromatolites or the living ones of Shark Bay. However, stromatolites have not been nearly as common since late Proterozoic times (around 700 million years ago) as they were throughout much of Precambrian times.

The reason for this is competition for space on the seafloor. Seaweeds (marine algae) became increasingly common from late Proterozoic times, as did mobile animals, which ploughed the sediment surface and burrowed into it. Today, stromatolites are largely restricted to lakes and shallow marine environments with extreme conditions that deter competition and predators. Stromatolites do however occasionally make brief comebacks after major extinction events. Back in the Grand Canyon, its Precambrian strata still had something new to contribute to our understanding of Precambrian life.

Chuaria and Precambrian amoebae

Overall, the 1700 m (5000 ft) or so of Chuar strata repeat an alternating pattern of shale and carbonate strata in 'bundles' some hundreds of metres thick. The stromatolite horizons occur sporadically within the carbonate strata. In between are thick sequences of interlayered shales (laminated muds) and thin sandstones. The latter are often covered with ripple marks and sometimes mudcracks, showing that the original sediment surfaces were occasionally exposed to the air and dried out. Within the shales Walcott spotted some tiny black specks, which aroused his curiosity.

Like any fossil hunter, he well knew that many interesting fossils are very small, especially those that occur first in the rock record. To look for them, you have get down on your hands and knees and put your nose to the rock. Walcott was lucky: some of these black specks were up to 5 mm wide, huge by micropaleontologists' standards. They appeared as round or oval discs made of some carbonaceous material, which must have puzzled Walcott considerably. But at least they boosted his confidence so that he could write in 1891 'that the life in the [Precambrian] seas was large and varied there can be little, if any doubt ... It is only a question of search and favourable conditions to discover it.' Eventually, in 1899, he formally named his Chuar fossils *Chuaria circularis* and described them as a kind of primitive shellfish called a brachiopod (or lamp-shell).

Brachiopods look like molluscan clams, but belong to a separate and different group of sea-dwelling shellfish. Although most brachiopods have calcareous shells like clams, there are small, primitive forms known from Cambrian strata that had organic shells, some of which were indeed circular in plan. Walcott thought that this was where his *Chuaria circularis* belonged. But even these apparently convincing Precambrian fossils did not make much of a stir. Walcott was wrong in thinking that his little Precambrian discs were brachiopods, but was right in thinking that they were organic in origin.

The true nature of *Chuaria* was not realised for nearly 100 years, not until 1985, when it was redescribed as the flattened and carbonised remains of an unusually large and spherical unicelled algal cyst, called an acritarch. *Chuaria* has now been found at many levels within the Chuar strata where it is generally microscopic (ranging in size from 5 mm down to 70 microns; a micron is a thousandth of a millimetre or four millionths of an inch) and occurs with other kinds of microscopic acritarchs. We now know that similar microfossils occur in late Proterozoic (Neoproterozoic) strata around the world dating from around 800–700 million years ago.

Again, it was chemical preparation of shales that revealed these microfossils. Shales are essentially muds and largely composed clay minerals that are remarkably resistant to chemical attack, which is partly why they are so good for making ceramics. Often the organic component of shales is very dilute and so the clay minerals have to be got rid of by drastic chemical treatment in order to concentrate enough organic material for observation under the microscope.

When muds such as these are many hundreds of millions of years old and have been buried beneath many kilometres of younger strata, they are lithified into hard, almost slaty shales. The only way to get rid of the clay minerals is to physically break the shale into small pieces in a rock crusher, then treat them with a very nasty chemical called hydrofluoric acid. This is highly dangerous, as it is colourless and has no odour but gives off a highly toxic gas and can dissolve flesh and bone quite readily. Plastic or wax is about the only material that can safely contain it. Even so, it may take several treatments and gentle heating (in special fume cupboards) to remove the clays, leaving a black sludge, if there was any organic material in the rock to begin with.

The 'organics' have to be oxidised using another cocktail of dangerous chemicals, then washed clean and permanently preserved in some liquid such as glycerine. If there is any fossil material left intact, it can be observed with a high-power microscope. Surprisingly, despite the very rough treatment, some microfossils are amazingly well preserved. So much so that some biologists have in the past refused to believe that certain Precambrian material is fossil at all, but rather think that it is modern contamination. Such contamination can indeed happen, but nowadays preparation techniques are rigorous enough to avoid such mistakes.

Even more interesting than the acritarchs are some strange, flask-shaped microfossils discovered in the 1970s. This time the microfossils were recovered by less drastic preparation techniques. The fossils occur in carbonate nodules – oval-shaped limestones that develop within the original mud sediment before it is flattened into shale. As a result, any fossil material within the nodules is protected from flattening. Another bonus is that the carbonate of the limestone can easily be dissolved by less noxious acids such as acetic or dilute hydrochloric acid. Nodules from one shale horizon yielded astonishing numbers of tiny (37–170 microns long) vase-shaped microfossils.

Using this extraction technique, Harvard student Susannah Porter recovered many thousands of specimens. At least 10,000 specimens were present in a sugar-cube-sized piece of nodule. Made of organic carbon, the teardrop-shaped flasks have an opening at one end and Porter was able to show that the vases were made by a kind of amoeboid unicell (*Melanocyrillium*) that lives within minute shells of their own making. It now turns out that such protists were common in late Proterozoic strata and their increasing abundance through Earth Time tells us that life in the oceans was becoming more diverse and complex by 750 million years ago.

Algae and cyanobacteria were the main micro-organisms that used light energy from the sun to photosynthesise organic compounds essential for their existence. Such organisms are called primary producers and form the base of the food chain for all other organisms. The evolution of the amoebae marks the next step in the development of the food chain, as they fed on the algae and bacteria. Susannah Porter also found that some of the amoebae shells have holes bored in them showing that they, in turn, were attacked and eaten by some as yet unknown predators. This is the oldest fossil record of such animals in Earth Time and records the formation of this important step in the evolution of life. Perhaps it also records the beginning of the arms race. Luckily, the event can be dated accurately to around 750 million years ago by the radiometric analysis of minerals in a volcanic ash that covers the shale and nodule layer in the Canyon.

Another gap in the Canyon's record

We now know that there is a huge time gap between the top of the Chuar Group (the upper part of the Grand Canyon Supergroup) and the overlying sediments that were laid down in Cambrian times. Like the underlying and older Unkar sediment, the Chuar strata were also laid down in shallow seas, with sediments ranging from muds and sandstones to stromatolitic carbonates (originally calcium carbonate limestone, but subsequently altered to a magnesium carbonate rock called dolostone). There are frequent signs of exposure of the sediment surface to the air such as mudcracks, but red beds are less common than in the Unkar strata. For continued shallow-water sedimentation like this, the whole basin of deposition has to have been slowly sinking at roughly the same rate as it was being filled with sediment.

Several other features, such as the presence of pull-apart faults that developed during sedimentation, show that the basin of sedimentation was actively sagging and stretching. This can only happen when the underlying, basement rocks are being pulled apart on a regional or larger scale. Furthermore, the uppermost 60 m of Grand Canyon Supergroup sediments are made up of a dramatic sequence of red beds with angular pebble breccias (called the Sixty-mile Formation). They reflect exposure at the surface and terrestrial conditions, with some substantial uplift and erosion related to block faulting, which is also typical of extensional basins.

Some experts argue that this sedimentary record of deposition on a newly formed western continental margin to Laurentia is the handiwork of the big extensional event that signalled the break-up of Rodinia. The possibility is supported by paleomagnetic evidence showing that palaeopoles for Laurentia began to diverge from those of East Gondwana (Australia–Antarctica–India) after about 720 million years ago.

The missing snowballs

Another small detail missing from the Canyon record is any record of Precambrian glaciation. In recent decades, the idea that the late Precambrian Earth was encompassed by at least one global glacial event has become a topic of much debate. This so-called Snowball Earth theory has generated a lot of academic heat and many questions have been raised over the nature of the supporting evidence. Buckets of academic cold water are constantly being thrown on the wilder aspects of the theory.

As long ago as 1949, Sir Douglas Mawson first suggested that the occurrence of very ancient glacial deposits in the Flinders Range of South Australia indicated that a glaciation had extended into much lower latitudes than ever thought possible. Mawson also suggested that climate amelioration following deglaciation paved the way for the evolution of the first multicelled animals.

Sir Douglas Mawson, 1882–1958, English-born University of Sydney-trained geologist in the University of Adelaide (1905–52) and explorer with Shackleton's Antarctic expedition (1907–9), Australasian Antarctic Expedition (1911–14, 1929–31), knighted 1914.

———————•———————

By then, Mawson knew that a protégé of his, Reg Sprigg, had recently found evidence for such animals in associated rock strata from the same region of South Australia (see below). However, Mawson believed that the position of the continents was fixed. As it became clearer that this was not so and that instead continents had moved or 'drifted' considerable distances, Mawson's ideas were dismissed. It was assumed that, when Australia was restored to its original position at the time, it would be near the pole and the ancient glacial deposits would be more easily explained.

———————•———————

Reginald Claude Sprigg, 1919–94, University of Adelaide-educated South Australian economic geologist and student of Mawson's, who worked for the South Australian department of mines then formed his own company in 1954. Elected youngest fellow of Royal Society of Australia at age of 17.

———————•———————

When in 1964 Cambridge geologist Brian Harland reviewed the growing evidence from around the world for a glaciation in late Precambrian times, he found evidence that seemed to indicate the occurrence of perhaps two separate glaciations spreading from the poles into low latitudes. The problem was that nobody knew where exactly the continents were positioned in late Precambrian times. Although there was some palaeomagnetic support for the idea, the data were not generally accepted as good enough to support such a revolutionary idea. But now we have somewhat better information, thanks to the painstaking accumulation of palaeomagnetic and radiometric data from these ancient rocks. Altogether, these data allow us to have a better idea of the placing and timing of individual continent positions relative to the poles. However, it is important to

Brian Walter Harland, 1917–2003, British, Cambridge-trained geologist who
taught in China (1942–6) before returning to Cambridge. He specialised in the
geology of Spitsbergen and the Arctic in general and was one of the first to claim
that there had been widespread glaciation in Precambrian times.

---

realise that the state of our knowledge is still very incomplete and far from
satisfactory. Nevertheless, there is a lot of new evidence to show that something
very odd was going on with global climates at the time, even if it did not amount
to global Snowball Earth conditions.

There is only one really secure, well-dated and reliable low-latitude data
point and that is for the Sturtian age Elatina glacial deposits of South Australia,
plus another possible one of similar age in Oman (around 723 million years old).
These rocks can be very difficult to date and so much has happened to them
since they were originally deposited that it can also be frustratingly difficult to
establish their original positions relative to the poles of the time. The ongoing
research and data gathering is all part and parcel of the general attempt to
reconstruct the distribution of past continents and plate movements, along with
the formation and break-up of ancient supercontinent agglomerations such as
Rodinia.

The Snowball Earth theory has now grown to such an extent that some experts
suspect that there might have been at least three late Proterozoic glaciations,
first between 740 and 700 million years ago (called the Sturtian), followed
by the Marinoan (650–630 million years ago) and the Gaskieran between 590
and 580 million years ago. In addition, there may also have been a restricted
glaciation right at the end of Proterozoic times around 550 million years ago and
a much older one around 2.3 billion years ago when banded iron formation was
common.

The story of how a global glaciation could have happened goes like this.
When an equator-spanning supercontinent like Rodinia begins to break up,
tectonic uplift of land surfaces greatly increases the rate and extent of weathering
and erosion. Carbon dioxide from the atmosphere mixes with rainwater to form
weak carbonic acid, which reacts with freshly weathered debris of carbonate-rich

rocks such as limestone, converting it to soluble bicarbonate. Not only is carbon dioxide removed from the atmosphere, but the dissolved bicarbonate is flushed into the oceans, where it combines with calcium and magnesium to reprecipitate and produce huge volumes of new carbonate sediments. These sink to the seabed and are 'locked up', forming a vast store of the Earth's carbon budget.

As carbon dioxide is a greenhouse gas, the removal of very large volumes from the atmosphere leads to significant and rapid cooling. Descent into an icehouse state initiates glaciation and the formation of ice caps. Incoming light energy from the Sun is very effectively reflected back from large ice surfaces (the albedo effect) and feeds back further cooling of the atmosphere (perhaps as low as minus 50 degrees Celsius) and growth of the icecaps. This in turn leads to runaway glaciation extending into tropical low latitudes, perhaps even encompassing the globe in a kilometre-thick layer of ice to produce a Snowball Earth. Most of the life on Earth is wiped out. But as suddenly as the glaciation formed it can come to an end.

While glaciation is doing its worst, global volcanoes still blast out large volumes of gases such as carbon dioxide into the atmosphere; even ice caps cannot prevent the process. In addition, land surface processes of weathering and erosion would have been literally frozen and put on hold. As a result, the associated chemical cycles that normally consume atmospheric carbon dioxide would have come to a halt, allowing this greenhouse gas to accumulate. Gradually the atmospheric carbon dioxide is replenished. And once a critical threshold is reached (estimated to require around 350 times present carbon dioxide levels), the atmosphere–ocean system suddenly flips from an icehouse into greenhouse or hothouse state, as some prefer to call it. Temperatures rise so rapidly (perhaps as high as 50 degrees Celsius) that within a few hundred years most of the ice melts. Sea levels rise and renewed weathering and erosion of 'de-iced' landscapes rapidly flushes bicarbonate into the oceans, quickly depositing a thick blanket of carbonate sediment, now preserved as cap carbonates on glacial deposits.

For this Snowball Earth theory to be correct, a number of features need to be observed. For instance, there should be global synchronisation of glaciations at all latitudes. This is still very difficult to prove, as many of the so-called glacial deposits cannot be reliably dated. Even with the rapidity with which glaciation and deglaciation are thought to have happened, for it to be global, it would have to be long lasting, in the order of 10 million years. Again, timing is problematic without good dating and it is now turning out that some sections have several diamictites (glacially derived sediments) interlayered with sandstone strata, which does not seem to fit the expected pattern. The radical changes in carbon dioxide levels should be reflected in the rock record, along with evidence for greatly enhanced weathering. New measures of weathering derived from independent isotope studies (of the element strontium) do not support the very high levels of weathering suggested by the model.

The main sedimentary signatures of late Proterozoic glaciations are first pebble-filled mudrocks that are called diamictites, and in this context they are interpreted as glacial in origin. Unlike deposits of the geologically recent Pleistocene ice ages, these ancient diamictites are invariably sandwiched between limestones that form the second signature. The limestone strata were deposited as carbonates characteristic of warm waters and warm climates, with virtually no intermediate sediments in between. In addition, there are some sedimentary iron formations that are making their last appearance in the rock record.

The discovery and interpretation of some late Proterozoic-age diamictites as glacial deposits was fundamental to the claim that there had been glaciation in this interval of Earth Time. For some diamictites there is no doubt about their glacial origin. They not only contain ice-scratched angular pebbles and boulders, but they are also associated with other glacial features such as glacially striated rock pavements and dropstones. The latter are pebbles and boulders that have fallen from sea ice into more normal marine sediments. However, in the rush to join the Snowball bandwagon, many other diamictic conglomeratic sandstones have been called glacial, with very little supporting evidence for the attribution. Critics of the 'full-on' Snowball theory claim that out of 85 diamictite deposits from around the world, dated at between 800 and 500 million years old, only some 16 are reliably glacial in origin.

The presence of limestones immediately adjacent to the diamictites is part of the supporting evidence for low-latitude positions of glaciated regions. Furthermore, the reappearance of limestones immediately after the diamictites seems to indicate very rapid climate change. However, the composition of the limestones is not exactly the same. Analysis of their carbon isotopes shows that there was a considerable organic contribution from sea-dwelling creatures to limestones found below the glacial deposits, but very little contribution to the limestones immediately above.

High positive carbon isotope ratios in limestones are also associated with large areas of shallow tropical seas. And these in turn are more abundant when supercontinents such as Rodinia rift and break apart. During such rifting, the total length of coastlines more than doubles as shallow seas flood around the margins of the new, smaller continental blocks or plates. The high rates of burial of organic carbon also locked up very large amounts of atmospheric carbon dioxide, contributing to the ice-house effect with its rapid and drastic cooling leading to a glacial event. Then, if the glacial event was globally extensive, the covering of sea ice would have shut down primary production in the oceans and led to the shutdown of marine ecosystems.

By contrast, the cap limestones above the diamictites generally have very low negative carbon isotope levels. At first these negative values seemed to agree with the Snowball model, in that they suggested continuing low organic productivity in the oceans, thus the organic component. Alternatively, the postglacial ocean may have continued to be depleted in the kind of organisms, such as cyanobacteria and algae, which were the source of the organic carbon.

However, recent more detailed analyses show that the lower strata of the cap limestones exhibit high positive ratios and the negative excursion does not 'kick in' until some way through the deposits. Depositional rates of the limestones could have been enhanced as a result of rapid heating of tropical waters and greatly increased biological productivity. But at the same time, increased weathering of continental rocks removes carbon dioxide from the atmosphere.

The removal of large volumes of this greenhouse gas would have led to global cooling. Descent into an icehouse state would have initiated glaciation. Another possibility that is much in vogue at the moment is that large quantities of methane, which has low carbon isotope values, were suddenly released from permafrost sediments that contain large volumes of frozen gas hydrates such as methane.

However, recent more detailed sampling and analysis of the distribution of carbon isotopic values through the carbonates show some puzzling complications. Positive values continue upwards into the base of the carbonates immediately above the glacial deposits. This strongly suggests that, contrary to what has been claimed, there was continuing organic production through the glacial phase. Furthermore, the claim that the brief negative carbon isotope 'excursion' was related to increased weathering has not been supported by analysis of strontium isotopes, which are also involved in the process.

Iron-rich sediments were last seen around 2 billion years ago in Earth Time and their reappearance at this late stage, when levels of oxygen in the atmosphere and oceans were close to those of the present, might seem rather strange. The answer given by Paul Hoffman and Dan Schrag, some of the main promoters of the Snowball Earth hypothesis, is that a covering of sea ice shut down the primary production of oxygen in the oceans by photosynthesising micro-organisms such as algae and cyanobacteria. Furthermore, they claim that the 'icing' on the oceans also prevented the diffusion of oxygen from the atmosphere into ocean water, promoting the deposition of iron-rich sediment in ocean waters.

That there were significant glacial events in late Precambrian times is not in doubt. But recent detailed examination of some of the critical evidence for their extent and influence on life does not seem to be quite clear cut as originally 'advertised'. There is certainly good evidence that there was no total ice blanket, there were probably significant 'uniced' areas of landscape and open areas of ocean, and life was not shut down. The Snowball Earth hypothesis has not melted away, but it is in the process of reinvention and transformation. So far, the Canyon deposits do not provide evidence for these events, but there is geological evidence not far away in eastern California.

California fills the gap

In California, sedimentation continued from late Proterozoic times right through into the beginning of the Palaeozoic Era and its initial period, the Cambrian. Altogether some three kilometres of Neoproterozoic sediments (ranging in age from 1.0–0.542 billion years ago) accumulated in shallow marine seas, depositing sands, silts and carbonates with the occasional invasion of land-derived river-borne sediment from the east and southeast. Most interesting of all are strata known as the Kingston Peak Formation, which includes sandstones, volcanic rocks and limestones with different kinds of conglomerates, including a diamictite. Overall, the strata result from the rifting apart of Rodinia and crustal stretching around 700 and 600 million years ago.

In Death Valley National Park, near Saratoga Spring, diamictite conglomerates can be seen to contain a variety of pebbles of different size, shape and composition, all 'floating'; that is, surrounded by finer-grained sediment. These characteristics are very different from those of a typical beach conglomerate. Instead, they reflect deposition from sediment-laden and land-derived ice as it floats out to sea and melts. Similar diamictites are found in the nearby Ibex Hills. Limestones typical of wave- and current-agitated shallow, warm waters occur below and between diamictite horizons. The sequence is capped by another kind of limestone known as the Noonday Dolomite. This was also deposited on a shallow marine continental shelf margin, but in quiet waters with thin rhythmic layering thought to have been produced by the growth of algal mats over the sediment surface.

Measurement of carbon isotope values through the limestones shows positive values below, between and immediately above the diamictites. The only negative values are found higher up in the Noonday Dolomite, repeating the distribution seen in similar rocks in Namibia and Australia. So these late Proterozoic deposits repeat the pattern that has been found worldwide at this level and that is seen as evidence for an extensive if not necessarily global ice age at this time.

The uppermost, postglacial sequence of Proterozoic strata in Death Valley is called the Stirling Quartzite. It was from here that some of the oldest fossil shells in the world were found in the 1960s and 1970s. They are therefore of considerable interest.

For around 200 years one of the base lines of historical palaeontology has been the argument that the fossil record of shelled organisms begins with a 'bang' or explosion in diversity at the beginning of Cambrian times. Hundreds if not thousands of fossil collectors around the world have spent vast amounts of effort examining earliest Cambrian-age strata and the immediately older sedimentary rocks below. All seemed to confirm the view that shelly fossils first appeared in the earliest Cambrian-age strata. But in the late 1950s, the discovery of some tiny tubular and mineralised fossils in late Proterozoic strata in Brazil showed that the story is more complex and more interesting.

A sharp eye is needed to spot the fossils, as well as sufficient knowledge and inquisitiveness to give them a second glance. At first, they are not very impressive, just tiny, gently curved tubes a few millimetres wide and a centimetre or two long. Looking more closely, the tubes turn out to have thin walls, partly stiffened with carbonate mineral deposits. The tubes expand upwards and have growth lines on the outside, which are developed into circular flanges in some species. Just in terms of their form, they look quite like the tubes of a group of living marine 'worms' called the pogonophorans, but we have no soft-part evidence to support such an affinity. Indeed, there are reports that some Chinese fossil tubes of this general kind also have a simple branching pattern. If this is correct, then they are not pogonophorans but might rather have a link with the sea anemones, a group of primitive animals that later gave rise to the corals.

At first, the Brazilian specimens were thought to be a kind of calcareous alga. Then more were found in Namibia, southern Africa, and called *Cloudina* after Preston Cloud, an American pioneer of Precambrian palaeontology. Further finds in South America led to the realisation that they are not calcareous algae but the fossilised living tubes of a distinct group of extinct animals that together are now referred to as cloudinids. They have a global distribution in late Proterozoic strata and in some localities they are so common that they built reef-

---

Preston Ercelle Cloud, Jr., 1912–91, American palaeontologist, after the navy trained at George Washington University and Yale, joined the United States Geological Survey in 1941, professor at Yale (from 1946–8), returned to the survey until 1961 when he moved to a succession of university posts in California. Pioneered the study of Precambrian microfossils and his book, *Cosmos, Earth, and Man*, was published in 1978.

like mounds on the seabed. In Namibia, the reef mounds also contain another slightly skeletonized small organism called *Namacalathus*. This has a tubular stalk leading to a globular structure with six side openings, giving a hexagonal symmetry and a single, slightly larger opening at the top. So the pre-Cambrian evolution of mineralised skeletons was not a singularity restricted to the cloudinids, but extended to at least one other kind of organism.

So far, no shells of typical early Cambrian organisms have been found associated with the cloudinids and their 'friends'. Despite the more ancient and precocious development of skeletonisation, the idea that the main biological revolution occurred at the base of the Cambrian may still be correct. Nevertheless, late Proterozoic strata contain another palaeontological surprise that was not recognised until the 1950s — the so-called Ediacarans.

Soft-bodied Ediacarans

As with so many apparent first discoveries in Earth Time, detailed investigation reveals some previous unsung and forgotten record that predates the generally accepted 'first' find. So it is with the strange soft-bodied and extinct Ediacaran organisms. Back in 1877, two English geologists, E. Hill and T. G. Bonney, found and described some 'curious arrangements of concentric rings which have been supposed to be organisms' on some ancient seabed surfaces in the late Precambrian sandstones of Charnwood Forest near Leicester, England. These subsequently turned out to be genuine Ediacaran fossils, but at the time Bonney and Hill dismissed them as inorganic.

The real recognition of these novel fossils had to wait until the late 1940s, when an Australian mining geologist, Reg Sprigg, was reassessing the economic value of some abandoned lead-silver mines in the Ediacaran Hills of the Flinders Range north of Adelaide, South Australia. Among the hillside outcrops of sandstone strata of the Rawnsley Quartzite, Sprigg found remarkably well-preserved impressions of some very organic-looking structures. There was no sign of any hard parts and the preservation was curious: the fossils seemed to form positive casts filled with sand. Although his palaeontological knowledge

Rev. Thomas George Bonney, 1833–1923, theologian (Canon of Manchester), petrologist and professor of geology at University College, London (from 1871), president of the Geological Society of London (1884).

――――――――――― • ―――――――――――

was not great, he was a widely experienced field geologist and knew that they were quite unlike any other fossils he had ever seen.

Over the next few years Sprigg published reports of his finds and suggested that they might be the remains of some kinds of jellyfish. Although he thought they were probably of early Cambrian age, he did also claim that they might be among the oldest fossil evidence for animal life. However, his reports were published in an Australian scientific journal that was not widely read outside of that country and it took some time before the palaeontological world began to sit up and take notice of what was a remarkable and very important find.

On the other side of the world, back in Charnwood Forest in April 1957, a schoolboy enthusiast by the name of Roger Mason rediscovered similar fossils to those dismissed as inorganic by Bonney and Hill. The low sandstone crags in this part of Leicestershire are ideal for clambering and climbing over. They were a favourite after-school haunt of Roger and his friends and on one of these excursions Roger's companion, knowing of his palaeontological interests, alerted him to some fossils on the rock surface.

Fortunately, Roger Mason told academic palaeontologist Trevor Ford of Leicester University of the discovery and showed him a paper rubbing he had made of the fossil. Ford was initially sceptical, but the clearly organic form reproduced by the rubbing persuaded him to take a look for himself. He was quickly convinced and in the following year published a description and illustrations of the fossils. One of the most striking of the new fossils was a strange little plume or feather-shaped frond that Ford called *Charnia masoni* after the location and Roger Mason. Most importantly, Ford could argue convincingly that the Charnwood fossils were late Precambrian in age rather than early Cambrian as the Australians thought. The Ediacaran 'bandwagon' slowly began to roll. Now, over 50 years later, there is an amazing amount of information about these strange fossils, but there is still a very real uncertainty about what kind of organisms they were.

One of the favourite early interpretations saw them as some kind of jellyfish, and indeed a number of them did have circular dish and blob shapes. But when palaeontologists tried to replicate the preservation of soft-bodied recent jellyfish in sand, they were singularly unsuccessful. It seemed that the Ediacarans must have had tougher body tissues than living jellyfish. Another approach was predicated by the evolutionary Darwinian expectation that the ancestors of the major groups of invertebrate sea creatures from jellyfish through molluscs and arthropods to echinoderms must be present in these latest Precambrian strata. Otherwise, where would all the Cambrian shelly fossils have come from? As a result, the various Ediacaran forms were at first shoe-horned into these groups and claimed to represent the soft-bodied ancestors of coelenterates (jellyfish, sea anemones), segmented worms, trilobite arthropods, sea urchins (echinoderms) and so on. The radical alternative explanation is that they were some kind of failed evolutionary experiment.

The last few decades have seen Ediacaran fossils turning up all over the world in latest Proterozoic strata dated at between 575 and 541 million years ago. Some forms are widespread, while others are endemic to a few nearby localities. Overall, the diversity has increased enormously with some 100 species now known. Apart from vastly increasing our knowledge about their diversity, this global distribution has revealed Ediacarans with less common modes of preservation, especially in fine-grained muddy sediments, such as seen in Newfoundland, Canada and in the White Sea region of Arctic Russia. Such occurrences have given new insights into their mode of life and biology.

The form of the Ediacarans varies from simple blobs, discs and sac shapes to ribbons and fronds up to 2 m in length. They are the first large creatures to have lived on Earth. Some of them lived within the seabed sediment, others could move slowly over the sediment surface like some sort of flatworm, and yet others were anchored in the sediment with leaf and ribbon-shaped, stiff but flexible fronds projecting up into the water in a manner reminiscent of living seapens (pennatulaceans). Many had strangely quilted bodies, some of which were filled with sand during life, while some were very like primitive sponges. But as yet there is no consensus on whether they form a mixture of known and unknown animal groups or whether they are all extinct 'aliens'. In that case, where did the Cambrian invertebrates come from?

Curiously, although Californian strata of late Proterozoic age are thought to extend through this time interval and the sediments are quite similar to those in which many Ediacarans have been found, none has yet been uncovered in the Californian strata. However, a few have been found not too far away over the border to the south in Mexico and somewhat further away in North Carolina. By far the most interesting Ediacarans of Laurentia are to be found in Newfoundland, a rocky island off the northeast coast that is a paradise for geologists.

Ediacarans, including *Charnia masoni*, were first found in southeastern Newfoundland in 1969. They occur within a 6-km-thick succession of late Proterozoic strata that record a depositional transition from a deep marine basin through shallow coastal to land-based alluvial deposits. The most abundant fossils were found at Mistaken Point in strata containing a volcanic ash that was radiometrically dated at around 565 million years old. Ediacarans continue to occur sporadically throughout another kilometre and half of strata below this.

The lowest and therefore oldest known Ediacarans still include *Charnia masoni* and another similar frond called *Charnia wardi*. This latter species is the biggest Ediacaran, growing from an anchorage in the sediment to nearly 2 m long. Numerous fronds of both species have been found lying parallel to one another, bent over and flattened onto the seabed by a submarine current before being covered by a volcanic ash deposit. Over a kilometre below the lowest-known Ediacarans some glacial diamictite deposits, around 595 million years old, are found interbedded with the predominantly marine deposits. If this date is correct, it indicates that these earliest Newfoundland Ediacarans are perhaps 580–570 million years old. As such, they are not only the biggest Ediacarans known but also the oldest by some 5 or 10 million years.

The Ediacarans seem to appear suddenly in late Proterozoic time, already significantly larger and more complex than any previous life form. In addition, they seem to appear 'fully fledged' within some 15 million years of a glaciation that is supposed to have shut down primary production in the oceans of the world. But is this the reality of the situation? Is it just that we have not yet found older Ediacarans nor the organisms from which they evolved? If this is true, then they will be even closer in age to the glaciation. If so, does this weaken the case for a catastrophic impact on life by the last 'snowball' event? Perhaps the Ediacarans evolved before the last glaciation? We just do not know yet, just as we do not really know what kind of organisms the Ediacarans represent. Despite all the uncertainties, one thing is sure: the glaciations were real and the evolution of the Ediacarans mark a critical stage in the story of life on Earth, which may be linked in some way to these major environmental changes.

This exploration of early Earth Time has been detailed and has taken us well beyond the confines of the Grand Canyon. If it is necessary to excuse such attention, I think it can easily be justified when we remember that the Precambrian does represent by far the greatest proportion of Earth Time. The rock strata laid down over the 4 billion years and more of early (Precambrian) Earth Time is one of the last great unexplored regions of the Earth's surface, apart perhaps from the deep oceans. The last few decades have seen remarkable advances in our understanding of the remote past and I guarantee that the next few decades will bring yet more surprises from Precambrian strata.

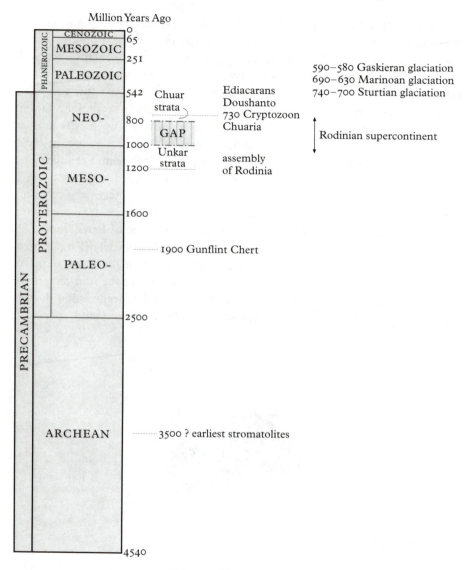

Archean to Neo-proterozoic.

12

The Cambrian arms race

The youngest strata of the Precambrian sequence in the Canyon are dramatic, often red-coloured coarse boulder conglomerates, breccias and alluvial sediments (called the Sixty-mile Formation). Among the jumble of boulders, some individual blocks are tens of metres in size and are comprised of huge chunks of strata from older parts of the succession. Evidently something dramatic went on in late Precambrian time when these rocks were being formed. Geologists who have studied these rocks in detail reckon that earthquakes must have frequently shaken the region as repeated fault movements uplifted landscapes a metre or so at a time over thousands of years. The landscape was broken up as fault cliffs rose up with steep and unstable slopes. Every now and again a cliff would collapse, with huge blocks crashing and sliding downslope. Slower but equally powerful changes were made as whole masses of rock debris, mobilised by frequent earth tremors, crept and slumped downslope over distances of kilometres.

The dating of these events is not well constrained, but it was around 700 million years ago. Since these inhospitable landscapes did not support any life at the time, there are no fossils to help us match deposits across the region or give them a relative age.

Above the Sixty-mile Formation lies a widespread sequence of marine sandstones (the Tapeats Sandstone) and shales (the Bright Angel Shale). In places, these do

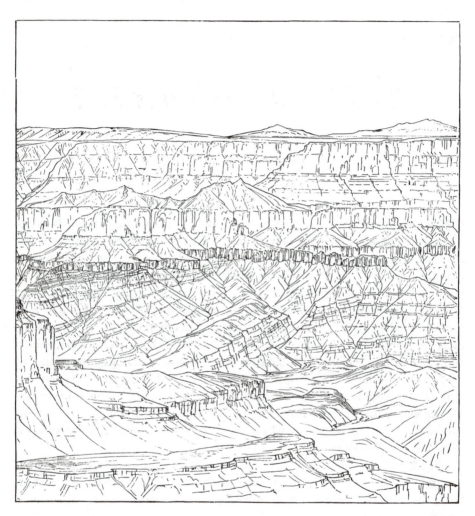

A drawing from a photograph illustrating the unconformity between the Cambrian age Tapeats sandstone and the underlying tilted Precambrian strata.

contain fossils that signify an early Cambrian age, around some 520 million years old. As we have seen, the timing of the beginning of Cambrian times is known now to be close to 542 million years ago. So there is a very large time gap in the Grand Canyon succession between the last 700-million-year-old Precambrian deposits to be preserved and the earliest Cambrian ones, which were laid down on top of them some 180 million years later. Why should this be and what was going on in the interval?

John Wesley Powell was struck by the way the strata in the bottom of the Canyon are tilted and truncated, as if planed off by some immense invisible force before having Palaeozoic strata 'spread over their upturned edges'. This striking feature is a magnificent example of what geologists call an angular unconformity. Powell was aware that such structures have great geological significance and he had a pretty good idea of what that significance was.

Over 80 years before Powell first clapped eyes on the Canyon, the sight of a similar rock formation at Siccar Point on the east coast of Scotland provided a kind of epiphany for the mathematician John Playfair. In 1788, the sight of these wave-swept rocks produced such an effect on Playfair and his geological guide James Hutton that Playfair wrote how 'the impression made will not easily be forgotten' with 'the palpable evidence presented to us, of one of the most extraordinary and important facts in the natural history of the earth'. What was it about these rocks that so astonished them?

The site is certainly attractive in a bleak sort of way on a wild stormy day, but by no stretch of the imagination does it compare with the Grand Canyon. And yet the influence of Siccar Point on our understanding of the Earth's history has arguably been just as great, if not more so. Playfair explains:

we felt ourselves necessarily carried back to the time when the schistus on which we stood was yet at the bottom of the sea, and when the sandstone before us was only beginning to be deposited ... from the waters of a superincumbent ocean. An epocha still more remote presented itself, when the most ancient of these rocks, instead of standing upright in vertical beds, lay in horizontal planes at the bottom of the sea, and was not yet disturbed by that immeasurable force which has burst asunder the solid pavement of the globe.

They were looking at an angular unconformity that stimulated Playfair to further reflect that 'the mind seemed to grow giddy by looking so far into the abyss of time'. It was Hutton's exploration and explanation of the rocks that generated these famous words. And it was Hutton who was instrumental in unshackling our view of Earth history from biblical constraints.

By the time Powell encountered the same phenomenon in the depths of the Canyon, the received wisdom of the time suggested that such an unconformity implied that the Precambrian strata were first folded by immense compressive tectonic pressures. The large-scale compression also elevated the rock strata to form landscapes that were subject to long-term weathering and erosion. Over many millions of years, the rocks were worn away and reduced to form new sedimentary debris. This in turn was carried away by wind and water and dumped in the encroaching ocean, which lay not too far away to the west. The hills and valleys of the landscape were gradually reduced to sea level and eventually the sea returned and lay down a new succession of marine deposits. However, we now know that there are important differences in the developing story.

Critically, the main tectonic event here was not compressive but extensional; that is, stretching of the crust on a regional scale that is linked to the break-up of the supercontinent of Rodinia between 750 and 550 million years ago. It was this stretching motion that led to extensive faulting, as most rocks are brittle and do not easily stretch; although it has to be said that rocks that have been heated within the Earth do become plastic enough to stretch. Some sediments that are still soft and have not been lithified into brittle rocks can also be stretched. By around 550 million years ago a new seaway was established between Laurentia and the ancestral Pacific Ocean, a seaway formed as global sea levels rose and flooded onto the deeply eroded landscapes of the Precambrian.

The original recognition of Cambrian Earth Time, as we have seen, had a troubled history in mid-nineteenth-century Britain, but by the time Walcott arrived in the Grand Canyon, the Cambrian System was firmly re-established and acknowledged as this first period of the Palaeozoic Era by geologists around the world.

Cambrian floods

The thickness of the sands (Tapeats Sandstone, 30–100 m) deposited by the ocean waters as they lapped and flooded eastwards onto the Laurentian continent was partly controlled by the residual Precambrian topography and also their relationship with the overlying muds of the Bright Angel Shale (82–137 m thick). Again, we encounter an important geological concept, that of a cross-time relationship known technically as 'diachronism' (see box). The two types of strata interfinger and the time boundaries cut through them. There is a problem in dating the strata because the basal sands only preserve what are known as 'trace fossils' – tracks, trails and burrows left in the sediment by mobile organisms, mostly various kinds of worms but also at times by trilobites, snails and other shelled creatures. It is generally (but not always) impossible to put a relative date to these, but they can be very useful in aiding our understanding of the depositional environments.

Luckily, the transitional strata with the overlying shales do contain some rare shells (body fossils) that establish a late Early Cambrian age (perhaps around 520 million years ago) for some of the sandstones and a mid-Cambrian age (perhaps around 510 million years ago) for others. Near the top of the lower Cambrian in California there is a famous sand deposit, known as the Zabriskie Quartzite, which is riddled with small vertical, sediment-filled fossil burrows, not unlike those found on modern intertidal beaches. However, the distinguishing feature of these burrows is that they are simple single vertical tubes (several centimetres long and between 0.5 and 0.25 mm in diameter) known as *Skolithos*. They occur almost worldwide at the base of the Cambrian and are generally regarded as the dwelling or resting burrows of some unknown suspension feeding organism. The varying age reinforces the view that these are diachronous facies. The other implication is that some of the lower sands are perhaps of early Cambrian age. However, to get an idea of what life was like at the beginning of Cambrian times we have to look elsewhere.

Diachronism

Basically, the concept of diachronism (meaning 'across time') is very simple and readily understandable, as it still potentially occurs in any sedimentary environment. For instance, marine shoreline deposits typically include pebbly beach conglomerates that pass seawards into contemporary intertidal sands and offshore muds. The offshore decrease in sediment size is directly related to the decreasing energy in the depositional environment from wave and surf power to quieter water below wave base (apart from storm-generated events). All these different deposits (sedimentary facies) can be laid down at the same time over a distance from beach to offshore of maybe no more than a kilometre.

When sea level is rising and flooding in over a landscape, the beach and other zones migrate both inland and overlap on top of one another through time as they move inland. The long-term net result is a basal layer of conglomerate extending inland, covered by a layer of sand and then mud. When that is turned into hardened rock strata, the geologist is confronted with a succession of three types of strata that may have taken hundreds of thousands, if not millions, of years to accumulate. It will not be immediately evident that the boundaries between the conglomerate, sandstones and mudstones are not time planes. The true time planes cut through all three deposits, which are thus diachronous facies. Resolving the time planes can be very difficult and require detailed examination of any fossils and other data.

The palaeontological evidence can be hard to come by and differentiate. Typically conglomerates do not preserve any fossils and intertidal beach sands are difficult environments for life. Because they are constantly being reworked by waves and tidal currents, such sands tend to be inhabited by organisms that live in the sand and can rebury themselves if disturbed, such as worms, crustaceans (shrimps and crabs) and active clams such as razor and wedge-shells. The offshore quieter muds are host to yet different organisms, so that each facies tends to have its characteristic biota. Historically, it took some time for palaeontologists to realise that this is what happens.

The arms race takes off in the Cambrian

There are just a few areas around the world that still preserve the passage from the latest Precambrian into Cambrian times with more or less continuous sedimentation of marine deposits. One of these is in Siberia, which is an ancient and discrete entity that only later became 'welded' onto Asia. In late Precambrian times Siberia was close to the equator and broke away from the Rodinian supercontinent as it fell apart. Because of its position in low latitudes, a succession of shallow- and warm-water carbonate deposits accumulated on the margins of Siberia. These now form cliffs of limestones exposed along the banks of the Siberian rivers, which flow into the Arctic Ocean. Luckily, the occurrence of some lavas in the lower part of the succession provides us with a very accurate date for the beginning of Cambrian times – 542 ± 1.0 million years ago.

For several decades, Russian geologists and palaeontologists have been trying to tell the rest of the world how wonderful and important these rocks are for understanding the beginning of the Cambrian story. But thanks to frigid relationships and lack of communication during the Cold War, it is only relatively recently that the Siberian rocks have become widely appreciated. Meticulous measurement of the strata and layer-by-layer collecting of their fossils have revealed a remarkable history of burgeoning life in the oceans.

The first sign of life is found in crinkly laminated limestones, similar in kind to stromatolitic mounds, and similarly constructed by intertidal successions of bacterial mats. A few meandering trails are preserved across the sediment surfaces. Clearly, by this time there were also free-moving, elongate worm-like organisms some tens of millimetres long in existence. For relatively large organisms like this to be capable of sinuous movement across a sediment surface in search of food, they have to be multicelled with differentiated tissues and perhaps specialised body organs. In other words, they have to be quite complex and sophisticated in their body organisation, more so than the Ediacarans found in more ancient strata. Recently, there have been a number of claims of sinuous trace fossils being found in more ancient strata, but their organic nature is disputed.

As the carbonates pass up into sands and then muds, so the fossils change. To begin with there are tiny, millimetre-sized, hollow cones, but increasing numbers of tiny shells, plates and other weird mineralised structures of different shapes appear over the next few tens of metres. Although they are just a millimetre or so in size, some are nevertheless recognisable as the shells of sea creatures that are still familiar today, such as spiral-shelled snails, bivalved lamp shells (brachiopods), plus a lot of others, such as the extinct archaeocyathans, which are only recognisable to fossil experts. The archaeocyathans formed some of the first reef structures in shallow tropical waters, had small conical porous shells and were probably related to the sponges.

These are the fossilised remains of increasingly complicated animals that have already separated into major biological groups (technically known as phyla – singular phylum) with very different bodily organisation. As they are already separate, the question arises of how long ago they split into these fundamentally different groupings.

Historically, the biological argument was based on an understanding of anatomy, embryology and development of the different organisms. Charles Darwin was already aware of the implications of this biological argument with respect to the fossil record when he was writing *The Origin of Species*. The presence of separate kinds of well-differentiated organisms appearing in the earliest Cambrian strata seems to require a long Precambrian evolutionary 'gestation' and ancestry, but where are the fossils to support such a conclusion?

Darwin had a much greater problem than we do today. As we have seen, when he was preparing his theory of evolution in the mid-nineteenth century, there were no known Precambrian fossils. Darwin had to produce some very good reasons for this absence and devoted two whole chapters of *The Origin* to detailing why the geological and fossil record could be excused for not preserving the critical evidence for late Precambrian life. His answer was that the rock record was riddled with 'holes', gaps in successions of strata that represented significant periods of Earth Time. If no strata were preserved during a particular epoch, there would be no fossils and thus no record of the animals and plants that lived during that interval. Darwin used a book metaphor to describe the situation. He characterised the testimony of the rocks as:

a history of the world imperfectly kept, and written in a changing dialect; of this history we possess the last volume alone, relating only to two or three countries. Of this volume, only here and there a short chapter has been preserved; and of each page only here and there a few lines.

Since there was good evidence to suggest that this was in fact the case for much of the geological record, Darwin felt able to claim:

> if my theory be true, it is indisputable that before the lowest Silurian stratum was deposited, long periods elapsed, as long as, or probably far longer than, the whole interval from the Silurian age to the present day; and that during these vast, yet quite unknown periods of time, the world swarmed with living creatures.

As we have seen, when Darwin was writing this, the hegemony of Murchison's Silurian 'empire' was in full swing. Sedgwick's Cambrian had been eclipsed as the oldest fossil-bearing strata and subsumed into the Silurian. Murchison claimed that life began in 'his' Silurian and such was his influence that Darwin and many other geologists happily went along with the idea. Darwin knew that his theory of evolution would not be acceptable to his old geological mentor. With Sedgwick already a potential opponent, matters could be no worse than they were.

Now that we have a fossil record extending back deep into Precambrian times and early Earth Time, there is not so much of a problem. But the question has not been completely resolved. Relatively complex multicellular organisms turn up well over a billion years ago, and we have the variety of relatively large Ediacaran creatures around 560 million years ago. So can the ancestors of complex animals such as the molluscan snails and arthropod trilobites be found among them? Although the scientists who first examined the Ediacarans tried 'shoehorning' them into these groups of living animals, the modern opinion is that this will not do. Neither the ancestors of the annelid worms, molluscs nor arthropods can be discerned with confidence among the soft-bodied Ediacarans, so where are they?

Modern genetic studies have raised the possibility that we can time the evolutionary separation of groups of organisms by measuring the genetic 'distance' between their living representatives. If we can obtain some measure of the rate of evolution in the groups and know the 'distance', then we can estimate when the original split (divergence time) occurred – providing that the rate of evolution did not change. This 'molecular clock' sounds very promising and a lot of work has been done to measure important evolutionary developments like when the early branches of the animal 'tree' first arose. The first estimates were getting on for a billion years ago, but after squeals of complaint from palaeontologists, the measures were refined and came down to a more sensible 750–700 million years ago. If this is in any way correct then it reinforces the problem with the fossil record.

Even if we allow that the first shelled creatures such as the 550-million-year-old *Cloudina* represent some complex invertebrate group such as the molluscs, there is still a gap of 150–200 million years in the late Proterozoic when we have little or no fossil record that can reasonably be related to the missing ancestors. The problem is compounded by the fact that they would almost certainly have been entirely soft bodied and therefore generally difficult to preserve, unless we can find some strata with exceptional states of preservation. There is some hope that further study of the 590–600-million-year-old Doushanto fossil embryos will reveal the presence of identifiable representatives of invertebrate groups such as the molluscs or annelids. The problem is that at early stages of cleavage and cell division one embryo cannot be distinguished from another in the fossil state. The alternative argument, followed by some palaeontologists, is that the molecular clock is wrong and that there really was a very early Cambrian 'explosion' of invertebrate life with very rapid rates of evolution and diversification.

Trace fossils provide some of the strongest supporting evidence for this argument. By their very nature, they record the activities of soft-bodied creatures and they are often well preserved in sandy deposits typical of shallow waters. A great deal of research has gone into the analysis of this very particular kind of fossil and its interpretation. Burrow form and pattern can now be quite securely related to the level of organisation of the animal that made it. For instance, the construction of upright U-shaped burrows that terminate at a seabed surface are characteristic of complex invertebrates such as polychaete worms.

Such burrows are present in some of the earliest Cambrian beach sands but not in older Proterozoic sands, suggesting that they did not evolve until the beginning of the Cambrian. Details of the fossil forms that appear successively within the earliest Cambrian strata also suggest that aspects of the evolutionary explosion are recorded. For instance, the trilobite arthropods do not appear in the oldest Cambrian layers but rather some 20 million years later, whereas small cap-like shells made of calcium phosphate that belong to a kind of lampshell (brachiopod) do occur quite early, after some 13 million years. A couple of million years later, the first shelled molluscs (for example clams and snails) appear. But our best view of the Cambrian explosion is seen far away from the Grand Canyon, in China and the Canadian Rockies.

New windows on Cambrian life

Walcott was always something of a workaholic and fortunately his wife did not seem to mind. Even their honeymoon involved geological fieldwork! Having risen to become Director of the US Geological Survey in 1894, Walcott was not only one of the most important geologists in America but one of the most important and influential scientists. His organisational and 'manhandling' skills, well honed and tempered by his years working for James Hall, led him to appointment as Secretary to the Smithsonian Institution in Washington DC from 1907 to 1927, one of the most powerful scientific organisations in the world. Although his first academic 'passion' was research, especially on Cambrian fossils, much of his time was diverted into administration and attending endless committees, so much so that his private journals are full of complaints that there were only 'odd moments spent with Cambrian brachiopods'. Nevertheless, he did manage to escape from time to time.

His geological work in the Canadian Rockies began in 1907 and involved serious hiking and riding over high passes. On August 31st, 1909 Walcott, his wife and his young son were making their way along the ridge connecting Mount Field and Wapta Mountain in British Columbia, when Walcott's trained eye spotted some fossils on the frost-shattered blocks of rock littering the mountain scree slopes. Although the muddy sediment and its fossil content was intensely flattened and slightly metamorphosed to a slaty condition, Walcott recognised that he was looking at Cambrian fossils with a curious mode of preservation that seemed quite promising.

His accidental discovery of what became known around the world as the Burgess Shale fauna opened a whole new window on life in Cambrian times. Over the next few years, Walcott returned again and again to the locality because its fossil novelties seemed inexhaustible. He excavated a small quarry into the mountainside so that he could methodically work his way through the most fossiliferous layers. In the process, he uncovered some 70,000 specimens, all of which were shipped back to the Smithsonian.

Despite his other duties, Walcott managed to describe over 100 new species from the Burgess Shale, but he recognised that it was only the tip of the iceberg. Surprisingly, the Burgess riches hidden away in the Smithsonian did not receive much further attention until the 1960s and then it was British trilobite enthusiast Harry Whittington who really began the renaissance in the study of the Burgess fossils. Whittington had been well placed at Harvard to research the Smithsonian fossils, but when he took up the famous Woodwardian

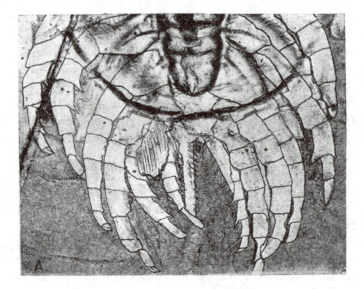

Detail of the tail of a Cambrian trilobite from the Burgess Shale showing preserved soft parts such as the typically arthropodal jointed pairs of legs and gills.

professorship in the University of Cambridge, England, he supervised a succession of research students to look in detail at the different fossil groups, how they lived and died, and what the original seabed environment was like. More recently, Canadian palaeontologists have been able to reclaim their fossil heritage and make their own investigations.

This remarkable locality with its ancient seabed muds and huge diversity of early life is now a World Heritage Site. The fossil fauna is dominated by arthropods (around 50 per cent of both species and biomass), all of which are extinct and few of which are familiar except for the trilobites. This diversity of arthropods shows well-developed ecological specialisations from burrowing to grazing seabed sediment to a variety of carnivores, including metre-sized anomalocarids that were top predators and active swimmers. It is now thought that all these animals were caught up in a submarine collapse of the seabed and

Although highly flattened the preservation of soft parts in the Burgess Shale fossils such as this trilobite provided new insights into the biology of these extinct arthropods.

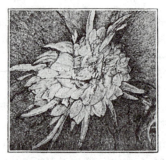

Wiwaxia, a strange mollusc-like organism from the Burgess Shale which has its upper surface covered with long flat blade-like plates, presumably for protection from predators.

Canadia, a bristly polychaete.

Aysheaia, a *Peripatus*-like lobopod.

Pikaia, a segmented chordate-like animal originally thought to be an annelid worm.

avalanche of mud into deeper water. When it finally came to rest, a wonderful sample of Cambrian life was trapped and entombed, all jumbled up within the mud. What was a catastrophe for the biota was a stroke of good luck for palaeontologists.

Sponges, echinoderms and worms each comprise about 10 per cent of the biomass and the remaining 20 per cent is made up of a variety of other organisms. Unlike the Ediacarans, most of the Burgess animals can be assigned to major living groups. Not so long ago, it was thought that many of the Burgess animals were quirky evolutionary 'one-offs' that became extinct without issue. Much of the problem arose from the severe flattening of the fossils, which has made interpretation of their original form extremely difficult. But now we have a much better understanding thanks to finds of similar fossils elsewhere, which also demonstrate that there was nothing unusual about the Burgess animals, life really was like that in mid-Cambrian times. Dating the strata was also a considerable problem, but now a relatively secure age of around 505 million years ago places it in mid-Cambrian times, some 37 million years into the period.

One of the most interesting and enigmatic of the Burgess shale animals was a tiny (4 cm long) elongate leaf-shaped creature called *Pikaia*, which has some resemblance to the living lancelet *Branchiostoma* (previously known as *Amphioxus*). For over a century zoologists have recognised that the lancelet is a primitive chordate with certain features in common with all backboned animals, such as a single main nerve cord running along its back, supported by a stiffening rod called a notochord and a series of paired muscles along the left and righthand side of its body – like a fish has. *Pikaia* seems also to preserve such features and was hailed as a possible ancestor to all backboned animals including ourselves, but it has recently been overshadowed by some exciting new Chinese finds.

Like the Burgess Shale on the margin of Laurentia, South China also lay within the tropics in early Cambrian times but on the other side of the world, and perhaps still clustered with the Gondwanan continents of Australia and India and so on. It was in 1984 that the amazing Chengjiang deposits were discovered by Chinese geologist Hou Xian-guang. The essential difference between the Chengjiang and Burgess strata is that the Chengjiang is preserved differently, with the result that the strata are easier to split open and many of the fossils are easier to see. Also the way the deposit and its fossils accumulated is quite different.

The Chengjiang muds were being laid down in the quiet coastal waters of a shallow sea. Periodically the oxygen levels in the waters were lowered to such an extent that many of the organisms died. At other times, it seems that influxes of freshwater from the land killed off the biota. The remains were quickly covered by more mud, which helped preserve fine details, including aspects of their soft tissues as also happened in the Burgess Shale. Importantly, the Chengjiang deposit is now known to be around 525 million years old. Being 20 million years older than the Burgess Shale, the evolution of the Chengjiang fossils thus predates those of the Burgess and adds significantly to our view of life in early Cambrian times.

Like the Burgess biota, there are some 100 so far known kinds of fossils and of these 60 per cent are arthropods, but here another 30 per cent are algae and bacteria, with the remaining 10 per cent belong to a diversity of other forms, from sponges to possible vertebrates. Most of the animals lived on and in the seabed. The burrowers included lampshells (lingulid brachopods that still have living relatives) with a long rootlike structure called a pedicle, which they used for burrowing and anchorage. In addition there were predatory priapulid worms. However, the top predators were the large anomalocarid arthropods similar to those found in the Burgess Shale. Most of the other arthropods, including trilobites, were active scavengers, some moving around on the seabed, some ploughing or scratching the surface sediment for tiny particles of food. Some were active swimming predators, but below the giant anomalocarids in the 'pecking' order. There were also a variety of other swimming and floating creatures including comb jellies (ctenophores), perhaps some jellyfish and probably vertebrates.

The free-swimming primitive vertebrates and vertebrate-like animals of Chengjiang are similar in size and general form to the Burgess Shale's *Pikaia*, but they are also more diverse and much more abundant and better preserved than *Pikaia*. Hundreds of specimens have been found for each of the two genera known. The *Myllokunmingia* specimens preserve traces of a single fin along the back, paired muscle blocks, paired filamentous gills and paired sensory structures in the head region, which are all primitive vertebrate characters, although there appear to be no hard skeletal structures.

The animal shares a number of characters with the living hagfish. *Yunnanozoon*, the other genus, is more problematic. It is not clear whether the body has paired muscle blocks or segments, there are structures that might be paired gonads, and the 'throat' region (pharynx) has arched filamentous structures that could be similar to the branchial arches seen in the living lancelet. Experts are still arguing over whether it is another primitive vertebrate, an even more primitive lancelet-like chordate or a representative of a related but completely extinct group.

With regard to our deepest ancestry, the most important aspect of these discoveries is that, by early Cambrian times, evolution had already advanced very close to the origin of the vertebrates. That this should be so makes the idea of the Cambrian 'explosion' even more remarkable or, alternatively, even more implausible. The argument is not yet resolved.

Yet another gap in the Canyon record

Modern analysis of the Cambrian strata in the Canyon indicates that there was a slowly subsiding continental shelf that received a wedge of sediments carried by rivers from eroding landscapes and dumped offshore. Beyond lay a widening ocean – the Paleo-Pacific, also known as the Panthalassic Ocean. These are all characteristics of what is known as a 'passive' or 'drifting' margin, where there are no major tectonic processes such as subduction of ocean floor rocks. There is good evidence that this passive margin existed on the western margin of Laurentia from early Cambrian times and persisted for at least 200 million years, until early Carboniferous times (around 359 million years ago) and perhaps for as long as 375 million years until the end of Palaeozoic times and the beginning of the Mesozoic Era and the Jurassic Period (around 199 million years ago).

During this 200-million-year interval of Palaeozoic Earth Time, Laurentia was periodically inundated by large-scale marine floods, which at times reached

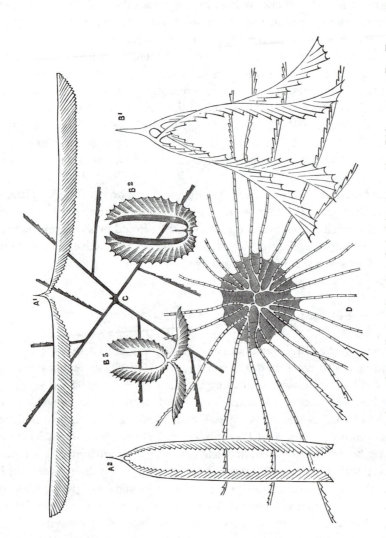

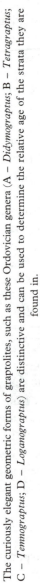

The curiously elegant geometric forms of graptolites, such as these Ordovician genera (A – *Didymograptus*; B – *Tetragraptus*; C – *Temnograptus*; D – *Loganograptus*) are distinctive and can be used to determine the relative age of the strata they are found in.

deep into the continent's interior. Each flood event lasted for tens to hundreds of millions of years and was terminated by major retreats of the seawaters (known as regressions to geologists). The receding waters exposed the recently deposited sediments to subaerial erosion and weathering, which in places removed much of what had been deposited and consequently erased that part of the stratigraphic record.

Although shallow seas invaded the southern margin of Laurentia from mid-Ordovician to late Silurian times (and are preserved today in and around New Mexico), the Grand Canyon region remained above sea level and does not preserve any record of sediments of any kind until late Devonian times. As we have seen, events on the opposite, southeastern and eastern margins of Laurentia resulted in a rich record of dramatically changing environments and life. The land was first invaded by animals and primitive plants during Ordovician times, although they were confined to freshwaters for a considerable period of time. The incredibly inhospitable nature of barren rocks and rock debris exposed to the atmosphere required a whole barrage of pre-adaptations before organisms could expose themselves on dry land.

The next marine transgression to leave any deposit in the Canyon's record began in early Devonian times and spread over much of the continent, eventually inundating the Canyon region. Renewed subsidence of the region meant that the seaways remained right through mid-Mississippian (lower Carboniferous) times, leaving a significant thickness of strata.

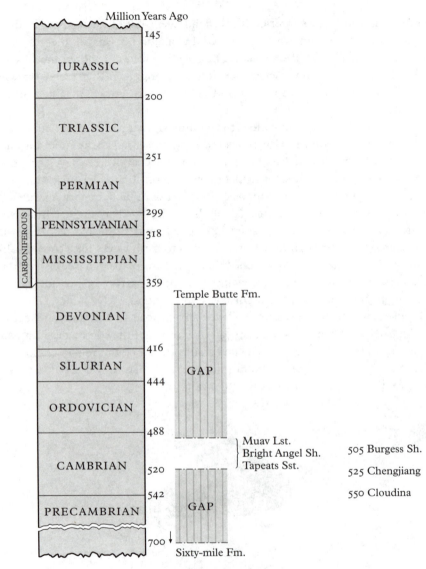

Million Years Ago

145

JURASSIC

200

TRIASSIC

251

PERMIAN

299

PENNSYLVANIAN

318

CARBONIFEROUS

MISSISSIPPIAN

359

DEVONIAN

Temple Butte Fm.

416

SILURIAN

GAP

444

ORDOVICIAN

488

Muav Lst.   505 Burgess Sh.
Bright Angel Sh.
Tapeats Sst.   525 Chengjiang

CAMBRIAN

520

550 Cloudina

542

PRECAMBRIAN

GAP

700

Sixty-mile Fm.

Precambrian to Devonian.

13

The Upper Palaeozoic – American style

DEVONIAN TO PERMIAN

Throughout much of the Canyon the mid and high parts of the rock walls are dominated by vertical red-stained cliffs, 150–250 m (500–800 ft) high. Powell commented:

> as it appears along the Grand Canyon it is always stained a brilliant red, for immediately over it there are thin seams of iron, and the storms have painted these limestones with pigments from above. Altogether this is the red-wall group. It is chiefly limestone. Let it be called the red wall limestone.

It subsequently became clear that the rock strata that Powell was describing actually span across more than 66 million years of Earth Time, from mid-Devonian to late Mississippian in age.

The less dramatic and often quite inconspicuous limestones that make up the Canyon's lower wall were differentiated as the Temple Butte Formation and have been dated as late Devonian in age (around 360 million years old). As we have seen so far, the rock record of the strata in the lower part of the Canyon has only taken us up into mid-Cambrian-age rocks (perhaps 510 or so million years old). Thus yet again we have another significant gap in the Canyon story, with some 150 million years missing between the Cambrian and late Devonian.

Neither the Ordovician nor succeeding Silurian periods of Earth Time are represented at all and the early Devonian is missing as well, so there must be another major unconformity. But there is no clear-cut or dramatic evidence of truncated strata, as we have seen before. Indeed, the unconformity can be very difficult to spot, even to a trained geologist. So what was going on?

In the western and central part of the Canyon, the Cambrian–Devonian gap is not at all obvious, with Cambrian and Devonian-age dolomitic limestones succeeding one another without an obvious break. However, in the eastern Canyon a trained eye can pick up the visual signs of what are known as channel fill deposits (up to 30 m deep and 120 m wide), cutting down into the strata below – telltale clues to a gap of some kind in the sequence of deposition. But the only way to measure the duration of such a gap is to find some fossils and these are few and far between. Back in the 1880s, Walcott's expertise as a field palaeontologist allowed him to find some – brachiopods, corals, snails and most usefully some fish remains. These latter are the fossilised, bony, scale-like skin plates of a curious and distinctly Devonian-age fish.

Called *Bothriolepis*, this was just one of many bizarre jawless (agnathan) fish that lived in the lakes and rivers of the vast Laurentian continent. They were some of the first fish to adapt to living in the freshwater rivers and lakes that traversed the otherwise barren landscapes of the continent's hot and arid interior. Laurentia straddled the equator at this time and although a variety of primitive land plants had evolved, they were all restricted to low-lying wetlands surrounding coastlines, rivers and lakes. Without soils, the landscapes were subject to intense weathering and erosion. But there was abundant life where there was water. Many of the jawless fish had thick, bony plates covering their bodies, forming a tough, leathery armour that helped protect them from large arthropod predators (such as the scorpion-like eurypterids) and life in the rough and tumble of fast-flowing waters. These armoured agnathans were so diverse and rapidly evolving that in some regions such as Baltic Russia their fossils can be used as age-related biozonal markers. By identifying particular species of armoured agnathans, it is possible to determine the exact part of Devonian Earth Time to which the strata containing them belong, at least to within a million or so years.

This mid 19th century reconstruction of Devonian Earth Time mixes marine fossils (molluscs and sea-lilies – bottom left) with a freshwater jawless fish (bottom right) and early primitive land plants (center right).

The presence of freshwater armoured agnathans here in shallow intertidal to subtidal carbonates, mixed with sea-living creatures such as brachiopods, shows that the agnathan remains were washed down by rivers and dumped in coastal sedimentary environments. So land was still not far away to the north and east, but in this part of the continent is not represented by any sedimentary equivalents of the Old Red Sandstone such as we have met before in Britain. In Greenland, however, river and lake sediments of late Devonian age contain some of the most interesting and important fossils in the history and evolution of backboned animals like us – the earliest-known four-legged animals.

Their initial discovery in the early decades of the twentieth century is a quite extraordinary story. In 1897 a Swedish engineer and balloonist called Salomon Andrée went missing while trying to reach the North Pole and an expedition was sent to Greenland to see if they could find any trace of him. They did not, but the party spotted some interesting-looking fossil bones on a bleak mountainside called Celsius Bjerg. Not until 1931 was Swedish geologist Gunnar Save-Soderburgh able to recover more samples. He handed them over to palaeontologist Erik Jarvik, who made a meticulous study of them, eventually published in 1952. *Ichthyostega* (meaning 'fish-roof') is a metre-long salamander or newt-like animal with a heavy, flat bony skull and four legs (known as a tetrapod). Jarvik portrayed it as the first animal capable of leaving the water and walking onto dry land, but he was only partly right. By the 1980s, Jenny Clack, a young Cambridge researcher, was reviewing the fossil evidence for the evolution of the first tetrapods. She had seen Jarvik's specimens and had some questions about his interpretation, but needed her own specimens as Jarvik was still working on them. As luck would have it, she discovered that some Cambridge geologist had collected fossils from the same area in Greenland and these turned out to be the remains of a closely related animal called *Acanthostega*. They were enough to warrant further collecting, which brought more specimens to light.

When eventually the tough sediment was cleared away from the bones, Clack and her coworkers Mike Coates and Per Ahlberg were amazed to find dramatic new evidence for the nature of the animals. *Acanthostega* did indeed have four limbs, but it also had gills and a flattened, fish-like tail, which meant that it was

Anders Erik Vilhelm Jarvik, 1907–98, Swedish palaeontologist and graduate of Uppsala, joined the Swedish Museum of Natural History (Naturhistoriska Riksmuseet) in 1934, becoming professor in 1960. He made pioneering and very detailed studies of extinct Palaeozoic fossil fish and early tetrapods.

---

unlikely that it ever ventured onto land. Instead, its limbs were an adaptation for survival in fast-flowing river waters and feeding on small arthropods and perhaps small fish. Also, the hands and feet did not have five fingers and toes, as Jarvik had claimed, but eight fingers and seven toes. Recently Jenny Clack and Per Ahlberg have described another new, closely related genus of tetrapod from Celsius Bjerg. The presence of at least three distinct animals living in the same environment at this time tells us that their ancestry must stretch back into the more distant past of middle or even early Devonian times.

Per Ahlberg later in 1991 found an even older tetrapod called *Elginopteron* in the Old Red Sandstones of northern Scotland and, in 2000, *Panderichthys* (meaning Pander's fish and named after Christian Pander, the nineteenth-century Russian palaeontologist), a Devonian lobe-finned fish of the kind from which these early tetrapods probably evolved. Just to make the story even more intriguing, fossil trackways have been found in Ireland and Australia, which show that there were tetrapods capable of moving across wet sediment beside the rivers and lakes of Devonian times. Unfortunately, no bones have yet been found associated with these trackways.

In recent decades the relative dating of these Devonian limestones has been aided by the discovery of marine microfossils known as conodonts (meaning 'cone teeth'). As we have seen (p. 177), these tiny, tooth-like fossils were originally discovered and correctly identified as belonging to some kind of extinct fish by Christian Pander. But for the following 120 years and more palaeontologists argued about what kind of organism they belonged to. The problem was that they were not found with any other 'fish-like' vertebrate remains such as backbones or scales. Nor did the so-called teeth seem to show any signs of wear, something that might reasonably be expected if they were indeed used for grasping, killing and cutting up prey.

Nevertheless, the widespread and common occurrence of conodonts in limestones of Palaeozoic age meant that a great deal of effort went into the study of their taxonomy and distribution in both time and space. It was realised that the conodonts occur as paired left and righthand elements and that there were a variety of forms from spiky cones to flat 'platform' elements that might belong to the same parent animal. Many different form-species were distinguished, based purely on morphological distinctions of individual paired elements. Some of these turned out to have restricted time ranges, which make them very useful for separating successive strata in the same way that ammonites and graptolites do.

Identification of conodonts from low levels in the Temple Butte limestones in Matkamiba Canyon indicates the presence of the *Polygnathus assymetricus* biozone, which is of late Givetian age. Givetian is the uppermost of two international stages recognised in the middle Devonian whose boundaries have been calculated from evidence elsewhere to range from 391.8 ± 2.7 million years to 385.3 ± 2.6 million years old. Thus the Givetian stage spans some 7 million years and we can reasonably date this occurrence of conodont fossils and the limestone strata containing them, with some considerable accuracy, at around 386 million years old. Late Frasnian conodonts, some 376 million years old, occur near the top of the Temple Butte limestones, showing that the whole formation was deposited over a period of about 10 million years. The ability to make such accurate estimates is the result of many years of research by numerous scientists around the world – conodont palaeontologists, biostratigraphers specialising in Devonian sediments, and specialists in radiometric dating.

The top of the Temple Butte strata and its junction with the overlying Redwall Limestone is marked by an irregular erosion surface, sometimes with a pebble conglomerate. This tells us that there was a temporary retreat of the seas, of sufficient duration to allow some weathering and erosion of the uppermost Temple Butte strata before the sea next flooded the land. What regional uplift there was must have been gentle, because there are no significant angular discordancies between the strata above and below the unconformity, but there was enough time for some locally prolonged weathering and erosion.

The Redwall Limestone

Powell was greatly impressed by the outcrop of the Redwall Limestone:

> sometimes this stands in two, three, or four Cyclopean steps – a mighty stairway. More often the red wall stands in a vertical cliff 1,600 feet high. It is the most conspicuous feature of the grand facade and imparts its chief characteristic. All below is but a foundation for it; all above but an entablature and sky-line of gable, tower, pinnacle, and spire ... broken into vast amphitheaters, often miles around, between great angular salients. The amphitheaters also are broken into great niches ... vast chambers and sometimes royal arches 500 or 1,000 feet in height.

Analysis of the limestone sediments shows that they were laid down in a widespread shallow continental shelf sea. The massive carbonate cliffs of the Redwall Limestone look as if they were laid down in one prolonged phase of offshore deposition on a gradually subsiding seafloor. However, detailed examination shows that even here there were two phases of deposition separated by a temporary withdrawal of the sea. Overall the carbonates were laid down over a large area and are preserved today over much of the Colorado Plateau and southern Rockies. But again, the seas began to withdraw at the beginning of late Mississippian times. The recently formed limestones were exposed to subaerial weathering, which lasted for some millions of years, sufficient for the development of karst landscapes.

As we will see, limestones can be chemically weathered by dissolution in slightly acidic rainwater. Deep fissure and cave systems channelled water into a west-flowing drainage system. Some caverns were enlarged to such an extent that they collapsed, creating surface hollows and narrow channels up to 120 m deep in which younger terrestrial and nearshore lagoonal sediments accumulated. Some of the east–west extending channels have been traced for up to 130 km (80 miles). The upper Mississippian strata formed from these sediments include terrestrial red soils and a variety of marine strata, known as the Surprise Canyon Formation.

A late 19th century reconstruction of a Mississippian (Lower Carboniferous) tropical seabed crams together a host of marine life from primitive sharks to sea-lilies, corals and various kinds of shellfish.

In places the lower limestones are rich in fossils, showing that the shallow seas were inhabited by an abundance and diversity of shellfish similar in kind to those found in the Carboniferous limestones of Europe, but belonging to different genera and species. Corals, calcareous algae, moss-animals (bryozoans) and sealilies (crinoids) grew attached to the seafloor and helped baffle the currents, providing shelter and less mobile surface sediments, making them more suitable for settlement and habitation by brachiopods, bivalves, snails, trilobites, ostracods and fish. Occasional stem fragments of clubmoss are found, showing that land was probably not far away. Tropical storms carried the floating plant fragments out to sea, where they eventually became waterlogged and sank to the seabed.

The more varied sediments that were laid down in the second phase of deposition (the Surprise Canyon Formation) contain an even richer and more diverse fossil biota, one of the best found in the Canyon's strata overall. These sediments infill the channels eroded into the underlying Redwall limestones and range from conglomerates through sands and silts to lime muds. Over 60 species of marine shellfish, similar to those of the Redwall Limestone, are known along with some shark teeth. Again, conodonts have been used to pin down the exact biostratigraphy. Besides the remains of sea creatures, the remains of land-derived plants are common in places, with numerous logs of clubmoss and seedfern, and some 12 species have been identified so far.

As we have seen, the record of fossil plants can be highly problematic because of their fragmentation before burial. Consequently, attempts to reconstruct what the original forests looked like is fraught with difficulty. Nevertheless, the North American forest gives us some remarkable insights where there is rare preservation of significant numbers of tree stumps and even trunks *in situ*, in other words 'in place' – where they lived. It is the wonderful rock record of Nova Scotia and New Brunswick that preserves the critical information.

The remains of Mississippian (Lower Carboniferous) fossil forests are exceedingly rare, but over 700 fossil trees are known in New Brunswick. Most are clubmosses (lycopsids of the *Protostigmaria-Lepidodendron* type), which grew in extremely dense stands on delta wetlands. Nevertheless, they were still occasionally swept by forest fires and flooded by seawater. The forest grew in clumps of relatively small trees with trunk diameters of 3–12 cm and heights of up to 12 m. Estimated densities of between 10,000 and 30,000 trees per hectare (1–3 trees per sq m) have been calculated, much higher than most modern forests because their canopies minimised light competition. Being Lower Carboniferous in age these were the precursors to the main Upper Carboniferous (Pennsylvanian) Coal Measure forests and are therefore of great importance in helping our understanding of how such forests developed.

Adolphe Brongniart's illustration of the headwall of a French opencast coalmine at Treuil, St Etienne, showing sediment filled casts of large tree trunks still in their original life position, growing out of a coal seam into the sandstone strata above.

The Coal Measure forests of Nova Scotia have been world famous since the middle decades of the nineteenth century, when they were visited by Charles Lyell and William Dawson. In Pennsylvanian times vast tracts of these peat-forming tropical rainforests stretched from Kentucky to the Urals in an almost continuous belt. The overall biomass of these coal measure forests was considerably greater than the earlier Mississippian-age ones. In Nova Scotia, shoreline exposures of the strata preserve sediment-filled casts of tree trunks of *Lepidodendron* and *Sigillaria* several metres high, although originally they stood up to 30 m high. In places there are hollow tree stumps burned out by wildfire. Lyell and Dawson found the first skeletal remains of land-living primitive reptile relatives, such as *Hylonomus*, within the stumps.

The American Carboniferous

When Walcott came to try to correlate these Canyon strata with those elsewhere in the continent and abroad, he and his fellow American geologists of the 1890s were confronted with an extensive and confusing proliferation of stratigraphic names. Different successions of strata were being recognised across the vast length and breadth of the continent. Questions frequently arose concerning how local and regional units might be correlated with those described by geologists elsewhere, especially with those of Europe where so much of Earth Time was first carved up into systems and periods. To try to reduce the confusion, the United States Geological Survey published a whole series of *Correlation Papers* in which these matters were discussed at length. When it came to the Carboniferous, Henry Shaler Williams proposed the name Mississippian for a series of strata that correlated with the lower Carboniferous (Mountain Limestone) of Europe. He described the American strata as predominantly composed of limestones lying above Devonian strata and below the coal measures. He chose an exposure of strata in the upper Mississippi River Valley as being typical of the series. Furthermore, he chose some Pennsylvanian coal-bearing strata as typical of his upper series and called it Pennsylvanian, making the two series subdivisions of the Carboniferous System, as recognised elsewhere.

Henry Shaler Williams, 1847–1918, Yale-trained palaeontologist, first worked in his family business (1872–9) then returned to palaeontology at Cornell (from 1879–92), then Yale, where he was Dana's successor (1892–1904) before finally returning to Cornell (1904–12). He proposed the names Mississippian and Pennsylvanian respectively for the lower and upper part of the Carboniferous System in America.

———————————— • ————————————

A decade later, T. C. Chamberlin and R. D. Salisbury raised the two series to system level in their popular and influential *Textbook of Geology*. They claimed that there was an unconformity separating the two series and sufficient difference in the kinds of strata found to warrant this higher-level distinction. A whole new generation of American geology students were weaned on this text and many of them joined the expanding body of professional geologists staffing the various state surveys and other geological organisations and commercial companies. The scheme had the added benefit of giving an American dimension to the stratigraphic subdivision of Earth Time, which was otherwise dominated by all these systems derived from European strata. By the 1930s most of the state surveys had adopted the scheme, but not until May 14th, 1953 did the national organisation, the United States Geological Survey, adopt the terms officially. The rest of the world still uses Conybeare and Phillips's 1822 modification as Carboniferous of D'Omalius d'Halloy's 1808 name Terrain Bituminifere.

However, there is now also an international agreement that this American division be formally recognised, the only problem being that the Pennsylvanian/

———————————— • ————————————

Thomas Chrowder Chamberlin, 1843–1928, classically educated at Beloit College, Wisconsin where he became professor of geology (1873–82), Wisconsin state geologist and chief of the glacial division (1876–1904), first professor of geology in Chicago (1892–1919) and co-author (with R. D. Salisbury) of the influential *Textbook of Geology*. President of the Geological Society of America (1894) and founded the *Journal of Geology* (1893). He supported the idea of multiple glaciations and a planetismal origin for the Earth.

Mississippian boundary does not exactly coincide with the boundary between the Mountain Limestones (Lower Carboniferous or Dinantian as it is also known) and Coal Measures (Upper Carboniferous or Silesian as it is also known) of Europe, but occurs within the lower part of the Silesian. The small print of the agreement has yet to be worked out.

The Canyon's brilliant red cliffs

A series of brilliant red and red-brown cliffs and steps rise for the best part of 1000 feet (330 m) above the Redwall Limestone. Altogether a variety of sandstones, limestones, muds, pebble beds and evaporites are known by geologists as the Supai Group and contain five separate recognisable formations. The formation is one of the basic units of geological mapping and the distinction of successive strata. It consists of a sequence of strata that have enough features in common to allow them to be mapped as a unit distinct from those above and below. The varying hardness of the separate rock types results in differential weathering to produce alternating cliffs of relatively hard sediment, such as sandstone and limestone, and steps of softer, more easily weathered rocks such as mudstone and evaporites. Their strong red colouration has provided the insoluble iron-based pigments that have so spectacularly stained the underlying Redwall Limestone.

We now know that there is yet another unconformity of some 15–20 million years duration separating the Supai strata from the Redwall below. Furthermore, the Supai's 50-million-year timespan from around 320–270 million years ago takes us from the uppermost part of Mississippian Earth Time up through the Pennsylvanian and across the border into Permian Earth Time. It is a chronological journey that also turns out to be full of holes – more gaps in the stratigraphic record. These reflect an increasingly unstable geological environment with fluctuating sea levels and constantly migrating coastlines, producing alternations of marine–intermediate–terrestrial environments of deposition. But there are no signs of the coal deposits that typify Henry Shaler Williams's type Pennsylvanian and the upper Carboniferous of Europe. Nor is there a clear boundary with Murchison's Permian. If Earth Time had been carved up here, the major systems and periods would have been very different.

The overall regional depositional slope seems to have been down from land in the east to a seaway in the west, with marine transgressions proceeding from west to east and the reverse for regressions. The increasing abundance of sandstones and decrease in limestones reflect the changing environments of deposition. It can be very difficult to determine exactly how some sandstones were originally laid down. The problem is that deposition on broad coastal sandflats can produce very similar structures as deposition in some desert situations. The general accepted interpretation is that many of the sands were laid down on a broad coastal plain with a hinterland to the east of arid and semi-arid landscapes. But recently some of the sandstones have been reinterpreted as true eolian sands laid down in desert conditions. As we shall see, there are younger strata a little higher in the Canyon that preserve a much more spectacular record of desert sands.

Although there are fossils in the Supai strata, especially in the seabed deposits, few of them are useful for accurate correlation and relative dating. The most common remains are trace fossils – marks left by any kind of past 'activity' by plant or animal, so they range from feeding marks to trackways and burrows. Fine-grained sandstones and mudstones can be particularly good substrates for preserving trace fossils. Indeed, much of the evidence for the kinds of animals that lived on land during Permian Earth Time comes from trace fossils preserved in desert dune sandstones, animals such as scorpions and millipedes. However, the best evidence is found in the higher and younger Coconino Sandstone. It is surprising how much information about the extinct life of the past can be recovered from trace fossils – once you know how to read the signs. The problem is that rarely are there associated fossil remains that identify the organism that made the trace. The fossils that provided the first clues to the relative age of the strata were marine lampshells (brachiopods) and unicelled fusilinids. Correlation with similar strata beyond the Canyon that contain typical Permian-age plants and conodonts seems to confirm the overall age diagnosis.

Desert sands

The sandstones of the Coconino Formation form one of the most conspicuous rock outcrops in the Canyon. In the central part of the Canyon the sandstones are up to 183 m (600 ft) thick and reach as much as 305 m (1000 ft) along the Mogollon Rim near Pine in Arizona, but they also thin down to less than 20 m (65 ft) in other parts of the Canyon. The difference is probably due to differential rates of subsidence of the basin of deposition.

The sandstones' most spectacular feature is the dune cross-bedding, which is clearly visible from a considerable distance. Great downward-curving concave sets of lines traverse the sandstones with slopes of up 30 degrees over vertical thicknesses of up to 20 m (66 ft). They are readily explicable as the forward-facing (downwind) slopes (the so-called foresets) of large-scale desert dunes. Many other types of sedimentary structures associated with desert conditions can be observed, ranging from small-scale ripple marks that covered the surface of the larger dunes right down to rainprints that record the occasional rainstorm. The orientation of many of these structures reflects the prevailing winds of the time.

Modern studies of the dynamics of sand movement and deposition in hot deserts has verified that there was a Sahara-like dune field extending across this region and as far north as Montana in early Permian times. The whole formation records the advance and passage of a major sand sea across the region, with prevailing winds from the north and a migration southwards. Its existence at this time verifies the palaeomagnetic evidence that places Laurentia on the equator at this time. And the fossil record of tracks and trails preserved in the sands provide evidence that it was, as expected for such a geographical position, a hot, dry desert.

Traces of desert life

Such sands very rarely preserve any body fossils of plants or animals, but that does not mean that there was no life in and around the desert. Instead, it

The lower strata illustrated here are part of the Coconino Sandstone and show the large-scale sand dune cross-bedding typical of this Permian age desert deposit.

reflects the difficulty of preserving their remains in such environments. Even if occasional body parts or bones are dessicated and buried, the porosity of the sands means that even after burial, percolating groundwater will destroy the remains, either making them unrecognisable or removing them altogether.

As we know from studies of modern deserts, it is surprising just how much life can survive in such extreme environments. Anywhere that water collects, however briefly, whether it is from dew or occasional storms, attracts and promotes life. Cooler night-time temperatures encourage nocturnal animals and cooler subsurface temperatures encourage animals that can burrow in the loose sand. What the Coconino Sandstone does preserve remarkably well are the traces of that desert life; the only problem is how to identify what organisms made them.

Modern experimental work has helped enormously with the interpretation of fossil traces. A range of actively mobile living animals, which provide appropriate analogues for the fossil ones, have been observed moving over different sediment substrates under varying conditions of temperature, humidity and slope. Even scorpions are affected by the surface temperature of the sand and modify the way they walk over the sand accordingly. One Coconino scorpion trace that preserves marks made by the tail is very similar in form to that made by a modern scorpion (*Centruroides*) when the temperature is around 15 degrees Celsius (60 degrees Fahrenheit). At higher temperatures, the tail is lifted clear of the hot sand and does not leave a trace.

The form of the trace is also greatly affected by the cohesiveness of the sediment, which in turn is controlled partly by composition but also by the presence of moisture. Clean, clear-cut prints are left by animals crossing damp sand. The sand does not have to be under water, but can have its surface moistened by dew, and even the delicate footprints of millipedes, isopods, spiders and scorpions can be preserved. The remarkable eight-'footed' spider prints are similar to those made by living desert-dwelling spiders such as tarantulas, wolf spiders or trapdoor spiders.

In addition, the prints of small primitive reptiles have also been found. The form and preservation of some of the latter indicate that they were climbing dune slopes made of loose sand. Experiments show that the slopes have to have angles less than 27 degrees to preserve the prints, otherwise avalanching by the loose sand completely destroys them. Some 10 different 'ichnogenera' have been described, with even more 'ichnospecies'. Because there are no skeletal remains associated with the tracks, they cannot be directly linked to known species based on skeletal remains, but nevertheless it is useful to try to distinguish between different kinds of traces, hence the use of ichno – meaning trace – genera and species. Some of the footprints clearly show signs of five toes on the hindlimbs and four on the forelimbs, indicating that the fifth is reduced in size or specialised in some way and held above the substrate.

One of the major problems of the Coconino is that of placing it in time. With no biostratigraphically useful fossils and no rocks that can be radiometrically dated, the detailed age is problematic, but it is bounded by known early-Permian-age strata. As we shall see, the overlying Toroweap strata have been assigned to the late Artinskian stage, around 278 million years old.

Changing environmental conditions mark the top of the Coconino and beginning of the deposits of the Toroweap Formation. Once again, the seas reinvaded the region from the west.

Near the top of the ladder

For the visitor to the Canyon looking out and down from the viewpoints, the top of the Canyon's layered pile of strata is marked by the 90–120 m (300–400 ft) high grey-stepped cliff of the Kaibab Formation limestones. Different sedimentary rocks with varying resistance to weathering and erosion produce the stepped profile. The cliff rises above a scrubby vegetated slope developed in the underlying Toroweap Formation. The uppermost Kaibab strata form the bedrock for much of the surrounding Kaibab and Coconino plateaux and are among the most accessible of the Canyon rocks from numerous trailheads. Since Jules Marcou first recorded their presence in 1856, geologists have studied the limestones and shales that make up the Toroweap and Kaibab strata in great detail. Late nineteenth-century geologists such as G. K. Gilbert and Walcott saw the Kaibab and Toroweap strata as forming a single unit called the Aubrey Limestone.

A great deal is now known about the original deposits and the environments in which they were laid down.

Although not striking or outstanding in its outcrop, the Toroweap Formation strata show the largest geological diversity of any of the Canyon's recognisable rock units. The rocks cover some 65,000 sq km (25,000 sq miles) of Arizona and their deposition marks the beginning of a marine incursion. The result is a complex succession of up to 150 m of strata formed from sands, lime-muds, evaporites (gypsum and dolomite) and red beds, which reflect shallow marine, tidal flat, sabkha and eolian sand-dune environments of deposition. The shoreline moved back and forth across the region, which is why the deposits now seen in the Canyon vary so much.

Fossils are most common in the limestone deposits of the open shallow seas, which supported a diversity of Permian seabed life, much as we have seen before. The preserved remains consist almost entirely of shelly hard parts of animals that lived sessile lives on the seabed and fed by filtering tiny organic particles from the surrounding seawater, such as lampshells (brachiopods), moss

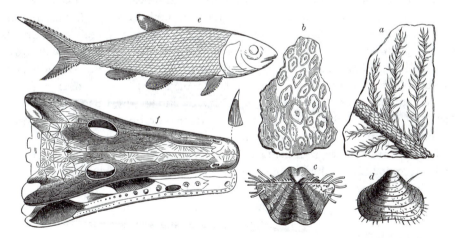

Life in Permian times included older Carboniferous-like organisms such as extinct plants (a and b), brachiopods (c and d), and crocodile-like labyrinthodont amphibians and a more modern Mesozoic-like fish (e).

animals (bryozoans), sealilies (crinoids) and occasional horn corals. Some trace fossils such as borings and burrows indicate that they were also of course many soft-bodied animals around that are otherwise not preserved.

The shallower-water, near-shore carbonates and evaporites were deposited in much more biologically stressful environments. Marked changes in temperature, salinity and oxygen content of the seawater can only be tolerated by really tough animals that are specially adapted to life in such conditions. There are not many of them, but there are a few snails and clams that can cope. They tend to be opportunistic species that can produce very high numbers of offspring. With a lack of competition from other organisms, they can flourish but are susceptible to mass kills when conditions suddenly deteriorate. Such local extinction events leave abundant shells in the sediment and these have a high fossilisation potential.

The Kaibab Formation forms a caprock up to 150 m (500 ft) thick to the Grand Canyon and, whether they realise it or not, it is the rock outcrop that most visitors first see. The Kaibab outcrop forms the surface of the Kaibab and Coconino plateaux into which the deepest parts of the Canyon are carved. This is also where most of the scenic viewpoints and trailheads are situated, so it is also where most visitors go. To the uninitiated it might seem surprising that the youngest rock strata of the Canyon are still predominantly seabed sediments over 265 million years old and belong to the Permian System of Palaeozoic Earth Time. We will return to the question of why are there no younger strata preserved here. Outcrops of Kaibab strata have been found over a region stretching eastwards from Las Vegas in Nevada and southwards from the Deep Creek Mountains in Utah, with some subsurface outcrops proven by drill holes in southern Utah where they contain oil.

To the untrained eye, sedimentary rocks like this can be difficult to understand and interpret because they have suffered many changes as they have developed from loose seabed deposits into hard sedimentary rocks. If we could have flown over the region 265 million years ago we would have seen low-lying land away to the northeast, with coastal sand-dune fields giving way seawards to a muddy shoreline with offshore sand bars and a shallow sea (between 10 and 100 m deep), floored with a mixture of sand and shell fragments and deeper water off to the west. At any one time all these different deposits (known as facies, see p. 298) were being laid down in different parts of the region. The problem for geologists is how to work out what deposits are of similar age, or how to draw timelines through the piles of sedimentary strata. It can be very difficult, depending on how fossiliferous the strata are and whether the fossils from one facies can be matched with those of another contemporary facies.

Life in these mid-Permian-age seas was remarkably varied and abundant, as can be seen from some highly fossiliferous strata within the Kaibab Formation. Again, a non-expert examining fossils in the rocks or beachcombing for shells here 265 million years ago would have had difficulty identifying the exact animal group to which many of the fossils belong. Indeed, some of them, such as the seamosses (bryozoans) and sealilies (crinoids) look a bit more like some curious kind of plant than animal. Since the 1930s, specialist palaeontologists have collected and described large numbers of fossils belonging to their own particular interests from these strata.

We know that the seabed was populated by 'meadows' of sponges, fan-shaped seamosses, corals and sealilies, which grew rooted in the sediment and attached to bits of shells. They helped secure the loose seabed sediment and baffled the water currents, providing shelter for a host of other animals. Tiny shelled unicells called forams and small shelled, shrimp-like ostracods occupied the top layer of the sediment, while various worms burrowed into it. Lying on the seabed were different kinds of shelled organisms, some of which look a bit like clams but are actually a different kind of animal called a lamp-shell (brachiopod), which still survives today but with nothing like its Permian numbers and diversity. Like clams, it made its living by sitting around filtering tiny bits of organic matter from the seawater.

A similar mode of existence was employed by other seabed life such as the more familiar-looking clams, snails and tusk shells (scaphopods). But then scurrying around among the more sedentary life were strange, king-crab-like creatures called trilobites, which are familiar to all fossil collectors but otherwise unknown even to many biologists. With their jointed limbs and hard exoskeletons, the trilobites were a group of marine arthropods not far from extinction.

Other active and mobile creatures included the squid-like nautiloid cephalopods, which carried a long, cone-shaped shell that aided swimming by providing buoyancy and streamlining. Locally they were abundant, swimming in fast-moving shoals for protection. The top predators were fish, which ranged from a variety of sharks to primitive bony fish whose teeth and scales accumulated in the sediment when they died. Strangest of all the swimming creatures were the tiny eel-shaped conodonts, which were very abundant and provided food for many of the smaller fish. But the conodonts were themselves carnivores and armed with a mouthful of spiky tooth-structures. They had no jaws and the whole tooth apparatus was extended to grasp the prey; as it was retracted the teeth closed and chopped the prey into pieces and delivered the bits into the gut.

The conodonts are another extinct group and generally all we find of them is their tiny teeth (about 1 mm long). Because conodonts were so abundant and their teeth are often well preserved and show lots of specific variation, their fossils are very useful in helping match contemporary strata regionally and even across oceans. Indeed, conodonts have been used to constrain the time range (estimated to be between 270.6 ± 0.7 and 268.0 ± 0.7 million years ago) of the Kaibab strata with recognition of Roadian-stage species.

All these Kaibab fossils are just the remains of organisms that can be preserved in sedimentary rocks. There were of course many other, entirely soft-bodied creatures that would have been present, ranging from jellyfish to worms and so on. The presence of numerous sponges and corals and the general abundance and variety of life suggest that these deposits were laid down in warm tropical waters. And many characteristics of the sediments support such an interpretation. There are evaporite minerals such as gypsum that only form where there are the high water temperatures and evaporation typical of the tropics. This interpretation is verified by independent geophysical evidence showing that during mid to late Permian times the American part of North America lay between the equator and 30 degrees North, some 10 degrees south of its present position.

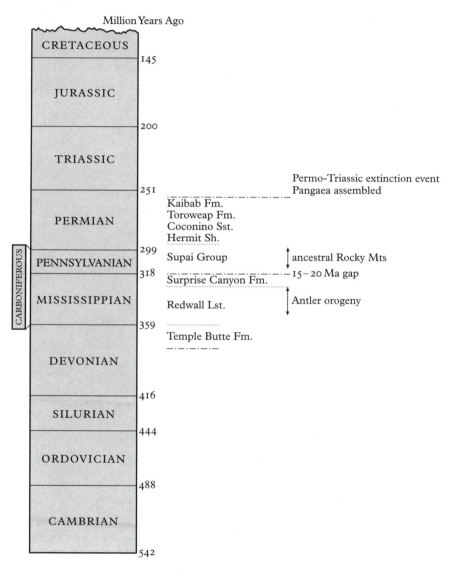

Million Years Ago

CRETACEOUS	
	145
JURASSIC	
	200
TRIASSIC	
	251
PERMIAN	
	299
PENNSYLVANIAN	
	318
MISSISSIPPIAN	
	359
DEVONIAN	
	416
SILURIAN	
	444
ORDOVICIAN	
	488
CAMBRIAN	
	542

CARBONIFEROUS

Permo-Triassic extinction event
Pangaea assembled

Kaibab Fm.
Toroweap Fm.
Coconino Sst.
Hermit Sh.

Supai Group   ancestral Rocky Mts

Surprise Canyon Fm. 15–20 Ma gap

Redwall Lst.   Antler orogeny

Temple Butte Fm.

Devonian to Permian.

14

The Missing Mesozoic and the Making of the Canyon

MIOCENE TO PLEISTOCENE

In the immediate Canyon area, the rock record stops in Permian times over 250 million years ago, although Earth Time has continued ever since. It is Permian-age rock strata that mostly form the present bedrock of the plateau landscape immediately surrounding the Canyon. We have climbed through about a mile's (1.6 km) thickness of Precambrian and Palaeozoic strata from the bottom of the chasm to the rim with its Permian-age strata. And although we come to an abrupt halt in our ascent through Earth Time, there is evidence to show that another mile's worth of Mesozoic and Cenozoic strata were originally laid down in the region, but have since been stripped away by the very processes that created the Colorado Plateau and reactivated an ancient river to cut the Grand Canyon.

The bad news for the aficionados of dinosaurs is that, as a result, the 'terrible lizards' and their relatives have been cut out of the story. Not only that, but the two major extinction events that frame the beginning and end of the Mesozoic Era have also been wiped off the record here. We cannot completely ignore these major episodes in Earth Time, but they really require another book or two to do them justice.

337

Mind the gap – the small matter of the Permo-Triassic extinction...

Neither Murchison nor any other mid-nineteenth-century geologists spotted any sign that the end of Permian times was marked by the biggest extinction event in the history of life. Perhaps as few as 10 per cent of species survived beyond the end of the Permian, so there really was a huge turnover in life forms. It is not as if Murchison and his contemporaries were not concerned about the changes in fossils from one group of strata to the next; they were. It was because it was the presence of such changes that they were using to justify distinct 'systems' of strata.

Part of the problem was that although the concept of catastrophic revolutions in the history of life was not new, such 'revolutions' had generally been dismissed as a reality by the 1830s. Catastrophism was associated with the outmoded ideas of the Diluvialists and the very idea of 'revolution' was too closely associated with the all too real and recent horrors of French Revolution for comfort. Since the dénouement of the Flood as a significant event in the history of life, gradualism, as propounded by Lyell, was the generally accepted historical process underpinning Earth processes and the rock record. Extinction of species and even whole groups of organisms such as the trilobites, graptolites or ammonites was accepted, but their loss was not connected to any specific large-scale catastrophic events.

Indeed, the most innovative idea about the history of life, the Darwin/Wallace theory of evolution, required slow, gradual progression and change rather than any dramatic collapses and subsequent 'explosions' of renewed life. Detailed records and descriptions of fossils and their distribution in time and space was only just beginning in the mid-nineteenth century. Nobody was in a position to review the overall state of the record yet, but it was not long before such overviews were possible.

Curiously, it was Darwin's attack, in *The Origin of Species*, on the imperfection of the fossil record that in 1860 prompted one of the first and most informative of the early overviews of the record by John Phillips. In 1860 Phillips was President of the Geological Society and had been invited to give the prestigious Rede

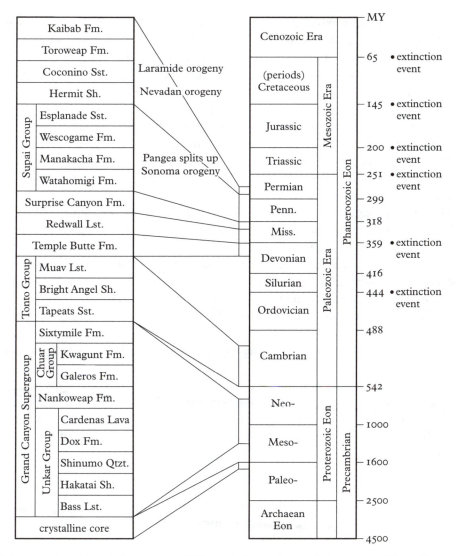

The succession of Grand Canyon strata (left) matched with the complete sequence of Earth Time to show the number and duration of the gaps in the Canyon record.

lecture at the University of Cambridge, entitled 'Life on Earth: Its Origin and Succession'. Phillips took the opportunity to review what was then known about the fossil record and how it could be viewed in the light of Darwin's expanded theory of evolution. He argued that Darwin had grossly overstated the imperfection of the record. More importantly, he thought the record good enough to test Darwin's claim that there had been extremely slow changes between species over the great length of geological time. Phillips said that despite the vastness of the geological timescale, there was no fossil evidence for Darwin's minute transitions. Furthermore, the growing body of data seemed to show that even the earliest fossils found in the rock record were representatives of complex organisms.

Phillips expanded his lecture into a short book, which was illustrated by a famous diagram of the changing diversity of life throughout geological time (see p. 204). Although he showed that life had an overall increase in diversity from the beginning of the Palaeozoic Era to the present, it had also suffered two very marked dips. These dramatic declines in diversity marked the end of the Palaeozoic and Mesozoic Eras and, of the two, the end-Palaeozoic collapse was the greatest. But Phillips was not using the diagram to argue that there had been extinction events; rather, he wanted to show that the history of life could be divided into three great eras that were of more general application than the proliferation of regional divisions of strata.

The Palaeozoic Era (meaning 'ancient life') had in fact been named by Sedgwick in 1838 and Phillips himself had coined the terms Mesozoic ('middle life') and Kainozoic ('recent life') back in 1840. The following year, Phillips justified his division in typically convoluted nineteenth-century prose as follows:

If we ask ... whether any dependence is certainly proved between the antiquity of the strata and the forms of plants and animal remains which they contain, we receive a satisfactory answer. There is proved to be a real and constant dependence of this nature, such that in every large region yet studied, where fossils occur in strata of very unequal geological age, there are whole groups of organic forms which occur only in the oldest strata, others which prevail only in the middle, and some which are confined to the upper deposits.

If instead of classifying the strata by mineral or chemical analogies, we resolve to employ the characters furnished by successive combinations of organic life which have appeared and vanished on the land and in the sea, we shall obtain an arrangement of remarkable simplicity, more precise in application, and less disagreeably harsh in definition, than that which has been so long followed. We shall have three great systems of organic life, characterizable and recognizable by the prevalence of particular species, genera, families, and even orders and classes of animals and plants, but yet exhibiting, clearly and unequivocally, those transitions from one system of life to another, which ought to occur in every natural sequence of affinities, dependent on and coincident with a continuous succession of physical changes, which affected the atmosphere, the land and the sea.

By 1840 enough was known about the fossil record for Phillips and other palaeontologists to realise that extinct fossil groups such as trilobites and graptolites were ancient life forms restricted to strata of the Palaeozoic Era. The middle life of the Mesozoic Era included distinctive 'saurians' – extinct reptiles such as ichthyosaurs, plesiosaurs, pterosaurs plus the puzzling giants *Iguanodon* and *Megalosaurus* that, in 1840, had yet to be characterised as dinosaurs. Finally, the Kainozoic Era (generally referred to as Cenozoic these days) of 'recent life' has its mammals, birds and flowering plants.

The renaissance of mass extinction as a significant mechanism for change in the history of life had to wait for the best part of 100 years. While the turnover in kinds of animals and plants was recognised, it was taken as a matter of fact without much exploration of why it had happened. It was the question of why the dinosaurs died out that finally prompted the renewed investigation of the possible causes for mass extinctions.

But the most puzzling mass extinction event is that marking the end of Permian times. Although it seems to be by far the most catastrophic extinction, no single cause has yet been identified, but a number of contributing factors are known. Plate movements had assembled the continents into a supercontinent known as Pangea, which stretched almost from pole to pole. Continental shelf seas were drastically reduced in area, as was the available ecospace for the main diversity of marine life that makes up the fossil record. For instance, the Palaeozoic corals were completely wiped out so that primary production and marine diversity built around reefs were devastated.

Many of the landscapes of the continental interior of Pangea were inhospitable environments for the still emerging land-living plants and animals. Continental climates produced vast areas of aridity with huge deserts inimicable to life. Plant communities on land were not wiped out overnight, but progressively collapsed until there was not much left except a few ferns and clubmosses. There were major episodes of volcanism with vast outpourings of plateau lavas, especially in Siberia, which could have caused climate change. But as yet no single 'smoking gun' has been identified, despite the expenditure of a lot of effort looking for one. There are many experts who would dearly like to find evidence for a large meteor or asteroid impact because it would help bolster the arguments about the other big extinction event that closed the Mesozoic Era, namely the end-Cretaceous impact event.

...and the end-Cretaceous extinction

Here there is no doubt that a large (11 km wide) rocky 'missile' from outer space blasted into an area now known as Chicxulub in the Yucatan region of Mexico around 65 million years ago and made a big hole, generated shockwaves, tsunami, wildfire and climate change. This event does indeed coincide with a major extinction event in which the dinosaurs and some of their relatives were wiped out, along with the ammonites and many other sea creatures. The big question asks how an impact event in one part of the world could have had such a global impact? There have been many other impacts in Earth Time, some of them just as big, but they have not apparently caused significant extinctions of life. And as far as we know, the biggest extinction event, that of the end Permian, cannot be linked to an impact, so was there something special about the end-Cretaceous event or was it perhaps just one ingredient in another multifactor catastrophe? The end Cretaceous was also marked by vast outpourings of plateau lavas, especially in the Deccan region of India, which again may have instigated climate change.

The whole problem of such extinction events is intriguing and important for our understanding of the history and evolution of life. Do not believe all you read about such events. Even experts who have devoted the best part of their working lives to the study of major extinctions are still trying to assess the details and put together workable scenarios. Take the question of wildfire after the Chicxulub impact. It is often taken for granted that thermal radiation was so great that global wildfire destroyed much of the land vegetation and therefore terrestrial primary production. The supporting evidence is supposed to be the widespread occurrence of fossil charcoal and soot in the appropriate sediments. However, recent re-examination by British palaeobotanists Margaret Collinson and Andrew Scott of the critical sections in North America, where the wildfire should have been at its worst, does not support this argument. The amount of charcoal is actually less than background levels found in adjacent Cretaceous strata and there are abundant fossil plant remains to be found in the boundary layers that show no sign of charring by wildfire.

Dinotimes

East of the Grand Canyon, the Navajo Reservation exposes spectacular Triassic-age strata that contain the trackways of large terrestrial vertebrates. To the southeast in New Mexico, over 1000 skeletons of small, bipedal dinosaurs were found buried within Triassic river sediments of the Chinle Formation by American palaeontologists George Whitaker and Edwin Colbert in 1947. The so-called Grand Staircase plateaux region of northern Arizona and southern Utah includes famous conserved landscapes such as Vermilion Cliffs, Zion National Park and Glen Canyon National Recreation Area. The strata of this region were originally laid down in depositional environments that fluctuated from wind-blown desert sands to the deposits of rivers, lakes and shallow seas. The 186-million-year-long record of Mesozoic life that they contain is remarkable.

It ranges widely from huge petrified trees and remains of many different kinds of dinosaurs to smaller, back-boned animals such as primitive mammals, as well as aquatic beasts from crocodiles to fish.

During the era whole new groups of reptiles (not just the dinosaurs but also the flying pterosaurs and marine reptiles such as the ichthyosaurs and plesiosaurs) evolved and became extinct. The mammals evolved, as did the birds along with the flowering plants. This varied saga of changing life and environments is also seen over a huge swathe of the North American continent, especially within the midwest and stretching right up through Canada to Alaska, forming a vast depositional basin that was periodically flooded by marine waters to form a midcontinental seaway that cut the continent in half. So what happened to this rock record of life and changing environments in the Canyon region? There is good evidence that the strata were originally deposited here, but what process could remove over a mile of rock? Clearly, there must have been regional vertical uplift, but to get an idea of what went on we have to have a closer look at the Colorado River itself.

The Colorado River

Unlike many of the world's important rivers, the Colorado has no significant link to the development of ancient human settlement or society. But of North American rivers, it is only exceeded by the Mississippi in length and is vital to some substantial modern settlements such as Los Angeles, Las Vegas and Phoenix, which through human engineering are 'watered' by the Colorado. These human habitations are located in inhospitable environments that could not naturally support their populations without the benefit of Colorado water. But the supply is finite and the development and control of the Colorado 'tap' have many interlinked social, political and technological problems.

Scientifically, the river and its role in the development of the Canyon have been of great importance in our understanding of the more general problem of how rivers and their valleys evolve. Early investigations in Europe were bedevilled with unappreciated complications resulting from the development of high-latitude landscapes under ice age conditions. Charles Darwin seriously overestimated the possible duration of part of the geological record because he was trying to make calculations based on data from small, postglacial rivers sited in glacially enlarged valleys. With the benefit of hindsight, we can see that he had the right approach but wrong choice of location from which to derive his data.

Early ideas

Since Darwin's days in the mid-nineteenth century, there have been two contrasting ideas about how river systems have developed. The most 'primitive' one is that there has been little overall change and that a river has a drainage pattern that is fairly fixed by the geological conditions since its initial development. Alternatively, a river system can be seen as a constantly changing entity that has evolved from certain ancestors and gives rise to descendent progeny whose 'appearance' will depend on changing factors such as climate and earth movements.

For several decades after the Powell expedition, the general view was that the Colorado must have been born with a course more or less similar to its present one. The extent of the uplift, downcutting and erosion was seen as so great that the whole system must be very ancient and probably began at the beginning of Tertiary times, some 60 or more million years ago, following the retreat of the great inland seas. By the 1930s, it had become clear that no evidence could be found for an ancient, early-Tertiary Colorado drainage system along the present pattern. Still constrained by the single ancestral model, the conclusion had to be that the whole system must instead have developed in late Tertiary times.

The whole basis of the interpretation was thrown into doubt in the late 1960s when it was recognised that there were early Tertiary drainage systems, but that they departed from the present pattern locally. Problematically, it seemed that the river had an early Tertiary age in its upper reaches but a late Tertiary age in its lower reaches. Furthermore, there was evidence that for at least part of its course the river had flowed in an opposite direction; that is, towards the northeast. All this new data and reassessment of old data led to the inevitable conclusion that the old model for the development of the drainage system was seriously flawed. It was replaced by the realisation that there were different phases in the history of development that could be radically different from one another. The antiquity of the upper reaches of the drainage system was accepted by most experts, but there were arguments about the lower reaches. Could it be possible that in late Tertiary (Pliocene times) a new stream that emptied into the Gulf of California could have eroded headwards and captured the ancestral Colorado somewhere in the area of the eastern Canyon today and only then begun to carve the gorge out?

Although there is still no complete consensus on the river's history, there is a general acceptance of the capture of an ancestral drainage pattern by a young river connected to the Gulf of California. This led to the carving out of the Grand Canyon in a matter of just a few million years, no more than five and probably less. The cross-section of a gorge has a much smaller area than that of most normal V-shaped river valleys and so there is a much smaller total volume of rock material to be removed from a gorge. Nevertheless, the excavation of this immense gorge was still a remarkable feat and testament to the extraordinary power of natural forces and processes.

Before the river's flow was regulated in the 1960s, the average daily discharge was close to 17,000 cubic feet per second (cfs), but rose to 77,500 cfs during annual floods and exceptionally as high as 300,000 cfs in rare flood events such as occurred in 1884. Such figures may not mean much, but as a comparative measure at a discharge of 32,000 cfs, 1000 tons of water are moving down the river channel every second. The average elephant weighs 5 tons, so it is like a 200-strong herd flitting past every second, or thirty 30-ton sauropod dinosaurs. The average daily load of sediment carried by the river exceeded 300 tons during normal flow, so imagine the volumes carried by major floods. Present control on the river has reduced sediment load to some 50 tons a day. The rapidity of the erosion was promoted by regional uplift of nearly 1 km (0.6 miles) since the formation of the lower river.

Over one 220-mile downstream stretch, the river drops about 540 m from 944 m (3116 ft) to 405 m (1336 ft). But water being a low-viscosity fluid,

The avalanching of rock debris fans from the canyon walls carries large boulders into the Colorado River where they form rock 'gardens' and rapids.

the 'slope' consists in detail of a series of steep and turbulent rapids separated by many relatively tranquil pools. The rapids often form where rock debris from the canyon slopes cascades down into the river, forming debris fans and constricting its flow. Such constrictions increase flow rate and speeds of up to 33 ft per second (10 m/s) have been measured at Hermit rapids. And kayaks have been filmed shooting the Crystal Rapids at similar speeds, i.e. 36 kph (22 mph).

The rock material in debris fans varies from small silt and sand particles up to metre-sized boulders. The maximum-sized debris moved by normal flow is cobble-sized, but when stream flow reaches 5000 cfs its power is sufficient to move boulders up to 2 m (7 ft) in diameter. So flood discharges such as the 92,000 cfs recorded in 1983 would have a considerably greater efficiency in moving boulders and everything smaller from debris fans. The boulders are moved out of the constricted flow of the rapids and build up downstream where the flow widens and slows down to form what are known as 'rock gardens'.

Normally the river carries fine grains of sediment and 'washes' these from the Canyon downstream. During annual floods larger, cobble-sized rock debris is moved inexorably towards the sea, and then there are those rare flood events that have a higher order of magnitude and can make radical changes to the river channel by moving even large boulders and flushing out huge volumes of finer sediment. It is only in recent decades that these different levels and frequencies of transport and removal of rock debris have been appreciated. Furthermore, it is likely that in the recent past high-magnitude floods were more frequent when rainfalls were higher. But the Colorado has also seen another, even more dramatic form of damming and flooding – that produced by volcanic eruptions.

Lava dams

On August 25th, 1869 John Wesley Powell wrote:

> we have no difficulty as we float along, and I am able to observe the wonderful phenomena connected with this flood of lava. The canyon was

doubtless filled to a height of 1,200 or 1,500 feet, perhaps by more than one flood. This would dam the water back; and in cutting through this great lava bed, a new channel has been formed, sometimes on one side, sometimes on the other ... As we float down we can see that it ran out into side canyons ... What a conflict of water and fire there must have been here! Just imagine a river of molten rock running down into a river of melted snow. What a seething and boiling of the waters; what clouds of steam rolled into the heavens! Thirty-five miles today. Hurrah!

Powell's geological expertise allowed him to realise the implications of what he was seeing. But even his geological experience fuelling his vivid imagination could not have extended to the totality of what happened. The quenching effect of molten lava streaming into cold water causes it to contract so rapidly that it explodes. These events would indeed have been remarkable sights; so much for any idea of long-term tranquility in the gorge. The other important aspect that Powell could not have conceived of is the timescale. Radiometric dating of the lava flows has emphasised their geological youthfulness, and the fact that they have all been breached by the Colorado's erosive power has provided independent measure of the extraordinary rapidity with which the Canyon has been excavated.

Today, anyone can view the spectacle from Toroweap, providing that they can interpret what they are seeing – one of the most dramatic displays of past volcanic activity in the whole continent. Over the last 1.5 million years some 150 lava flows have poured into the Canyon, with some flows being 200–300 m (600–900 ft) thick. Some originated on the Uinkaret Plateau and cascaded over the North Rim into Toroweap Valley and Whitmore Wash. Others flowed more directly into the Canyon, creating spectacular lava falls over the rim of the inner gorge into the river some 300 m (900 ft) below. Inevitably, as Powell realised, some of these flows filled the gorge, forming natural dams.

Research has shown that these dams were up to 600 m (2500 ft) high, fifteen times as high as Niagara Falls and with twice the volume of discharge. One of the lava dams extended for 135 km (84 miles) along the Canyon. Behind them the waters of the Colorado backed up to fill huge lakes, just like modern manmade reservoirs such as the Mead and Powell lakes. Some of the natural lava-dammed lakes were so big that they back-filled upstream beyond the upper reaches of the Canyon into Utah, beyond the upstream extent of today's Lake Powell. When ponding water eventually overtopped a dam forming a waterfall, a new gorge would be eroded through the lava, leaving remnants attached to the Canyon side walls.

There would have been a critical point when headward erosion cut through enough of the dam to weaken it sufficiently to cause a catastrophic collapse. Calculations – based on comparative measures from Niagara Falls, which has cut through 18 km (11 miles) of rock in 8000 years – suggest that most of the lava dams would have been destroyed within 20,000 years of their formation. At least 13 such lava dams, formed over the last million years, have been identified and their total life probably amounted to not much more than 250,000 years. Over this time the Colorado cut down through a total thickness of some 3390 m (11,300 ft) of hard basaltic lava.

The alternating filling and catastrophic emptying of lava-dammed lakes has also left a patchy record of high-level lake and river deposits, often stranded as terraces high on the Canyon sides above present water levels. Detailed study of these deposits helps reconstruct the development of the river system and preserves important records of early human activity. Lakeside 'beach' sediments contain remains of agriculture, stone buildings and even sometimes signs of more short-term camping by prehistoric people. Most of the archaeological artefacts are associated with the Anasazi people and date from 1000–1150 AD, although some are as much as 2800 years old. Modern river and poolside beaches are also used for camping by the thousands of rafters who ride the Colorado rapids these days.

A critical feature of river valley formation is the rate of retreat and enlargement of the valley sides. Weathering and erosion of the Canyon walls deposit debris in the valley bottom. The Colorado River then removes the rock debris so effectively and rapidly that the stream channel has little chance to be protected from further downcutting by the accumulation of sediment, as happens in the middle and downstream portions of most river systems. Where canyons such as the Grand Canyon form, and the river is still contained within a relatively narrow channel at the base of the gorge, the rate of downcutting is relatively high compared with the retreat of the valley sides. Again, measures obtained from dated lava flows and their erosion show that the erosive energy contained within the Grand Canyon system is so great that the Canyon walls are retreating at a rate of one or two miles per million years. The history of erosion and slope retreat in the Canyon has been set off and governed by tectonic uplift. Such movements, especially where they are related to major faults, are essentially episodic and occur in pulses. Individual fault movements, even on major faults, only amount to a matter of a metre or so at a time. However, they tend to occur in clusters, which can add up to tens of metres separated by quiet periods with little activity.

Shaking the ground

The rocks of the Grand Canyon are dislocated by a number of active major faults whose history of movement extends back over the last 4 million years. The underlying forces are those of stretching in a northeast–southwest direction, resulting in fracture of the brittle crustal rocks. The region is part of a seismically active belt (called the Intermountain Seismic Belt) that runs north–south through central Utah. Over the last 50 years there have been five earthquakes with a magnitude of 9.0 or more on the Richter scale. By comparison, the earthquake that devastated San Francisco in 1906 is estimated to have reached 8.3 on the Richter scale. Only the remoteness of the Canyon and the lack of large-scale human habitation have prevented such quakes from receiving much attention.

Deposits and their dating

The erosion and enlargement of the Canyon have involved the cutting down of the river channel and the recession of the Canyon walls. The rock debris derived from these processes would soon accumulate and choke the Canyon, were it not for a continuing removal of the debris by the river, which has flushed it downstream. As we have seen, research over the last few decades has shown that all these processes can be very complex and that the history of events is far from being the gradual one that was originally envisaged. On-going processes, such as river flow, can be directly observed and measured, as can regular and predictable events such as seasonal storms and associated floods.

However, unpredictable and rare events, such as avalanches and debris flows, are much harder to observe, especially in such a large area, much of which is very difficult to access. Debris flows, for instance, have rarely been observed, but their effects and deposits are important features in the Canyon, especially where they have formed large fan deposits. To uncover and reconstruct the history and development of the Canyon, scientists have had to investigate any signs of past processes recorded within the present topography and deposits of the Canyon. And then the scientists have to interpret their significance, not an easy task at the best of times but one that is made especially difficult when the age of the features is hard and sometimes impossible to discern. However, the problems of dating have spurred investigators to come up with a number of ingenious methods.

Modern understanding of the processes of surface weathering has allowed the development of various techniques for measuring the length of time over which rock debris and sediment on the debris fan surfaces has been exposed to the elements. Wind-blown sand can, over time, polish the exposed surface of boulders. Splitting, spalling and disintegration of boulders, especially those made of sandstone, also happen over time. But most useful is the solution of limestone boulder surfaces exposed on the fan surface.

Rainwater, which has been weakly acidified by atmospheric carbon dioxide to form carbonic acid, will over time slowly etch limestone. Experiments have shown that dissolution happens at a rate of about 2.6 mm per 1000 years. The oldest known are a few limestones on fan surfaces at the mouths of the Forster and Fossil Canyons and these have 17.4-mm-deep solution pits, which makes them around 4700 years old. By comparison, the youngest fan surfaces dated by this method are between 500 and 600 years old, having pits averaging 1.2 mm deep.

Interestingly, the average age difference between large debris fans within the Canyon is around 820 years (with a range of between 500 and 1200 years), which shows what rare events they are. In addition, analysis has shown that, over the last 4000 years of Holocene time, there were five separate phases when large-scale debris flows were particularly common; that is, around 800, 1500, 2100, 2900 and 4000 years BP. Some 75 per cent of dated fan surfaces are less than 2900 years old and it is likely that these phases coincided with increased rainfall, but it has yet to be proven.

This rarity of occurrence is why the chance of observing a large-scale debris flow happening is very low, and yet these are major events that have a considerable impact on the development of the Canyon. Despite their rarity, luckily a few debris flows have been observed and recorded.

Debris flows

The deposition of a layer of sand or gravel cannot be dated chronologically unless it contains some sort of 'clock' that actually recorded the act of deposition. The most common type of 'clocks' for such deposits are fossils which contain organic carbon that can be dated by radiocarbon methods. Unfortunately, such fossils tend to be very rare in these kinds of deposits. Analysis of pebble type can be very useful in telling us where they originated from. For instance, some pebbles of a distinctive igneous rock are known to have travelled all the way from sources in mountains of the Colorado Plateau and San Juan Mountains. And sometimes deposits have enough distinctive characters that allow them to be matched with similar deposits of known age elsewhere, in which case a similar age can be given, albeit cautiously.

The great 'watershed' in the recent development of the Colorado system and the Grand Canyon was the closure of the Glen Canyon Dam in 1963, which had a profound effect on the flow of the river. Flow was reduced drastically, as was the capacity of the river to carry away sediment and rock debris from the Canyon bottom. Sediment will gradually fill up the reservoir behind the dam, but it has an estimated 'shelf life' of 1200 years. Anyway, the Holocene history of the canyon can be sharply divided into pre- and post-dam phases.

From the human historical point of view, the most interesting of the pre-dam deposits are those that can be dated using 'fossils', including both natural and human artefacts. The oldest radiocarbon date of 4500 years BP comes from the upper Marble Canyon. Natural driftwood found in some of terrace deposits mostly belongs to the western honey mesquite tree (*Prosopis glandulosa* var. *torreyana*) and has no value for relative dating, but can be radiocarbon dated. Rare cottonwood fragments with tell-tale beaver cutmarks tend to be restricted to some older and higher terraces. The presence of milled driftwood cut by modern methods indicates younger deposits.

The oldest datable archaeological artefacts are ceramics from between 800 and 900 AD, technically known as Pueblo I. Younger, Pueblo II and early Pueblo III ceramics indicate that deposition of the older river deposits ended between 1150 and 1200 AD, which probably coincided with Anasazi people leaving the area. The causes of the alternating deposition and erosion are not fully understood, but probably relate to changes in climate. Ultimately, the water in the Colorado system is derived from melting snow up in the Rocky Mountains, while the sediment mainly comes from tributaries draining the Colorado Plateau. Consequently, any significant climate change in either area could have had an effect in the Canyon.

Interestingly, modern deposition within the last few decades that cannot be resolved by radiocarbon dating can sometimes be dated using tree-ring dates. Post-dam construction deposits can be dated by modern artefacts such as drink containers. Partly degraded plastic containers along with beer and soda-pop cans without disposable tabs generally date from the 1980s.

Overall, the history of the Colorado River system is a dramatic one that resembles a Darwinian evolutionary model based on natural selection (of drainage patterns) and survival of the fittest (streams), externally guided by tectonic movements rather than the genetic mutations of biology. There is competition between drainage systems with changes in gradient. Those with increased gradients are favoured, but there is also struggle for survival through headward erosion and capture. The result has been a succession of drainage

Ancient lake terrace deposits form beaches containing wood and artefacts up to 4000 years old reflecting their use by humans in the past.

patterns that change with time, so much so that the descendants bear little resemblance to their ancestors.

Grand Canyon late Pleistocene

Much of the recent geological history of the Grand Canyon region is cryptic – it is hidden away in the several caves that penetrate limestone strata throughout the Canyon. For many years now the caves have been prospected for their fossil remains, which provide us with vital clues about life in the Canyon over the last few tens of thousands of years (to around 50 ka) through the latter part of the Pleistocene ice ages. Fossils recovered from the caves tell us that previous inhabitants of the Canyon included condors, big cats, mountain goats, shrubox, camels, horse, wolves, packrats, ground squirrels, voles, lizards and snakes, not to mention hosts of bugs and of course the plants on which they all ultimately depended. Last but not least, humans have occupied some of the more accessible caves, leaving artefacts dating back some 4000 years. Within the overall story of the latter part of the ice ages in North America, the picture provided by the Canyon is a very particular one. However, we shall digress where necessary to get a wider view.

The Colorado River's deep incision into the strata underlying the region has exposed thick limestones that are entirely of pre-Mesozoic age. There are two main sequences of limestones separated by a 350-m-thick succession of clastic sedimentary rocks (sandstones, siltstones and shales). The uppermost and younger carbonate sequence is made up of some 225 m of mid-Permian-age limestones, dolomites and gypsum-rich evaporites comprising the Kaibab and Toroweap Formations. The lower and older carbonates descend from the massive Redwall Limestone of Mississippian age, through the Devonian Temple Butte Formation into thin-bedded and shaly carbonates of the Cambrian-age Muav Limestone.

Rocks of this kind, which are mostly made of limey (calcium carbonate) minerals, can be slowly dissolved even by slightly acidic rainwater to produce distinctive fretted-surface landforms known as karst (as we have seen, derived from the Slovenian word 'kras' meaning stone). Dissolution continues as water makes its way underground with the opening and enlargement of fissures, pipes and channels, which may eventually collapse to form caverns. The processes of karst formation have happened throughout Earth Time and there is an important distinction to be made between previous 'palaeokarst', which is no longer active, and present active karst development. There is evidence for both in the Canyon limestones.

Ancient 'palaeokarst' developed mostly during gaps in the deposition of sedimentary strata, when the region was elevated above sea level to form a terrestrial landscape open to the processes of weathering and erosion. I will mention these 'palaeokarst' phenomena here because many of them have been reactivated in more recent times.

One of the best-developed 'palaeokarst' surfaces lies at the top of the Redwall Limestone. During late Mississippian times (around 325 ma), North America and western Europe straddled the equator. High sea levels flooded vast areas of the continent with warm and shallow seas in which a huge diversity of marine life flourished. Then regional uplift brought some of these newly deposited and lithified carbonate sediments above sea level, to be exposed to an equatorial climate. The prevailing high temperatures and often torrential rainfall rapidly produced intense karstification of the landscape of the kind seen today in Tsingy de Bemaraha, a World Heritage Site in Madagascar.

Numerous surface solution hollows called dolines opened and fed water underground, where it flowed laterally and dissolved extensive interconnected cave networks in the limestones. Similar processes are at work today, forming karst landscapes in subtropical Florida. The sea returned in late Mississippian times and deposition continued through Pennsylvanian into Mesozoic times, burying the karst landscape beneath several hundred metres of sediment. This heavy loading caused collapse, infill and cementation of the ancient karst surface and its subsurface cavities.

Renewed uplift to the south of the Canyon in Triassic times around 230 ma reactivated the circulation of underground water through the Redwall Limestone. The result was that some of the old solution pipes, which had been blocked with limestone collapse debris, were opened up by solution and many of the open vertical pipes extended towards the surface. Some of these pipes are now over

700 m deep and extend through the remaining Palaeozoic strata and into younger Mesozoic deposits that existed at the time. Importantly, some of these pipes became mineralised with the deposition of minerals of economic value such as copper ores (Grandview pipe) and uranium ores (Hack Canyon and Orphan pipes).

Regional uplift continued through late Cretaceous and early Tertiary times when the incision of the Colorado River began. Inevitably, this substantial elevation of the landscapes and their groundwater rejuvenated underground flow and exhumation of ancient caves in the Redwall Limestone. As a result, some of these, such as the Horseshoe Mesa caves, have over 1000 m of open passageways. Continuing elevation of the regional crust and lowering of the water table has now left these caves high and dry some 1200 m above the present level of the Colorado River. Nevertheless, there are still active springs close to river level that drain groundwater from the Redwall Limestone. Massive and beautiful travertine deposits, such as Travertine Falls below the South Rim of the Canyon, have built up around the outflow of some springs (such as the Havasu and Blue springs).

Travertine is a rock made of calcium carbonate that is spring deposited. When carbonate-rich water is exposed to warm and dry air it loses carbon dioxide to the atmosphere and its calcium carbonate, previously dissolved by the water, is reprecipitated. The resulting deposits often form terraced cascades where the water has already been heated underground. World-famous examples are to be seen in the thermal springs, such as the Minerva Terrace in the Yellowstone National Park, Wyoming, and at Antalya and Pamukkale in western Turkey. The former comprise the largest freshwater carbonate deposits in the world and the latter's spectacular terraces were declared a World Heritage Site in 1988.

Rainwater falling on the plateau surrounding the Canyon drains vertically through solution conduits so that there are hardly any horizontal caves in the Permian-age Kaibab and Toroweap Formation carbonates and evaporites. Water then moves through the underlying Pennsylvanian-age Supai Group clastic strata into the lower Palaeozoic-age carbonates. The largest caves here have passageways that have been surveyed over distances of 2000 m. Roaring Spring Caves supply water for the tourist facilities at both the North and South Rims of the Grand Canyon National Park.

Most of the caves seen today within the Canyon lie within the upper part of the Redwall Limestone. They are ancient ones that have been re-excavated by modern processes, but only for a short distance back from the present cliff faces, and their original deeper recesses are still blocked.

Given the topography of the Canyon, many of the caves can only be accessed by small, agile animals such as rodents or those capable of flight such as birds (especially raptors) and bats, and of course specially equipped human climbers and cavers. Many caves have small entrances that restrict the size of their inhabitants, but a few are larger with walk-in entrances accessible to larger animals such as mountain goats and felids (cats) such as pumas and occasionally horses and camels. However, remains of the latter are usually restricted to single bones brought into caves by scavengers such as wolves and felids. Naturally occurring caves provide refuge from enemies and the elements and have been used by animals and humans ever since there were animals around to occupy them.

Fossil evidence from cave deposits tells us that even during the glacial maximum between 25 and 18 ka (thousands of years ago), the region was more wooded than it is today with a mixture of broad-leaved deciduous trees and conifers such as juniper, pine, ash and Rocky Mountain maple. Animals present ranged from woodland snakes to camels and Harrington's mountain goat. With improving climate and warmer and drier conditions, shrubs such as roses appeared, while currant (Ribes) and sumac (Rhus) disappear around 12 ka. An extinction of local large animals such as Harrington's mountain goat and the Shashta ground sloth occurred around 15 ka. This may reflect a final crash of their populations in the face of changes in the plant cover, which could no longer support viable populations of animals of this size. Analysis of sediment and faeces from packrat middens that contain plant pollen suggest that the vegetation changed in stages.

The most famous of the Canyon's caves was discovered in 1936 by Willis Evans, a National Park Service employee, at the base of the Muav Limestone about 200 m (700 feet) above the river. Rampart Cave, as it became known, turned out to be a real treasure trove of Pleistocene life, with exceptionally well-preserved remains of a variety of animals ranging from the desiccated guts, hair, dung, claws and bones of the Shasta ground sloth *Nothrotheriops shastense* to remains of camel, mountain goat and extinct horse. According to Evans, the remains still smelled quite fresh and 'fragrant' when they were excavated. Analysis of the sloth dung has given a wealth of information on the animal's diet and way of life. More than 72 kinds of plants have been identified from the pollen, seeds and other plant fragments in the dung, showing that the sloths were omnivorous browsers. By eating such a variety of plant material they avoided the build-up of toxins specific to any one plant. Even the remains of parasites have been preserved in the dung. Fossil evidence, mostly from caves, indicates that the Shasta ground sloth ranged from northern California right down into Mexico and for nearly 100,000 years from $111,900 \pm 13,000$ to $15,030 \pm 210$ years ago.

Most of the cave floor deposits seem to have virtually ceased accumulating around 20 ka, which is the age of the cave floor surfaces apart from a thin veneer of more recent pollen and dust. The development of the modern dry climate conditions has helped preserve the quality and quantity of cave deposits and their contained fossils.

The giant ground sloth

Up to 6 m (20 ft) long and weighing about 3 tons, the giant ground sloth was a remarkable beast that has its own special place in our history on a number of accounts. The surviving sloths are primitive placental mammals famous for their 'slothfulness' and common habit of hanging upside down from tree branches by their specially hooked claws. But they were not always like this.

The ground sloths first evolved in South America and took the opportunity to move into North America when the two continents were first connected by the Panamanian 'land bridge' in late Miocene times, around 9 million years ago. Another wave of sloths made the trip north in late Pliocene times (about 2.4 million years ago). They were an important member of the extraordinary two-way exchange of organisms, both plants and animals, which must have passed one another on this remarkable intercontinental 'freeway'. Sloths evolved into several groups and numerous species (13 in North America), but the last died out at the end of the last glacial around 11,500 years ago.

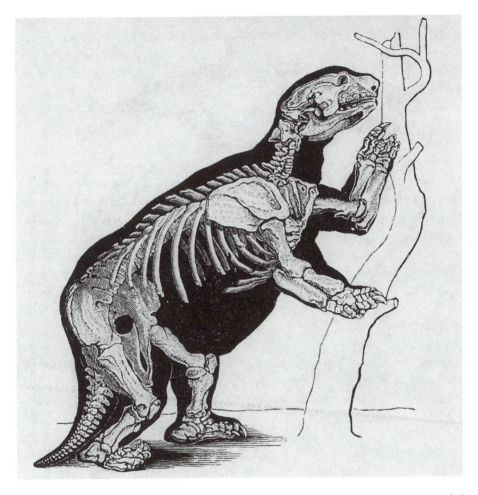

Giant ground sloths such as *Mylodon* were amongst the largest mammals in the Americas, now their much smaller living descendents are confined to South America.

There was a two-way traffic of giant sloths between South and North America, this is a reconstruction of the giant Shasta sloth whose remains were found in a canyon cave in the 1930s.

The fossil record of ground sloths in North America is largely confined to the deposits of various kinds of natural cavities in limestone landscapes such as caves, sink holes and fissure fills. The bulk of American limestone solution features are found in Florida, northern California and in a belt from Missouri east through Kentucky and Tennessee to Maryland, with a scattering across the southern states from Arizona to Texas. Of these, caves are the most important because sometimes the cave environment has remained incredibly stable and provides excellent cool, dry and dark conditions for the preservation of ancient biological materials. From the abundance of the remains of certain kinds of sloths in caves, it seems that some of them must have used the caves as dens. Consequently, even soft tissues such as bits of skin, nails and tendons and dung have been preserved in caves.

The discovery of fossil sloths in the Americas dates back to the eighteenth century. One of the many interests of that great American polymathic hero Thomas Jefferson was the investigation of the life of the past. In 1799 he wrote:

> It is well known that the substratum of the country beyond the Blue Ridge is limestone, abounding with large caverns ... In digging the floor of these caves ... in the county of Greenbriar, the labourers at the depth of two or three feet, came to some bones, the size and form of which bespoke an animal unknown to them.

Those West Virginian bones were later described as belonging to one of the sloth species that frequented caves, namely *Megalonyx jeffersoni*, which has the longest history of all the sloths in North America, surviving from 9 ma to late Pleistocene times around 14 ka. The Shashta ground sloth (*Nothrotheriops*

Thomas Jefferson, 1743–1826, trained and practised as a barrister, joined the revolutionary party and drafted the Declaration of Independence (1776), sent to France with Franklin (1784), appointed secretary of state by Washington (1789), third President of America (1801) when the slave trade was prohibited, sponsored Lewis and Clark, retired 1809 and helped found the University of Virginia (1825).

shashti) encountered earlier is one of the commonest sloths to be fossilised, frequently occurring in cave deposits. Other sloths were adapted to a variety of environments, including arid deserts.

The first discovery of giant ground sloth bones occurred in eighteenth-century Paraguay. The bones from a complete skeleton were reassembled and an engraving of the rhinoceros-sized animal found its way via Madrid in Spain to Paris and 'landed' on the desk of Georges Cuvier, anatomist *extraordinaire*. From the engraving Cuvier was able to make a detailed analysis and comparison with the skeletal remains of the humbler and much smaller surviving tree sloth that still inhabits south Central and the northern part of South America. By using his skills as a comparative anatomist, Cuvier demonstrated similarities (correlation of parts) between the characteristic skull, jaws and clawed limbs of the fossil and extant sloths to show that they were closely related. But also in this pioneering use of the technique for the analysis of the remains of extinct creatures, he concluded that the rhino-sized fossil, which he named *Megatherium* (meaning 'huge beast'), must have had a radically different life style from the tree sloth.

In addition, Cuvier used the fossil ground sloth, along with the mammoth and mastodon, as the first good examples that extinction had taken place. He argued that the Earth's surviving menagerie of large, land-living animals were well enough known to assume that these grand beasts had vanished. Thomas Jefferson was not so sure. He had long been interested in fossils, especially those of the mammoth and mastodon. Although remains of these extinct elephant relatives are not preserved within the Canyon, the eighteenth-century discovery of their remains in North America was of considerable significance in the history of our knowledge of past life and its interpretation.

'Elephants' in America

Bones of elephant-like animals were first discovered in the Ohio Valley in 1739 by a French-Canadian colonist Baron Charles de Longueuil, who was also a major in the army of Louisiana. De Longueuil was dispatched to assist

Jean-Baptiste Le Moyne de Bienville, governor of New Orleans, attack the Chicksaw Indians. The remains of three elephant-like animals were found in a swamp beside the Ohio river, near what is Louisville today. Longueuil retrieved a tusk, a leg bone (femur) and some molar teeth. When the campaign was over in 1740 he sent the bones to Paris, where they became the subject of much scientific speculation. One of the teeth was first described by Jean Guettard, a Swiss geologist, in 1752. In a paper to the French Académie des Sciences that was accompanied by the first attempt at a geological map of America, Guettard asked, 'What animal does it come from? Does it resemble fossil teeth of that size which have been found in various parts of Europe?' At the time he had to admit that 'those are two points on which I was unable to shed any light'.

Jean Etienne Guettard, 1715–86, Swiss geologist who studied medicine in Paris and was keeper of natural history collections for the Duke of Orléans and published a mineralogical map of France and England.

But 10 years later in 1762, a young French anatomist, Louis Daubenton, compared the remains with those of an elephant and a Siberian mammoth. He claimed that the femur and tusks, although of different sizes, were otherwise so similar that they belonged to the same species, some variety of elephant like the mammoth. Daubenton, like most naturalists of his time, believed that species were fixed entities, that there was no such thing as extinction, and that any variation was no more than differences of breed or race. Consequently, the marked differences of the molar teeth from those of elephants could only mean that they belonged to some other species. Since they bore some resemblance to hippopotamus teeth, he concluded that the remains of two quite different animals had been mixed together.

New discoveries at Big Bone Lick in what is now Boone County, Kentucky, southwest of Covington (near Cincinnati), soon resurrected the argument over what subsequently became recognised as a distinct species, *Mammut americanum*, the American mastodon. From the 1750s, large numbers of bones were recovered from marshy ground surrounding a salty spring beside the river in the upper Ohio valley. We now know that many animals, attracted to the site by the salt lick, became mired in the marsh and perished there. Over subsequent decades bones collected from the site were dispersed all over the place, including some that, in 1767, reached London. Others were excavated from Big Bone Lick by William Croghan, a Dublin-born Irish protestant whose family had settled in Pennsylvania in 1741.

William Croghan, 1770–1830, Dublin-born Irish protestant trader whose family emigrated to America and settled in Pennsylvania in 1741. He collected fossils as a hobby, especially from Big Bone Lick in Ohio, and communicated with Franklin about them.

From the size and shape of the bones and tusks, Croghan concluded that 'they are the bones of elephants'. After many adventures, which included being held captive by American Indians, Croghan arrived in New York with his precious bones. From there he sent specimens to London, both to the Scots physician and pioneer of comparative anatomy William Hunter and to another American polymath who combined politics and science and was living in London at the time, Benjamin Franklin. From his study of the bones and teeth, Hunter argued that they did indeed belong to a single species but a very unusual one – a carnivorous elephant. Furthermore, wrote Hunter, 'though we may as philosophers regret it, as men we cannot but thank heaven that the whole generation is probably extinct'.

A friend of Franklin's, the English naturalist Peter Collinson, had also studied Croghan's specimens and reported his thoughts about them to the Royal

---

William Hunter, 1718–83, Scots physician to Queen Charlotte, pioneer of comparative anatomy and collector of natural history whose specimens were acquired by Glasgow University and form the basis of the Hunterian Museum there. Brother of John Hunter, also a physician and collector.

Benjamin Franklin, 1706–90, American polymath and statesman, apprenticed to his brother as a printer, then journalist and publisher, appointed postmaster of Philadelphia (1737), began experiments on electricity (1746), elected to the Assembly, sent to England as diplomat (1757–75), to Paris in 1776 to seek assistance against the British, and on Independence was made American ambassador (1783–5), returned to be President of the state of Philadelphia.

———— • ————

Society in 1767. Collinson also thought that the remains were those of a single kind of unknown animal related to the elephants, because the molars with protuberances were always found with the tusks and other elephant-like bones. However, the detailed anatomy of the molars suggested to him that they belonged to a plant eater.

To begin with, Franklin agreed with Hunter's diagnosis and added that since elephants 'now inhabit naturally only hot countries where there is no winter', how could such animals inhabit the Ohio valley and Siberia? Apparently, concluded Franklin, 'the earth had anciently been in another position, and climates differently placed from what they are at present'. The following year, 1768, Franklin, who was an acute observer, reconsidered the subject and came around to Collinson's line of thought.

it appears to me that animals capable of carrying such large heavy tusks must themselves be large creatures, too bulky to have the activity necessary for pursuing and taking prey

Furthermore, the knob-like protuberances on the molar surfaces 'might be useful to grind the small branches of trees, as to chew flesh'.

———— • ————

Georges-Louis Leclerc, Comte de Buffon, 1707–88, French son of a wealthy lawyer and also studied law, but devoted himself to science. Director of the Jardin du Roi (1739) and author of a 44-volume *Natural History* (1749–67), made Comte de Buffon by Louis XV.

The most famous naturalist of the time was the French aristocrat Georges-Louis Leclerc de Buffon and Collinson submitted his conclusions concerning the Ohio animal to him in 1767 as a series of questions or problems. The tusks are elephant like but the teeth more resemble those of the hippopotamus. If they did belong to a single animal, then it was clear that animal was very different from any that were living and was therefore 'lost'. There are no elephants living in America and anyway they only lived in hot countries such as India and Africa. How could such a paradox be explained?

Buffon gave his answers and explained his reasoning in *Les Epoques de la Nature*, published in 1778. He reverted to the idea that the remains belonged to

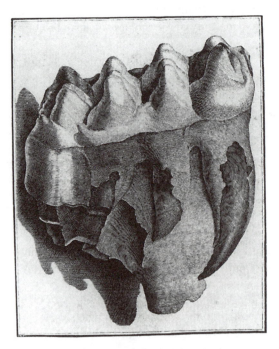

The huge fossil cheek teeth found in Ohio in the 18th century puzzled naturalists such as Buffon because they have a bumpy 'mammilated' surface typical of a hippo and yet were found associated with elephant-like tusks.

both elephant- and hippo-related animals. Indeed, he refused to accept the common co-occurrence of the different skeletal remains and thought that he could detect the presence of three different species! But more important was his consideration of the problem of their occurrence in countries with severe winters and the question of their extinction. Although he was 77 years old when he wrote *Les Epoques de la Nature*, it was a monumental work and perhaps Buffon's most enduring scientific legacy. In it he framed the whole of Earth history and performed experiments from which he calculated its age as 75,000 years. Buffon divided his version of Earth Time into seven epochs, within his concept of a slowly cooling Earth to which we will return (see p. 401).

For Buffon the presence of elephant remains in high latitudes such as Siberia was important supporting evidence. He argued that during the fifth episode of the Earth's cooling, in a chapter entitled 'When Elephants and Other Southern Animals Lived in Northern Lands', high regions became habitable first and were occupied by life that could tolerate the heat. But as these regions cooled further, the animals were forced to migrate to lower latitudes such as America and Europe and then on further to the tropics. Finally, in the seventh epoch humankind appeared. Buffon also argued that the Ohio animal was extinct, having perished as a victim of climate change associated with the cooling of the Earth.

Although in modern terms Buffon was wrong in many of his conclusions, his line of reasoning presented an important breakthrough in how naturalists came to view the Earth and its history. His eminence and influence were such that he could 'afford' to distance himself from religious dogma. He argued that we could 'compare nature with herself and work back from her present, known state, to several epochs of a more ancient state'. His 'actualistic' approach avoided divine intervention and miracles. It was to become a guiding principle of modern science and of particular importance within the earth sciences.

Buffon's epochs of nature

To begin with the Earth was an incandescent mass whose elements hardened into what Buffon called a 'vitriscible' rocky state as it cooled. There was a general flood, which on retreat left fossil shells embedded in its sedimentary deposits. The large quadrupedal animals followed next and to Buffon their global distribution showed that the continents must have been joined as a single mass. The sixth epoch saw the continents separate and finally in episode seven mankind appeared.

Buffon used an ironworks on his estate at Montbard near Dijon to heat iron spheres of different sizes. During these experiments, he timed their cooling and from this data calculated how long it would take an Earth-sized iron sphere to cool. His published results claimed that the Earth must be at least 75,000 years old, but his unpublished notes show that he thought the figure to be some 40 times longer; that is, around 3 million years. His reticence may show that he was not entirely immune to criticism and was worried that such an extreme age might leave him open to ridicule by his contemporaries, who generally believed in an age of not much more than 'six or eight thousand years', derived from various versions of the biblical chronology.

Buffon was attempting an all-embracing and systematic history of the Earth, following the earlier philosophical tradition of producing theories of the Earth. But his method was already outmoded: the new science of the latter part of the eighteenth century was demanding more precise facts and explanations. It was the next generation of rising stars of natural philosophy such as Johann Friedrich Blumenbach in Germany and Georges Cuvier in France who were to carry the study of Earth history and ancient life forward into the next century.

———————— • ————————

Johann Friedrich Blumenbach, 1752–1840, German anthropologist, professor of medicine and curator of natural history at Göttingen. He collected and measured human skulls from around the world, which he used as a quantitative basis for a racial classification around a caucasian ideal form.

———————— • ————————

It was Blumenbach who, in 1799, first gave scientific names to the Siberian and North American ancient elephant relatives. Somewhat confusingly, he called the former *Elephas primigenius* (now known as *Mammuthus primigenius*) since he thought it was a species of elephant, and the latter he called *Mammut ohioticum* (now known as *Mammut americanum*). However, Cuvier was dissatisfied with these designations, especially the latter.

Cuvier had been studying elephants and their fossil relatives for some time and realised that he could use the huge and distinctive beasts as an excellent example of a more important issue, the question of extinction. In 1796 (or year IV of the French Revolutionary calendar) Cuvier had declared that such a study would 'shed light for us on the obscure and intriguing history of the revolutions of the globe'. A young French Protestant from Monbeliard near the Swiss-German border, Cuvier had studied in Germany and then tutored the children of a Norman Lutheran family in Caen during the revolutionary years of the early 1790s.

When the Paris-based academic institutions were reformed, Cuvier, although only 26 years old, gained a position in the Muséum National d'Histoire Naturelle, which replaced the Jardin du Roi. The museum was rapidly being filled with the spoils of war as France's newly emboldened armies tramped around Europe and the Mediterranean. Furthermore, it was staffed by some of the most illustrious names in natural philosophy, such as the geologist Barthélemy Faujas de Saint-Fond and the zoologist Jean-Baptiste Lamarck. Full of ambition and determined

Jean-Baptiste de Monet, Chevalier de Lamarck, 1744–1829, army officer, worked in a Paris bank while studying medicine and botany, keeper of the Jardin du Roi (from 1774), professor of invertebrate animals in the National Museum of Natural History in Paris. He developed a transformationalist evolutionary theory and was author of *Zoological Philosophy* (1809) and *System of Invertebrate Animals* (1815–22).

to make his mark among such illustrious colleagues, Cuvier employed the new techniques he had learned in Germany in his 1796 *Treatise on the species of elephant, both living and fossil*. He demonstrated by detailed anatomical comparisons that the living Indian and African elephants have significant differences that make them quite separate species and compared them with fossil remains from Siberia that represented a third and indubitably 'lost species'.

Cuvier developed what he called 'comparative anatomy', whereby the skeleton, body parts, function and life style were seen as both interdependent or integrated and yet structured and organised on the same principles across the animal kingdom. For instance, animals that ate meat would have teeth suitable for that purpose and claws for catching and holding prey. But at the same time, the same sets of limb bones could be identified between animals that ran on the ground, swam in the sea or flew through the air.

The fossil animals that were to play a key role in Cuvier's development of comparative anatomy and the question of extinction were first the giant ground sloth (*Megatherium*) of Paraguay, which Cuvier described in 1796 (see p. 364), and secondly the elephants. He returned to the tougher question of the Ohio animal in 1806. By analysing its anatomy he was able to show that it was much further removed from the elephants than the mammoth and yet should not be confused with the latter. Accordingly, he placed it in a separate genus that he named *Mastodon*, meaning 'breast-tooth' and referring to the rounded tubercles on the surface of the molar teeth.

In addition, Cuvier began to discuss the character of the event that had caused the animal's extinction. Furthermore, he extended his discussion to include a number of other large fossil mammals, including species of rhinoceros, hippopotamus and tapir, whose remains were found widespread in superficial deposits of the Americas, Europe and Asia. Not only mammoth but also rhinoceros remains with hair and other tissues preserved in frozen ground had been reported from Siberia by reliable authorities such as Prussian explorer and naturalist Peter Pallas. For Cuvier this was evidence that the animals could not have been swept into the region by flood events, but must have lived there and been suddenly overwhelmed by some catastrophic event or sudden revolution.

Peter Simon Pallas, 1741–1811, medically trained Prussian naturalist, professor at the academy of sciences in St Petersburg, explored from the Urals to Siberia (1768–74, 1793–4) and wrote *Zoographica Russo-Arctica* (1811–31).

———— • ————

Since marine shells were often found closely associated with the bones of land-living animals, Cuvier argued that it was a brief and transient incursion of marine waters that had overwhelmed them. Although this might sound like a reworking of the Noachian Flood idea, Cuvier also pointed out that since the bones were only found in low-lying areas, the incursion had also been restricted geographically and was not universal.

Meanwhile, back in America, the polymathic Jefferson managed to combine his duties as third President of America with his scientific interests. He supported Charles Willson Peale's 1803 search for giant fossil bones in a technically difficult, water-logged excavation in Orange County, New York. Peale eventually cobbled together bones from several nearby sites and separate skeletons to reconstruct a 'single' entire mastodon skeleton for his museum in Philadelphia. Some 30 ft 6 in long from its tail to the tip of its tusks, and standing 11 ft 10 in tall at the shoulder, it was a very impressive beast and attracted the attention of a lot of Philadelphians. Wild speculation in the press promoted the idea that the 'mammoth' might be over 100 ft long and 100 ft high. Even Jefferson was not immune to the hype and suggested that it had been 50–100 ft long and 40–80 ft high. Remember, this was well before anyone knew that the really monstrous dinosaurs existed and this was one of the biggest land animals known.

Needless to say, when confronted by Peale's reconstruction, some members of the public were less than overwhelmed. A Mrs Anne Royall commented that

———— • ————

Charles Willson Peale, 1741–1827, American painter and naturalist, started as a silversmith then became a student of Benjamin West in London (1867–8). Settled in Philadelphia and became a Democratic member of the assembly, painted and exhibited his 'Portrait Gallery of the Heroes of the Revolution' (1782) and opened the Peale Museum of natural history in 1786.

while 'the skeleton is indeed as large as is represented it had not that formidable, dread-inspiring aspect which my romantic turn led me to expect, and with which I expected to be overwhelmed: I beheld it without surprise or emotion.' What is more, two sceptical gentlemen slipped under the guard rail and scraped one of the huge 'bones' with his penknife and swore, according to Mrs Royall, that 'it was nothing but wood'.

Even so, an epidemic of mammoth fever swept America and some of Jefferson's Massachusetts admirers made a mammoth cheese weighing 1235 lb and delivered it to Washington in a four-horse waggon. Jefferson was suitably appreciative and exhibited the cheese in the East Room of the White House, which he duly nicknamed the 'mammoth room', but he had to wait some time before he could fill it with real 'mammoth' bones.

Jefferson's geopolitical 'savvy' and palaeontological interests led to his further sponsorship of the Meriwether Lewis and William Clark 1804–6 exploration of the American West. Part of their remit was to collect any fossil bones they might come across and to investigate whether any mammoths were living in the remote wooded and forested territories west of the Missouri. In addition, they were to check up on persistent rumours that there were Welsh-speaking, white-skinned people known as the Madocians living in the far west. They were supposed to be descendants of the Welsh Prince Madoc who, it was claimed, discovered America in 1170. Jefferson was disappointed on both counts, but in 1807 William Clark did recover some 300 fossil bones from Big Bone Lick. We now know that they included the remains of both mammoth and mastodon along with extinct species of bison, deer and oxen. They were shipped down the Mississippi and in 1803 installed in Jefferson's 'mammoth room'.

Meriwether Lewis, 1774–1809, American soldier and explorer, led an unsuccessful expedition up the Missouri (1792), private secretary to President Jefferson (1801) and joined with William Clark to explore west of the Mississippi (1804–6) and made the first overland journey to the Pacific coast. Governor of Louisiana from 1806.

William Clark, 1770–1838, co-leader of the Lewis and Clark expedition (1804–6); grew up on his father's slave-run Virginia plantation, joined militia (1789–96) and served with Meriwether Lewis, inherited family estates. Asked by Lewis to accompany him on their pioneering expedition, subsequently appointed brigadier general and superintendent of Indian affairs for Louisiana by Jefferson.

———————————— • ————————————

The President only had another year to run in office and so employed a Philadelphia anatomist, Dr Caspar Wistar, to sort the bones. Wistar selected a few for Jefferson to keep as ornaments in his Monticello home. Others were to go to the American Philosophical Society and the remainder he gifted to the National Institute of France, because Jefferson remembered that the French sample of bones from the Ohio animal was not very great. Needless to say he did not think that the British warranted any such gift and it was not until the 1840s that London would possess any fine examples.

Albert Koch was a German from Saxony who, like so many Europeans, emigrated to America in the 1830s. And Koch, like many other German immigrants, settled in St Louis. He set himself up as a collector and dealer in fossils. Presumably he must have had some training back in Germany and he called himself Dr Koch. By 1836 he had opened the St Louis Museum, which he stuffed full of any curiosities he thought might induce visitors to pay to see them. The objects ranged from wax effigies of famous people to live alligators and a grizzly bear. He also travelled around the region, always on the lookout for the next interesting object. Early in 1840, he heard of some bones unearthed in Benton County, Missouri and managed to excavate the nearly complete skeleton of a mastodon from the banks of the Pomme de Terre River. He attempted to make a proper scientific job of the excavation and recorded the type of sediment it was buried in and the associated fossils, which were plants. 'All of the

———————————— • ————————————

Albert Koch, German born, emigrated to America in 1830 and settled in St Louis as an entrepreneur and collector. Opened a private museum in 1836 and toured with prize exhibits to Europe, visiting London in 1841.

vegetable remains,' he wrote, 'are tropical or very low southern production. They consisted of large quantities of cypress burs, wood and bark; a great seal of tropical cane and tropical swamp moss.'

Koch had recovered a particularly fine mastodon specimen and set about mounting it for exhibition. Ever the showman, aware of public demand for the extreme, he 'stretched' his skeleton with extra ribs and backbones so that it became 32 ft long and 15 ft tall. For increased dramatic effect, he attached the tusks to the skull so that they curved up and back over the animal's head. Opening in St Louis, the fantastic exhibit then went on the road to Louisville and by October 1841 was in the Masonic Hall in the city of Philadelphia, home to the internationally famous American Philosophical Society, founded by Benjamin Franklin in 1743. One of the country's best-known experts on fossils, Dr Richard Harlan, told the members that Koch was exhibiting 'one of the most extensive and remarkable collections of fossil bones of extinct mammals that have hitherto been brought to light in this country'. He praised Koch's efforts while also pointing out the errors of reconstruction. By the end of the year Koch and his mastodon, which he variously called *Missourium* and *Missouri leviathan*, were on display in the Egyptian Hall, in London's fashionable Piccadilly.

Apart from the generally curious British public who flocked to see Koch's display, there were some more informed and critical visitors such as the famous geologist and author of the *Principles of Geology*, Charles Lyell. Another was the rising star of early Victorian science, the anatomist Richard Owen, who first described the unique features of a group of extinct reptiles that he called the Dinosauria. On February 23rd, 1842 Owen discussed Koch's reconstruction at a meeting of the Geological Society of London, one of the oldest societies devoted purely to the science of geology in the world. Owen 'rubbished' Koch's claim that he had discovered a new giant animal and pointed out that it was simply a mastodon that had been incorrectly reconstructed. Owen had spotted all the 'add-ons', the inflated stance and misplaced tusks, and produced his own reworking of the skeleton in the form of a huge 7-ft-long drawing. Leonard Horner was in the audience and reported the goings-on to Lyell in a letter.

However, the niceties of Owen's argument were lost on London's public, who thronged to see Koch's fossil show in such numbers that it did not close

By the mid 19th century enough fossil bones had been found to show that the Americas had been inhabited by a variety of large extinct elephant-like animals called mastodons, as illustrated in John Collins Warren's *The Skeleton of the Mastodon Giganteus of North America* (Boston, 1852).

until the following summer, when Koch took the exhibits on the road again to Dublin in Ireland and then to Germany. In May 1844 Koch, on his way home to America, stopped over in London to close a business deal. Owen might have done his damndest in criticising Koch's reconstruction, but Owen also knew a fine specimen when he saw one. He encouraged the British Museum to buy the mastodon and some other fossils. Koch also got a good deal, receiving a downpayment of US$2000, with a further US$1000 a year for the rest of his life, which ended up totalling US$23,000.

As soon as the museum had its hands on the specimen, it stripped away the 'excess baggage', repositioned the tusks correctly and put it back on public display as *Mastodon americanum*, now known as *Mammut americanum*. It is one of the finest mastodon skeletons in existence and in reality, the beast stood some 8–10 ft in height and weighed some 4–5 tons, not much different from the African elephant.

Quite undaunted by any criticism of his reconstructions, Koch had no sooner returned home than he was again on the lookout for any spectacular fossils that might drum up a crowd for his museum. In February 1845, he spotted a huge backbone sitting in a farmer's fireplace in Clarke County, Alabama. On hearing that such bones frequently turned up in surrounding fields, he made further inquiries and soon heard of a skeleton across the Tombigbee River at the Washington Old Courthouse and dug it out. Even though it was already some 90 ft long, as usual Koch could not resist the temptation to make it even bigger and better by adding more bones from other sites.

By the end of that summer he had put together a skeleton that was over 114 ft long in the Apollo Rooms on Broadway in New York. With Koch's claim that it was a gigantic sea serpent, which he called *Hydrargos sillimani*, the exhibit was an instantaneous success. Charles Lyell, who was visiting the country, called on Koch to find out as much as he could about the geology of Alabama. Lyell knew well enough about Koch's abilities and tendencies and wrote to Horner about the latest monster. In fact, similar bones had already been excavated from elsewhere in Alabama in the 1830s and some of them had reached England, where they had been examined by Owen. The 'sea serpent' was a sea mammal, a large extinct whale that Owen described and named *Zeuglodon cetoides* at a meeting of the London Geological Society on January 9th, 1839.

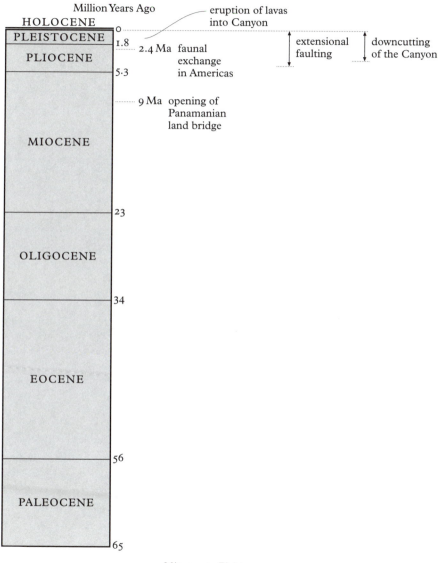

Miocene to Pleistocene.

15

Peopling the Americas

30 TO 10 THOUSAND YEARS

How and when the Americas were originally peopled is one of the great archaeological puzzles. As Samuel Haven, author of *Archaeology of the United States*, commented in 1856, 'after the discovery of America, the minds of the learned and ingenious were much exercised to account for its habitation by men and animals'. As soon as Europeans first encountered other humans in the Americas, there were questions about who they were and where they had come from. To Spaniards of the sixteenth century the ready-made answer was that they were one of the lost tribes of Israel. In their wanderings these Israelites had accidentally found a northern land connection into the continent. Since then the problem of by whom, when and where the Americas were first peopled has indeed exercised the minds and preoccupied the professional lives of many scientists over many generations and still the picture is not entirely clear.

There have been several false starts in the hunt for remains of the first 'North Americans' that have been swept under the academic carpet of embarrassing mistakes. One of the most famous was the 'astounding discovery' in the early 1920s of 'Nebraska Man', as the find was nicknamed. Hailed around the world as a 'missing link', 'a prehistoric Columbus' of huge importance in human evolution, the fossil was officially blessed with the scientific name *Hesperopithecus*, meaning 'western ape'. Males and females were even reconstructed by the English anatomist Sir Grafton Elliot Smith and depicted in the *Illustrated London News*

381

as naked, stick-wielding 'ape-humans' occupying a Nebraskan landscape filled with early horses and camels. All this was achieved on the basis of one fossil cheek tooth found in Pliocene deposits, which were, at the time, thought to be around a million or so years old.

———— • ————

Sir Grafton Elliot Smith, 1871–1937, Australian-born and trained anatomist and specialist on the brain and its evolution, professor in Cairo (1900), Manchester (1909) and London (1919), expert on mummification and one of those who thought 'Piltdown Man' genuine, knighted 1934.

———— • ————

The discovery gained extra prominence because of the ongoing row over the proselytisation of evolution in schools in the USA. The well-known American palaeontologist and evolutionist Professor Henry Osborn of the American Museum of Natural History joined the fray by welcoming the find and remarking that 'the Earth spoke to Bryan from his own state', adding that 'this little tooth speaks volumes ... evidence of man's descent from the apes'. The Bryan in question was an anti-evolutionist Nebraskan politician William Jennings Bryan. 'Nebraska Man' even featured in the notorious Scopes trial of 1925, when Tennessee teacher John Scopes was tried for breaking the state law against teaching Darwinian evolution. *Hesperopithecus* was introduced as part of the fossil evidence for the existence of prehistoric humans.

Surprisingly, considering the potential importance of the find, it was not until 1927 that the original site was re-excavated in the hope of finding further bones. To the surprise and delight of the investigators, they found a jaw and further

———— • ————

Henry Fairfield Osborn, 1857–1935, Princeton-trained American vertebrate palaeontologist, fossil hunter and evolutionist, professor of biology at Columbia (1891), United States Geological Survey (1900–24) and president of the American Museum of Natural History (1908–33). His 1910 textbook *The Age of Mammals* was highly influential.

skeletal remains, but their joy soon turned to dismay as they realised that they were all bones and teeth of an extinct Pliocene pig.

In defence of the scientists, it has to be said that a worn pig molar can look remarkably like a human one. However, the 1920s were a curious time in the investigation of human prehistory. Fossil evidence for any 'linkage' between the apes and humans was very scarce and a lot of scientists desperately wanted to be the first to find the so-called missing link. Normal critical judgement was often suspended when confronted with such finds and even crude forgeries such as the 1911 discovery 'Piltdown Man' in England was accepted by experts such as Sir Grafton Elliot Smith.

However, we now know that extinct human relatives (*Homo erectus*) did migrate out of Africa as long ago as late Pliocene times. Some of them even got as far as China and Java in southeast Asia, but not as far as the New World. If they had, the story of human evolution would have been even more complex and interesting than it already is.

Clovis hunters and Monte Verde

The more orthodox twentieth-century answer to the question of when and how the Americas were first 'invaded' or colonised by humans was that by around 13.5 ka (12,000–14C or radiocarbon date), migratory Siberian hunters arrived in Alaska on foot from northeast Asia. They are known as the 'Clovis' people, because of their distinctively fashioned stone spearheads that were first found in the 1930s at Clovis in New Mexico. Small bands of Clovis hunters walked across the narrow Bering Strait close to the Arctic Circle when the sea level was lower and it was dry land. The broad flat plain of the Bering Strait is commonly referred to as Central Beringia.

A further major problem was how, having arrived on the North American continent, the 'Clovis' people then made their way south. The vast Laurentide ice sheet covered central and eastern Canada and spread as far south as Ohio, Indiana, Illinois and Pennsylvania, apparently blocking any inland route. The coastal route was thought to be equally impassable, because the Cordilleran

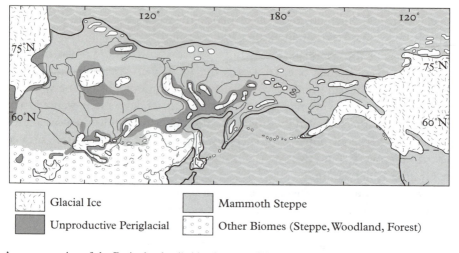

A reconstruction of the Beringian landbridge between Siberia and North America during the Last
Glacial Maximum c. 18,000 years ago, with lowered sealevels and ice cover.

glacier covered much of the Pacific coast as far south as Seattle. Even where the
coastline was free of ice, the high Coastal Ranges come down to the sea with
precipitous seacliffs, thus blocking any coastal passage.

However, in the 1960s, investigation of the eastern margin of the Cordilleran
glacier and the western margin of the Laurentide ice sheet indicated that there
might, at times, have been a long, narrow ice-free corridor between the two
great ice barriers. The idea certainly grabbed the popular imagination and was
soon reconstructed as a kind of 'superhighway' between cliffs of ice. Once opened,
it was imagined that a sudden flood of big-game hunters would have flowed down
the corridor following migratory animals such as mammoth, caribou, musk-ox
and bison right into the ice-free heartlands of North America. But in recent
decades the picture has become a lot more complicated and interesting.

The timing of the glaciation precludes the existence of any ice-free corridor
between 22,000 and 13,500 years ago, so how did the Clovis hunters enter the
continent and spread south by around 13.5 ka? Fragmentary but growing evidence

suggests that the Clovis hunters were not the first people to set foot on the continent. In addition, detailed investigation of the northeast Pacific coastline of Canada has raised the possibility that the earliest human immigrants into the continent might have taken an offshore coastal route rather than an inland one.

Recent modelling of the complex interactions between climate change, ice movements, the rise and fall of sea level and migrating coastal environmemts with their plants and animals suggests that the British Columbian coastal terrain was ice free by around 16 ka (13.8 ka–14C years). Edible molluscs, fish such as herring and sea mammals (seals and sea lions) were also present and easily obtained as food. Although on the British Columbian mainland sea levels were up to 120 m higher than during the glacial maximum, they were more than 150 m lower out on the Queen Charlotte Island archipelago because of differential ice loading and offshore upward bulging of the continental crust. Exposure of the offshore islands to marine climate influences meant that they were ice free from around 16 ka until 12 ka (10.25 ka–14C years), when rising sea levels drowned the coastal route. But by then the inland ice-free corridor was well established.

Sea levels began falling around 100,000 years ago, rose again during the warm interval 50–23 ka, and eventually dropped to some 90 m below the present level during the glacial maximum around 18 ka. The desolate Beringian dry-land connection between the Asian and American continents was exposed over the whole of this interval and remained so until around 15.5 ka, when climate warming began. There is fossil evidence that some 22 species of mammal migrated from Asia via Beringia into the Americas, including mammoth, musk-ox, caribou, moose, grizzly bear, polar bear and saiga antelope. Rising sea levels gradually reduced the Beringian connection until it was finally submerged around 10 ka.

One might imagine that humans could have used the new 'freeway' as long as 40,000 years ago. But there is absolutely no material evidence for such an early entry by humans into the continent. Indeed, there is frustratingly little evidence at all for any human habitation in the Americas before 15,000 years ago, and there are very few finds older than 14,000 years ago. Particularly frustrating is the lack of human bones; most of the evidence comes from much more easily preserved stone tools. Part of the reason may be that the evidence is now below sea level on the Beringian plain or the drowned Pacific coast strip of Alaska and Canada. Be that as it may, the main reason probably has to do with the very inhospitable climate and environment of Beringia, which was not accessible even for tough Siberian hunters until the glacial ended and climate began to improve.

No sooner had the last glacial reached its coldest phase around 18,000 years ago than the climate began to swing back into a warm phase punctuated by fits and starts and reversals. Until very recently, the earliest archaeological evidence for human occupation of Siberia dates back to around 21 ka around the shores of Lake Baikal, over 4000 km to the southwest of the Beringian plain. But in 2004 Russian archaeologists announced the discovery of a spectacular new find of 30,000-year-old (27,000–14C years) artefacts in northern Siberia (near Kazachie on the Yana River) and 500 km inside the Arctic Circle.

The artefacts found at the Yana site include spear foreshafts fashioned from mammoth ivory and rhino horn, which are remarkably similar to those ivory foreshafts made by the American Clovis people over 15,000 years later. Foreshafts allowed hunters to replace broken spear points quickly and reuse the spears. However, the woolly rhino became extinct around 17,000 years ago and did not colonise the Americas, and so the Clovis people had no option but to use the more brittle mammoth ivory. Problematically, there are also stone tools that do not bear any resemblance to Clovis ones, so there remain big questions as to the possible direct connections between these Yana River Siberians and the Clovis people. The debris of animal bones (some 800) found at the Yana site includes the remains of mammoth, bison, reindeer, horse, large lion-like predatory cats and plant fossils, which all point to a cool, dry steppe climate with grasses, and stands of larch and birch. But this was before the climate descended into the cold depths of the last glacial. What happened to the Yana people when the last glacial took grip and transformed their 'happy hunting grounds' into a desolate tundra wasteland significantly colder than it is today we will never know, but they certainly did not stay in the Yana River valley; that would have been suicidal.

Yana is the first well-documented site on the Asian side of Beringia that predates the last glacial. At last it offers good evidence to suggest that modern humans had penetrated this far north and east before the last glacial. But having

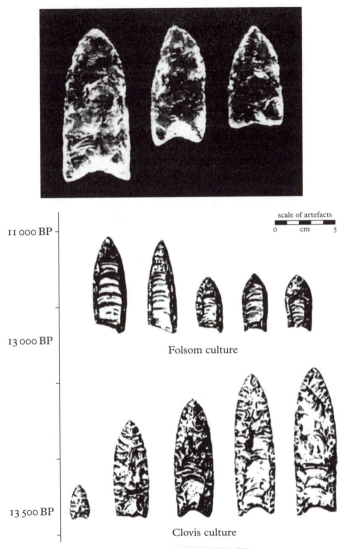

scale of artefacts

0   cm   5

11 000 BP

13 000 BP

Folsom culture

13 500 BP

Clovis culture

Subtle changes in these exquisitely crafted stone points are recognised as the product of two successive cultures of big game hunters in North America the Clovis and Folsom peoples. The upper quartz points were found associated with mammoth bones at the Lehner Ranch site in New Mexico. The razor sharp points were bound and 'glued' to a wooden shaft some 2 m (7 ft) long, perhaps with a detachable foreshaft to make a formidable weapon.

got this far north and east, did they also venture the extra 2600 km further east across into Alaska well before 20,000 years ago? The old question of exactly where in Siberia the first occupants of the Americas came from now has a possible answer. It is an answer that supports the other evidence from archaeology, palaeoanthropology (such as the study of Native American teeth), DNA and the linguistic 'history' of native 'Indian' Americans that the first 'Americans' were Asiatic Siberians. But there is also emerging evidence for successive pre-Clovis waves (or perhaps it would be better to say small ripples) of immigrants.

It is highly unlikely that there was any mass rush to cross into an imaginary 'promised land'. On a clear day the mountains of Alaska can just be seen from the coast of Siberia. It is only 80 km (50 miles) between Chukotskoye Nagorye in northeast Siberia and the western tip of the Seward Peninsula in Alaska, a narrow strait covered by a shallow sea today. Nevertheless, confronted with a desolate barren plain and high snow- and ice-covered mountains beyond, the incentive to venture into such an unknown and inhospitable territory probably precluded all but the most adventurous or perhaps most 'foolhardy'.

Initially, a few isolated small bands of hunters probably followed migratory animals out across the plain of Central Beringia. Active pursuit of game would have been very difficult on this featureless plain without cover and hunting may well have been confined to tracking down stragglers from the herds. Alternatively, they might have followed the coastal strip where they would always have access to shellfish. The very mobility of the hunters and the animals has left virtually no archaeological 'imprint' on the landscape. And, even if it did, so much of Beringia is once again under water and out of reach.

So far, the earliest traces of these pre-Clovis settlers comes from the Bluefish Caves in the Yukon, perhaps dating back to at least 15,750 years ago and maybe as long ago as 20 ka. Canadian archaeologist Jean Cinq-Mars first spotted the limestone caves near the Bluefish River from a helicopter back in 1975. The variety of chewed bones (mammoth, bison, horse, sheep, caribou, moose, saiga, musk-ox) shows that the caves were primarily dens used by predators such as lion and cougar and scavengers such as wolves and bears, but some of these bones also look as if they have been fashioned by human hands, although not all experts agree. And there are stone artefacts – small flakes called microliths and the remains of the stone nodules they were broken from. Similar artefacts have been found elsewhere in Alaska, but none is any older than about 13 ka. Unfortunately, the Bluefish Caves do not provide really secure evidence for pre 13.5 ka settlement in Alaska, although they are the best available for this region at the present. There is a scattering of other putative pre 13.5 ka sites much further south, but many of these also have problems. And there is the problem of how anyone managed to negotiate their way through the glacier-bound northlands.

The presence of the famous ice-free corridor between the ice sheets and glaciers has recently been thrown into doubt, especially prior to 14,700 years ago and the re-establishment of significantly warmer climates. The corridor would have had to be some 1500 km long, not a distance that could be quickly travelled on foot even by the hardiest of hunters. There would have been no firewood and precious little to eat. And yet there is some evidence for pre-Clovis people living south of the ice front at least 14 ka ago, first at the Meadowcroft rock shelter in Pennsylvania.

Situated in Cross Creek Valley, a branch of the Ohio River, the rock shelter was first excavated in 1973 and the subsequent 30 years of detailed investigation have yielded some tantalising clues to early habitation. A woven plait of fibre that could have been part of a basket was dug out and has been dated at around 23 ka. Younger layers above contained stone tools and animal bones dated to around 18 ka. You might think that this would be unequivocal evidence for early settlement, but the problem is that the animals are temperate ones such as deer, chipmunk and squirrel that fed on oak, hickory and walnut trees. The site is only 80 km south of the ice front and should have been tundra at around 18 ka.

Meadowcroft is in the middle of a coalmining region and the sediments are all contaminated with coal dust, which some experts believe has resulted in much older dates than they should be. But the excavator, James Adovasio, still protests that the dates are real and that the sediments are not contaminated with coal dust, so the jury is still out on this one. There is another site called Pedra Furada in northeast Brazil that has been claimed to be more than 40 ka old, but this seems even less acceptable to most archaeologists. The one other site that has really made people begin to accept the possibility of pre-Clovis people is that of Monte Verde.

Monte Verde nestles on the narrow Chilean coastal plain, caught between the mountains of the Andes and the island-studded Pacific coast. Buried beneath the peaty banks of the Chinchihuapi Creek 30 km from the coast lie the remains of abandoned huts, work surfaces, hearths, cooking debris and rubbish dumps, all dated to between 14.5 and 13.8 ka. The rapid growth of peaty sediments over the site has preserved not just flaked stone artefacts but also some of the hut timbers, wood tools, animal bones (including the elephant-like extinct mastodon) and pieces of hide, along with knotted fibres.

It was in the late 1970s that Tom Dillehay, an archaeologist at the University of Kentucky, began to follow up a find of bones made by the local Gerardo Barria family in the early 1970s. Dillehay started a programme of excavation at the site that was to take his team over 20 years to complete. By the time they had finished they had uncovered clear evidence for a small streamside settlement with two rows of timber-framed and skin-covered dwellings – a far cry from the frozen northern tundra. The Monte Verde people actually lived much closer to the Antarctic Circle (3500 km to the south) than the Beringian Arctic Circle (some 15,000 km to the north). They 'enjoyed' a cool temperate climate with abundant trees, shrubs, herbs and wild roots and tubers, including wild potatoes.

Although initially there was considerable scepticism about the nature of the find and more especially about its age, Dillehay's meticulous work and careful documentation have gradually won over many but not all of the critics. There is also some scant evidence from possible stone and wood artefacts for an even earlier occupation at the site dated at 33 ka by scattered charcoal, but Dillehay himself is, as yet, cautious about this until more ground has been excavated.

The argument now concerns how long it might have taken the Monte Verde people to make their 15,000 km journey from Beringia down to southern Chile. It has to have been in the order of several thousand years, since they would have been unlikely to move more than a few kilometres a year as they would have been encumbered with babies and children. Even at 5 km per year it would take 3000 years, meaning that they were in Beringia around 17.5 ka, but since the region was still in the final throes of a glacial that is highly unlikely. It is therefore more reasonable to speculate that they crossed Beringia before the last glacial. If so, then the Americas were occupied prior to 22 ka, before the last Wisconsinan glaciation took hold.

Historically, the first evidence for the prehistoric settlement of the Americas was made back in 1908. Near Folsom, New Mexico, a cowboy named George McJunkin spotted some large animal bones and unusual-looking stones apparently embedded in deposits in the dry gully of a creek that flows down Wild Horse Valley from Johnson Mesa. Torrential rains in 1908 had washed the loose sediment out of the creek, exposing the heavy bones and stones. McJunkin dug them out and took them back to his ranch, where they languished for some 17 years. Luckily, instead of eventually being thrown out, in 1925 they found their way to Jesse Figgins, director of the Denver Museum of Natural History in Colorado, who recognised the bones as those of a large extinct bison.

Figgins was intrigued, decided to investigate the site and was soon rewarded with the discovery of two stone spear points. He showed them to the Czech immigrant Ales Hrdlicka, who encouraged his excavations but told him to leave any future finds of stone artefacts undisturbed *in situ*. In other words, they were to be left exactly as they were, exposed in the sediment, so that they could be inspected by experts.

———————— • ————————

Ales Hrdlicka, 1869–1943, Bohemian-born anthropologist, studied medicine in America and became a homeopathic physician. Began a reassessment of sites associated with Native Americans, developing the idea that they originated in Asia. He joined the American Museum of Natural History, then the National Museum in Washington (Smithsonian Institution).

———————— • ————————

By summer 1927 Figgins had a result and the experts duly gathered to examine a well-formed spear point in close association with bison bones. Barnum Brown, a famous palaeontologist at the American Museum of Natural History and finder of dinosaurs, was one of the experts and duly declared that 'the answer to the antiquity of man in the New World is in my hand'. He was wrong, but it was a good 'sound bite' and brought plenty of publicity to the find, jettisoning Figgins to national fame in the process. At the time there was no direct method of dating the find, only informed guesswork, and Figgins reckoned that the kill site might be around 10,000 years old. He was very nearly right and today, thanks to radiocarbon dating, we know that the Folsom points were made between 13 and 11 ka. Just five years later, in 1932, a new find surfaced in New Mexico, at Clovis, whose people we have met before.

Barnum Brown, 1873–1963, fossil collector, especially of dinosaurs, who worked all over the Americas, India and Ethiopia, financed first by the Sinclair Oil company. Hired by Henry Fairfield Osborn for the American Museum of National History in 1897 and discovered the first skeleton of *Tyrannosaurus rex* in 1902.

Two amateur collectors found beautifully fashioned stone points lying in dried-up lake-bed sediments along with animal bones. In the 1930s further sites with similar points closely associated with bones were found nearby at Blackwater Draw and up in Colorado at Dent, where mammoths had been the prey rather than bison. By the mid-1950s more Clovis sites had been found, including one at Naco in southern Arizona where a nearly complete mammoth skeleton was associated with eight Clovis points. There is evidence of bone regrowth, suggesting that none of the spear wounds killed the beast and it survived for some time before dying, perhaps from natural causes or perhaps from the long-term effects of the attack. And then the remains of eight mammoths and twelve spear points were found nearby at the Lehner Ranch.

When the first reliable dates became available for these Clovis sites, none was older than 13.5 ka. The Clovis hunters thus predated the Folsom people and became generally regarded as the first human occupants of the Americas. These Clovis pioneers soon took on an iconic status. Apparently on foot and armed with no more than stone-pointed spears, these people regularly took on giant mammoths and must have killed enough of them to make the effort and danger worthwhile. A further question arose: had people such as the Clovis hunters also been unwittingly responsible for an 'overkill', not just of the mammoths but also many other large and medium-sized mammal species, known as the Pleistocene 'megafauna' of the Americas?

The 'overkill' hypothesis has been most vigorously promoted by Paul Martin of Arizona State University, who argues that the Clovis hunters entered the continent from Beringia, travelled down the ice-free corridor to arrive beyond the receding icefront around 13.5 ka. Small groups of hunters, 'old hands at hunting woolly mammoths and other Eurasian animals', according to Martin, then fanned out through the forests, woodlands and across the prairies within a few hundred years. They indulged in a veritable *Blitzkrieg* or feeding frenzy, which rapidly decimated their prey populations.

Martin further argued that this protein bonanza soon produced a boom of little 'Clovises', with their population increasing at rates of 3–4 per cent a year, who in turn grew up into more successful hunters until the populations of their prey animals finally crashed. But not all experts agreed. What of the role of climate change? Such high rates of population increase with low infant mortality are unheard of among other hunter-gatherers. As we shall see the Clovis people may well have helped the megafauna on their way but, as so often happens in science and life, the story is turning out to be more complicated than first thought.

Pleistocene extinctions

One of the biggest questions that has emerged from our investigation of Pleistocene time is whether it was climate change or human intervention that wiped out the magnificent beasts of the Ice Ages. The mammoth, woolly rhino, giant cave bears, giant deer, sabre-tooth cats and herds of wild horse, cattle, bison and reindeer that covered the Americas and Eurasia and were so evocatively figured by our ancestors in cave paintings, rock drawings and portable carvings have mostly disappeared, but what caused their demise? Did they just fall by the wayside, victims of climate change, or were they pushed to extinction by our forebears? There are many other ideas about the possible causes of these extinctions, including a current fashion for invoking pandemics of disease. Nevertheless, however uncomfortable it might seem, the front-runners are still those skilled modern human hunters who first colonised the Earth beyond Africa. Climate change or possibly a combination of human intervention and climate change is the second main option.

You might reasonably think that it should not be too difficult for scientists to answer this question but it is surprisingly complex. There is no doubt that the Pleistocene so-called megafauna of large and medium-sized mammals of the northern hemisphere suffered an extinction event after the latter part of the Ice Ages. Over the last few tens of thousands of years a significant proportion of the megafauna has gone and the process is not finished yet. This time interval might seem distinctly protracted, but on a geological time scale it is still very quick.

To begin with, the primary suspect was actually climate change. The idea was that drastic changes in vegetation had a major effect on the large numbers of plant eaters, which were dependent on fairly specific food types such as the grasses on which the mammoths, horse, cattle and bison depended. With warmer and wetter climates at the end of the last glacial, the vaste cold steppe grasslands were gradually overgrown by encroaching scrub, herbs and eventually forest, leading to severe reductions and terminal decline of the grass eaters. There was a knock-on or cascade effect. Populations of top carnivores such as the big cats, which depended on the plant eaters, consequently crashed as well. But what of the role of our ancestors, who we know were hunters and serious meat eaters (see p. 384)?

The Americas seemed to provide an ideal test of the problem because of the late arrival of modern humans in the continent, either around 12,000–14C years ago (around 14 ka calendar years, see p. 412) or perhaps, as we have seen, much earlier, around 22 ka. Could the megafaunal extinction event be chronologically tied to the arrival of these hunters? Of all the big beasts of the ice ages, the mammoth has attracted most attention and there is plenty of fossil evidence for the existence of various species of mammoth and other elephant relatives in the Americas. Their huge bones tend to fossilise quite well and their massive cheek teeth are particularly resistant to subsequent (post-mortem) destruction.

The discovery of many animal bones at a number of American sites seemed to support the idea that the early human occupiers of the continent were ruthlessly efficient big-game hunters. It has been claimed that the remains of whole family groups or even herds are present at some of these sites. However, it can be very difficult to prove whether the animals did actually belong to single groups and were slain by a single 'mass kill', or whether they were 'recruited' more gradually over a longer period of time.

A number of American sites preserve the remains of groups of mammoths ranging from 5 to over 100 individuals. Some of these sites (e.g. Waco, Texas, dated at c. 28 ka) have been shown to be the result of natural mass mortality (for example drowning in flood waters) before humans arrived on the continent. Others, such as Freisenham Cave, are clearly natural accumulations (for example a sabre-tooth cat den, dated at 20–17 ka) formed over a considerable time. But there are also a number of sites that are younger than 13 ka and preserve human artefacts along with the mammoth remains.

Much of the linkage between the animal remains and humans comes from stone tools associated with the mammoth bones, but these do not necessarily prove that the two were exactly contemporaneous, let alone that the humans killed the animals. Even the common occurrence of cut marks on the bones does not prove that the humans hunted down and killed the animals, although they do strongly suggest a close association in time. Cut marks on the bones are usually associated with the act of butchering or defleshing a carcass, but the animal may have already been dead or dying. Killing a healthy mammoth with spears was not easy; it was a lot safer to take on beasts that have already been killed by other predators or are dying from natural causes. Very rarely is there any obvious cause of death, although there are a few cases where sharp worked stone points have been found embedded in animal rib cages.

Luckily, a new, sophisticated application of isotope analysis can help answer a number of these problems. Measurement of variation in carbon, oxygen and strontium isotopes from the enamel of mammoth cheek teeth allows differentiation between mass kills that took place over a short period of time and longer-term accumulation of the remains of individual animals. Carbon isotopes can reflect differences in the plant material consumed, oxygen isotopes track local climates and variations in strontium isotopes reflect soil types. The greater the variation in the isotopes, the less likely are they to have lived and died together.

The technique has been tested out at two prehuman American sites in Texas – Waco (c. 28 ka), where the remains of some 23 mammoths and a single camel have been found, and Freisenhahn Cave (c. 20–17 ka), with over 100 individuals. At Waco most of the skeletons are articulated and the animals must have died where they are found, within a single layer of silty clay. The bones are well preserved and show little sign of post-mortem disturbance, suggesting that they were rapidly buried soon after they died. Age analysis shows that they were predominantly adult females and juveniles along with one adult male, a sex and age profile typical of living groups of elephants in which the adolescent and older males separate from the females and babies until one or more of the females comes into oestrus and is sexually receptive to adult males, or at least a dominant male who can exclude any rivals.

By comparison, the Freisenhahn Cave site contains a large variety of bone material including bison, horse, peccary, tapir, dog and large cats, as well as mammoth teeth. Radiocarbon dating shows that accumulation continued over a period of some 3000 years. Detailed analysis of the jumble of dismembered bones shows that the site was a sabre-tooth cat (*Homotherium serum*) den. Parts of carcasses were dragged back to the cave by the big cats so that they could be consumed without having to constantly protect their food from the attentions of other predators and scavengers.

The carbon isotopes from the Waco site were tightly clustered, whereas those from Freisenhahn showed a significant level of variance. This supports the interpretation of the Waco site as a natural 'mass kill', which probably resulted from a group of closely related animals being caught and drowned together by a single flash flood. In contrast, the cave accumulation consists of unrelated animals being 'recruited' one by one over a long period of time.

The same techniques have also been applied to sites where the association of Clovis hunter artefacts with mammoth remains has been used to argue for accumulation by human-generated mass kills. A recent study tested three Clovis sites (Blackwater Draw, New Mexico – 6 animals, 13–11 ka; Miami, Texas – 5 animals, 11.4–10.5 ka; and Dent, Colorado – 13 animals, 11.2–10.9 ka).

Surprisingly high levels of variability in each of the isotope systems indicate that the accumulation of mammoth remains at all three sites was not the result of mass kills, but rather represents slow accumulation over a number of years. From this evidence it seems that the Clovis hunters of the Great Plains did not slaughter entire family groups of mammoths but rather hunted or scavenged individual animals. However, there are still some other Clovis sites, such as Lehner and Murry Springs in Arizona, which need to be tested before we can say the same for all known 'mass' mortalities linked to the Clovis hunters.

But this result does not necessarily discount the idea that human hunters were not entirely responsible for the extinction. It just may not have been as dramatic as television and hype-driven reconstructions would prefer. Modelling of the viability of declining prey populations suggests that even small numbers of mobile hunters can, within centuries, reduce large herds of slow-reproducing megaherbivores such as the mammoth (and of course bison within historical times) to unsustainable population numbers.

In recent years the global scenario for this Pleistocene extinction has been broadened to include the southern hemisphere. The timing of extinctions of the megafauna of Australia and New Zealand convincingly supports the idea of a human hunter-driven event. For instance, the unusual flightless avifauna of New Zealand, including the moas, survived until the 'late' arrival of humans around AD 1000.

Thousands of Years Ago

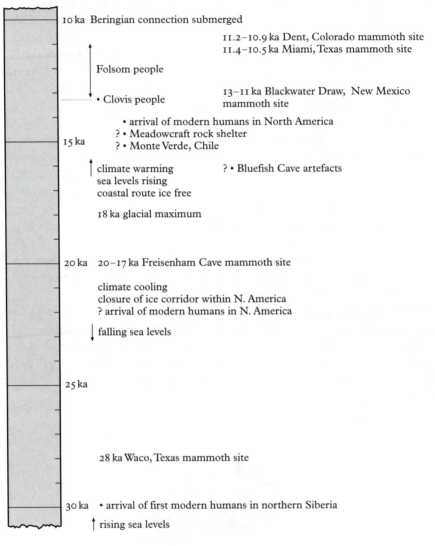

30 to 10 thousand years.

16

Rock of ages –
Dating rocks and fossils

ARCHEAN TO CENOZOIC

As we have seen, one of the major problems that the investigation of Earth Time's geological past faced was that of chronological dating of strata and their contained fossils. The mapping, sequencing and correlation of strata allowed for no more than a relative dating. For many British geologists, James Hutton had opened the way to a realisation that the age of the Earth must be very great and could not be defined by or derived from any biblical source. By Darwin's day there was a sense that the history of the Earth had to extend back over many hundreds of millions of years. But there was no hard evidence and influential physicists such as William Thomson, Lord Kelvin, doubted such long time-scales. Not until the beginning of the twentieth century did a method for dating rocks begin to emerge, and even then it proved to be enormously unreliable until the theoretical and technical advances of the 1940s and the Second World War.

A sense of age for rocks and fossils was a major problem, ever since the seventeenth century when a number of spuriously accurate estimates were made for the age of the Earth. In Europe, these calculations were inevitably based on the assumption that the Old Testament was a reliable historical document. The most famous scholarly attempt to work out the date of Creation was made by James Ussher, protestant Archbishop of Armagh, Ireland.

James Ussher, 1581–1656, protestant Archbishop of Armagh, Ireland, scholar, fellow and professor of divinity in Trinity College, Dublin; author of *Annals of the Old Covenant from the First Origins of the World*, 1650, in which he calculated the date of the world's origin as 4004 BC.

4004 BC and all that

In reality, Ussher's was just one of many such calculations. He had the prestige of being a renowned scholar, Professor of Divinity and Vice-Chancellor of Trinity College, Dublin. He used not only Old Testament sources but also contemporary knowledge of the Julian calendar, devised by the Renaissance scholar Joseph Justus Scaliger, astronomical calculation and extra-biblical sources. Scaliger's Julian period was taken to have started on a hypothetical day, January 1st, 4713 BC, which he thought predated all known historical events. According to Ussher's 1650 *Annals of the Old Covenant from the First Origin of the World*, the world began the night before Sunday October 23rd in year 710 of the Julian calendar – 4004 years before the birth of Christ.

However, as long ago as the fifth century, biblical scholars had noticed that there were problems with the Old Testament account, such as the creation of light before the creation of the Sun (Genesis 1:3, 16) and the fact that the moon is not light emitting but light reflecting. It was also long recognised that there are different components to the Genesis account. In addition, growing scholarly interest in the classical world and the Middle East, during the eighteenth century, led to a reassessment of prehistory and a questioning of the Old Testament chronology. Nevertheless, for the majority of believers the idea that the creation took just six days also became firmly entrenched in western culture. However, by the end of the eighteenth century, there were a number of more scientific attempts to calculate the Earth's age.

The French natural philosopher and experimenter Comte de Buffon mustered a number of lines of evidence to support his ideas about the cooling of the Earth and the time it had taken to do so; in other words, the age of the Earth. The existence of the bones and tusks of elephants in far northern latitudes such as Siberia indicated to Buffon that in earlier times the Earth must have been as hot as Africa. By 1778 Buffon, as we have seen, divided Earth history into seven epochs, echoing the days of creation in the Genesis narrative, with man only appearing in the last epoch, which suggested to Buffon that there was therefore a substantially long period of prehistory or prehuman time.

Buffon also tried an experimental approach, building on ideas developed by Isaac Newton. Heating a number of iron cannonballs of different sizes to white heat, Buffon timed how long they took to cool. He found Newton's conjecture that the cooling time was proportional to the diameter of the sphere was correct. However, Buffon disagreed with Newton's calculation for the cooling time of an iron ball the size of the Earth and reckoned that it would have taken 96,670 years and 132 days, almost twice as long as Newton's calculation.

Buffon was not entirely satisfied with the result. He was aware that the Earth was made of other materials with different cooling rates and that the Sun contributed heat to the Earth, which would have prolonged its cooling time. By 1779, he arrived at his final calculation of 74,832 years for the age of the Earth. Buffon reckoned that some 60,000 years had passed before the Earth was cool enough to be first inhabited by life and then steamy jungles had stretched as far north as Siberia. Not for another 10,000 years was it fit for humans. According to Buffon:

> thus we are persuaded, independently of the authority of the sacred books, that man has been created last, and that he arrived to take the sceptre of the earth only when it was found worthy of his empire.

Despite Buffon's work and that of Newton before him, Ussher's 4004 BC date was still widely accepted and even printed in Bibles as an historic truth. Not surprisingly, the notion of a 6000-year-old Earth persisted into the nineteenth century and beyond as an established 'fact' for some fundamentalist Christians. It was still being quoted in the infamous 1925 Scopes trial between American creationists and evolutionists in Dayton, Ohio.

By the latter part of the eighteenth century, James Hutton had shown from his study of stratification and rates of sedimentation that Ussher's 6000 years was not nearly enough time for observed rates of geological processes. Hutton, a Scottish philosopher of nature, proclaimed from his examination of strata that he could see 'no vestige of a beginning, no prospect of an end'. By the latter part of the nineteenth century, Lyell and Darwin were using rates of erosion and deposition to estimate that the Earth was hundreds of millions of years old. In the first edition of his book *On the Origin of Species*, Darwin estimated that it had taken 300 million years for the erosion of Weald, which involved just the relatively recent (geologically speaking) strata of the Cretaceous and Tertiary systems.

Darwin considered that evolution had proceeded by a succession of gradual changes and splitting of descendent species from common ancestors. Consequently, he needed as much time as he could get for all the changes that must have taken place to evolve backboned animals from single-celled protists and within the vertebrates to have evolved humans from fish. And then again, he argued that the origin of life must have preceded the first protists by a huge amount of time. By the 1850s Darwin knew that fish fossils had been found in Old Red Sandstone (Devonian) strata. He also knew that Devonian strata were overlain by many miles of younger stratified rocks and must therefore be very ancient, so how much more ancient must the origin of protists have been?

Such geological efforts were severely criticised by the eminent Belfast-born physicist William Thomson, Lord Kelvin. In 1862, Kelvin dismissed Darwin's published calculation – 'what then are we to think of such geological estimates as 300,000,000 years for the "denudation of the Weald"?' Furthermore, Kelvin argued that as the age of the Earth was constrained by the age of the cooling Sun, it was to be expected that its inhabitants 'cannot continue to enjoy the light and heat essential to their life, for many years longer, unless sources now unknown to us are prepared in the great storehouse of creation'.

——————————— • ———————————

William Thomson, Lord Kelvin, 1824–1907, Belfast-born Scottish physicist and inventor, trained in Glasgow, Cambridge and Paris. He returned to Glasgow as professor (1846–99). One of the greatest scientists of his day, Thomson devoted considerable effort to calculating the age of the Earth and was highly critical of the estimates made by geologists. Created baronet in 1892.

Scientifically, Kelvin was a strict empiricist and despised 'woolly thinking' and vague speculation without hard data, of the kind that Darwin was using. In addition, Kelvin was no friend of evolutionary theory. Like Buffon before him, Kelvin thought that he could use physics to discover how long it had taken for the Earth to cool to its present temperature from the initial heat of its formation. Knowledge of the common rocks of the Earth, their melting points and conductivity had advanced enormously since Buffon's days. Kelvin realised that a simple iron ball model was inadequate and that most of the rocks of the Earth seemed to be comprised of silicate minerals, whose ability to conduct heat was very different from that of iron.

Kelvin's preliminary calculations gave the age of the Sun as around 20 million years and that of the Earth somewhere between 200 and 1000 million years, but he wanted to refine his calculations and did not publish these figures. He was aided by a new theory of heat conduction developed by the French mathematician Joseph Fourier (1768–1830) and assumed that the initial temperature of the molten rock from which the Earth cooled was 3871 degrees C (7000 degrees F). Kelvin was informed by John Phillips that temperature increases downwards into the interior by 0.55 degrees C (1 degree F) for every 15 or so metres (45–60 ft). From this, in 1862 Kelvin calculated that it had taken 98 million years to reach its present state. But he also stated that if his assumptions did not hold then the Earth's age was likely to range anywhere between 20 and 400 million years old.

However, Kelvin was not at all happy with this result because it seemed to be far too long. His concern arose from the prevailing view that the Sun was probably no more than some 40 million years old and the age of the Earth should not be greater than that of the Sun. Over the following decade Kelvin constantly reworked his calculations and each time managed to revise the age downwards to 40 and then later to around 20 million years (in 1893), which was in line with the prevailing ideas about the age of the Sun. Such was Kelvin's influence that his measures were readily accepted by most scientists, apart from some geologists who still thought that they were a serious underestimate.

As the role of radioactivity in maintaining the internal heat of the Earth was not known, Kelvin's measure was indeed a serious underestimate. It is often stated that the discovery of radioactivity and its role in maintaining the internal temperature of the Earth finally broke the straitjacket of Kelvin's influence. But this view fails to take into account Kelvin's dogmatism in linking the age of the Earth to that of the Sun. Ideas about solar energy and the Sun's compositional homogeneity were not overthrown by the discovery of radioactivity. Not until the recognition of thermonuclear fusion in the 1930s was the paradox fully resolved. Nevertheless, it was the discovery of radioactivity and the subsequent development of 'radiometric dating' that eventually made it possible to break Kelvin's stranglehold on the generally accepted age of the Earth.

Radiometric dating

The discovery that natural radiant energy was a much more complex phenomenon than previously thought with various different sources dates back to the last decade of the nineteenth century. In 1895 Röntgen discovered a new kind of radiation, which he called X-rays, and apparently 'aroused an amount of interest unprecedented in the history of physical science' according to J. J. Thomson, Head of the Cavendish Laboratory in Cambridge, reporting to professional colleagues the following year. We now know that it was indeed a remarkable breakthrough and one that was to bring great benefits and dangers that were not initially appreciated, dangers that were also to arise with the other newly discovered forms of radiation.

In 1896 the brilliant French physicist Henri Becquerel discovered that crystals of a uranium salt accidently placed on top of a wrapped and unexposed glass photographic plate caused the plate to blacken as if it had been exposed to light. Becquerel realised that the crystals were spontaneously emitting some unknown type of energy similar but different to X-rays. The radiation was solely due to the radium and, unlike light energy, could not be reflected. He also

Wilhelm Konrad von Röntgen, 1845–1923, Prussian-born, Nobel prize-winning physicist (1901), studied in Zurich and was professor in Strasbourg, Giessen, Würzburg, where he discovered X-rays in 1895, and Munich (1899–1919).

Sir Joseph John Thomson, 1856–1940, Nobel prize-winning (1906) British physicist who discovered the electron, thus opening up the study of atomic structure, Cambridge-trained and became Cavendish professor there (1884–1919) and made the laboratory world-famous.

discovered that a lump of radium mineral that he carried around in his pocket burned his skin. But it was the young Polish scientist Marie Curie and her French husband Pierre who made a study of these strange 'Becquerel rays'. Marie Curie made the all-important discovery that the radiant energy emitted by the uranium salt was an inherent property of the element uranium and together with her husband Pierre named the new phenomenon 'radioactivity'. In addition, Marie Curie found that the element thorium also emitted similar radiation.

When the Curies examined two naturally occurring uranium ores, pitchblende and chalcolite, they discovered that the radiation emitted was more intense than the uranium or thorium content of their ores, indicating the presence of other radioactive elements. Following laborious separation processes of fractional crystallisation, they managed to distinguish the presence of polonium and the much more radioactive uranium.

However, it was a brilliant New Zealander, Ernest Rutherford, working with British chemist Frederick Soddy, who made the breakthroughs that were to lead to the development of radiometric dating. From experiments on thorium compounds in 1902, Rutherford and Soddy discovered that the activity of a substance is directly proportional to the number of atoms present. From this observation, they formulated a general theory that predicted the rates of radioactive decay and went on to suggest that the gaseous element helium might be a 'decay' product of a radioactive element. At that time it was not known how

Antoine Henri Becquerel, 1852–1908, French Nobel prize-winning physicist (1903) and expert on fluorescence who discovered 'Becquerel rays', later known as radioactivity.

Marie and Pierre Curie, 1867–1934 and 1859–1906 respectively, French physicist couple (she was Polish born), worked on magnetism and radioactivity (a term she coined in 1898), jointly awarded Nobel prize for physics with Becquerel in 1906. She gained a second Nobel for chemistry in 1911 for isolating pure radium.

———— • ————

many elements were radioactive nor what their decay products might be, since radioisotopes had yet to be discovered and there was no instrument available that could measure radioactivity. Nevertheless, Rutherford's brilliant insights allowed him to suggest that radioactivity might be used as a 'clock' to date the formation of some naturally occurring minerals and therefore the rocks that contained them.

Rutherford had enormous respect for Kelvin and when addressing a meeting that the great man was attending, referred to Kelvin's 1862 claim that the Sun could not keep shining unless 'the great storehouse of creation' contained some unknown source of energy. Rutherford and others had now discovered that hidden source – the energy emitted by radioactive elements as they decay within the rocks of the Earth, which is sufficient to counteract and significantly slow down the rate of cooling. He tried to placate Kelvin by portraying the old man's prophetic and prescient disclaimer as the hallmark of a very great scientist – 'that prophetic utterance refers to what we are now considering tonight, radium!' But Kelvin never really accepted the role that radioactive elements played in the creation of the Solar System, a process that we now understand as stellar nucleosynthesis.

———— • ————

Ernest Rutherford, Baron, 1871–1937, New Zealand born and educated, Nobel prize-winning (1908) physicist who discovered and described the radioactive 'decay' process with Soddy and predicted the existence of the neutron. Joined Cavendish laboratory in Cambridge (1895), professor in McGill University, Canada (1898), Manchester (1907). Assisted by Niels Bohr, Cambridge (1919), where he succeeded J. J. Thomson.

Frederick Soddy, 1877–1937, English radiochemist, Oxford trained, worked with Rutherford at McGill University, Canada and became professor of chemistry at Glasgow, Aberdeen and Oxford, discovered and named 'isotopes' and awarded Nobel prize for chemistry in 1921.

In 1905, Rutherford wrote that 'if the rate of the production of helium by radium (or other radioactive substance) is known, the age of the mineral can at once be estimated from the observed volume of helium stored in the mineral and the amount of radium present'. On this basis he determined the very first radiometric date for a fergusonite mineral, which gave a Uranium-Helium age of around 497 million years and one of 500 million years for a uraninite mineral from Glastonbury, Connecticut. But Rutherford wisely cautioned that these were minimum ages because some of the helium gas would undoubtedly have escaped during the processing of the materials. He suggested that calculations based on lead might be superior:

if the production of lead from radium is well established, the percentage of lead in radioactive minerals should be a far more accurate method of deducing the age of a mineral than the calculation based on the volume of helium for the lead formed in a compact mineral has no possibility of escape.

In the same year, an American radiochemist, Bertram Boltwood, went on to provide the first reasonably accurate means of dating the formation of certain minerals within the Earth. Boltwood studied at Yale then in Germany and, on returning to America, worked to improve the analytical techniques of radiochemistry pioneered by his friend Rutherford, who at this time was

Bertram Boltwood, 1870–1927, American radiochemist, studied at Yale and in Germany, returned to Yale as professor (from 1897). He developed understanding of the uranium decay series and analytical techniques, which allowed the first measures of geological age based on Pb : U ratios.

at McGill University in Montreal. Boltwood made a systematic analysis of radioactive uranium-bearing rocks and noticed that generally both helium and lead were present, with the lead being the stable end product of the decay chain from uranium.

Boltwood went on to develop a technique that allowed him, with the aid of a geiger counter, to measure decay rates and with some chemical apparatus to analyse the remaining lead and uranium concentrations and the ratio of the radioactive isotopes. Initially, he tried out his new method on 10 uranium minerals from rocks whose relative geological age was roughly known, publishing the results in 1907. These samples ranged in age from 2200 million years for a thorianite (thorium and uranium oxide) from Ceylon (now known as Sri Lanka) to 410 million years for a uraninite (uranium oxide) from Glastonbury, Connecticut. The oldest date increased the age of the Earth by an order of magnitude. Although by modern standards these results were not very accurate, for instance the age of the Glastonbury uraninite has been recalculated to 265 Ma, Boltwood's technical developments were of enormous importance. Now the physicists really had to take notice and admit that Kelvin was way off the mark. It began to seem that the geologists had been right all the time to argue that the Earth must be much, much older than 20 million years or so.

By 1910, a British geologist, Arthur Holmes, was pursuing a similar approach and embarked on a lifetime's quest 'to graduate the geological column with an ever increasingly accurate time scale'. He calculated the age of a Norwegian rock, which contained several radioactive minerals, as 370 million years. As the rock was known to have originated within the Devonian geological system, he thus provided the first date for that geological system and period of time. In retrospect, this was the most accurate of the early radiometric dates and, if Holmes had had the resources to continue his work, radiometric dating would

Sir Arthur Holmes, 1890–1965, English pioneer geochronologist and professor of geology in Durham (1924–43), then Edinburgh (1943–62), who first worked out a geological timescale based on radiometric dates and measures of the total thicknesses of the different systems of strata.

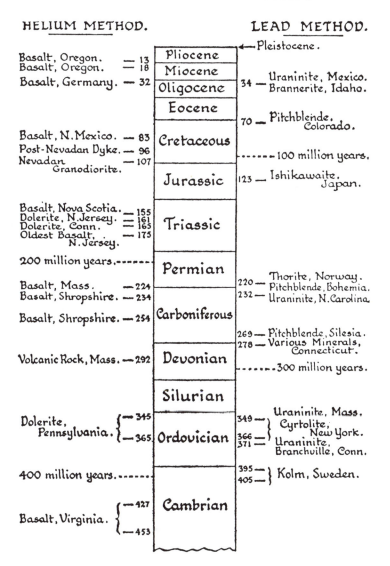

The timescale of Phanerozoic Earth Time as presented by Arthur Holmes in 1937 with U–Pb and U–He data.

have progressed much faster than it did. Holmes also recalculated some of Boltwood's published data and arranged them to produce the first geological timescale. He was to improve on this scale continuously for the rest of his professional life.

Refinements

Since Holmes's initial work in 1911, many improvements have been made to the process of radiometric dating. Of major importance was the discovery in 1913 that the atoms of a chemical element can exist in two or more different forms, called 'isotopes', which are the same chemically but have different atomic masses. Some isotopes are stable, and it is only the unstable ones that undergo radioactive decay. Of crucial importance for radiometric dating purposes, different unstable isotopes of the same element often have very different half-lives. For example, most uranium consists of the isotope U238, with a half-life of 4.5 billion years, but about 0.7 per cent is the isotope U235, with a half-life of 713 million years. Lead comes in several stable isotopic forms – some that occur in minerals only through the decay of other, radioactive isotopes, and others that that were present in the minerals from when they first formed. It became apparent to Holmes and others that for better accuracy, it would be necessary to measure isotope ratios (for example U238 to its decay product, the lead isotope Pb206), rather than just uranium to lead.

This discovery of isotopes initially complicated the process of radiometric dating, but in time made it more precise. One initial effect was a reappraisal of Holmes's time scale – as a result of not compensating for these (then unknown) factors, his computed ages were too high. Nevertheless, researchers were beginning to realise that radiometric methods held promise for reassessing the Earth's age. In 1921, Henry Russell obtained 4 billion years as a rough approximation to the age of the Earth's crust, based on an average of its maximum age calculated from its total uranium and lead content, and a minimum age based on the oldest known (at that time) Precambrian minerals. Arthur Holmes later revised Russell's calculation, based on different estimates of the amount of uranium and lead in the crust, giving an age of between 1.6 and 3 billion years. Over the following years, several more different ages for the Earth's crust were computed and published. These included 3.4 billion years (Rutherford, 1929); and 4.6 billion years (Meyer, 1937). Meanwhile, older and older rocks were being found in different parts of the world.

By the 1940s, it became apparent that to calculate an accurate age for the Earth, one piece of data was still needed – the ratio of different isotopes of lead in the Earth's crust at the time of its formation. Holmes made isotope measurements on some ancient lead ore-bearing rocks from Invigtut in Greenland and by 1946, these gave an age of 3015 million years, which was the first really reliable estimate of a minimum age for the Earth. Holmes went on to estimate that the origin of the uranium, from which the lead was derived, must be around 4460 million years ago, but he thought that origin was within the gas cloud from which the Earth was formed, rather than being the date of the Earth's origin.

A decade later, following the end of the Second World War, American scientists Harrison Brown and Claire Patterson, who had worked on the Manhattan Project and the development of the atomic bomb, became interested in using meteorites to calculate the age of the Solar System. In 1953, Patterson managed to determine the lead isotope content of the Canyon Diablo meteorite, which blasted Meteor Crater in Arizona around 50,000 years ago. From this, he calculated an age of 4510 million years and compared it with an age of 4560 million years calculated for lead values from earth-bound granite and basalt rocks. He concluded that the similarity between the dates indicated that this was also the date at which the Earth first formed. By 1956 Patterson had made further measures from different meteorites and deep-sea sediments, which represented a generalised sample of Earth rocks. Again, the average worked out at 4.55 billion years, very close to Holmes's figure.

———————— • ————————

Claire Patterson, 1922–95, American chemist who worked with Harrison Brown on the Manhattan Project and after the Second World War, first at the University of Chicago then California Institute of Technology (from 1952), worked on the calculation of the Earth's age, finally settling on 4.55 billion years.

Towards an Earth Time scale

For Earth Time, Holmes's development of the geological time chart allowed him to publish in 1947 a graph based on the calculated radiometric ages of a number of rocks, which could each be fairly accurately tied into the known succession of strata within certain geological periods. Even so, there were only five reliably dated points between the Cambrian and present, ranging back as far as 450 million years to a point in mid-Cambrian times. However, a curve drawn between the points allowed rough estimates of the duration of each geological period to be made for the first time.

A major difficulty with radiometric dating is that most minerals that can be dated by this method are formed from an initially molten state within igneous rocks. There are exceptions, the most important being the radiocarbon method of dating certain archaeological materials. But because of the short half-lives of the daughter isotopes, the method cannot be used on materials older than about 50,000 years. Consequently, for the vast majority of Earth Time, igneous rocks are the main ones that can be reliably dated. Even then, we must always remember that there are error bars attached to all these dates. The problem for stratigraphers, who study the history of deposition of the sedimentary strata of the Earth, and palaeontologists, who study the fossils that such rocks contain, is how to relate the formation of igneous rocks to the deposition of sediments.

Stratigraphically, the most useful igneous rocks are volcanic, lavas and ash deposits, which can be found interbedded with fossiliferous sediments. The problem here is that the most common isotopes found within volcanic rocks are those of potassium and argon, which have shorter half-lives than uranium and lead. Nevertheless, K/Ar and Ar/Ar dating of volcanic rocks has proved immensely useful in dating Tertiary-age strata, especially those associated with the Great East African Rift valley and their human-related fossils. Whenever you see a date in years attached to some human ancestor, the chances are that it has been derived from some volcanic rock layer near where the fossil was found.

Without radiometric dates we would not be able to say anything about rates of geological or biological processes in the past. Prior to the late 1940s, most dating of rocks and geological time was little more than informed guesswork. It is

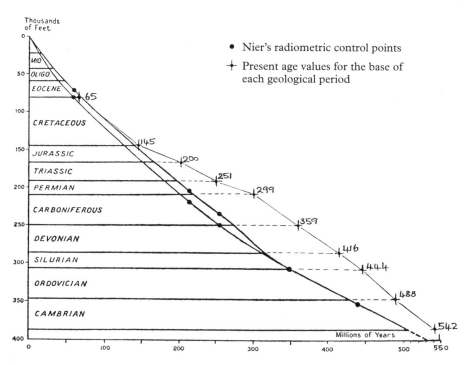

Holmes's 1947 version of the Phanerozoic Earth Timescale based on just five lead isotope ages originally determined by Alfred Nier, some of which are shown with alternative positions. Holmes arranged them against their geological positions in a vertical scale of the periods of Earth Time based on estimated thickness of the strata.

now known that the early formation of the Earth, as part of the accretionary disc around the Sun, began 4.57 billion years ago. Earth's early growth was protracted, being dominated by planetary collisions, and it was not until around 4.51–4.45 billion years ago that it reached its present mass, with a metal core and primitive atmosphere.

At present the Earth's oldest-known rock material is a 4.4-billion-year-old zircon crystal from Australia, dated by an Australian/American team in January 2001, using the U-Pb method. Zircon is a particularly tough and enduring

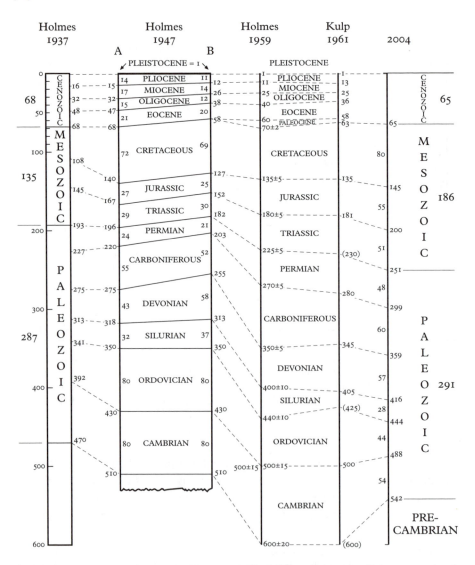

Comparison of a number of alternative Phanerozoic Earth Timescales produced since 1937, showing how they have developed.

mineral, resilient to change, and is generally formed in continental crust rocks. The composition of the zircon suggested to the researchers that the Earth's early growth was protracted over 100 Ma and that there must have been continental crust and water on the Earth's surface by 4300 Ma, much earlier than previously thought. However, most of the Earth's geological record extends back no more than 4000 Ma, to the end of the early intense phase of meteorite bombardment, which destroyed or reworked almost all the older material.

Million Years Ago

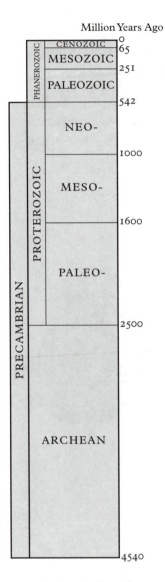

Archean to Cenozoic.

Earth Time – Conclusion

This exploration of the rock record of Earth Time has focused largely on the initial nineteenth-century division and grouping of strata. The 'brotherhood of the hammer' were highly territorial and ambitious as they hustled and bustled amongst the rocks and argued about how to carve up Earth Time. They hoped to promote themselves and secure lasting personal reputations by establishing their 'systems' as nationally and internationally recognised divisions of Earth Time. Like Charles Dickens's Mr Gradgrind they believed in facts rather than theories. But one of the major problems of geology as a science is that the interpretation of the seemingly 'rock-solid facts' can actually be highly variable. Disputes were and still are the name of the game and ranged from minor spats to long-running, bitter and highly personalised feuds between the protagonists. Whoever said that science was impersonal?

This historical carve-up used obvious differences between sequences of rock types and their fossils. The overall result was a piecemeal scheme of division, cobbled together over a considerable period of time by many different authors in various parts of the world who were making up the rules of the 'game' as they went along. By the end of the nineteenth century Earth Time was divided into five major 'eras': the Quaternary, which included the recent ice ages and present or Holocene time, the Tertiary (also known as the Cenozoic) or 'age of mammals', the Mesozoic or 'age of reptiles', the Palaeozoic, which included the 'ages of amphibians, fishes and primitive life' as well as the beginnings of life. Finally there was the Precambrian or Azoic, which was thought to be devoid of life.

Within these major divisions, a chronological sequence of systems was defined such as the Silurian and Devonian, based on distinctive and often regionally located successions of strata, with characteristic fossils. It was the actual rock and its varied content, including fossils, which provided the material basis that geologists were trying to place within the abstract continuum of Earth Time.

The fossils often represent particular episodes in the history of life. For example, the Devonian was thought to preserve the early development of the fishes and the Jurassic to preserve part of the dinosaur story along with that of their aquatic and flying relatives. Paradoxically, however, the Jurassic strata of the Jura Mountains, by which the period was first recognised, are mostly marine and do not contain many fossils of the terrestrial dinosaurs.

There was an inherent duality in the scheme. Although the chronology of Earth Time is essentially a continuum, it was recorded and represented by 'unit' sequences of rock strata (the study of which is called chronostratigraphy). It gradually became clear to geologists that the boundaries of successive units often represent gaps in the record of deposition. And when the matching of unit boundaries was attempted on a regional or global scale, it was evident that they were not necessarily synchronous and often overlap. The business of sorting out such discrepancies was and still is highly contentious as contenders vie with one another to promote the claims of their favoured stratigraphic successions.

It became quite clear why such problems were arising. At any one time, contemporary deposits are laid down in any number of different sedimentary environments around the world, ranging from desert sands to glacial moraine and tropical reef carbonates. The boundaries between different environments of deposition shift over time as for instance deserts, ice sheets or seas expand or shrink with continuous climate change and the movement of the continents and oceans.

Although the major divisions of Earth Time were established by the end of the nineteenth century, geologists had to spend the next hundred years and more trying to make the scheme more workable and sort out its inherent contradictions. Even by 1881 when the second International Geological Congress met in Bologna, everyone acknowledged that some sort of international agreement was necessary so that geologists around the world use the same divisional names for Earth Time in a consistent way.

For example, any reference to the base of the Devonian System of strata and the beginning of the Devonian Period of Earth Time is now 'based' on a fixed point in a continuous sequence of fossiliferous seabed sedimentary strata. Despite the fact that the Devonian System is so named after the county of Devon in southwest England, it was discovered that the sequence of strata from the top of the Silurian System is not present in Devon. Consequently, the base of the Devonian ended up located within an equally historic region, namely Joachim Barrande's Bohemia.

It took the best part of 100 years before the Bologna initiative became a practicality. Eventually, in 1972 the first internationally agreed system boundary to be formally marked was that of the Siluro-Devonian. The specific locality is the euphonically named Klonk section near the village of Suchomasty in the Czech Republic. Ceremonially marked with a 'golden spike' in 1972, the specific point is bed 20 in the section where fossil graptolites of the species *Monograptus uniformis* first appear in the strata. Just above this, limestone bed 21 contains trilobites belonging to the *Warburgella rugulosa* group, which are indicative of the Lochkovian stage, the earliest stage of the Devonian Period. The idea is that such points should be fixed in perpetuity but there are arguments that the scheme should not be over-rigid.

The base of the Devonian also demarcates the top of the Silurian System, but the base of the Silurian System has been formally marked with a golden spike at Dob's Linn in southern Scotland. Here the boundary is marked by the first appearance of the graptolite species *Parakidograptus acuminatus* and *Akidograptus ascensus* in a continuous succession of marine strata from the underlying Ordovician. It might seem slightly strange that the top and bottom of a system of strata are placed in different countries, but the passage of Earth Time is a global phenomenon. The purpose of a golden spike is to locate and define a level in a section where time and rock coincide.

Over the last 30 years, all but one of the system boundaries (the exception being the base of the Cretaceous System) for post-Cambrian (Phanerozoic)

Earth Time have been selected along with other important subdivisions such as epochs. But most important are the 90 or so stage divisions, the smallest and most fundamental units of formal Earth Time classification, 50 of which have been formally located so far (there were only 15 designated in 1990). Stages represent all rocks laid down during the time span assigned to that stage and are the only units to be represented by carefully selected type sections.

Essentially golden spikes mark the lower boundaries of stages and some also coincide with epoch and period boundaries. For instance, the golden spike at Dob's Linn, near Moffat in Scotland, placed 1.6 m above the base of the Birkhill Shale, not only marks the base of the Rhuddanian Stage and the Llandovery Epoch but also the base of the Silurian Period. The reason that the base of the Cretaceous Period has yet to be defined is that its basal stage, the Berriasian, has yet to have its lower boundary marked by a golden spike.

Since 1994 when the International Stratigraphic Guide was published, the specific geographical and geological rock contexts of stage boundaries within type sections have been referred to as Global Boundary Stratotype Sections and Points or more conveniently GSSPs. A breakdown of the locations on a national basis shows an interesting distribution that reflects a mixture of historical influences and geological/geographical considerations. The present geographical distribution of GSSPs is as follows: Australia 1, Canada 2, China 4, Czech Republic 3, Egypt 1, France 4, Germany 2, Italy 7, Morocco 1, Portugal 1, Spain 1, Sweden 2, Tunisia 1, UK 9, USA 5. Apart from their geological appropriateness, the GSSPs also have to be readily accessible to scientists and their immediate environments have to be secure from deterioration, damage or change in land use.

Most importantly, the grand hierarchical scheme of Earth Time subdivision has been tied into the radiometric scale with increasing accuracy since the pioneering work of Arthur Holmes in the late 1930s. But the problems of matching ages, based largely on radioisotopes generated within igneous rocks, to the sedimentary strata-based divisions of Earth Time ensure that this process will continue for some years.

In 1937 Holmes estimated that the base of the Cambrian system of strata and thus Cambrian time began around 470 million years ago. By 1959 his estimate had grown to 600 ± 20 million years, whereafter it has come back to 542 ± 1.0 million years ago. And Murchison's Silurian System, which at its apogee subsumed the Cambrian and included all strata from the base of the Devonian down to the top of the Precambrian, is now estimated to have had a duration of around a mere 27 million years from 443.7–416.0 million years ago to become one of the shortest periods of Earth Time.

Some boundaries are more securely dated than others so that the present chronology is still not finally set in 'tablets of stone'. The analytical errors associated with the otherwise precise dates for the Cenozoic, Mesozoic and Palaeozoic eras are 65.5 ± 0.3, 251.0 ± 0.4 and 541 ± 1.0 million years respectively. There are also direct dates on the base of the Carboniferous, Permian, Jurassic and Oligocene. But most other period or stage boundaries lack direct age control and so are based on interpolation between known dates and high-resolution biostratigraphic zonal schemes. The ages for this large group of Earth Time divisions are most likely to change over the next decades.

From uppermost Cambrian through to end Silurian times composite graptolite biozones were scaled with links to high-precision zircon and sanidine radiometric dates. The Carboniferous through to Permian is scaled from biozones based on conodonts, ammonoids and unicell fusulinids calibrated against a combination of U-Pb and 40Ar–39Ar radiometric dates.

From late Jurassic times the palaeomagnetic record of periodic reversals of the Earth's magnetic polarity has been mapped out in detail from ocean floor lavas (see p. 258). Known as chrons, the main couplets of normal and reversed polarity are numbered C1 to C34 from the present back to the Santonian stage of late Cretaceous times over 83.5 million years ago. Generated at spreading ridges between diverging tectonic plates, such ocean floor lavas preserve the contemporary magnetic field but their record does not extend back beyond Jurassic times. However, as there is also a spasmodic continental record of widespread outpourings of lava, a reliable paleomagnetic record of reversals can be extended back through Triassic times. Some other bundles of chrons have also been numbered such as M1–M37 from early Cretaceous (125.0 million years ago) back to the end of middle Jurassic times (161.2 million years ago). And then the palaeomagnetic record becomes increasingly patchy through the

Paleozoic but will be better known with future field investigation. Importantly, the geological record of reversals can help link marine and continental successions.

Radiometric dating of many reversals provides an important calibration for the scale and identification of specific reversals within the stratigraphic record and can help date parts of the record that otherwise have no directly available radiometric ages. For instance, the identification of the Olduvai phase of normal polarity between 1.95 and 1.77 million years ago, within the Matuyama reversal from 2.58 to 0.78 million years ago, has helped locate the Pliocene/Pleistocene boundary (at 1.81 million years ago) and date important hominid-bearing African sedimentary strata.

The idea that the periodicity of sediment cycles is astronomically tuned might seem far fetched, but it has become yet another chronometric tool that can be tied to the palaeomagnetic and radiometric timescales. Periodic changes in the Earth's orbit and precession cycle can be linked to climate change, especially relating to periodicity within ice ages. The idea dates back to the end of the nineteenth century and the Scottish James Croll, but its modern development originates with the brilliant Serbian astronomer Milutin Milankovich. Although the interaction of the different cycles is very complex, their impact can now be identified in the sedimentary record. For sediments deposited over the last 20 million years or so they are generally regarded as being accurate to within the duration of a precession cycle, i.e. about 20,000 years.

With the advent of radiometric dating it has become possible to encompass all the rocks of the Earth within the overall framework of Earth Time and

———————•———————

James Croll, 1821–90, self-taught Scottish scientist and Fellow of the Royal Society (1876), who after working as a carpenter, shopkeeper and salesman became janitor in Glasgow's Andersonian College where he developed his interest in climate change relating to the ice ages. He was employed by the Geological Survey of Scotland (1867–80) and correlated changes in the Earth's orbital eccentricity with the ice ages and attempted to link them to estimated variations in seasonal solar radiation in the two hemispheres. His influential textbook *Climate and Time* was published in 1875.

Milutin Milankovich, 1879–1958, Serbian astronomer, trained in Vienna before moving to Belgrade University where he, like Croll, recognised that periodic fluctuations in solar heat resulting from eccentricities in the Earth's orbit, tilt of the axis of rotation and precessional change influence whether the northern or southern hemisphere receives more radiation over a 20,000-year cycle. He also linked these astronomical cycles to the periodicity of the Quaternary ice ages.

———————————— • ————————————

its study, a subject long known as stratigraphy but previously confined to sedimentary strata. In addition, it is now possible to consider the abandonment of the old and rather confusing dual scheme of nomenclature. The time unit terms such as period and system for rock units can be quietly dropped, but whether this will actually happen is another matter.

At present, the 90 or so stage-level divisions of the Phanerozoic Eon encompass all Cambrian and younger strata and thus span 542 million years. So on average each stage is some 6 million years long. This represents a remarkable degree of refinement and precision. Within most stages the temporal distribution of particular fossil groups such as graptolites, trilobites, ammonites and unicell foraminifers has allowed the recognition of even finer subdivisions called biozones based on evolving species. We now know, thanks to the framework of radiometric dating, that many of these biozones had durations of a million years or less. Again, this is an astonishing level of refinement that has only been achieved by the painstaking researches of countless earth scientists all over the world.

While this approach to the division of Earth Time is very effective for Cambrian and younger strata, it does not work for most of the Precambrian because of the lack of recoverable or stratigraphically useful fossils. Consequently, a different kind of boundary stratotype has to be used, called the Global Standard Stratigraphic Age (GSSA). This is an abstract concept based on boundaries defined purely by linear age, so that the Archean is divided into four eras – Neo-, Meso-, Paleo- and Eoarchean. The three younger eras have bases defined by the following ages: 2800, 3200 and 3600 million years respectively.

The base of the oldest has yet to be defined because it requires agreement about what developmental stage should be selected within the early formation of the Earth and when that happened – should it be taken from when the first mineral materials have survived? It also has to be remembered that when dealing with radiometric dates derived from rocks that are billions of years old there are significant error bars on each measure that amount to 10 million years or more.

However, the youngest Neoproterozoic Era (one of three divisions of the Proterozoic) includes as its youngest system the Ediacaran with a base dated at 630 million years ago. This has a GSSP located at the base of the Marinoan cap carbonate in the Enorama Section of the Flinders Ranges, South Australia. So here the boundary has been selected on an event basis, namely the end of the Marinoan glaciation. There is hope that eventually these Precambrian GSSAs can be replaced by GSSPs as the stratigraphy of this huge chunk of Earth Time becomes better understood.

As we have seen, a constant problem with the understanding of Earth Time, the timing, duration and rates of its processes, is the thorny question of the resolution of dates and the estimation of uncertainties related to them. In recent years, much of the debate over mass extinction events and their causes has focused on the difficulty of recognising 'instantaneous' or even short-term events in the geological record.

For instance, around 55 million years ago the end of Palaeocene times and the boundary with the overlying Eocene was marked by an extinction event. There was a significant turnover in the newly emerging land mammals and ocean-dwelling micro-organisms. The rock strata from both land and sea environments of deposition record anomalous carbon isotope values across the boundary. Although the anomaly is only measured in a few parts per thousand, nevertheless it was a global event and must represent a release of somewhere between 1200 and 2000 gigatonnes of carbon into the atmosphere. The nature of the event and its global distribution suggested that at least its initiation was probably 'instantaneous'; the question was how long did it last?

Analysis of sediment cores from the deep ocean floor revealed cycles of deposition that can be linked to 19,000- and 23,000-year astronomical precession cycles. By relating the cycles to the carbon 'excursion' (or 'spike', as it is called), it became clear that the spike happened over a very short period of time (geologically speaking).

Recent research suggests that this large-scale event happened in a rapid single pulse that lasted no more than a few thousand years – a truly catastrophic event by anyone's standard. Such a conclusion can only be reached thanks to an accurate timescale. It then took another 120,000 years for the global carbon cycle to recover. The carbon excursion coincides with climate and faunal changes and has been linked to massive releases of methane hydrate into ocean waters from deep within ocean floor sediments (at least 300 m deep) where it is stored in a solid crystalline state. An estimated 14,000 gigatonnes of carbon are still locked up as hydrate in ocean floor sediments and, if quickly released, would have a severe impact on today's carbon reservoir of 42,000 tonnes.

While such resolution of Earth Time is remarkable for the 'deep' past, it is inadequate for the more recent past where dating can still be a real headache for scientists. The recent discovery of the extraordinary 'dwarfed' human species *Homo floresiensis* in Indonesia is a good example. The skeletal remains were found in cave deposits, which are often notoriously difficult to date accurately by any method. Samples of charcoal associated with the bones have been radiocarbon dated at around 18,000 years ago and other dating measures on the surrounding sediment indicate an age of around 38,000 years ago. Fossil remains of the extinct and also dwarfed elephant relative *Stegodon* are associated with the human-related bones. And independent evidence shows that *Stegodon* died out about 12,000 years ago. Consequently, all that can be said so far is that the little *Homo floresiensis* people lived from before 38,000 years ago to at least 18,000 years ago.

Over the last 200 years, much has been achieved in the building of the outlines of the Earth Time calendar and much more will be achieved. But it is important to remember that the construct of Earth Time and its divisions have been fabricated by humans. Uniquely, as far as we know, we are the only life forms to care about the past, whether it is the historic or prehistoric past of Earth Time. Our investigation of the past seems to be part of our continuing effort to understand ourselves and where we have come from. Our forebears felt the strong pull of the deep past and could not resist the temptation to investigate. The new science of geology provided them with the tools and methods to make the journey, however difficult it proved. The revelations of the antiquity of Earth Time and life are fascinating but often prove very uncomfortable for some.

The *terra incognita* of the depths of pre-Cambrian Earth Time, some 4 billion years' worth, are still largely unknown and present a wonderful challenge for future generations of those prepared to voyage into the remotest regions of Earth Time. Fortunately, unlike so many of the pioneers, you no longer have to be a wealthy gentleman amateur or clergyman to pursue the investigation of Earth Time – the future challenge is open to all. Good hunting.

Summaries of ratified GSSPs with locality maps and sections are to be found on the International Commission on Stratigraphy's (ICS's) website (http://www.stratigraphy.org). Details of the state of play with regard to the Quaternary and its subdivision can be found through the website of the International Union for Quaternary Research (INQUA) Stratigraphy and Chronology Commission (SACCOM; http://www.inqua.tcd.ie) and that of the Quaternary Palaeo-environments Group, Godwin Institute for Quaternary Research, University of Cambridge, UK (http://www-qpg.geog.cam.ac.uk).

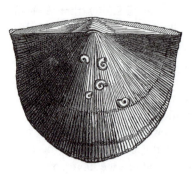

References

Benton, M. J. 2003. *When Life Nearly Died*. Thames and Hudson, London.

Berry, W. B. N. 1987. *Growth of a Prehistoric Time Scale, Based on Organic Evolution*. Blackwell, Palo Alto, California.

Beus, S. S. and M. Morales (eds). 2003. *Grand Canyon Geology*. (2nd ed.) Oxford University Press, New York.

Cadbury, D. H. 2000. *The Dinosaur Hunters*. Fourth Estate, London.

Cohen, C. 2002. The Fate of the Mammoth. University of Chicago Press, Chicago.

Collie, M. and J. Diemer. 2004. *Murchison's Wanderings in Russia*. British Geological Survey, Keyworth, Nottingham.

Davies, G. L. 1968. *The Earth in Decay: A History of British Geomorphology 1578–1878*. Macdonald & Co., London.

Greene, J. C. 1961. *The Death of Adam*. Mentor, New York.

Knell, S. J. 2000. *The Culture of English Geology, 1815–1851*. Ashgate, Aldershot.

Knoll, A. H. 2003. *Life on a Young Planet: The First Three Billion Years of Evolution*. Princeton University Press, Princeton.

Lewis, C. L. E. and S. J. Knell (eds). *The Age of the Earth: From 4004 BC to AD 2002*. The Geological Society, London.

Lyell, C. 1830–3. *Principles of Geology*. 3 vols. John Murray, London.

McGowan, C. 2002. *The Dragon Seekers: The Discovery of Dinosaurs during the Prelude to Darwin*. Little Brown, London.

Oldroyd, D. 1996. *Thinking about the Earth: A History of Ideas in Geology*. The Athlone Press, London.

Palmer, D. 1997. *Life Before Man*. Reader's Digest, London.

Palmer, D. 2000. *The Atlas of the Prehistoric World*. Marshall Publishing, London.

Palmer, D. 2000. *Neanderthal*. Channel 4 Books, London.

Palmer, D. 2003. *Prehistoric Past Revealed: The Four Billion Year History of Life on Earth*. University of California Press, Berkeley.

Peake, H. 1930. *The Flood: New Light on an Old Story*. Kegan Paul, London.

Phillips, J. 1844. *Memoirs of William Smith, LLD*. John Murray, London.

Powell, J. W. 1895. *Canyons of the Colorado*. Flood and Vincent, New York.

Rudwick, M. J. S. 1969. *The Meaning of Fossils*. Science History Publications, New York.

Rudwick, M. J. S. 1985. *The Great Devonian Controversy*. University of Chicago Press, Chicago.

Rudwick, M. J. S. 1992. *Scenes from Deep Time: Early Pictorial Representations of the Prehistoric World*. University of Chicago Press, Chicago.

Rudwick, M. J. S. 2004. *The New Science of Geology: Studies in the Earth Sciences in the Age of Revolution*. Ashgate, Aldershot.

Scott Baldridge, W. 2004. *Geology of the American Southwest: A Journey through Two Billion Years of Plate-Tectonic History*. Cambridge University Press, Cambridge.

Secord, J. A. 1986. *Controversy in Victorian Geology: The Cambrian-Silurian Dispute*. Princeton University Press, New Jersey.

Thackray, J. C. (ed.) 2003. *To See the Fellows Fight*. The British Society for the History of Science.

Torrens, H. 2002. *The Practice of British Geology, 1750–1850*. Ashgate, Aldershot.

Zittel, K. A. von. 1901. *History of Geology and Palaeontology to the End of the Nineteenth Century*. Walter Scott, London.

Index